THE PUBLIC PAPERS AND ADDRESSES

OF FRANKLIN D. ROOSEVELT

THE PUBLIC PAPERS
AND ADDRESSES OF
FRANKLIN D. ROOSEVELT

WITH A SPECIAL INTRODUCTION
AND EXPLANATORY NOTES BY
PRESIDENT ROOSEVELT

Volume Three

THE ADVANCE OF
RECOVERY AND REFORM
1934

RANDOM HOUSE · NEW YORK · 1938

The material in these volumes has been

compiled and collated by

SAMUEL I. ROSENMAN

Counsel to the Governor during the ad-

ministration of Franklin D. Roosevelt

as Governor of the State of New York

1929-1932

Contents

Contents

Contents

Contents

Contents

Contents

Contents

Contents

Contents

Contents

Contents

Contents

Contents

Contents

The Advance of Recovery
and Reform

Introduction

THE *Year of Crisis* had definitely passed by the time we entered the year 1934. The panic and fear which had descended upon the American people by March 4, 1933, had been completely dissipated as they realized that the Legislative and Executive branches of their Government were willing and ready to use all of the power and resources of the Nation to alleviate suffering, prevent further disaster, and rebuild the structure of economic life upon firmer foundations of social justice. In industry, in labor, in farming, things were steadily getting better. The improvement was evident not only by the general widespread feeling of increased well-being in practically all walks of life, but also by the statistics of business and agricultural output and values.

The steady course of improvement which began in March, 1933, reached its 1934 peak during the month of May, as shown by the leading economic indexes of the period. During that period employment in manufacturing industries increased 40 percent; average weekly earnings in these industries increased 28 percent; manufacturing payrolls increased 80 percent; industrial production increased 48 percent; freight car loadings increased 31 percent; and wholesale prices increased 22 percent. The 40 percent increase in manufacturing employment involved an addition of approximately 2,000,000 wage earners to the payrolls of the factories of the Nation. This amount of reemployment, taken together with the 28 percent increase of average weekly earnings, meant that there was being added to the pay envelopes of workers in manufacturing industry the sum of $61,500,000 each week.

Employment increased similarly in non-manufacturing business. The estimated increase from March, 1933, to May, 1934, in both manufacturing and non-manufacturing businesses, was 4,711,000 workers. In the same period cash income from farm products increased 48 percent. The value of new building construction permits issued increased 38 percent.

In comparison with these increases, the increase in the cost

3

of living, as indicated in the economic indexes, was only 6 percent.

But this year of advance of recovery was also a year of advance of reform. As I pointed out in the Introduction to Volume II, while we were determined in 1933 to bring about recovery for all economic groups and for all types of economic activity, we were equally determined to effect reform where abuses existed, in order to make our recovery a more lasting one.

During that first year and during 1934, the important reforms of 1933 still continued to promote and insure the revival of trade and agriculture. The sounder banking system and the insistence upon telling the truth in selling securities to the public; the abolition of child labor; the discouragement of sweated labor; the outlawing of unfair trade practices; the rational control of farm surpluses; the attainment of a sounder and fairer currency; the promotion of our good-neighbor policy with the rest of the world; the protection of public utility investors and consumers; the encouragement of more efficient industrial relationships through collective bargaining and through labor boards set up to prevent exploitation of labor — all of these were bringing about a nation-wide deeper sense of security and an increased confidence in the newer foundations of a more permanent economic structure, as the *Year of Crisis* faded away and as recovery proceeded.

What we had done in 1933 in the way of reform was supplemented and augmented by what we did in 1934: in adopting Federal supervision and regulation for securities and commodities exchanges; in our steps taken to stamp out crime, gangsters and racketeering; in the partial improvement of our Federal judicial procedure; in the reform of our foreign trade structure through reciprocal trade agreements; in the beginnings of our comprehensive program of making proper use of land, water and minerals throughout the United States through the establishment of the National Resources Board; in the reform of the use of the Great Plains of the United States by our regulatory grazing legislation; in the establishment of a sounder currency by our new gold and silver legislation; in the betterment of our treatment of the

4

Indians of the Nation; and, above all, in the beginning of our whole program of social security through the appointment of a Committee to devise and recommend a Federal system of old-age assistance, unemployment insurance and other forms of help to underprivileged groups.

With the passing of the dark days of early March, 1933, a small minority, which gradually grew in number, had begun to clamor that reform should cease. A great many of these people, in good faith, urged as the reason for this demand the fear that continued reform might jeopardize continued recovery. They still were unable to realize that permanent recovery was impossible without the eradication of the economic and social maladjustments which permitted wealth and prosperity to concentrate in the control of a few, while fully a third of our population continued unable to provide themselves and their families with decent food, clothing and homes.

But the most vociferous opponents of reform in this small minority were actuated not by any conscientious apprehension about further recovery, but by a realization that their own economic control and power, which they had enjoyed during the so-called boom era, were being destroyed. Through speculative use of other people's money, through the exploitation of labor which could not bargain on equal terms, through unrestrained power to manipulate corporate securities, finances and devices, this handful of men had been able to build up economic empires for themselves, which not only controlled the labor, property and lives of thousands of their fellow citizens, but in some cases dominated the processes of Government itself. They saw in the various changes of the two years 1933 and 1934 the beginnings of the crumbling of their own power.

This small minority became even more vocal as the recovery of 1934 increased. To promote their own advantage, they began a vast expensive campaign of propaganda (often with their stockholders' money) to appeal to the electorate of the Nation to stop the whole program of reform.

In the fall of 1934 there were to come the general Congressional elections—the first to be held since the election of 1932 which had swept the Democratic Party into office. The Congressional political campaign of 1934 was definitely a lining up of those on the one hand who wished to stop the New Deal in its tracks, and those on the other hand who wished to see it go further along the lines it had laid down. Even back in that campaign of 1934 we began to hear the same propaganda which later, in the Presidential campaign of 1936, became more vociferous though equally futile: "usurpation of power by the Executive"; "unconstitutional legislation"; "stifling taxation and debts"; "imminent Federal bankruptcy."

Even some of the members of my own party, who had been elected on the 1932 Democratic platform which was being carried out in 1933 and 1934, began to urge a change in the policies of the Administration lest, as they urged, the Congressional elections of 1934 turn against us. The great majority of my party, however, continued to stand on the platform on which they had been voted into office.

The forebodings of the few members of my own party, and the triumphant predictions of the opposition, that the elections of 1934 would be a repudiation by the electorate of the objectives and the methods which were being pursued in Washington, did not materialize. I am frank to say that I myself hardly believed that we would be able to maintain the same overwhelming majority of Congressmen as had been returned by the elections of 1932. The Senate was composed of 60 Democratic members, 35 Republican members and one Farmer-Labor member; and the House of Representatives was composed of 310 Democratic members, 117 Republican members, and 5 Farmer-Labor members. I felt very dubious that in an off-year such as 1934 this percentage could be increased or even maintained, though I felt confident that the overwhelming majority of the people of the United States clearly understood what we were doing and approved. I was hopeful, however, that we would be able to maintain a substantial majority.

I am frank to confess my surprise at the results of the 1934 elections under the circumstances. They resulted in a Senate of 69 Democrats, 25 Republicans, one Progressive, and one Farmer-Laborite; and in a House of Representatives consisting of 322 Democrats, 102 Republicans, 7 Progressives and 3 Farmer-Laborites—a Democratic increase of 9 Senators and 12 members of the House. The popular vote throughout the United States for members of the House was 17,519,821 Democratic and 13,434,-477 Republican; for United States Senators 12,465,340 Democratic and 10,968,146 Republican.

The elections of 1934 confirmed the belief of the leaders and members of the Congress, and my own belief,that the people were satisfied with our efforts to bring about a continuation of the *Advance of Recovery and Reform* which are outlined in the pages of this volume.

Franklin D Roosevelt

Washington, D. C.
November 15, 1937

1 (Annual Message to the Congress.
January 3, 1934

Mr. President, Mr. Speaker, Senators and Representatives in Congress:

I COME before you at the opening of the Regular Session of the 73d Congress, not to make requests for special or detailed items of legislation; I come, rather, to counsel with you, who, like myself, have been selected to carry out a mandate of the whole people, in order that without partisanship you and I may cooperate to continue the restoration of our national well-being and, equally important, to build on the ruins of the past a new structure designed better to meet the present problems of modern civilization.

Such a structure includes not only the relations of industry and agriculture and finance to each other but also the effect which all of these three have on our individual citizens and on the whole people as a Nation.

Now that we are definitely in the process of recovery, lines have been rightly drawn between those to whom this recovery means a return to old methods — and the number of these people is small — and those for whom recovery means a reform of many old methods, a permanent readjustment of many of our ways of thinking and therefore of many of our social and economic arrangements.

Civilization cannot go back; civilization must not stand still. We have undertaken new methods. It is our task to perfect, to improve, to alter when necessary, but in all cases to go forward. To consolidate what we are doing, to make our economic and social structure capable of dealing with modern life is the joint task of the legislative, the judicial, and the executive branches of the national Government.

Without regard to party, the overwhelming majority of our people seek a greater opportunity for humanity to prosper and find happiness. They recognize that human welfare has not increased and does not increase through mere materialism and luxury, but that it does progress through integrity, unselfishness, responsibility and justice.

In the past few months, as a result of our action, we have demanded of many citizens that they surrender certain licenses to do as they please in their business relationships; but we have asked this in exchange for the protection which the State can give against exploitation by their fellow men or by combinations of their fellow men.

I congratulate this Congress upon the courage, the earnestness and the efficiency with which you met the crisis at the Special Session. It was your fine understanding of the national problem that furnished the example which the country has so splendidly followed. I venture to say that the task confronting the First Congress of 1789 was no greater than your own.

I shall not attempt to set forth either the many phases of the crisis which we experienced last March, or the many measures which you and I undertook during the Special Session that we might initiate recovery and reform.

It is sufficient that I should speak in broad terms of the results of our common counsel.

The credit of the Government has been fortified by drastic reduction in the cost of its permanent agencies through the Economy Act.

With the twofold purpose of strengthening the whole financial structure and of arriving eventually at a medium of exchange which over the years will have less variable purchasing and debt-paying power for our people than that of the past, I have used the authority granted me to purchase all American-produced gold and silver and to buy additional gold in the world markets. Careful investigation and constant study prove that in the matter of foreign exchange rates certain of our sister Nations find themselves so handicapped by internal and other conditions that they feel unable at this time to enter into stabilization discussion based on permanent and world-wide objectives.

The overwhelming majority of the banks, both national and State, which reopened last spring, are in sound condition and

9

have been brought within the protection of Federal insurance. In the case of those banks which were not permitted to reopen, nearly six hundred million dollars of frozen deposits are being restored to the depositors through the assistance of the national Government.

We have made great strides toward the objectives of the National Industrial Recovery Act, for not only have several millions of our unemployed been restored to work, but industry is organizing itself with a greater understanding that reasonable profits can be earned while at the same time protection can be assured to guarantee to labor adequate pay and proper conditions of work. Child labor is abolished. Uniform standards of hours and wages apply today to 95 percent of industrial employment within the field of the National Industrial Recovery Act. We seek the definite end of preventing combinations in furtherance of monopoly and in restraint of trade, while at the same time we seek to prevent ruinous rivalries within industrial groups which in many cases resemble the gang wars of the underworld and in which the real victim in every case is the public itself.

Under the authority of this Congress, we have brought the component parts of each industry together around a common table, just as we have brought problems affecting labor to a common meeting ground. Though the machinery, hurriedly devised, may need readjustment from time to time, nevertheless I think you will agree with me that we have created a permanent feature of our modernized industrial structure and that it will continue under the supervision but not the arbitrary dictation of Government itself.

You recognized last spring that the most serious part of the debt burden affected those who stood in danger of losing their farms and their homes. I am glad to tell you that refinancing in both of these cases is proceeding with good success and in all probability within the financial limits set by the Congress.

But agriculture had suffered from more than its debts. Actual experience with the operation of the Agricultural Adjustment Act leads to my belief that thus far the experiment of seeking a balance between production and consumption is succeeding and has made progress entirely in line with reasonable expectations toward the restoration of farm prices to parity. I continue in my conviction that industrial progress and prosperity can only be attained by bringing the purchasing power of that portion of our population which in one form or another is dependent upon agriculture up to a level which will restore a proper balance between every section of the country and between every form of work.

In this field, through carefully planned flood control, power development and land-use policies in the Tennessee Valley and in other great watersheds, we are seeking the elimination of waste, the removal of poor lands from agriculture and the encouragement of small local industries, thus furthering this principle of a better balanced national life. We recognize the great ultimate cost of the application of this rounded policy to every part of the Union. Today we are creating heavy obligations to start the work because of the great unemployment needs of the moment. I look forward, however, to the time in the not distant future, when annual appropriations, wholly covered by current revenue, will enable the work to proceed under a national plan. Such a national plan will, in a generation or two, return many times the money spent on it; more important, it will eliminate the use of inefficient tools, conserve and increase natural resources, prevent waste, and enable millions of our people to take better advantage of the opportunities which God has given our country.

I cannot, unfortunately, present to you a picture of complete optimism regarding world affairs.

The delegation representing the United States has worked in close cooperation with the other American Republics assembled at Montevideo to make that conference an outstanding success. We have, I hope, made it clear to our neighbors that we seek with them future avoidance of territorial expansion and of interference by one Nation in the internal affairs of another. Furthermore, all of us are seeking the restoration of commerce in ways which will preclude the building up of large favorable trade balances by any one Nation at the expense of trade debits on the part of other Nations.

In other parts of the world, however, fear of immediate or future aggression and with it the spending of vast sums on armament and the continued building up of defensive trade barriers prevent any great progress in peace or trade agreements. I have made it clear that the United States cannot take part in political arrangements in Europe but that we stand ready to cooperate at any time in practicable measures on a world basis looking to immediate reduction of armaments and the lowering of the barriers against commerce.

I expect to report to you later in regard to debts owed the Government and people of this country by the Governments and peoples of other countries. Several Nations, acknowledging the debt, have paid in small part; other Nations have failed to pay. One Nation — Finland — has paid the installments due this country in full.

Returning to home problems, we have been shocked by many notorious examples of injuries done our citizens by persons or groups who have been living off their neighbors by the use of methods either unethical or criminal.

In the first category — a field which does not involve violations of the letter of our laws — practices have been brought to light which have shocked those who believed that we were in the past generation raising the ethical standards of business. They call for stringent preventive or regulatory measures. I am speaking of those individuals who have evaded the spirit and purpose of our tax laws, of those high officials of banks or corporations who have grown rich at the expense of their stockholders or the public, of those reckless speculators with their own or other people's money whose operations have injured the values of the farmers' crops and the savings of the poor.

In the other category, crimes of organized banditry, cold-blooded shooting, lynching and kidnapping have threatened our security.

These violations of ethics and these violations of law call on the strong arm of Government for their immediate suppression; they call also on the country for an aroused public opinion.

The adoption of the Twenty-first Amendment should give material aid to the elimination of those new forms of crime which came from the illegal traffic in liquor.

I shall continue to regard it as my duty to use whatever means may be necessary to supplement State, local and private agencies for the relief of suffering caused by unemployment. With respect to this question, I have recognized the dangers inherent in the direct giving of relief and have sought the means to provide not mere relief, but the opportunity for useful and remunerative work. We shall, in the process of recovery, seek to move as rapidly as possible from direct relief to publicly supported work and from that to the rapid restoration of private employment.

It is to the eternal credit of the American people that this tremendous readjustment of our national life is being accomplished peacefully, without serious dislocation, with only a minimum of injustice and with a great, willing spirit of cooperation throughout the country.

Disorder is not an American habit. Self-help and self-control are the essence of the American tradition — not of necessity the form of that tradition, but its spirit. The program itself comes from the American people.

It is an integrated program, national in scope. Viewed in the large, it is designed to save from destruction and to keep for the future the genuinely important values created by modern society. The vicious and wasteful parts of that society we could not save if we wished; they have chosen the way of self-destruction. We would save useful mechanical invention, machine production, industrial efficiency, modern means of communication, broad education. We would save and encourage the slowly growing impulse among consumers to enter the industrial market place equipped with sufficient organization to insist upon fair prices and honest sales.

But the unnecessary expansion of industrial plants, the waste of natural resources, the exploitation of the consumers of natural monopolies, the accumulation of stagnant surpluses, child labor, and the ruthless exploitation of all labor, the encouragement of speculation with other people's money, these were consumed in the fires that they themselves kindled; we must make sure that as we reconstruct our life there be no soil in which such weeds can grow again.

We have plowed the furrow and planted the good seed; the hard beginning is over. If we would reap the full harvest, we must cultivate the soil where this good seed is sprouting and the plant is reaching up to mature growth.

A final personal word. I know that each of you will appreciate that I am speaking no mere politeness when I assure you how much I value the fine relationship that we have shared during these months of hard and incessant work. Out of these friendly contacts we are, fortunately, building a strong and permanent tie between the legislative and executive branches of the Government. The letter of the Constitution wisely declared a separation, but the impulse of common purpose declares a union. In this spirit we join once more in serving the American people.

2 (Secretary of the Treasury Woodin Resigns. January 1, 1934

The following correspondence was made public today at the White House:

Tucson, Arizona,
December 13, 1933

Dear Governor:

It is with great regret that I am compelled to tender you my resignation as Secretary of the Treasury, to take effect at your convenience any time before January first.

The state of my health will not permit me to remain in this position.

I cannot express what a wrench it is to me to leave your official family and you must know how proud and happy I have been to have served you.

With great admiration and affection.

Faithfully yours,

W. H. WOODIN

The White House,
Washington, D. C., December 20, 1933

Dear Will:

That you feel you must definitely leave the Treasury post by the end of the year is, of course, a great sorrow to me; but I am even more saddened by the thought that the throat is still giving trouble. I know, however, that it is of the highest importance that you shelve all official cares, and that with your fine courage and constitution you will soon get wholly well. Remember that when that day comes you are wanted and needed in the service of the country. Your calm, practical and courageous action in the difficult days of last spring and summer will always be remembered.

All of us miss you greatly and all of us send you our devoted regards.

Henry Morgenthau, Jr., will go in on January 1, and I am happy in the thought that you so strongly approve the choice.

Take care of yourself.

Faithfully and affectionately yours,

FRANKLIN D. ROOSEVELT

Hon. William H. Woodin,
  Tucson, Arizona.

3 ❡ The Annual Budget Message. January 3, 1934

To the Congress of the United States:

I TRANSMIT herewith the Budget for the year ending June 30, 1935. It contains also estimates of receipts and expenditures for the current year ending June 30, 1934, and includes statements of the financial operations or status of all governmental agencies, including the Reconstruction Finance Corporation. The estimates herein given and included in the Budget have to do with general and special funds — the Government's moneys. They do not relate to trust and contributed funds, which are not Government moneys, except where expressly referred to as such.

GENERAL FINANCIAL POSITION

In my annual message to the Congress I have already summarized the problems presented by the deflationary forces of the depression, the paralyzed condition which affected the banking system, business, agriculture, transportation, and, indeed, the whole orderly continuation of the Nation's social and economic system.

I have outlined the steps taken since last March for the resumption of normal activities and the restoration of the credit of the Government.

Of necessity these many measures have caused spending by the Government far in excess of the income of the Government.

The results of expenditures already made show themselves in concrete form in better prices for farm commodities, in renewed business activity, in increased employment, in reopening of and restored confidence in banks, and in well-organized relief.

THE CURRENT FISCAL YEAR

(Ending June 30, 1934)

Exclusive of debt retirement of $488,171,500 for this year, Budget estimates of expenditures, including operating expenses of the regular Government establishments and also all expenditures

16

which may be broadly classed as caused by the necessity for recovery from the depression will amount this year (ending June 30, 1934) to $9,403,006,967. (See Budget Statement No. 3, table A.) This total falls in broad terms into the following classifications:

Expenditures for fiscal year ending June 30, 1934

General:

Departmental	$2,899,116,200
Legislative	17,718,500
Independent establishments	616,857,067
	$3,533,691,767
Less public-debt retirements	488,171,500
Total, general	$3,045,520,267

Emergency:

Public Works Administration	$1,677,190,800
Agricultural Adjustment Administration	103,250,000
Farm Credit Administration	40,000,000
Emergency Conservation Work	341,705,600
Reconstruction Finance Corporation	3,969,740,300
Tennessee Valley Authority	19,000,000
Federal Land Banks	52,350,000
Federal Deposit Insurance Corporation	150,000,000
National Industrial Recovery Administration	4,250,000
Total, emergency	$6,357,486,700
Total, general and emergency, less public-debt retirements	$9,403,006,967

As against these expenditures, which have either been appropriated for or for which appropriations are asked, the estimated receipts for this fiscal year (ending June 30, 1934) are $3,259,938,756. (See Budget Statement No. 2, table A.)

On this basis, including, however, certain additional expenditures for 1934 which are not included in the Budget estimates but which I believe to be necessary and amounting to $1,166,000,000 as shown in a subsequent table herein, the excess of expenditures over receipts will be $7,309,068,211. Interest charges on the borrowings in excess of Budget estimates will slightly increase this figure.

On the basis of these estimates, the public debt, in the strict sense of the term, at the expiration of this fiscal year will therefore amount to approximately $29,847,000,000, or an increase as shown above of $7,309,068,211.

However, as against this increase in the total debt figure, it is right to point out that the various governmental agencies have loans outstanding with a book value of $3,558,516,189 against which collateral or assets have been pledged.

In order to make clear to the Congress what our borrowing problem is for the next 6 months, permit me to remind you that we shall have to borrow approximately 6 billion dollars of new money and, in addition, 4 billion dollars to meet maturities of a like amount.

THE FISCAL YEAR 1935

(Ending June 30, 1935)

The Budget estimates of expenditures, exclusive of debt retirement of $525,763,800 and exclusive also of such sum as may be necessary for new and extraordinary recovery purposes, for the fiscal year ending June 30, 1935, amount to $3,960,798,700.

Again summarizing the main headings of these expenditures, they fall into the following items:

Expenditures for fiscal year ending June 30, 1935

General:

Departmental	$3,202,074,900
Legislative	18,734,500
Independent establishments	542,466,600
	$3,763,276,000
Less public-debt retirements	525,763,800
Total, general	$3,237,512,200

Emergency:

Public Works Administration	$1,089,883,100
Agricultural Adjustment Administration	5,000,000
Emergency conservation work	65,190,000
Reconstruction Finance Corporation	[1] 480,436,600
Tennessee Valley Authority	31,000,000
Federal land banks	12,650,000
Total, emergency	$ 723,286,500
Total, general and emergency, less public-debt retirements	$3,960,798,700

[1] Excess of credits—deduct.

It will be noted that many of these items such as public works fall under appropriations made in 1933, the actual expenditures not taking place until after June 30, 1934. (For details of above expenditures see Budget Statement No. 3, table A.)

The above figures do not include additional loans by the Reconstruction Finance Corporation. If its loaning authority is extended beyond June 30, 1934, it is contemplated that any additional loans by it would thereafter be taken from the new and additional recovery fund hereinafter referred to.

The estimates of receipts for the next fiscal year (ending June 30, 1935), exclusive of foreign-debt payments, of increased liquor taxes and of increased revenue flowing from amendments to the existing revenue law, amount to $3,974,665,479. (See Budget Statement No. 2, table A.)

Therefore, exclusive of debt retirement, these Budget estimates for the next fiscal year show a small surplus of $13,866,779. But it must be borne in mind that this surplus does not include any additional expenditures for extraordinary recovery purposes.

It is clear that the necessity for relief and recovery will still be with us during the year 1934-35. Additional relief funds will be necessary. Further needs of the country prohibit the abrupt termination of the Recovery Program. No person can on this date definitely predict the total amount that will be needed, or the itemizing of such an amount. It is my best judgment at this time that a total appropriation of not to exceed 2 billion dollars will, with the expenditures still to be made next year out of existing appropriations, be sufficient.

I shall therefore ask the Congress for appropriations approximating that amount.

This amount is not included in the Budget estimates. If appropriated and expended, therefore, it will change the small estimated surplus of 13 million dollars into a debt increase of nearly 2 billion dollars. It is only fair, of course, to say that such a debt increase would be partially offset by loans made against collateral and assets pledged.

Therefore, the total debt, if increased by the sum of 2 billion dollars during the fiscal year 1935, would amount to approximately $31,834,000,000 on June 30, 1935. It is my belief that so far as we can make estimates with our present knowledge, the Government should seek to hold the total debt within this amount. Furthermore, the Government during the balance of this calendar year should plan to bring its 1936 expenditures, including recovery and relief, within the revenues expected in the fiscal year 1936.

Let me put it another way: The excess of expenditures over receipts during this fiscal year amounts to over 7 billion dollars. My estimates for the coming fiscal year show an excess of expenditures over receipts of 2 billion dollars. We should plan to have a definitely balanced Budget for the third year of recovery and from that time on seek a continuing reduction of the national debt.

This excess of expenditures over revenues amounting to over 9 billion dollars during 2 fiscal years has been rendered necessary to bring the country to a sound condition after the unexampled crisis which we encountered last spring. It is a large amount, but the immeasurable benefits justify the cost.

The following table shows expenditures and receipts for the fiscal years 1934 and 1935 as contained in the Budget, plus the additional expenditures which will be made out of additional authorizations and appropriations here recommended. It shows, also, the estimated increase in the public debt and the book value of assets held as security against loans:

	1934	1935	2-year period 1934–35
Receipts[1]	$3,259,938,756	$3,974,665,479	$7,234,604,235
Expenditures (exclusive of debt retirement):			
General	2,530,720,267	2,486,768,200	5,017,488,467
Agricultural Adjustment Administration	514,800,000	750,744,000	1,265,544,000
Emergency[2]	6,357,486,700	723,286,500	7,080,773,200
	9,403,006,967	3,960,798,700	13,363,805,667
Additional expenditures from additional appropriations	1,166,000,000	2,000,000,000	3,166,000,000
Total expenditures	10,569,006,967	5,960,798,700	16,529,805,667
Increase in debt[3]	7,309,068,211	1,986,133,221	9,295,201,432
Estimated book value of assets held as security for loans	....	....	5,461,969,273

[1] These estimates of receipts are predicated on Federal Reserve Board average index of industrial production of 81 for the fiscal year 1934 and of 98 for the fiscal year 1935:

	Calendar year average	Fiscal year average
1929	119	118
1930	96	110
1931	81	87
1932	64	70
1933	[a] 76	67
1934	[b] 85	[b] 81
1935	....	[b] 98

[a] Partially estimated.

[b] Estimated.

[2] These include net expenditures after deducting Reconstruction Finance Corporation repayments in 1935 of $480,436,600.

[3] This figure does not include contingent liabilities such as Reconstruction Finance Corporation debentures issued to banks and other institutions.

APPROPRIATIONS

The Budget estimates of appropriations for 1935, exclusive of Agricultural Adjustment Administration benefit payments and refunds of processing taxes, but inclusive of all other appropriations for regular departments and independent establishments including interest on the debt and debt retirement, are $2,980,-293,833.60. When compared with Budget estimates of appropriations transmitted in the Budget for 1934, they show a reduction of $684,913,167.

A tabular comparative summary of receipts, estimates, appropriations, and expenditures, classified according to general and emergency items and listed by departments and under other general heads, appears in Budget Statement No. 1, Table B.

TAXES

The estimates of receipts take no account of the additional revenue which may be obtained from an increase in liquor taxes and from the proposed changes in the income-tax law. Since neither of these tax measures has come before Congress as yet, no accurate estimate can be made of their yield. However, if, as proposed by the Committee of Ways and Means, the tax on distilled spirits is increased from $1.10 a gallon to $2 a gallon, and the rates of tax on wines are also increased, the estimated revenue would be increased by approximately $50,000,000, assuming that consumption is not affected by additional gallonage taxes imposed by the States. Considerable additional revenue can also be secured from administrative changes in the income-tax law, which may amount to as much as $150,000,000 for a full year.

The estimates for the Post Office Department are predicated upon a continuation of the 3-cent postal rate for non-local mail. It is highly important that this rate be continued. I recommend its continuance.

ECONOMY LEGISLATION

The estimates of appropriations submitted in the Budget are predicated on the continuation of certain economy legislative provisions which I ask to be enacted and which are appended hereto. The most important is that having to do with reduction of compensation of Federal employees. It is eminently fair that, the cost of living having fallen as compared with 1928, the employees of the Government sustain some reduction in compensation. This is not inconsistent with our policy of advocating an increase in wages in industry. For wages there had fallen far beyond any reduction contemplated for Federal employees and in most grades are even now substantially below compensation paid Federal employees under the maximum reduction of 15 percent.

Among the legislative provisions appended hereto is one prohibiting automatic increases in compensation except in the Army, Navy, and Marine Corps. The personnel of these three services are engaged in a life service to their country. Some, by reason of the pay freezes, have sustained reduction in compensation of more than 25 percent. They are, therefore, in a different category from those in other governmental agencies. They should, in 1935, be released from the restrictions on automatic increases in compensation.

CONTROL

Up to now there has been no coordinated control over emergency expenditures. Today, by Executive order, I have imposed that necessary control in the Bureau of the Budget.

Heretofore, emergency expenditures have not been subject to audit by the Comptroller General of the General Accounting Office. Today I am, by Executive order, reposing in him the authority to conduct such an audit and to continue to audit each such expenditure. Hereafter, therefore, just as in the departmental expenditures, there will be, in emergency expenditures, a pre-Budget and a post-audit.

By reason of the fact that the Bureau of the Budget has had no control in the past over the various expenditures, obligations, and allotments made by the emergency organizations, the task of preparing the present Budget has been the most difficult one since the Budget and Accounting Act went into effect in 1921.

These difficulties, in future years, will be substantially minimized by the control which I have established.

* * *

It is evident to me, as I am sure it is evident to you, that powerful forces for recovery exist. It is by laying a foundation of confidence in the present and faith in the future that the upturn which we have so far seen will become cumulative. The cornerstone of this foundation is the good credit of the Government.

It is, therefore, not strange, nor is it academic, that this credit has a profound effect upon the confidence so necessary to permit the new recovery to develop into maturity.

If we maintain the course I have outlined, we can confidently look forward to cumulative beneficial forces represented by increased volume of business, more general profit, greater employment, a diminution of relief expenditures, larger governmental receipts and repayments, and greater human happiness.

For later budget message of this year, see Item 83, this volume, May 15, 1934.

4 ❡ The President Welcomes the First Ambassador of the Union of Soviet Socialist Republics. January 8, 1934

Mr. Ambassador:

I AM very happy to receive the letters accrediting you as Ambassador Extraordinary and Plenipotentiary of the Union of Soviet Socialist Republics and to welcome you in that capacity.

The foundation has now been laid for the development of genuinely friendly relations and close cooperation between the Governments of the United States of America and the Union of Soviet Socialist Republics. It will be your privilege and mine to work together in the task of building upon that foundation a permanent structure of friendship and collaboration.

A deep love of peace is the common heritage of the people of both our countries and I fully agree with you that the cooperation of our great Nations will inevitably be of the highest importance in the preservation of world peace. The successful accomplishment of this mutual task will be of immediate and lasting benefit not only to the people of our countries but to all peace-loving peoples everywhere.

I welcome you personally, Mr. Ambassador, with especial satisfaction. On more than one occasion during recent years you have shown your friendliness for the American people. This has not been unnoted or unappreciated by the Government of the United States and I consider it most auspicious that the Government of the Union of Soviet Socialist Republics should have selected as its first Ambassador to this country not only one of its most distinguished citizens but also one whose friendly feelings for this country are well known.

You may be assured, Mr. Ambassador, of reciprocally friendly feelings toward you on the part of the American Government and people. Members and officials of this Government will do all in their power to cooperate with you and will be glad to lend you every assistance that may contribute to the accomplishment of your mission, the success of which is greatly desired by my own as well as your Government.

I trust that you will inform His Excellency, the President of the Central Executive Committee, the Government, and the people of the Union of Soviet Socialist Republics that their kind messages of good-will are deeply appreciated and that I send in return sincere wishes for their peaceful progress and happiness.

5 ❧ White House Statement on Executive Order Fixing Reduction in Pay of Federal Employees. January 9, 1934

THE President today signed an Executive Order continuing the fifteen percent reduction in compensation of Federal officers and employees until June 30, 1934.

The Department of Labor reported two sets of findings. The first, based on the cost of living for families of wage earners and lower salaried workers in 32 cities scattered throughout the United States, reveals that the average cost of living for these groups in our population was, during the last half of 1933, 21.1 below the average of the base period of December, 1927, and June, 1928. In this set of findings the decline in the cost of living in the District of Columbia for similar families was 17.9.

The second set of findings resulted from a special study of the cost of living of Government employees in the District of Columbia and was made during the past three months by the Labor Department. These show a decline in the cost of living of 14.6 percent.

In view of the above and because the law provides for index figures covering all parts of the country, it is necessary to continue the present scale until June 30, 1934.

NOTE: The foregoing statement with reference to the Executive Order continuing reduction in pay shows the method of computation which was adopted after the Economy Act in fixing reductions in the salaries of Federal employees in accordance with fluctuations in the cost of living. This process is described in Item 12, Vol. II.

6 ❧ A Recommendation for Legislation to Guarantee Principal of Farm Mortgage Bonds.

January 10, 1934

To the Congress:

I HAVE already suggested to the Congress that one of our tasks, in the light of experience, is to improve and perfect previous legislation.

I now recommend that the Emergency Farm Credit Act of 1933 be amended to provide responsibility by the Government for the payment of the principal of, as well as interest on, bonds issued.

Two billion dollars of bonds were authorized. While the interest was guaranteed, the ultimate obligation of the Government for payment of the principal was not legally assumed. We should supplement what most of us frankly believe to be the moral responsibility of the Government by adding the necessary legal responsibility. The result of providing a bond on which both the principal and interest are guaranteed would be to put such bonds on a par with Treasury securities.

By setting up a corporation to issue these bonds, the important task of refinancing agricultural indebtedness can be continued on virtually a self-sustaining basis.

The Farm Credit Administration is expediting the disbursement of funds. In order that progress in making loans may be uninterrupted, I hope that the Congress will give attention to this subject as soon as possible.

It is true that technically the responsibilities of the Government will be increased by the amount of $2,000,000,000.00, but it seems in every way right that we thus publicly acknowledge what amounts already to a moral obligation. In any event, the securities to be offered are backed, not only by the credit of the Government, but also by physical property of very definite value.

NOTE: Because of the restricted condition of the money market it became necessary to provide Government assistance in raising money

27

with which to carry on the program of refinancing farm mortgages (see Items 29 and 54 of Vol. II).

The original Emergency Farm Mortgage Act of 1933 directed the Reconstruction Finance Corporation to make available to the Land Bank Commissioner the sum of $200,000,000 for the purpose of making the so-called Commissioner loans. It later became evident that the $200,000,000 would not be sufficient to meet the great number of demands for refinancing loans which had come in and were continuing to come in from farmers throughout the country.

The foregoing message recommended that the Government should raise the money by guaranteeing the principal as well as the interest of bonds issued for this purpose.

Pursuant to that recommendation the Federal Farm Mortgage Corporation Act was passed (Pub. No. 88, 73d Congress; 48 Stat. 344, approved January 31, 1934). Its aims were: (1) to assist in financing the Federal Land Banks during the period of emergency; and (2) to provide funds for Land Bank Commissioner loans.

The capital of the Federal Farm Mortgage Corporation was fixed at $200,000,000, and was subscribed by the Governor of the Farm Credit Administration on behalf of the United States. For the purposes of such subscription, the funds made available to the Land Bank Com-

missioner under §32 of the Emergency Farm Mortgage Act of 1933 and the mortgages taken by the Commissioner were transferred to the Corporation. The Corporation was authorized to issue bonds up to $2,000,000,000 to be fully and unconditionally guaranteed both as to interest and principal by the United States.

In this way the credit of the United States was used to raise money for the purpose of refinancing farm mortgages. As of November 30, 1937, the Corporation had bonds outstanding in the sum of $1,419,865,900.

Between May 1, 1933, and October 31, 1937, the Federal land banks and the Land Bank Commissioner made over 800,000 loans totaling over $2,200,000,000. There were outstanding on October 31, 1937, over 1,000,000 Federal land bank and Land Bank Commissioner loans totaling almost $2,900,000,000 including loans made by the Federal land banks prior to May 1, 1933.

In addition to loans made by the Federal land banks and the Land Bank Commissioner, other lending institutions and agencies under the supervision of the Farm Credit Administration made approximately for all purposes under its jurisdiction 2,700,000 loans for slightly more than $2,400,000,000. Loans outstanding of these institutions and agencies totaled approximately $500,000,000 as of Oct. 31, 1937.

7 ❨A Request for Senate Ratification of the St. Lawrence Treaty with Canada. January 10, 1934

To the Senate:

I REQUEST the consideration of ratification by the Senate of the so-called "St. Lawrence Treaty with Canada." Broad national reasons lead me, without hesitation, to advocate the treaty. There are two main considerations, navigation and power. Canada and the United States are possessed of a natural flow of water from near the center of the continent to the ocean — a flow which throughout the greater part of its length is today available for navigation by large-size vessels. A system of locks at the eastern end of Lake Superior, a dredged channel between Lake Huron and Lake Erie, and another series of great locks between Lake Erie and Lake Ontario provide free and adequate navigation to a point well down the St. Lawrence River. From there, a series of three rapids, all of them within a distance of 120 miles, now impede navigation by ocean-going vessels; but a Canadian canal already provides facilities for smaller ships. This Canadian canal now is used substantially up to its capacity.

Two of the three rapids are wholly in Canadian territory; the other is in the so-called "international" section. A great power development at the Beauharnois Rapids in Canada is already nearing completion and locks for ocean-going ships have been planned for and could readily be built at a low cost as part of the plan. This means that only two additional series of locks are required for a complete and continuous seaway from Duluth to salt water. I call your attention to the simple fact that Canada alone can, if it desires, build locks at the Lachine Rapids and at the international sector and thus provide a seaway wholly within Canadian control without treaty participation by the United States. This, however, would be a reversal of the policy of cooperation which the United States and Canada have continuously maintained for generations.

I want to make it very clear that this great international highway for shipping is without any question going to be completed in the near future and that this completion should be carried out by both Nations instead of by one.

I am sending you herewith a summary of data prepared at my request by governmental agencies. This summary, in its relation to the economic aspects of the seaway, shows from the broad national point of view, first, that commerce and transportation will be greatly benefited and, secondly, that local fears of economic harm to special localities or to special interests are grossly exaggerated. It is, I believe, a historic fact that every great improvement directed to better commercial communications, whether in the case of railroads into new territory, or the deepening of great rivers, or the building of canals, or even the cutting of the Isthmus of Panama, have all been subjected to opposition on the part of local interests which conjure up imaginary fears and fail to realize that improved transportation results in increased commerce benefiting directly or indirectly all sections.

For example, I am convinced that the building of the St. Lawrence Seaway will not injure the railroads or throw their employees out of work; that it will not in any way interfere with the proper use of the Mississippi River or the Missouri River for navigation. Let us be wholly frank in saying that it is better economics to send grain or other raw materials from our Northwest to Europe via the Great Lakes and St. Lawrence than it is to send them around three sides of a square — via Texas ports or the Mississippi, thence through the Gulf of Mexico, and thence from the southern end of the North Atlantic to its northern end. In this illustration, it is well to remember that a straight line is the shortest distance between two points.

I am satisfied that the treaty contains adequate provision for the needs of the Chicago Drainage District and for navigation between Lake Michigan and the Mississippi River. A special report from the Chief of Engineers of the War Department covers this subject.

On the affirmative side, I subscribe to the definite belief that the completion of the seaway will greatly serve the economic and transportation needs of a vast area of the United States and should, therefore, be considered solely from the national point of view.

The other great objective provided for in the treaty relates to the development of electric power. As you know, I have advocated the development of four great power areas in the United States, each to serve as a yardstick and each to be controlled by government or governmental agencies. The Tennessee Valley plants and projects in the Southeast, the Boulder Dam on the Colorado River in the Southwest, the Columbia River projects in the Northwest are already under construction. The St. Lawrence development in the Northeast calls for action. This river is a source of incomparably cheap power located in proximity to a great industrial and rural market and within transmission distance of millions of domestic consumers.

The Legislature of the State of New York by unanimous vote set up the necessary State machinery during my term as Governor of New York and the State stands ready to cooperate with the Federal Government in the distribution of power in accordance with what I believe is today a definite national policy.

Power in the international sector of the St. Lawrence cannot be developed without a treaty between the United States and Canada. On the other hand, Canada can develop a huge block of new power at the two other rapids which lie wholly within Canadian territory. Here again, as in the case of navigation, it is better in every way that we should maintain the historic principle of accord with Canada in the mutual development of the two Nations.

I have not stressed the fact that the starting of this great work will put thousands of unemployed to work. I have preferred to stress the great future advantages to our country and especially the fact that all of us should view this treaty in the light of the benefits which it confers on the people of the United States as a whole.

NOTE: The actual signing of the treaty for the development of the St. Lawrence River was postponed until July 18th, 1932, two days after

31

the adjournment of the Congress, thus definitely precluding its consideration by the Senate in 1932. (See note and Items in Chapter IV of Vol. I for the recent history of this development.) During the last week of the regular 1932 session, however, the Senate had adopted a resolution authorizing a subcommittee of the Committee on Foreign Relations to conduct an inquiry with respect to matters touching the St. Lawrence waterways treaty.

This subcommittee convened after the election on November 14, 1932.

On December 13 and 14, the Power Authority of the State of New York presented evidence before this subcommittee. It called attention to the long fight in New York State to prevent the exploitation of the St. Lawrence power resources by private interests, and to the crystallization of public sentiment in the State in support of public development. It further called attention to the adaptability of the resources to public development, to the economic soundness of the project insuring great benefits to the consumers of electricity and to the enormous waste of energy resulting from delay in its development.

The Power Authority further called attention to the importance of an understanding between State and Federal authorities on engineering plans, representation on agencies created by the treaty, and

on allocation of costs on a basis which would not place an excessive burden on the power project as distinguished from the navigation project. It recounted the difficulties it had faced in attempting to deal with the previous Administration on these points. It emphasized the contrast between this condition and that across the border, where the Dominion of Canada and the Province of Ontario had reached an agreement between themselves prior to the signing of the treaty.

The Power Authority pointed out that the Treaty, as drawn, embodied engineering plans which would have provided for a permanent diversion by the Aluminum Company of 25,000 c.f.s. to its Massena power plant, thereby reducing by 25 percent the United States share of the average flow of the river at the main dam. It called upon the Committee to eliminate this provision and to establish safeguards to prevent the assertion of any private right or claim to the waters of the St. Lawrence.

As a result of this protest, notes were exchanged between the United States and the Canadian Governments by which Canada agreed in advance to any modification of the plans with respect to the diversion through the Massena power canal that might be necessary to safeguard the rights of the State.

The subcommittee of the Senate Committee on Foreign Relations thereupon reported in favor of ratification of the proposed treaty, subject to the agreements, provisions and interpretations set forth in this exchange of notes. The subcommittee report also took cognizance of the agreement between the Power Authority and the United States Corps of Engineers, establishing $89,726,000 as the proper allocation of cost to the power project.

The full Committee on Foreign Relations accepted the report of the subcommittee and on February 21, 1933, favorably reported the treaty to the Senate.

After March 4, 1933, there was a complete reversal of the policy of thinly-veiled non-cooperation which had characterized the attitude of the preceding Administration toward New York's public power project. I continued the close relations with the New York Power Authority developed while I was Chief Executive of the State. I conferred frequently with Chairman Walsh and arranged for the Power Authority to cooperate with the State Department, the Federal Power Commission and other federal agencies handling various aspects of the Great Lakes-St. Lawrence project.

The new Congress, which convened on March 4, 1933, was dominated by the necessity of enacting immediate legislation to lift the country out of the depression and to remove glaring abuses in its social and economic life. In spite of this primary necessity, the Power Authority was able to secure the cooperation of the Senate Committee on Foreign Relations and the House Committee on Interstate and Foreign Commerce in the introduction of a joint resolution confirming the agreement reached February 7, 1933 with the United States Corps of Engineers covering allocation of the cost of the works in the International Section of the St. Lawrence River, as between navigation and power.

This resolution, entitled H. J. Res. 157, subsequently passed by the House of Representatives on April 26, 1933, contained the following important proviso approved by me:

"*Provided,* that no part of the United States' share of the water in the international rapids section of the St. Lawrence River shall be diverted for the benefit of any person or private corporation, nor shall the use of any part of said water or the rights pertaining to said water be sold, leased, or otherwise alienated to any person or private corporation for the generation of hydroelectric power."

Reference of this joint resolution to the Senate Committee on Foreign Relations for prompt consideration on its merits was blocked by some of those opposed to the treaty itself.

On June 8, 1933, I sent a letter addressed to Senator LaFollette

33

in the absence of Senator Pittman, the Chairman of the Senate Committee on Foreign Relations, who had just sailed as a delegate to the London Economic Conference, strongly urging the adoption of the resolution and favoring ratification of the treaty itself. During the last hours of the session, a final effort to pass this joint resolution as an amendment to the National Industrial Recovery Act failed. I promptly requested reconsideration of the vote by which this amendment was defeated, but in the closing hours of the session it was impossible to obtain this result without holding up the program of recovery legislation.

The Senate debates on the joint resolution above noted had revealed that opponents of the treaty were going to stress the need for a comprehensive economic survey of the proposed undertaking. I therefore decided that I would have such a survey ready to be used in connection with the formal submission of the treaty to the Senate.

After a conference at the White House, September 14, 1933, I announced the formation of an interdepartmental board to make such a survey of the project in all its aspects, including both navigation and power.

The Interdepartmental Board on the Great Lakes-St. Lawrence Project, with Chairman Frank R. McNinch of the Federal Power Commission as chairman, included representatives of the following cooperating Government agencies: Federal Power Commission, War Department, Department of Commerce, Department of Agriculture, Interstate Commerce Commission, and, with the consent of the Governor of New York, the Power Authority.

The Interdepartmental Board survey of the Great Lakes-St. Lawrence seaway and power project was completed early in January, 1934, and a summary of the data was submitted to me on January 10, 1934.

On the same day, in the foregoing message to the Senate, I requested consideration of ratification by the Senate of the so-called "St. Lawrence Treaty with Canada."

With the foregoing message I transmitted a summary of the extended report of the Interdepartmental Board. The full report was transmitted later and was subsequently printed in two volumes as Senate Doc. No. 116, 73d Congress, 2d Session.

The summary describes the project as follows:

"The Great Lakes-St. Lawrence Waterway is already in existence. Its development is not a question of initiating, but rather of completing, a project in the improvement of which the United States and Canada have whole-heartedly cooperated for generations. The vessels of both countries have navigated its waters freely and with equal rights since the Webster-Ashburton Treaty of 1842. Throughout this entire period it has been in the truest sense an international highway, unique in the fact that for more than a century no warship has floated in its waters. The United States and Canada have already with common accord expended many millions of dollars in its improvement and it now carries an enormous tonnage even in its most restricted sections.

"The waterway, which now extends from Duluth-Superior at the western end of the Great Lakes system to the Atlantic Ocean, a distance of 2,350 miles, has already been improved to a minimum depth of 21 feet except in the relatively short section of the St. Lawrence River which lies between Prescott-Ogdensburg and Montreal. In this 120-mile section there are now 47 miles of 14-foot canals. This constricted section forms a bottle neck which prevents the passage of ordinary ocean-going vessels and makes the port of Montreal virtually the head of ocean navigation and the transshipment point for inbound and outbound commerce.

"The pending Great Lakes-St. Lawrence deep waterway treaty is in substance an agreement between the United States and Canada to complete the improvement of the existing waterway to provide a minimum depth of 27 feet from the Great Lakes ports to the Atlantic Ocean.

"The major portion of the work provided for in the treaty between the United States and Canada will be done in the international rapids section of the St. Lawrence River, which forms the boundary between the State of New York and the Province of Ontario. Here two great dams will be constructed converting the existing turbulent rapids into deep pools where navigation will be unrestricted. Ocean-going vessels will be passed around these dams by canals having a total length of 10 miles with three locks capable of handling large ocean-going vessels without delay. The dams will also be used to generate 2,200,000 horsepower of electrical energy which will be shared equally between the United States and Canada."

Important conclusions of the Interdepartmental Board with regard to the economic justification for the seaway may be summarized as follows:

Estimated Commerce and Savings

1. The annual capacity of the proposed Great Lakes-St. Lawrence seaway is conservatively estimated at 25,000,000 tons, as compared with the 9,000,000 ton capacity of the existing 14-foot St. Lawrence canals. Traffic is already pressing the present capacity and enlargement must be undertaken if serious congestion of commerce is to be avoided.

2. The proposed improvement to a minimum depth of 27 feet will enable more than 70 percent of the world's ocean-going freight tonnage to use the proposed seaway. This will provide a waterway from Duluth to the Atlantic in which ocean-going vessels may move with unrestricted speed over approximately 97 percent of the total distance.

3. Comparison with the important ship canals of the world, including the Manchester, Kiel, Suez, Panama Canals and the North Sea Canal to Amsterdam, shows that the proposed seaway is completely practical for navigation by ocean-cargo vessels.

4. The net cost to the United States of completing the proposed seaway under the treaty is estimated at $182,726,000, which estimate assumes that the New York Power Project, to develop 1,100,000 horsepower on the United States side of the international rapids, will carry $89,726,000 as its share of the cost. The annual cost of operation and maintenance of the seaway, of interest on bonds at 4 percent, and of amortization in fifty years is estimated at only $9,300,000.

5. The potential export and import tonnage which will move via the seaway, based on 1929 conditions, is conservatively estimated in a special study prepared by the War Department at 13,000,000 tons per year, and the annual savings in transportation costs, as compared with present available routes, at approximately $79,000,000.

6. Potential exports via the waterway include wheat and grain products, meat and animal fats, manufactured iron, chemicals, automobiles, agricultural implements, and copper. Potential imports include sugar, rubber and rubber substitutes, coffee, bananas, kaolin, vegetable oil, manganese and pyrites.

7. In the 10 years, 1923 to 1932, inclusive, the domestic coastwise and intercoastal trade of the country comprised approximately four-fifths of the total water-borne commerce. In other words, the volume of domestic commerce was four times that of foreign commerce. This suggests that the ports on the country's other coasts will be more largely benefited by the growth of intercoastal commerce moving via the Great Lakes-St. Lawrence waterway than they can be injured by changes in the movement of foreign commerce occasioned thereby.

The New Seacoast and its Tributary Area

8. Completion of the waterway would create what is tantamount to a new sea coast for the United States, 3,576 miles in length of shore line reaching into the heart of the country, and converting thirty American cities located on the Lakes and on connecting channels into virtual seaports.

9. The seaway area is defined by a line on the map of the United States bounding the area adjacent to the seaway in which transportation costs to and from the markets of the world would be reduced by the improvement. It includes Ohio, Indiana, Michigan, Illinois, Wisconsin, Missouri, Iowa, Minnesota, North Dakota, South Dakota, Nebraska and Kansas in their entirety, and parts of New York, Pennsylvania, Kentucky, Colorado, Wyoming and Montana.

10. The population of the area to be served was, in 1930, forty-five million people, or more than 35 percent of the country's population. The area includes thirty cities of more than one hundred

thousand population each. The factory products in the area, as of that year, equaled in value 46 percent of the total of the United States as a whole. The acres of crop land within the area were 52 percent of the country's total, raising 50 percent of the total livestock, 52 percent of all the dairy cattle, 72 percent of all the hogs, 76 percent of all the corn, 84 percent of all the oats and 64 percent of all the wheat raised in the United States. Its wholesale trade amounted to about 33 percent of the national total.

11. The unimproved sections of the St. Lawrence River form a bottle-neck obstruction to navigation by ocean-going vessels which confines the commerce of the Great Lakes ports almost entirely to trade with each other and prevents their participation in intercoastal trade with Atlantic, Gulf and Pacific ports. Removal of these obstructions would stimulate coastwise and intercoastal shipping in the home market of the United States, which is confined by law to American bottoms. The opening of the Great Lakes region, with a capacity for production and consumption comparable with the North Atlantic States, must result in benefits not only to lake ports and their adjoining territory but also to the nation as a whole.

The Seaway Will Not Harm the Railroads

12. A reasonable forecast of the demand for railroad freight transportation by 1950, as compared with 1929, is an increase of 200,000,000,000 tons. The proposed seaway, therefore, cannot be viewed as tending to take away from the railroads a portion of their existing tonnage, but rather as a part of a program for expanding a coordinated transportation system designed to handle the country's increasing traffic most economically.

13. If the comparison is limited to the railroads paralleling the proposed seaway, the growth of traffic offered will exceed the potential seaway traffic ten times over, and these are the roads over which the traffic density is already greatest.

14. Analysis of detailed traffic trends, including a study of the experience of Western railroads, as a result of the opening of the Panama Canal, substantiates the statement that the seaway will not adversely affect the railroads of the country. It suggests, on the contrary, that the economic development which the new navigation route will stimulate will benefit rather than injure the roads.

The Power Project

With respect to the St. Lawrence power project to be constructed in conjunction with the seaway development in the International Section of the St. Lawrence River, the

37

report of the Interdepartmental Board may be summarized as follows:

1. The Great Lakes-St. Lawrence seaway project does not involve the United States in any expenditure whatever for power developments in those sections of the river which are entirely Canadian. The power in the most important Canadian section, i.e., the Soulanges Rapids section, is already being developed by Canadian private interests. This is no concern of the United States under the Great Lakes-St. Lawrence project but it does afford a cogent economic reason for the early development of power in the international rapids section, if the United States is to keep pace in providing cheap current for its rural and domestic consumers and for industry.

2. The St. Lawrence power project, so far as the United States is concerned, involves the development of approximately 1,100,000 horsepower in that section of the river which serves as the international boundary between the State of New York and the Province of Ontario. If the agreement with the New York Power Authority is confirmed, as embodied in the joint resolution which passed the House of Representatives but which failed to pass the Senate in 1933 as above indicated, that agency will assume responsibility for $89,726,750 of the total United States investment under the treaty. The corresponding power development on the other side of the river will be paid for by the Province of Ontario.

3. The international rapids section of the St. Lawrence River provides an exceptional opportunity for hydroelectric power development within transmission distance of the most important power market in the United States. It will assure power within a radius of 300 miles of the project at a cost low enough to stimulate industrial development and provide means for reducing electric rates to domestic and farm consumers throughout the entire area.

4. The remarkable uniformity of flow of water from the tremendous storage reservoir of the Great Lakes, consisting of 94,000 square miles, can be relied upon to make available, by generation on the United States side of the international boundary, 769,562 horsepower of primary energy and 141,798 horsepower of high-grade secondary energy, aggregating a potential annual output of approximately 5,700,000,-000 kilowatt hours of electricity, primary and secondary. This is equivalent to approximately one-half of all the electricity produced in New York State in 1932.

5. St. Lawrence power will be developed at very low cost. It is estimated that, including the costs of maintenance and operation, interest at 4 percent on the bonds, amortization within forty years, and allowance for depreciation, St. Lawrence power can be generated for

an annual cost of about $6,000,000 or $7.92 per horsepower year of primary energy and $5.54 per horsepower year of installed capacity.

6. On a publicly owned transmission line St. Lawrence power can be made available for base load power at 80 percent load factor at a total cost of 3.13 mills in Southern New York, and 3.8 mills in New York City. At 60 percent load factor the corresponding costs would be 4.2 mills for southern New York and 5.1 mills for New York City. These figures indicate that St. Lawrence power can be utilized over a wide area, at costs materially below those of generating that power by steam.

7. A ready market for St. Lawrence power is assured by the fact that the area within transmission distance, totaling 114,835 square miles, is one of the most densely populated regions in the country. It has a density of population of 213 per square mile, as compared with 40.5 per square mile for the country as a whole. Within the market area for power resides approximately 20 percent of the country's population.

8. The market area is also important in terms of the demand for power for industrial purposes, since it is responsible for about 28 percent of all factory production of the United States. In fact, the factories within transmission distance of the St. Lawrence power project

spent $422,000,000 for power and fuel in 1929.

9. Assurance of expansion in this great market for power is found in the growth of population, increasing per capita consumption of electricity, the increase in average residential use of electricity, extension of rural electrification, increased use of central-station power in factories, development of new industries dependent on large supplies of power, railroad electrification and highway lighting.

10. Scientifically determined trends suggest that the combined results of these factors will probably require an increase in the power supply of New York State from 14,000,000,000 kilowatt hours in 1930, to 21,000,000,000 kilowatt hours in 1940 and 28,000,000,000 kilowatt hours in 1950. This demand would absorb by 1940 the entire potential output of the St. Lawrence project if used as base-load power. In fact, authoritative forecasts from the electric industry anticipate an even greater increase in demand for power than this analysis shows.

11. The reduction in rates which will come from public development of power will itself increase the amount of power used. This is especially important in terms of encouragement to larger domestic use of electricity, as illustrated by Ontario municipalities, where residential bills averaging from 2.6 cents down to 0.8 cents per kilowatt hour are

associated with average residential consumption ranging from 816 to 4692 kilowatt hours per home per year.

12. Analysis of the relationship between power development and growth of industry in other regions shows that the installation of the proposed 1,100,000 hydroelectric horsepower on the United States side of the St. Lawrence River is likely to bring with it investment of over $500,000,000 in new industries, with employment for some 80,000 additional factory workers and a corresponding increase in population and in all lines of economic activity including rail transportation of raw materials and consumer goods.

13. The proposed development of St. Lawrence power by the Power Authority of the State of New York is primarily for the purpose of securing the lowest possible rates for domestic and rural consumers of electricity. It is the last opportunity available to provide the Northeastern section of the country with the benefits assured to other sections of the country through the development of the Tennessee Valley River basin, the Colorado River and the Columbia River.

The proposed treaty was defeated in the Senate on March 14, 1934, by a vote of 46 ayes and 42 nays, the required two-thirds affirmative vote not having been obtained.

See Item 34 of Vol. V for a further discussion of this proposed development.

8 ❬ Request for Legislation to Organize a Sound and Adequate Currency System. January 15, 1934

To the Congress:

IN CONFORMITY with the progress we are making in restoring a fairer price level and with our purpose of arriving eventually at a less variable purchasing power for the dollar, I ask the Congress for certain additional legislation to improve our financial and monetary system. By making clear that we are establishing permanent metallic reserves in the possession and ownership of the Federal Government, we can organize a currency system which will be both sound and adequate.

The issuance and control of the medium of exchange which we call "money" is a high prerogative of government. It has been such for many centuries. Because they were scarce, because they could readily be sub-divided and transported, gold and silver have been used either for money or as a basis for forms of money which in themselves had only nominal intrinsic value.

In pure theory, of course, a government could issue mere tokens to serve as money — tokens which would be accepted at their face value if it were certain that the amount of these tokens were permanently limited and confined to the total amount necessary for the daily cash needs of the community. Because this assurance could not always or sufficiently be given, governments have found that reserves or bases of gold and silver behind their paper or token currency added stability to their financial systems.

There is still much confusion of thought which prevents a world-wide agreement creating a uniform monetary policy. Many advocate gold as the sole basis of currency; others advocate silver; still others advocate both gold and silver whether as separate bases, or on a basis with a fixed ratio, or on a fused basis.

We hope that, despite present world confusion, events are leading to some future form of general agreement. The recent London agreement in regard to silver was a step, though only a step, in this direction.

At this time we can usefully take a further step, which we hope will contribute to an ultimate world-wide solution.

Certain lessons seem clear. For example, the free circulation of gold coins is unnecessary, leads to hoarding, and tends to a possible weakening of national financial structures in times of emergency. The practice of transferring gold from one individual to another or from the Government to an individual within a Nation is not only unnecessary, but is in every way undesirable. The transfer of gold in bulk is essential only for the payment of international trade balances.

Therefore it is a prudent step to vest in the Government of a Nation the title to and possession of all monetary gold within its boundaries and to keep that gold in the form of bullion rather than in coin.

Because the safe-keeping of this monetary basis rests with the Government, we have already called in the gold which was in the possession of private individuals or corporations. There remains, however, a very large weight in gold bullion and coins which is still in the possession or control of the Federal Reserve banks.

Although under existing law there is authority, by executive act, to take title to the gold in the possession or control of the Reserve Banks, this is a step of such importance that I prefer to ask the Congress by specific enactment to vest in the United States Government title to all supplies of American-owned monetary gold, with provision for the payment therefor in gold certificates. These gold certificates will be, as now, secured at all times dollar for dollar by gold in the Treasury—gold for each dollar of such weight and fineness as may be established from time to time.

Such legislation places the right, title and ownership to our gold reserves in the Government itself; it makes clear the Government's ownership of any added dollar value of the country's stock of gold which would result from any decrease of the gold content of the dollar which may be made in the public interest. It would also, of course, with equal justice, cast upon the Government the loss of such dollar value if the public interest in the future should require an increase in the amount of gold designated as a dollar.

The title to all gold being in the Government, the total stock will serve as a permanent and fixed metallic reserve which will change in amount only so far as necessary for the settlement of international balances or as may be required by a future agreement among the Nations of the world for a redistribution of the world stock of monetary gold.

With the establishment of this permanent policy, placing all monetary gold in the ownership of the Government as a bullion base for its currency, the time has come for a more certain determination of the gold value of the American dollar. Because of world uncertainties, I do not believe it desirable in the public interest that an exact value be now fixed. The President is authorized by present legislation to fix the lower limit of permissible revaluation at 50 percent. Careful study leads me to believe that any revaluation at more than 60 percent of the present statutory

42

value would not be in the public interest. I, therefore, recommend to the Congress that it fix the upper limit of permissible revaluation at 60 percent.

That we may be further prepared to bring some greater degree of stability to foreign exchange rates in the interests of our people, there should be added to the present power of the Secretary of the Treasury to buy and sell gold at home and abroad, express power to deal in foreign exchange as such. As a part of this power, I suggest that, out of the profits of any devaluation, there should be set up a fund of two billion dollars for such purchases and sales of gold, foreign exchange, and Government securities as the regulation of the currency, the maintenance of the credit of the Government and the general welfare of the United States may require.

Certain amendments of existing legislation relating to the purchase and sale of gold and to other monetary matters would add to the convenience of handling current problems in this field. The Secretary of the Treasury is prepared to submit information concerning such changes to the appropriate committees of the Congress.

The foregoing recommendations relate chiefly to gold. The other principal precious metal — silver — has also been used from time immemorial as a metallic base for currencies as well as for actual currency itself. It is used as such by probably half the population of the world. It constitutes a very important part of our own monetary structure. It is such a crucial factor in much of the world's international trade that it cannot be neglected.

On December 21, 1933, I issued a proclamation providing for the coinage of our newly mined silver and for increasing our reserves of silver bullion, thereby putting us among the first Nations to carry out the silver agreement entered into by sixty-six Governments at the London Conference. This agreement is distinctly a step in the right direction and we are proceeding to perform our part of it.

All of the sixty-six Nations agreed to refrain from melting or debasing their silver coins, to replace paper currency of small denominations with silver coins and to refrain from legislation that would depreciate the value of silver in the world markets. Those Nations producing large quantities of silver agreed to take specified amounts from their domestic production and those holding and using large quantities agreed to restrict the amount they would sell during the four years covered by the agreement.

If all these undertakings are carried out by the Governments concerned, there will be a marked increase in the use and value of silver.

Governments can well, as they have in the past, employ silver as a basis for currency, and I look for a greatly increased use. I am, however, withholding any recommendation to the Congress looking to further extension of the monetary use of silver because I believe that we should gain more knowledge of the results of the London agreement and of our other monetary measures.

Permit me once more to stress two principles. Our national currency must be maintained as a sound currency which, insofar as possible, will have a fairly constant standard of purchasing power and be adequate for the purposes of daily use and the establishment of credit.

The other principle is the inherent right of Government to issue currency and to be the sole custodian and owner of the base or reserve of precious metals underlying that currency. With this goes the prerogative of Government to determine from time to time the extent and nature of the metallic reserve. I am confident that the Nation will well realize the definite purpose of the Government to maintain the credit of that Government and, at the same time, to provide a sound medium of exchange which will serve the needs of our people.

NOTE: On January 15, 1934, the Secretary of the Treasury announced that a sufficient time had elapsed for the delivery of gold coin, gold bullion and gold certificates to the Treasury pursuant to the various Executive Orders since Executive Order No. 6102, April 5, 1933 (see Item 33, Vol. II), including the latest order on the subject, that of the Secretary of the Treasury of December 28, 1933. He accordingly fixed midnight of January 17, 1934, as the expiration of the period within which such gold should be delivered.

In the foregoing message to the Congress made on the same day, January 15, 1934, I further stated the future monetary policies of the Administration. It will be observed that the message also reaffirms certain essential points already made clear in the earlier acts of the Administration, in regard to hoarding and to governmental control of gold reserves.

I laid stress in this message on the two principles which were basic to the formulation of a monetary policy: (1) the maintenance of a sound currency which in so far as possible would have a fairly constant standard of purchasing power and be adequate for purposes of daily use and the establishment of credit; and (2) the right of Government to issue currency and to be the sole custodian and owner of the reserve of the precious metals underlying that currency, with the power to determine from time to time the extent and nature of the metallic reserves.

I pointed out that the free circulation of gold, except for the payment of international trade balances, is unnecessary, leads to hoarding and is dangerous to the financial structure in times of emergency. I suggested that the Secretary of Treasury should be given power, in addition to his then existing authority, to buy and sell gold at home and abroad, and to deal in foreign exchange as such. I also referred to the function of silver as a basis for currency. Pursuant to this message, the Congress passed the Gold Reserve Act of 1934 (Pub. No. 87, 73d Congress; 48 Stat. 337).

See Item 16 of this volume for a discussion of this Act and for a résumé of the monetary policy and program to date. The following press conference of the same date as this message (Item 9, this volume) also discusses the message and the subject of devaluation of the dollar.

On the same day as the message, January 15, 1934, I issued three Executive Orders, Nos. 6558, 6559, and 6560, not printed in these volumes.

The two last Executive Orders, in general, freed dealings in foreign exchange to a certain degree from their former license requirements. While they continued to prohibit foreign-exchange transactions except under licenses, the orders provided that unless prohibited by the Secretary of the Treasury foreign-exchange transactions and transfers of credit could be carried on without a license for (a) normal commercial and business requirements, (b) reasonable travel and personal requirements, (c) the fulfillment of legally enforceable obligations incurred prior to March 9, 1933.

9 ❡ The Eighty-eighth Press Conference (Excerpts). January 15, 1934

(Gold and Silver — Message to the Congress of January 15, 1934, Item 8 of this volume — Devaluation of the dollar.)

THE PRESIDENT: Are these the only people out of all the White House correspondents who know anything about finance? *(Laughter)*

Q. We are the only ones who admit that we do not. *(Laughter)*

THE PRESIDENT: The easiest way, I think, is for me to read this release to you. *(Referring to the preceding Item 8)*

MR. EARLY: They already have it.

THE PRESIDENT: I just want to say one or two things. In the first place, Steve wanted me to stress that all this is in confidence until the message is released and nothing is to be said in advance of the release.

Q. By the way, when will the release be made?

THE PRESIDENT: As soon as it gets up there to Congress. I don't know whether it is released up there before it is read by the Clerk or not, but I see by the heading "until its reading has begun in the Senate or in the House."

Now, in a nutshell, the first portion of this, down to the first line, might be called philosophical. In other words, it merely goes into the general theory that the issuance of money or currency or any medium of exchange is solely a Government prerogative and always has been since the days of Babylon or the time they used sea shells or coral beads in the South Sea Islands. In theory, coral beads are a perfectly good medium of exchange, perfectly good money as such, provided there is control over them. It becomes a question of control. Throughout history it has always been advisable, for the sake of stability, to have some basis behind the currency which, as a matter of practical fact through the ages, has been the precious metals, gold and silver.

Q. Might we assume that that is an argument against greenbacks — what you have just stated?

THE PRESIDENT: It certainly is an argument against starting of the printing presses. On the other hand, of course, as you know, there has been a very great difference of opinion as to what is a greenback and what is not a greenback. This is the easiest illustration — if we were to start tomorrow to pay off the deficit of this year just by printing greenbacks, they really would be greenbacks; there is no question about that.

On the other hand, a limited amount of non-interest-bearing five- and ten-dollar bonds to retire an outstanding debt and with provision for retirement of those new non-interest-bearing bonds would not be greenbacks.

What people fear about greenbacks is, of course, that some future Congress may take off the limit — take off the lid.

Then we come down to the next point which is the taking of the title to the gold by the Government. That follows out logically the theory that the Government is entitled to control the basis behind all currency.

Then the third point is the establishment of an upper limit within which I have to act. By that I mean that I could not stabilize at above 60 if this bill is put through. This bill does not stabilize at 60. It leaves me free to stabilize between 50 and 60.

And — this is just for information because I have noted one or two stories — there has been absolutely no doubt from the legal point of view of the authority under the previous Act to stabilize more than once and to put it at 50 or 60 or anything else I want, as often as I want.

Q. What Act is that?

THE PRESIDENT: Oh, last spring; the Banking bill. . . .

Then the third point in that same paragraph. It would set up a fund of two billion dollars for the purchase and sale of gold, foreign exchange, and Government securities.

Q. Might that be called a stabilization fund?

THE PRESIDENT: Well, that is only part of it. . . .

Q. The point I had in mind was this: that this would permit you to deal with foreign exchange without definitely fixing, permanently, the value of the dollar.

THE PRESIDENT: Let me give you a little background on this particular thing, because I think it is important. Last spring things went up much too fast in this country. Wheat went up to $1.25, which, undoubtedly, was altogether too high. That was caused by speculation. A great many manufacturers overproduced, the steel companies overproduced, the textile people overproduced, all for various reasons, trying to get in under the wire before the Code went into effect.

The result was a perfectly natural one. There was quite a big drop in commodity prices of all kinds around the middle of July. That was a perfectly healthy thing. But a little bit later on, somewhere around September, there began a very definite drift of commodity prices downward. That was caused by a great many factors. It was caused by people who did not approve of N.R.A. codes, it was caused by some of our foreign friends who were deliberately trying to increase the exchange value of the dollar and decrease the exchange value of the franc — there were a good many foreign elements that entered into it.

The result was that by the tenth or fifteenth of October we were in a definite downward drift which, if carried out, would have been a serious thing. Wheat, which should have a normal value of 85 or 90 cents had got down to 60. Cotton had got down to below 9 cents a pound and there was a rather determined drive against prices. The whole line was down.

That was when we took action on gold. I have forgotten what gold was at that particular point; it was around 4.60, as I remember it. It was around 4.60, and the tendency was for it to go to 4.50, 4.40 or 4.30; and because of the pressure on the other side, if left alone it might perhaps eventually have gone back to the figure that the British Treasury and the Bank of England were taking as the stabilization figure away back last May and June, about 3.90 to the pound.

We then started to purchase gold. There are various ways of maintaining foreign exchange. You can either purchase bills of exchange, etc., or actually buy the gold. This move today was in prospect at that time, and obviously it was to the interest of the United States to buy gold. So we bought gold and have been buying it ever since in fairly large quantities and the result has been that the exchange has gone up to well over five dollars and has maintained itself there largely because of the American purchase of gold.

It has, I think, been felt by people on the other side as well as here that if we had not pursued the gold-purchase policy, the actual exchange-value rate on gold would be four dollars instead of five dollars.

The other result of maintaining the dollar-pound and dollar-franc ratio as high as it has been was our ability to get rid of a great many of our export surpluses. Cotton has been moving out. Of course, you know one of our objectives is to eliminate the very large surplus which has been overhanging the domestic prices. The same thing applies to wheat and everything else. Our objective has been to get rid of the surpluses. We got rid of a great deal of cotton and we got rid of a great deal of copper, for instance. At the same time the import trade has increased enormously during the past three months, since the dollar has gone down in terms of pounds. The result has been a very excellent one from a general economic domestic point of view.

This revaluation of not more than 60 percent and not below 50 percent should enable us to maintain a fairly reasonable exchange ratio with other Nations. The reason it has to be done this way is what I said in the message to Congress, that there is at the present time no willingness on the part of the other Nations to go back on a fixed basis. In other words, to put it the other way around, Great Britain has been pursuing what you call the Professor Warren theory for perhaps two and a half years. That is the thing that some of our people forget very definitely. They have a managed pound, abso-

49

lutely managed, far more so than we have ever thought of managing the dollar. . . .

Q. What is the purpose of purchasing Government securities along with gold and exchange?

THE PRESIDENT: I suppose the easiest way to answer that, the purchase of Government securities, is to ask the question, "Is it right or proper that a handful of people who did not happen to like what was going on or who wanted to use a club in order to get something of their own through — that such private individuals should have the right, without check, at their own sweet will, to dump Government bonds into the market and artificially depreciate the price of Government bonds? Is it moral that private individuals should have that right?"

Q. Was there short-selling of Government bonds?

THE PRESIDENT: I couldn't tell you whether there was short-selling or not but there were, undoubtedly, certain individuals — this does not by any means apply to the overwhelming majority of the bankers in the United States — but there were individuals who recommended to their clients that they should get rid of Government bonds and in most of those cases there were ulterior motives.

Now, the fact that the Government would be given the right to purchase Government bonds means that a private effort of that kind could be check-mated right away. This is protective armor for any Government, and we ought to have it.

Q. Does the setting up of that two-billion-dollar fund depend on the profits of revaluation?

THE PRESIDENT: Yes. . . .

The last part of the message relates to silver. It expresses the thought that silver has also been used from time immemorial as a metallic base, that it is still used by half the population of the world as such, that it is used by us and is a crucial factor in international trade, and that it cannot be neglected. Further on, I say that Governments can well employ silver as a basis for currency and I look for a greatly increased use. I also describe the existing situation with respect to the agreement among the 66 Nations and the fact that we have put our part of the agreement into effect. I also say that I am withholding any recommendations to the Congress for further extension at this time because I want to know the results of the London agreement and the results of the rest of our monetary measures.

Q. Can you tell us anything about the legislation that is to be offered in connection with this?

THE PRESIDENT: There has been drafted what might be called a purely tentative method of arriving at the things recommended in the message. I am perfectly frank in telling you that I haven't even read it. In other words, it is to save the committees trouble and to give them something to "chew on" in order to carry out the recommendations. It is not an Administration bill. It is just to help the committees.

Q. On this gold policy, there is no thought in mind of the Treasury, with its gold stocks, issuing money on the basis of 40 percent reserve?

THE PRESIDENT: No. The idea is, of course, that for this money turned in the Federal Reserve Banks are given certificates that there is gold in the Treasury, dollar for dollar, and that on those certificates the Federal Reserve Banks can issue their own currency to their member banks.

Q. Do you look for any immediate effect on domestic prices from the mere passage of this legislation?

THE PRESIDENT: I don't know; I have no idea.

Q. The profit from this operation clearly is to go to the Treasury?

THE PRESIDENT: Yes. Right on that point, there has been a divergence of opinion amongst some of the bankers — not by any means all — and on the part of a few politicians who have wondered whether the Government had any right to take this profit or whether the profit should accrue to the stockholders of the banks. Of course, so far as I can see, there is no question on that at all. We asked individuals to turn in their gold and get paper money for it. We also asked all the corporations to do it, and substantially all did as requested. I cannot see a great deal of difference between a bank and a private corporation. The constituent bank is owned by private individuals, and if we were to pursue that policy of letting the stockholders of the banks take this profit, it would mean that the Government would be handing them a great big Christmas present.

I am very careful to point out in this message that such legislation places the right, title and ownership of our gold reserves in the Government itself. It makes clear the Government's ownership of any added dollar value of the country's stock of gold which would result from any decrease of the gold content of the dollar which may be made in the public interest.

But, in order to be fair, I point out that the Government would lose such dollar value if the public interest in the future should require an increase in the amount of gold designated as a dollar.

Q. It is your idea to have a permanent policy, retaining the limits within the 50 and 60, revaluing within those limits from time to time?

THE PRESIDENT: As far as any human being can say "permanent."

Q. And continue to hold all the gold?

THE PRESIDENT: Certainly, to hold all the gold. . . .

Q. This would not increase the currency-issuing power of the Federal Reserve at all?

THE PRESIDENT: The thing to remember is that every bank statement — the statements of the member banks, the State banks, and the twelve Federal Reserve Banks, their statements are in terms of dollars and there is absolutely no change in their statements. It does not give them less reserve or more. They have the same number of dollars.

Q. Would you mind phrasing in words of one syllable to millions of unlettered people, to most of whom this would be Greek, how the Government would derive these profits that there is so much talk about?

THE PRESIDENT: Let's put it this way: We have been trying to bring the purchasing power of the dollar back, approximately, to the level in which the average of the debts of the country were incurred so that the average of people can pay off those debts in a dollar that has approximately that same purchasing power. One method — the most practical method — of doing it, is to cut the theoretical gold content of the dollar. Now, you can only make that practical and fair if the Government has all the gold. The number of dollars in the banks of the country will be exactly the same as they were before and the Government — as the currency-issuing power — will have the same weight of gold in the Treasury, but in terms of actual dollars for the Treasury, it will represent 80 percent more or 100 percent more, depending on what we revalue at. . . .

Now, there is one other thing. Of course, in terms of foreign exchange, the dollar is today worth, in terms of gold, only about 63 cents.

Q. Can you make any use of this profit other than the two-billion-dollar fund you set up?

THE PRESIDENT: That is for the future.

Q. Have you any authority to issue currency against it?

THE PRESIDENT: No.

Q. And the profit does not represent a base of currency in the Federal Reserve?

THE PRESIDENT: No. We keep it in the Treasury.

Now, off the record, just for your information — I have to keep it off the record because it involves another branch of the Government — we do not intend to encourage Congress to spend the billions of the profit. (*Laughter*)

Q. If anything like that were done, it would be up to Congress to take action?

THE PRESIDENT: We asked them to take action on the two billions.

Q. Congress would have to pass further legislation if you wanted to make use of the profit?

THE PRESIDENT: Yes.

Q. Do you hope that this will encourage international stabilization?

THE PRESIDENT: I hope so.

Q. If you use a bullion system —

THE PRESIDENT: This is a bullion system. We will not coin any gold coins except such as might be necessary to make up small amounts less than a bar of gold. Loose change.

Q. In other words, I don't see how you can make an artificial gold price effective unless exchangeable in some form.

THE PRESIDENT: The bullion and small change would be used for foreign settlements. Those take place every six months or a year.

Q. Did you say that the export embargo was removed?

THE PRESIDENT: No, no. Of course, after the whole system gets into bullion, obviously the export embargo would be removed to the extent that if we do have an unfavorable trade balance at the end of the period, we would ship out bullion to pay unfavorable trade balances.

Q. There is no relaxation of the order, then?

THE PRESIDENT: No.

Q. Everybody in the country is wanting to know how it is going to affect him.

THE PRESIDENT: How?

Q. He wants to know whether it is going to increase his buying power or increase his wages — how much it is going to be felt.

THE PRESIDENT: Probably very little. Probably certain commodity prices will go up to a certain extent and it will enable people, knowing that Congress has said between 50 and 60, to make contracts ahead with far greater assurance than at the present time, because today it is between 50 and 100.

Q. And now it will be definitely between 50 and 60?

THE PRESIDENT: That bill makes it between 50 and 60.

10 ❨ The Eighty-ninth Press Conference (Excerpts). January 17, 1934

(Party officials practicing law in Washington.)

Q. Mr. President, quite a few of us have been writing stories about the activities of National Committeemen practicing before the Departments, and some have gone so far as to say that it is embarrassing the Administration. Have you anything to say on that?

THE PRESIDENT: I think if we can avoid reference to individuals, it is all right to talk about the general principle. I have felt all along that it is not quite in accord with the spirit of the Administration that any individual who holds a high Party position, such as National Committeeman, should earn a livelihood by practicing law, because, in a sense, he holds himself out as having access to the back door of the Administration. It just "is not done." . . .

11 ❨ White House Statement on Means to Prevent Monopolistic Practices under N.R.A. Codes. Executive Order No. 6569. January 20, 1934

THE President today signed an Executive Order (No. 6569) to provide a practical and rapid way for making effective those provisions of the National Industrial Recovery Act that were designed to prevent persons, under the guise of purported sanctions contained in codes of fair competition or independently or in defiance of such codes, from engaging in monopolistic practices or practices tending to eliminate, oppress or discriminate against small enterprises.

Where a complainant shall have been dissatisfied with the disposition of his case by the agency of the Government which he may have invoked, the complainant may press his case before the Federal Trade Commission. If this Commission has no jurisdiction to handle the complaint, it is to be referred to the Department of Justice. Under such a method, grievances arising out of codes of fair competition or based upon violations of those portions of the anti-trust laws of the United States that prohibit monopolistic practices, can be adequately aired and settled by disinterested governmental agencies in accordance with the principles set forth in the recovery legislation. The Federal Trade Commission, in handling such complaints, will follow the procedure set forth in its organic act — a procedure that is informal, not costly to the complainant, and expeditious.

These agencies, equipped with wide knowledge of and long experience in issues of this nature, will be able to carve an ordered and just solution of the pressing economic problems necessarily raised by the application of the principles inherent in the recovery program. Conceptions as to what practices are monopolistic and are beyond the allowable area of the National Industrial Recovery Act will thereby be enabled to rest upon realistic foundations of the place to be accorded to concentrated capital and cooperative effort in our modern economic civilization. The result should be a coherent body of law, protective of the large consuming interests and yet broad enough to afford the necessary play for industry to act as a unit, free from the pressure of unrestrained and wasteful competition. Such pathways lead to industrial peace in the fullest sense of that word, a peace that will be just to the various contending interests and which will afford a permanent basis for our economic reconstruction.

NOTE: Of course the real victims of monopolies are always the consumers, who are forced to pay excessive prices unless the Government itself protects them.

The rebuilding of the purchasing power of all classes of our population was the cornerstone of our program of recovery from the very beginning. This required first the raising of income. But the creation of conditions by which a larger portion of the population could obtain larger incomes would not be effective if the increase in the cost of necessities of life proceeded at a faster pace. The farm and industrial programs of the Administration which were building up the incomes of producers and workers could result in a general increased capacity to consume only if they were used in such a way as not to inflate prices unduly. As a protection against this frustration of the recovery program, the Administration at an early period created several new offices and charged them with the specific duty of safeguarding the interests of consumers not only in the matter of prices but of policies affecting the quantity and quality of goods produced and distributed.

The creation and operation of these consumer agencies represented a new principle in government. It was the recognition of the right of consumers to have their interests represented in the formulation of government policy and in the administration of laws affecting the production and distribution of goods. I think it can be safely stated that never before had the particular problems of consumers been so thoroughly and unequivocally accepted as the direct responsibility of government. The willingness to fulfill that responsibility was, in essence, an extension and amplification of the meaning and content of democratic government.

On July 22, 1933, a Consumers' Advisory Board was set up in N.R.A. to protect the interests of consumers as code provisions were being formulated and administered.

As has been pointed out, the initiative in code-making, and the administration of approved codes remained in the hands of organized producers and sellers. The natural result was that codes were directed to remedying the evils most observed by such groups rather than the evils suffered by consumers. While the protection of purchasers was one of the functions of the N.R.A., little could be done affirmatively. Effort was limited to approving or disapproving suggested provisions of codes. The N.R.A. was able to eliminate code provisions that might have fostered monopoly, but it was unable to enforce the inclusion of provisions which would make monopoly illegal.

The N.R.A. provided that approved codes were to be exempt from the anti-trust laws. At the same time it provided that before the President approved a code he must be convinced that its provisions were not designed to permit monopolies, or to eliminate or oppress smaller enterprises. In the conflict inherent in the ambiguities of these provisions, every reasonable effort was made to prevent provisions and practices savoring of monopoly.

The Board did maintain constant vigilance for consumers' interests in the formulation and administration of codes. Proposed provisions which would lead to price fixing or price maintenance were closely examined. Only when facts and circumstances showed a clear necessity for price maintenance clauses and only where a maximum amount of consumer protection was provided would the consumer adviser approve the code.

The Consumers' Advisory Board drafted and urged the adoption of orders safeguarding the rights and privileges of cooperative buying associations. Proposed prohibition of quantity discounts, for example, threatened the very existence of consumers' cooperatives. By an active campaign, the Board was successful in obtaining exemption from these clauses for farmers' and consumers' cooperatives (see Item 148, Vol. II).

In general, the Board became the Washington representative for consumers throughout the Nation. Letters giving information and calling attention to specific cases of profiteering, unfair combinations, and other violations were carefully investigated. Hundreds of specific cases of unfair code administration were settled to the advantage of the consumer through the active intervention of the Board.

The Board was instrumental in forming the local consumers' councils, which have continued since the termination of N.R.A. and which give promise of affording a real medium for the expression of consumer needs.

The Board provided an impetus to the study and development of standards for consumers' goods. Independent organizations, whose interest in standards was aroused, have since been increasingly active along these lines. It brought into the foreground the consumers' interest in production, employment and wage rates. It developed a better understanding on the part of income receivers as to their interests as consumers, and, together with the Consumers' Counsel Division of the Agricultural Adjustment Administration, has been largely responsible for the subsequent cooperative efforts at self-protection by consumers.

It was reconstituted as the Consumers Division of the National Recovery Administration on July 30, 1935, by Executive Order No. 7120 (see Vol. IV, Item 98).

Recognition of consumer interests in the agricultural recovery program was implicit in the Agricultural Adjustment Act as was its recognition in the National Industrial Recovery Act. It was one of the stated purposes of A.A.A. to "establish a balance between production and consumption of farm products." In the administration of this Act, the Secretary of Agriculture created the office of Consumers' Counsel on June 27, 1933, for the purpose of representing the interests of consumers at every stage in the activities of the A.A.A. It was believed essential that both producers' and consumers' interests be represented by trained economists, highly skilled in research and in the interpretation of economics. Basically the long-time concerns of both groups coincide, since the consumer wants the producer to receive the kind of return for his produce that will insure the continuance of an adequate food supply, and the farmer wants the consumer to be able to buy an adequate volume of farm products.

In the approach toward this common ultimate goal, however, conflict on particular points inevitably appears, and in such instances it has been the function of the Consumers' Counsel to represent the consumer and assist in finding the point of maximum justice to him and to the producer. Once a production program, a marketing agreement, or license is in effect, it becomes the function of the Consumers' Counsel to observe its operation and determine whether or not the results anticipated at the time it was framed are actually being obtained. Where it appears that they are not, the Counsel has a double duty: to urge reconsideration of the program within the A.A.A., and to give publicity to the facts as they exist.

The office of Consumers' Counsel is still functioning as a division of the A.A.A. and issues a bi-weekly illustrated bulletin for the general reader which is called the "Consumers' Guide," and which has the double purpose of educating non-farm consumers on the economic problems of the farm population and their relation to the general welfare, and to promote the more effective use of purchasing power.

In the exercise of its duties, the office of Consumers' Counsel has participated in the economic analyses, conferences, and hearings in-volved in the formulation of plans for and the administration of the provisions of the agricultural program. At hearings on any phase of this program the Consumers' Counsel and his staff present testimony, and question witnesses with a view to establishing the consumers' position with respect to the program. Under its second function, the Consumers' Counsel office assembles and makes public factual material on changes in supplies and prices of foods and other farm products; and attempts to assist in the self-protection of consumers by publishing information intended to advise them in wise and economical buying.

Inevitably in the course of its work, this office has found itself confronted with such problems as price-fixing, spreads between the producer and consumer, and methods of bringing about more effective distributive processes between the farm and the city. The Consumers' Counsel office has advocated, as a general policy, reduction of spreads wherever possible and has scrutinized agreements, codes, and licenses to detect provisions which might result in Government sanction of increased spreads. It has supported the position of the Administration that such arrangements should not become merely instruments for securing monopolistic advantages.

The foregoing statement, setting forth the provisions of Executive Order No. 6569, is an example of other efforts made by the Administration to prevent monopolistic practices under the codes. A few months later, by Executive Order No. 6632, I set up an independent body to investigate the complaints that monopolies were resulting from N.I.R.A. (see Item 39, this volume).

(See Item 98, Vol. IV, for a further discussion of activities in behalf of consumers.)

12 ❡ Letter Limiting the Lending Power of the Reconstruction Finance Corporation.

January 21, 1934

Dear Jesse:

I HAVE approved the bill, S. 2125, 73d Congress, 2d Session, "To continue the functions of the Reconstruction Finance Corporation, to provide additional funds for the Corporation, and for other purposes."

It is my understanding that the bill does not confine the total lending authority of the Reconstruction Finance Corporation to the sum of $850,000,000 specified therein, but that the extension of the life of the Corporation automatically makes available to it the amount of any repayments received during the period of such extension and that you may make commitments and expenditures under the indefinite provisions of the Reconstruction Finance Corporation Act. It is to be noted that the bill does not confine the payments on account of commitments and agreements entered into by the Corporation to the period ending February 1, 1935, but provides for payments over a period of one year after the date of such commitments and agreements.

In order to confine all additional expenditures required to be made in 1935, which were not expressly provided for in the Budget, to the amount indicated in my Budget Message, I find it necessary to advise you that my approval of this bill is given with the distinct understanding that the cash withdrawals from the Treasury by the Corporation for the fiscal year 1935, including any debentures issued for the purchase of preferred stock and capital notes of banks, and exclusive of the funds which you may be called upon to allocate to other agencies of the Government as provided by law, will not, without my prior approval, exceed the sum of $500,000,000, and that no commitments or agreements shall be made so that expenditures may be made thereon after June 30, 1935. Your estimates of repayments for the fiscal year 1935 indicate that this total authorized expenditure of $500,-000,000 may for the most part be made out of repayments.

Cordially yours,

Hon. Jesse Jones
Chairman, Reconstruction Finance Corp.
Washington, D. C.

13 ⟪ White House Statement on Payments Due Americans from Germany. January 22, 1934

THE President talked with the German Ambassador about payments due to Americans by German States, municipalities and corporations, which payments now pass by decree through the German Treasury.

The President asked definitely that American creditors be given the same treatment as the creditors of other Nations.

In addition, the President told the Ambassador of his desire that commercial relations be stimulated between the United States and Germany.

14 ⟪ Radio Address on the Occasion of the President's First Birthday Ball for the Benefit of Crippled Children. January 30, 1934

TONIGHT I am very deeply moved by the choice of my birthday anniversary for the holding of Birthday Balls in so many communities, great and small, throughout the country. I send you my greetings and my heartfelt thanks; but at the same time I feel that I have the right to speak to you more as the representative on this occasion of the hundreds of thousands of crippled children in our country.

It is only in recent years that we have come to realize the true significance of the problem of our crippled children. There are so many more of them than we had any idea of. In many sections there are thousands who are not only receiving no help but whose very existence has been unknown to the doctors and health services.

A generation ago somewhat the same situation existed in relation to tuberculosis. Today, because of constant stressing of the subject, the Nation understands the tuberculosis problem and has taken splendid steps not only to effectuate cures but also to prevent the spread of the disease.

The problem of the crippled child is very similar. Modern medical science has advanced so far that a very large proportion of children who for one reason or another have become crippled can be restored to useful citizenship. It remains, therefore, only to spread the gospel for the care and cure of crippled children in every part of this kindly land to enable us to make the same relative progress that we have already made in the field of tuberculosis.

As all of you know, the work at Warm Springs has been close to my heart, because of the many hundreds of cases of infantile paralysis which have been treated there. It is a fact that infantile paralysis results in the crippling of more children and of grown-ups than any other cause. Warm Springs is only one of the many places where kindness and patience and skill are given to handicapped people. There are hundreds of other places, hospitals and clinics, where the surgeons, doctors and nurses of the country gladly work day in and day out throughout the years, often without compensation.

Warm Springs, through the generous gifts which are being made to the Foundation tonight, will be able to increase its usefulness nationally, especially in the field of infantile paralysis. We shall be able to take more people and I hope that these people will be able to come to us on the recommendation of doctors from every State in the Union. I want to stress, however, that the problem of the crippled child is so great that in every community and in every State the local facilities for caring for the crippled need the support and the interest of every citizen. Let us well remember that every child and indeed every person who is restored to useful citizenship is an asset to the country and is enabled "to pull his own weight in the boat." In the long run, by helping this work we are contributing not to charity but to the building up of a sound Nation.

At Warm Springs the facilities are available, insofar as beds and funds permit, to the rich and to the poor.

The fund to which you contribute tonight will undoubtedly permit us to extend the facilities of Warm Springs in a greater degree than before. I like to think and I would like each one of you who hears me to remember that what you are doing means the enriching of the life of some crippled child. I know and you know that there could be no finer purpose than our will to aid these helpless little ones.

Today so many thousands of welcome telegrams and postcards and letters of birthday greetings have poured in on me in the White House that I want to take this opportunity of thanking all of you who have sent them. From the bottom of my heart I am grateful to you for your thought. I wish I could divide myself by six thousand and attend in person each and every one of these birthday parties. I cannot do that, but I can be and I am with you all in spirit and in the promotion of this great cause for which we all are crusading.

No man has ever had a finer birthday remembrance from his friends and fellows than you have given me tonight. It is with a humble and thankful heart that I accept this tribute through me to the stricken ones of our great national family. I thank you but lack the words to tell you how deeply I appreciate what you have done and I bid you good night on what is to me the happiest birthday I ever have known.

NOTE: Each year during my term as President, a National Committee has sponsored so-called Birthday Balls on January 30th, which is my birthday. The purpose of the balls has been to raise funds for the helping of crippled children not only at the Foundation at Warm Springs, but all through the country. These gatherings have resulted in great assistance not only in treating infantile paralysis and other diseases which cripple children, but also in research as to the causes and prevention of the diseases.

On May 9, 1934, I expressed my thanks again for the proceeds of these balls and pointed out how the funds were going to be allocated (see Item 78, this volume).

15 ❡ White House Statement on Presidential Proclamation (No. 2072) Fixing the Weight of the Gold Dollar. January 31, 1934

1. ACTING under the powers granted by Title 3 of the Act approved May 12, 1933 (Thomas Amendment to the Farm Relief Act), the President today issued a Proclamation fixing the weight of the gold dollar at 15$\frac{5}{21}$ grains nine-tenths fine. This is 59.06 plus percent of the former weight of 25$\frac{8}{10}$ grains, nine-tenths fine, as fixed by Section 1 of the Act of Congress of March 4, 1900. The new gold content of the dollar became effective immediately on the signing of the Proclamation by the President.

Under the Gold Reserve Act of 1934, signed by the President Tuesday, January 30th, title to the entire stock of monetary gold in the United States, including the gold coin and gold bullion heretofore held by the Federal Reserve Banks and the claim upon gold in the Treasury represented by gold certificates, is vested in the United States Government, and the "profit" from the reduction of the gold content of the dollar, made effective by today's Proclamation, accrues to the United States Treasury. Of this "profit" two billion dollars, under the terms of the Gold Reserve Act and of today's Proclamation, constitute a stabilization fund under the direction of the Secretary of the Treasury. The balance will be converted into the general fund of the Treasury.

Settlement for the gold coin, bullion and certificates taken over from the Federal Reserve Banks on Tuesday upon the approval of the Act was made in the form of credits set up on the Treasury's books. This credit due the Federal Reserve Banks is to be paid in the new form of gold certificates now in course of production by the Bureau of Engraving and Printing. These certificates bear on their face the wording:

> "This is to certify that there is on deposit in the Treasury of the United States of America ——— dollars in gold, payable to bearer on demand as authorized by law."

They also will carry the standard legal tender clause, which is as follows:

> "This certificate is a legal tender in the amount thereof in payment of all debts and dues, public and private."

The new gold certificates will be of the same size as other currency in circulation and the only difference, other than the changes in wording noted above, is that the backs of the new certificates will, as used to be done, be printed in yellow ink. The certificates will be in denominations up to $100,000.

In his Proclamation of today the President gives notice that he reserves the right, by virtue of the authority vested in him, to alter or modify the present Proclamation as the interest of the United States may seem to require. The authority by later Proclamations to accomplish other revaluations of the dollar in terms of gold is contained in the Gold Reserve Act signed on Tuesday.

2. The Secretary of the Treasury, with the approval of the President, issued a public announcement that beginning February 1, 1934, he will buy through the Federal Reserve Bank of New York as fiscal agent, for the account of the United States, any and all gold delivered to any United States Mints or the Assay Offices in New York or Seattle, at the rate of $35.00 per fine troy ounce, less the usual Mint charges and less one-fourth of one percent for handling charges. Purchases, however, are subject to compliance with the regulations issued under the Gold Reserve Act of 1934.

3. The Secretary of the Treasury today promulgated new regulations with respect to the purchase and sale of gold by the Mints. Under these regulations the Mints are authorized to purchase gold recovered from natural deposits in the United States or any place subject to its jurisdiction, unmelted scrap gold, gold imported into the United States after January 30, 1934, and such other gold as may be authorized from time to time by rulings of the Secretary of the Treasury. No gold, however, may be purchased which has been held in noncompliance with previous acts or orders, or noncompliance with the Gold Reserve Act of 1934, or these Regulations. Affidavits as to the source from which the gold was obtained are required, except in the case of nuggets or dust of less than five ounces, where a statement under oath will suffice. In the case of imported gold, the Mints may purchase only that which has been in customs custody after its arrival in the Continental United States.

The price to be paid for gold purchased by the Mints is to be $35.00 per troy ounce of fine gold, less one-fourth of one percent and less Mint charges. This price may be changed by the Secretary of the Treasury at any time without notice.

The Mints are authorized to sell gold to persons licensed to acquire it for use in the industries, professions, or arts, but not to sell more than is required for a three months' supply for the purchaser. The price at which gold is to be sold by the Mints will be $35.00 per troy ounce, plus one-fourth of one percent. This price also may be changed by the Secretary of the Treasury without notice.

16 ❦ Presidential Proclamation (No. 2072) Fixing the Weight of the Gold Dollar. January 31, 1934

WHEREAS, by virtue of Section 1 of the Act of Congress approved March 14, 1900 (31 Stat. L. 45), the present weight of the gold dollar is fixed at 25.8 grains of gold nine-tenths fine; and

WHEREAS, by Section 43, Title III of the Act approved May 12, 1933 (Public, No. 10, 73d Cong.), as amended by Section 12 of the Gold Reserve Act of 1934, it is provided in part as follows:

"Whenever the President finds, upon investigation, that (1) the foreign commerce of the United States is adversely affected by reason of the depreciation in the value of the currency of any other Government or Governments in relation to the present standard value of gold, or (2) action under this section is necessary in order to regulate and maintain the parity of currency issues of the United States, or (3) an economic emergency requires an expansion of credit, or (4) an expansion of credit is necessary to secure by international agreement a stabilization at proper levels of the currencies of various Governments, the President is authorized, in his discretion —

"(a) To direct the Secretary of the Treasury to enter into agreements with the several Federal Reserve Banks and with the Federal Reserve Board whereby the Federal Reserve Board will, and it is hereby authorized to, notwithstanding any provisions of law or rules and regulations to the contrary, permit such Reserve banks to agree that they will, (1) conduct, pursuant to existing law, throughout specified periods, open market operations in obligations of the United States Government or corporations in which the United States is the majority stockholder, and (2) purchase directly and hold in portfolio for an agreed period or periods of time Treasury bills or other obligations of the United States Government in an aggregate sum of $3,000,000,000 in addition to those they may then hold, unless prior to the termination of such period or periods the Secretary shall consent to their sale. No suspension of reserve requirements of the Federal Reserve Banks, under the terms of section 11 (c) of the Federal Reserve Act, necessitated by reason of operations under this section, shall require the imposition of the graduated tax upon any deficiency in reserves as provided in said section 11 (c). Nor shall it require any automatic increase in the rates of interest or discount charged by any Federal Reserve Bank, as otherwise specified in that section. The Federal Reserve Board, with the approval of the Secretary of the Treasury, may require the Federal Reserve banks to take such action as may be necessary, in the judgment of the Board and of the Secretary of the Treasury, to prevent undue credit expansion.

"(b) If the Secretary, when directed by the President, is unable to secure the assent of the several Federal Reserve Banks and the Federal Reserve Board to the agreements authorized in this section, or if operations under the above provisions prove to be inadequate to meet the purposes of this section, or if for any other reason additional measures are required in the judgment of the President to meet such purposes, then the President is authorized —

*　　　*　　　*

"(2) By proclamation to fix the weight of the gold dollar in grains nine-tenths fine and also to fix the weight of the silver dollar in grains nine-tenths fine at a definite fixed ratio in relation to the gold dollar at such amounts as he finds necessary from his investigation to stabilize domestic prices or to protect the foreign commerce against the adverse effect of depreciated foreign currencies, and to provide for the unlimited coinage of such gold and silver at the ratio so fixed, or in case the Government of the United States enters into an agreement with any Government or Governments under the terms of which the ratio between the value of gold and other currency issued by the United States and by any such Government or Governments is established, the President may fix the weight of the gold dollar in accordance with the ratio so agreed upon, and such gold dollar, the weight of which

68

is so fixed, shall be the standard unit of value, and all forms of money issued or coined by the United States shall be maintained at a parity with this standard and it shall be the duty of the Secretary of the Treasury to maintain such parity, but in no event shall the weight of the gold dollar be fixed so as to reduce its present weight by more than 50 per centum. Nor shall the weight of the gold dollar be fixed in any event at more than 60 per centum of its present weight. The powers of the President specified in this paragraph shall be deemed to be separate, distinct, and continuing powers, and may be exercised by him, from time to time, severally or together, whenever and as the expressed objects of this section in his judgment may require; except that such powers shall expire two years after the date of enactment of the Gold Reserve Act of 1934 unless the President shall sooner declare the existing emergency ended, but the President may extend such period for not more than one additional year after such date by proclamation recognizing the continuance of such emergency"; and

WHEREAS, I find, upon investigation, that the foreign commerce of the United States is adversely affected by reason of the depreciation in the value of the currencies of other Governments in relation to the present standard value of gold, and that an economic emergency requires an expansion of credit; and

WHEREAS, in my judgment, measures additional to those provided by sub-section (a) of said section 43 are required to meet the purposes of such section; and

WHEREAS, I find, from my investigation, that, in order to stabilize domestic prices and to protect the foreign commerce against the adverse effect of depreciated foreign currencies, it is necessary to fix the weight of the gold dollar at $15\frac{5}{21}$ grains nine-tenths fine,

NOW, THEREFORE, be it known that I, Franklin D. Roosevelt, President of the United States, by virtue of the authority vested in me by section 43, Title III, of said act of May 12, 1933, as amended, and by virtue of all other authority vested in me, do hereby proclaim, order, direct, declare, and fix the weight of the gold dollar to be $15\frac{5}{21}$ grains nine-tenths fine, from and after the date and hour of this Proclamation. The weight of the silver dollar is not altered or affected in any manner by reason of this Proclamation.

This Proclamation shall remain in force and effect until and unless repealed or modified by act of Congress or by subsequent Proclamation; and notice is hereby given that I reserve the right by virtue of the authority vested in me to alter or modify this Proclamation as the interest of the United States may seem to require.

NOTE: The Gold Reserve Act and the Proclamation which followed were the culmination, for the time being, of the monetary program initiated in March, 1933.

In order to show the relationship of the various measures, taken during this period of ten months, to each other and to our underlying objectives, I summarize our aims and the successive steps by which they were put in course of accomplishment. (See also Items 13, 16, 33, 42, 120, 146 and 187A of Vol. II and Items 8, 9, 89 and 146 of this volume.)

This was what we wanted to do:

1. To attain and, once attained, to maintain reasonably equitable and stable income relationships among the different groups: workers, farmers, business men, investors, etc.
2. To prevent marked fluctuations or sharp trends in wholesale price levels.
3. To maintain a reasonably stable cost of living.
4. To foster steadily increasing employment, more widespread income and purchasing power, and an orderly expansion of business activity.
5. To maintain such position of the dollar with reference to other currencies, as would encourage an increasing domestic and foreign trade, and thereby help raise the standard of living and promote peace.
6. To eliminate broad fluctuations in exchange rates without sacrificing sovereignty over our monetary policy.
7. To facilitate the smooth and easy adjustment of international payments and foster stability of foreign monetary systems.
8. To avoid competitive depreciation of currencies.
9. To restrict the "unjustified enrichment" — the unearned profit from gold and foreign exchange — which at other times here and at all times in most other Nations was permitted to fall to a privileged few as a result of governmental monetary action.

10. To make more effective the control of our monetary system and of the metallic reserves of gold and silver used as its base; and to make clear that it belongs where the Constitution says it does — in the Congress rather than in the hands of the bankers and the speculators.

The various steps we took to accomplish these objectives had necessarily to be guided by three principles:

a. The country's monetary system was in a seriously disrupted condition when our program started. The first actions taken had to be emergency measures designed to make immediate provision for preventing the system from going to pieces completely.

b. The relation of our monetary system to the commerce, industry, and finance of the Nation is such that progress can only be made gradually and by successive steps in order to avoid unnecessary dislocations and disruptions in the business of the country.

c. The things we were trying to do had never been done in the same way before. We were not dealing with theories, but with facts. It was sometimes necessary, therefore, to make our program effective step by step and to observe and analyze the effects of one step before we could be certain we were right in taking the next one.

I shall outline again the successive steps we took, already partly enumerated in Volume II; and it will be seen that each one of them was actuated by one or more of the considerations I have already described.

1. In connection with the banking holiday, banks and Government officials were generally prohibited from paying out gold; the export of gold was forbidden and steps were taken to eliminate hoarding of gold and currency. (See Vol. II, Item 8.) This was an emergency measure, but it was also the first of the steps in transferring to the Federal Government the more effective control and regulation of the monetary system, including monetary gold, and in restricting the private profits of a privileged few out of the Government's action.

2. Gold and gold certificates were required by Executive Order to be surrendered to the Treasury. (See Vol. II, Item 33.) This will at once be seen to have been the next step toward these ends. There was a comparatively small group of individuals who at that time owned gold or obligations payable in gold, or were able to speculate in foreign exchange, and who therefore, if we had not taken this step, would have been in a position to profit as a result of the misfortunes of the great mass of our citizens and as a result of the measures taken by the Government to alleviate those misfortunes and to correct the conditions responsible for them. Calling in privately owned gold, prohibit-

71

ing the enforcement of "gold-clause" obligations, and regulating foreign exchange were all designed to help prevent such results as well as to accomplish our other objectives.

3. The issuance of licenses to export gold was discontinued and dealings in foreign exchange were subjected to examination and regulation. (See Vol. II, Item 42.) This was a development of that aspect of the monetary program which relates to the foreign exchange value of the dollar. This foreign exchange value — that is, the amount of foreign currency such as francs, pounds or marks which can be exchanged for a dollar — is intimately and inevitably connected with our foreign trade. The condition of that foreign trade is, of course, in turn reflected in our own domestic situation, directly through the amount of manufactured products and raw materials which we are able to sell abroad and through the prices we in turn have to pay for imported material; and indirectly by the effect which our foreign trade necessarily has on our own price level, on our own volume of domestic activity and on our own standard of living.

Certain considerations must be borne in mind in any discussion of how the monetary program was related to our domestic price level. The American dollar is, like almost all other national currencies, related to gold. In our own situation

that relationship, prior to 1933, took the form of a legal definition of the dollar in terms of grains of gold. This created a definite and determinable parity between the dollar and gold and, through the dollar, a relationship between gold and the price level. In other words, it was always possible, given the dollar price of the commodity in question, to determine how many grains of gold would buy a bushel of wheat, a bale of cotton, or any other commodity. It therefore was apparent that any undervaluation of gold in terms of dollars would be related to the question of undervaluation of commodities in terms of dollars. The suspension of gold payments, followed by a progressively rising dollar-price for gold, was therefore designed to contribute to the rise in commodity prices which we felt was essential to restore the purchasing and debt-paying ability of the American people.

As noted, a further part of the program was to achieve a price level which would not be subject to major fluctuations, once an appropriate level had been reached. A contribution to this, it was contemplated, would be to fix, definitely, the gold value of the dollar, at least for the time being, after that value had been raised to an apparently sufficient point. It was therefore desirable to change the price of gold gradually during an interim period; and it was also desirable that prior to ultimate stabilization these prices should be temporary rather than permanent or semi-permanent. In order to accomplish this, the Government instituted a gold-buying program at gradually increasing prices.

4. The President was authorized by the Congress in the so-called "Thomas Amendment" to the Farm Relief Act to "devalue" the dollar — that is, to reduce the number of grains of gold constituting the statutory gold content of the dollar. (See Vol. II, Item 54.) This was done in order to provide the machinery by which an official and stable gold content for the dollar could be fixed. This authority, however, was not exercised until I issued the Proclamation of January 31, 1934, to which this note is appended. The gold content could not be fixed lower than 50 percent, and, as will be seen later, the upper limit was afterwards fixed by law at 60 percent, of the previous gold content. The Proclamation of January 31, 1934, fixed the gold content at 15-5/21 grains nine-tenths fine as compared with 25-8/10 grains nine-tenths fine and, therefore, was a reduction of about 59.6 percent. That Proclamation, therefore, did not exhaust the possibility of further devaluation since the dollar could, under the law, be reduced the further 9.6 percent that remains before reaching 50 percent.

5. "Gold clauses" — that is, provisions for payment of money obligations in gold coin or in gold — were declared invalid by the Congress. (Joint Resolution of June 5, 1933.) This was another measure designed to prevent unfair profits from accruing to a very small group of creditors and the placing of unfair burdens not only on the corresponding debtors, but on the general tax-paying public as a whole. It assured payment of the dollar amount of the obligation rather than of a purely fictitious gold "value."

6. The sale on consignment of newly-mined domestic gold (August 29, 1933) and, later (October 25, 1933), the purchase by the Reconstruction Finance Corporation of newly-mined domestic gold were authorized (see Vol. II, Item 120). These purchases made possible the gradually increasing gold price to which I have already referred. From October 24, 1933, to January, 1934, this price increased from $29.80 to $34.45, the latter price thus paving the way for the action that was taken by the Proclamation of January 31, 1934.

7. The Gold Reserve Act was passed on January 30, 1934. It was essentially an act designed to amplify and consolidate the instruments which had been devised up to that time for monetary control. Its aim was to provide that nicety of balance between fixity and freedom in the monetary system which would bring about a sufficient amount of stabilization, and yet

leave room for the protection of domestic price levels and the value of the dollar in foreign markets from "accidents of international trade, international policies of other Nations, and political disturbances in other countries," as set forth in my address as early as October 22, 1933 (see Vol. II, Item 146).

The Act was another decisive step by which the United States took "firmly in its own hands the control of the gold value of our dollar," as mentioned in that speech. It also gave the President wide authority with respect to fixing the weight of the silver dollar and subsidiary coins and to the issuance of silver certificates.

Some of the outstanding provisions of the Act were:

(a) It transferred title to all gold owned by the Federal Reserve Banks to the United States Government. This was the final step in the concentration in the Federal Treasury of all of the country's monetary gold.

(b) It limited the President's power to devalue the dollar by fixing an upper limit of 60 percent. This placed the range in which the new gold content could be fixed at between 50 and 60 percent of the former weight, and was one of the recommendations contained in my message to the Congress of January 15, 1934. (See Item 8, this volume.)

(c) It established a Stabilization Fund of $2,000,000,000 out of the profit which was to accrue from devaluation. (Reduction in the gold content of the dollar resulted in a "profit," in that the gold in the Treasury represented, after devaluation, a number of dollars increased by the percentage of devaluation.) The Stabilization Fund was established "for the purpose of stabilizing the exchange value of the dollar." By means of the Fund, the Secretary of the Treasury, with the approval of the President, was authorized to deal in gold and foreign exchange and such other instruments of credit and securities as he might deem necessary for stabilization purposes. The enactment of this provision furnished another means whereby the foreign exchange value of the dollar could be controlled and by which the dollar could be kept at its appropriate place in relation to other currencies. After three years of operation of the Stabilization Fund, I may be pardoned for expressing gratification at the successful results that have been achieved through it. These results include not only the maintenance of the stability of the American dollar but the introduction of a powerful new factor working for stability in international exchange and serving as an instrument on the one hand of international cooperation and, on the other, of protecting the foreign exchange situation against speculative attacks which in the past have interfered with legitimate financial and commercial transactions.

(d) It revised and clarified previously existing provisions of law granting to the Secretary of the Treasury the power to buy and sell gold. As we have already seen, purchases and sales of gold by the Treasury are a further means by which the relationship of the dollar to gold and, therefore, to foreign currencies and commodity prices, can be regulated.

(e) It authorized the Secretary of the Treasury, with the approval of the President, to regulate dealings in gold and prohibited activities not permitted by such regulations. The purpose of this section was to bring gold transactions permanently under the supervision of the Federal Government in order to prevent the hoarding of and private speculations in monetary gold which had, prior to March, 1933, so seriously hampered the Government's control of its monetary system. The regulations issued pursuant to this provision have been amended from time to time.

(f) It abolished gold coin as a component of our monetary system, and provided that no gold coin should be issued in the future, that all monetary gold should be formed into bars, and that, generally speaking, no currency of the United States should be redeemed in gold except as directed by the Secretary of the Treasury with the approval

of the President, and then only in gold bullion.

8. The day after approving the Gold Reserve Act of 1934, I issued the foregoing Proclamation fixing the weight of the gold dollar at 15-5/21 grains of gold nine-tenths fine. On the same day, purchase of gold by the Treasury was authorized at $35 per ounce less one-fourth of one percent, and it was announced that gold would be sold at $35 per ounce plus one-fourth of one percent for export to foreign central banks "whenever our exchange rates with gold standard currencies reached the gold export points so fixed." The monetary value of gold so fixed by the Proclamation and the price set for Treasury purchases and sales were approximately equal to the foreign exchange equivalent of the price of gold in the international markets at that time.

The Proclamation pointed out that the right was reserved by the President to alter or modify the terms of this Proclamation by virtue of his authority if the interest of the United States might seem to require it.

No further policy-making steps were taken by the Administration in regard to gold until the three-party arrangement of September 25, 1936 (see Vol. V, Item 135). During this period, confidence in the American dollar was completely revived, and much of the capital which had been exported prior to March 4, 1933, was returned to this country. Indeed foreign capital began to come here for safekeeping. The domestic price level revived, foreign trade improved, and income relationships began to readjust themselves.

17 ❡ White House Statement Approving Study to Establish a Uniform Federal Aviation Policy. February 2, 1934

THE President today approved the suggestion made by the Secretary of Commerce that, in view of the rapid development of aviation in several Federal branches, an inter-departmental study should be made for the purpose of establishing a uniform Federal aviation policy.

The study would seek to ascertain to what extent coordination may be effected and greater efficiency attained in promoting and fostering aviation for military, commercial, air mail and private flying purposes.

The study also would endeavor to determine to what extent aviation may be utilized by all governmental agencies with the view to saving time and money.

The President authorized Secretary Roper to initiate the study in cooperation with Members of the Cabinet who are charged with the various phases of aviation.

18 ❡ The Export-Import Bank of Washington Is Created. Executive Order No. 6581. February 2, 1934

WHEREAS the Congress of the United States has declared that a national emergency exists by reason of widespread unemployment and disorganization of industry; and has declared it to be the policy of Congress to remove obstacles to the free flow of interstate and foreign commerce which tend to diminish the amount thereof, to provide for the general welfare, by promoting the fullest possible utilization of the present productive capacities of industries, to reduce and relieve unemployment, to improve standards of labor, and otherwise to rehabilitate industry; and

WHEREAS in order to meet said emergency and to provide the relief necessary to protect the general welfare of the people the Congress has enacted, *inter alia,* the following acts:

1. National Industrial Recovery Act, approved June 16, 1933;
2. Reconstruction Finance Corporation Act, approved January 22, 1932;
3. Bank Conservation Act, approved March 9, 1933; and

WHEREAS in order effectively and efficiently to carry out the provisions of said acts it is expedient and necessary that a banking corporation be organized with power to aid in financing and to facilitate exports and imports and the exchange of commodities between the United States and other Nations or the agencies or nationals thereof;

Now, THEREFORE, under and by virtue of the authority vested in me by the National Industrial Recovery Act of June 16, 1933, it is hereby declared that an agency, to wit: a banking corporation, be created pursuant to Title 5, Chapter 9, Section 261 of the Code of the District of Columbia, under the name of Export-Import Bank of Washington.

The governing body of said corporation shall consist of a board of trustees composed of five members, and the following persons, who have been invited and who have given their consent to serve, shall act as incorporators and shall handle the concerns of the corporation for the first year:

Daniel C. Roper,   Secretary of Commerce
Robert F. Kelley,   Chief of the Division of Eastern European Affairs, Department of State
Chester C. Davis,   Administrator, Agricultural Adjustment Administration
Stanley Reed,   General Counsel, Reconstruction Finance Corporation

77

Lynn P. Talley,   Executive Assistant to the Directors of the Reconstruction Finance Corporation.

The operations of the corporation shall be carried on in the District of Columbia, and the main office of the corporation shall be at 1825 H Street N.W., Washington, District of Columbia.

The amount of capital stock of the corporation shall be $11,-000,000, divided into classes and shares as follows:

(a) $1,000,000 par value of common stock, divided into 10,000 shares of the par value of $100 each; and

(b) $10,000,000 par value of preferred stock, divided into 10,000 shares of the par value of $1,000 each.

The Secretary of State and the Secretary of Commerce are hereby authorized and directed to cause said corporation to be formed, with such certificate of incorporation, and bylaws, as they shall deem requisite and necessary to define the methods by which the corporation shall conduct its business.

The persons above named are authorized and directed to subscribe for all of the common capital stock for the use and benefit of the United States, of which amount five shares may be held in the respective names of the initial trustees and their successors if required by the law under which said banking corporation is incorporated.

There is hereby set aside for the purpose of subscribing for the common capital stock of said corporation the sum of $1,000,000 out of the appropriation of $3,300,000,000 authorized by Section 220 of the National Industrial Recovery Act and made by the Fourth Deficiency Act, fiscal year 1933, approved June 16, 1933 (Public No. 77, 73d Congress).

It is hereby further directed that any common stock in said corporation standing in the name of the United States shall be voted by such person or persons as they — the Secretary of State and the Secretary of Commerce — shall appoint as their joint agent or agents for that purpose. Any vacancies occurring in the initial board of trustees shall be filled by the board of trustees, subject to the approval of the President of the United States.

NOTE: The N.I.R.A. granted authority to the President to cause the creation of a banking corporation such as that authorized by the foregoing Executive Order.

As the depression years continued, and as the various Nations of the world made efforts to manage their currency and to regulate the flow of import trade, the number of medium and long-term foreign loans by private banks naturally declined, until by this time they had practically ceased. The net result was a serious curtailing of foreign business.

Most of the important trading Nations of the world saw the necessity for providing governmental credit facilities for the foreign trade of their citizens. The purpose of the Export-Import Bank was to aid in financing exports between the United States and any foreign country or its citizens.

The first bank, authorized by the foregoing Order, was organized to assist in financing the trade which was expected to result from the recognition by the United States of the Union of Soviet Socialist Republics. Its board of trustees properly took the position, however, that such credits should not be provided unless and until there was a satisfactory settlement of the debts and claims between the United States and the Soviet Union. In good faith, pending such settlement, the facilities of the bank were in fact reserved for the Soviet trade for a year.

The working capital of the bank was provided out of the $3,300,-000,000 authorized by the N.I.R.A. The preferred stock of $10,000,000 (later increased to $20,000,000) was subscribed and held by the R.F.C. The common stock of $1,000,000 was held by the Secretary of State and the Secretary of Commerce in their official capacities. The original board of five trustees was increased to a maximum of nine by Executive Order No. 6601-A, February 14, 1934.

In order to provide credits for trading with the Republic of Cuba, the Second Export-Import Bank of Washington, D. C., was created on March 12, 1934, pursuant to Executive Order No. 6638, dated March 9, 1934. As it became apparent that credit facilities were needed in financing trade with other countries, this second Export-Import Bank soon expanded its activities to include all foreign Nations except the Soviet Union. The common capital stock of this second bank was also held by the Secretary of State and the Secretary of Commerce in their official capacities; and its preferred stock was likewise subscribed and held by the R.F.C.

The Congress ratified the creation of these banks on January 31, 1935 (Section 9 of Public No. 1, 74th Congress), and continued them until June 16, 1937, or such earlier date as might be fixed by the President by Executive Order. By the same statute the Congress facilitated the operations of the banks by adding certain powers, such as the right to discount obligations.

After the unsuccessful termination of the negotiations with the Soviet Union in April, 1935, and upon the recommendation of the trustees, I directed the dissolution of the second Export-Import Bank on May 7, 1936, by Executive Order No. 7365, so that all of its business and outstanding commitments and loans could be transferred to the first Export-Import Bank of Washington. This transfer was completed on June 30, 1936, from which date there was only one Export-Import Bank instead of two.

By Section 2 of Public No. 2, 75th Congress (approved January 26, 1937), the termination date of this Export-Import Bank of Washington was extended from June 16, 1937, to June 30, 1939.

The Export-Import Bank sought to establish a flexible credit system to supplement, rather than replace, the facilities of private commercial banks. At the beginning of its operations, its commitments were more or less of an experimental nature.

It now operates principally and successfully in three major fields:

1. Short term credits in connection with the exportation of agricultural products, especially cotton and tobacco, where credit facilities are not readily available through private banks. In line with the general policy of supplementing rather than competing with banks, these loans are usually arranged by appointing the exporter's own bank as agent for the Export-Import Bank.

2. Extension of longer term credit to American firms desiring to export industrial products, particularly heavy machinery and railway equipment. This is usually accomplished through the purchase by the bank of the obligations of the foreign purchaser, representing up to 50 percent, and in some cases up to 75 percent, of the credit extended to the purchaser by the American seller.

3. Loans to American exporters where foreign Governments have failed to provide their own citizens with sufficient exchange to permit them to meet their dollar obligations. Advances of this character are usually made against the guaranty of the foreign Government concerned, or of a responsible foreign bank, or both.

In addition to the foregoing, the bank has, from time to time, purchased the obligations of foreign governmental agencies themselves, such as the notes of the Republic of China, which were held by the R.F.C. and F.C.A., arising from the sale of cotton, wheat and flour to China before the organization of the banks.

By December 31, 1936, the loans, authorized by the two Export-Import Banks since their creation, totaled $111,000,000.

In the absence of adequate credit

facilities by commercial banks, our Government must continue to cooperate with foreign traders, if foreign markets are to be maintained in the face of the many obstacles which have grown up in recent years against foreign trade. In addition to extending actual credit facilities, the Export-Import Bank has, by example, by participation, and by friendly intervention, induced commercial banks gradually to return to the field of foreign-trade financing. Experience has shown that we can furnish a reasonable amount of greatly needed Government assistance with very little actual risk.

The bank is now under the general administration of a Board of eleven trustees elected by the stockholders with the approval of the President.

19 ⟨ Extemporaneous Remarks to the State Directors of the National Emergency Council. February 2, 1934

I AM glad you have undertaken this very great task. As you know, we have felt for a long time that it was necessary to tie in, in some way, the entire emergency program which, in its many ramifications, we have been undertaking from time to time. We felt also that this work of disseminating information and preventing the crossing of wires, had to be done through decentralization. That is why you are here. You are the great decentralizers for the Federal Government and, in a sense, also, you are the coordinators between the Federal Government, the State and the local governments. That being so, I think that probably the future success of this program is more in your hands than in the hands of any other group.

Frank Walker, as National Director, has explained to you the various responsibilities you have. If you do not mind, I want to give you a few personal observations, based on certain experiences — four years in Albany, war work here during the Wilson Administration, and a certain amount of experience in the last few months.

One of the most difficult tasks that I know anything about is to avoid the results of certain perfectly normal and natural human impulses — impulses based on selfishness, impulses which take certain forms well known to most of us, such as trying to get special authority or special credit or individual applause or aggrandizement. Another thing we run into is the thought on the part of some people, of trying to make political capital out of relief work, out of the building up of what is in many ways a new relationship not only of government to citizen but also the relationship between employer and employee — the problem of taking care of human needs. Where we have fallen down in these past months, I would say in about 90 percent of the cases, the falling down has been caused, quite frankly, by individuals who try to get either personal or political credit out of something that ought not to have either of those factors in it in any shape, manner or form.

This work has nothing to do with partisan politics — nothing at all. A great many of you are Republicans, a good many are Democrats; quite a number do not belong regularly to one party or the other. We are not the least bit interested in the partisan side of this picture.

We do want you to be absolutely hard-boiled if you find any local person within your own States who is trying to get political advantage out of the relief of human needs. You will have the backing of this Administration 100 percent, even if you hit the biggest political boss in the United States on the head in carrying out this general program. It is important for the country to realize that relief — the carrying out of the principles behind the National Recovery Act, the carrying out of public works and all of the other ramifications — is based on a conception that is far beyond local politics or the local building-up of either a political machine or a party machine or a personal machine.

That is one of the things you will have a hard time in fighting. I think you will be able to get the help and enthusiastic support of at least 90 percent of the people within your own States if that idea can be thoroughly and completely fixed at the very inception of your work.

People are going to rush to you with all their troubles. That will relieve us in Washington very greatly.

You will require extraordinary patience and long hours and a smile at all times in carrying out the policy not just of the Administration in a narrow sense, but the policy of what I think is the overwhelming majority of the American people today. We are all behind this broad program, with few exceptions. We think it has done good. We believe we are on our way. We believe it is working out pretty well in all sections of the country.

I was interested in talking yesterday to the president of one of the greatest railroads of this country. I asked him how his road was doing. His reply was that while his road was carrying more freight and more passengers, the important fact was that the freight they were carrying revealed increases in every single classification of freight. That is the best illustration of the fact that we are building up economically in every section of the country, including practically all industries.

We know the human factor which enters so largely into this picture. We are trying to apply it to all groups needing aid and assistance and not merely to just a few scattered or favored groups. That is why we want from you the kind of information and kind of reports that will keep us in touch with the broad picture in every one of the forty-eight States.

I wish I could sit in with you in all the meetings you are having. When you return to your home States, you carry my very definite and distinct blessing. I hope you will not only keep Frank Walker informed, but through him, you will keep me in touch with the problems as you find them. Let us also have any suggestions you may have to make so we can give additional help from this end whenever necessary.

It has been fine to see you. Perhaps later in the spring, after you have been at work five or six months, we shall have another meeting in Washington.

NOTE: The National Emergency Council, in order to decentralize its administration and to function more efficiently, designated State directors for each of the States. On February 2, 1934, these directors all gathered in Washington for a general discussion with Mr. Frank Walker, the Executive Director of N.E.C., and I took this occasion to discuss with them some of their duties as State directors.

20 ❡ The President Agrees to Help Arbitrate the Peru-Ecuador Boundary Dispute.
February 6, 1934

THE Ambassador of Peru and the Minister of Ecuador have called upon me by instruction of their respective Governments to request, in accordance with the terms of the Ponce-Castro Protocol concluded between Peru and Ecuador on June 30, 1924, that this Government give its consent to the sending of delegations from Ecuador and Peru to Washington to discuss the adjustment of their common frontier. The Protocol provides that should the delegations be unable through direct negotiations to fix a definitive line, they will determine by common consent those zones the sovereignty over which is reciprocally recognized, as well as a zone to be submitted to the arbitral decision of the President of the United States.

It has been a source of intimate satisfaction to me to consent to the request made by the Governments of these great Republics, who have thus given most convincing and encouraging evidence of their determination to settle their long-standing boundary controversy through friendly discussion and in accordance with the most enlightened principles of international practice. Their decision should be a matter of encouragement to the Governments and the peoples of the entire continent.

In this connection it is heartening to recall that the Governments of Colombia and Peru are likewise undertaking to settle the controversy involving their common frontier through friendly negotiations being held at Rio de Janeiro.

The outstanding achievement of the Montevideo Conference was its unanimous work in strengthening the inter-American machinery for the peaceful adjustment of controversies which might arise among the American States. No Nations of the world have more effective means at their disposal for the peaceful solution of disputes than the Republics of this hemisphere. It would be a cause of the greatest rejoicing to friends of peace throughout the world if the armed contest resulting from a disagreement over frontiers in the Chaco, which is still continuing, would likewise yield to peaceful methods of adjustment. A continued resort to war, in view of the manifold agencies of peace which are available, would be a blot upon the civilization of this continent.

I am greatly encouraged that the Governments of Colombia, Ecuador and Peru give this convincing demonstration that they share our belief that such boundary disputes are eminently susceptible of pacific and friendly settlement.

NOTE: The boundary dispute between Peru and Ecuador involves the two former Spanish colonial provinces of Jaen and Mainas. It dates back to the early part of the nineteenth century. Since then there have been many attempts to settle the dispute, all without success.

In 1924, there was signed the Protocol mentioned in the foregoing statement.

In the meantime, negotiations were to continue between the disputants themselves in an effort to arrive at a peaceful solution of the boundary question.

The negotiations between the parties were not brought to any conclusion; and on July 6, 1936, an agreement was signed to transfer the seat of the negotiations to Washington. Special delegations were constituted for that purpose.

The inaugural session of the conference between the Ecuadoran and Peruvian boundary delegations was held on September 30, 1936, and on that date I made an address to the conference, printed as Item 140 of Vol. V.

2 1 ❰ The President Asks for Legislation to Help the Sugar Industry. February 8, 1934

To the Congress:

STEADILY increasing sugar production in the continental United States and in insular regions has created a price and marketing situation prejudicial to virtually everyone interested. Farmers in many areas are threatened with low prices for their beets and cane, and Cuban purchases of our goods have dwindled steadily as Cuban shipments of sugar to this country have declined.

There is a school of thought which believes that sugar ought to be on the free list. This belief is based on the high cost of sugar to the American consuming public.

The annual gross value of the sugar crop to American beet and cane growers is approximately $60,000,000. Those who believe in the free importation of sugar say that the two cents a pound tariff is levied mostly to protect this sixty million dollar crop and that it costs our consuming public every year more than two hundred million dollars to afford this protection.

I do not at this time recommend placing sugar on the free list. I feel that we ought first to try out a system of quotas with the threefold object of keeping down the price of sugar to consumers, of providing for the retention of beet and cane farming within our continental limits, and also of providing against further expansion of this necessarily expensive industry.

Consumers have not benefited from the disorganized state of sugar production here and in the insular regions. Both the import tariff and cost of distribution, which together account for the major portion of the consumers' price for sugar, have remained relatively constant during the past three years.

This situation clearly calls for remedial action. I believe that we can increase the returns to our own farmers, contribute to the economic rehabilitation of Cuba, provide adequate quotas for the Philippines, Hawaii, Puerto Rico and the Virgin Islands, and at the same time prevent higher prices to our own consumers.

The problem is difficult but can be solved if it is met squarely and if small temporary gains are sacrificed to ultimate general advantage.

The objective may be attained most readily through amendment of existing legislation. The Agricultural Adjustment Act should be amended to make sugar beets and sugar cane basic agricultural commodities. It then will be possible to collect a processing tax on sugar, the proceeds of which will be used to compensate farmers for holding their production to the quota level. A tax of less than one-half cent per pound would provide sufficient funds.

Consumers need not and should not bear this tax. It is already within the executive power to reduce the sugar tariff by an amount equal to the tax. In order to make certain that American consumers shall not bear an increased price due to this tax, Congress should provide that the rate of the processing tax shall in no event exceed the amount by which the tariff on sugar is reduced below the present rate of import duty.

By further amendment to the Agricultural Adjustment Act, the Secretary of Agriculture should be given authority to license refiners, importers and handlers to buy and sell sugar from the various producing areas only in the proportion which recent marketings of such areas bear to total United States consumption. The average marketings of the past three years provide on the whole an equitable base, but the base period should be flexible enough to allow slight adjustments as between certain producing areas.

The use of such a base would allow approximately the following preliminary and temporary quotas:

	Short tons
Continental beets	1,450,000
Louisiana and Florida	260,000
Hawaii	935,000
Puerto Rico	821,000
Philippine Islands	1,037,000

Cuba	1,944,000
Virgin Islands	5,000

6,452,000

The application of such quotas would immediately adjust market supplies to consumption, and would provide a basis for reduction of production to the needs of the United States market.

Furthermore, in the negotiations for a new treaty between the United States and Cuba to replace the existing Commercial Convention, which negotiations are to be resumed immediately, favorable consideration will be given to an increase in the existing preferential on Cuban sugars, to an extent compatible with the joint interests of the two countries.

In addition to action made possible by such legislative and treaty changes, the Secretary of Agriculture already has authority to enter into codes and marketing agreements with manufacturers which would permit savings in manufacturing and distributing costs. If any agreements or codes are entered into, they should be in such form as to assure that producers and consumers share in the resulting savings.

NOTE: The domestic sugar industry in 1933 had reached the same depressed state as had the rest of agriculture. Surpluses of sugar and general decreased demand had lowered prices below possibility of profit for producers of sugar within the continental limits of the United States and also in our insular possessions. Previous attempts to maintain the domestic market by tariff measures had failed to help continental producers, and had merely shifted the American market from Cuba to the insular possessions of the United States, where production increased enormously. Duty-free sugar from the Philippines, Hawaii and Puerto Rico kept on increasing. The continental beet and cane sugar crops also kept increasing. By the same token, the income of domestic sugar producers steadily went down. The average return to sugar-beet growers fell from $7.14 per ton of beets in 1930 to $5.13 in 1933. With the decline in income, wages paid to the field hands dropped accordingly. After 1929 returns to sugar-beet processors also declined.

A further result of the prior protectionist policy on sugar was the destruction of the valuable Cuban market for United States exports. Since Cuba could not ship sugar to America, she could not buy the products of American farms and factories. For example, in 1928, when Cuba shipped 3,125,000 short tons of raw cane sugar or its equivalent to the United States, she was able to purchase the products of 1,738,300 acres of American farm land. By 1932, however, Cuban shipments of sugar had fallen to 1,834,500 short tons of raw cane sugar or its equivalent, and with it she could purchase the products of only 921,000 American acres. This meant that American farmers had lost an export market in Cuba for farm products from 817,000 acres of land.

An attempt was made in 1933 to aid domestic producers through use of the marketing agreement powers of the Agricultural Adjustment Act. Sugar had not been included among the original basic agricultural commodities named in the Agricultural Adjustment Act (see Vol. II, Item 20). Therefore, the provisions relative to marketing agreements were relied upon to help the producers. Conferences and hearings were held during 1933, which resulted in an agreement on the part of the producers and processors, providing in part for the establishment of sugar quotas, the proposed execution of marketing agreements and codes of fair competition for various branches of the sugar trade. The Secretary of Agriculture, however, refused to approve the agreement

on the ground that (1) there was no adequate provision for benefits to farmers except through price enhancement; (2) the aggregate benefit to farmers was relatively small in relation to the aggregate cost to consumers; (3) the quotas established were in excess of the probable consumption; (4) no effective control of the amount of production was provided; (5) the Government's ability to protect consumers' interest was virtually limited to the President's power to terminate the whole agreement; (6) the benefit of price increases would have accrued to processors in an amount equal to or exceeding that which accrued to farmers.

After disapproving this sugar agreement, the Administration examined various alternative procedures for helping domestic cane and beet growers.

The first obligation was to the farmers and laborers. I, therefore, sent the foregoing message to the Congress, suggesting trying out a system of quotas, with the threefold object of protecting consumers, protecting the continental industry and providing against further expansion. To do this, I recommended that sugar beets and sugar cane be made basic agricultural commodities, so that a processing tax could be levied, the benefits of which could be used to compensate farmers for holding their production down to the quota level. To keep this tax from falling upon the consumers, I suggested that the rate of the tax should not exceed the amount by which the Executive under its powers would reduce the tariff on sugar. In my message I suggested preliminary and temporary quotas for the continent and for the insular possessions and Cuba. I recommended also that the Agricultural Adjustment Act be amended to permit the Secretary of Agriculture to license refiners, importers and handlers of sugar to buy and sell from the various producing areas only in accordance with such quotas. I suggested using as a basis for fixing quotas the average marketing of the past three years.

Pursuant to the foregoing recommendations, the Congress passed the Jones-Costigan Act (Pub. No. 213, 73d Congress; 48 Stat. 670) which I approved on May 9, 1934, with a statement printed as Item 76, this volume.

2 2 ⟨ Another Step to Protect Investors and to Eliminate Destructive Speculation — Recommendation for the Securities Exchange Commission. February 9, 1934

To the Congress:

I N MY message to you last March proposing legislation for Federal supervision of national traffic in investment securities I said:

"This is but one step in our broad purpose of protecting investors and depositors. It should be followed by legislation relating to the better supervision of the purchase and sale of all property dealt with on exchanges."

This Congress has performed a useful service in regulating the investment business on the part of financial houses and in protecting the investing public in its acquisition of securities.

There remains the fact, however, that outside the field of legitimate investment, naked speculation has been made far too alluring and far too easy for those who could and for those who could not afford to gamble.

Such speculation has run the scale from the individual who has

risked his pay envelope or his meager savings on a margin transaction involving stocks with whose true value he was wholly un-
familiar, to the pool of individuals or corporations with large resources, often not their own, who sought by manipulation to raise
or depress market quotations far out of line with reason. All of
this has resulted in loss to the average investor who is of necessity personally uninformed.

The exchanges in many parts of the country which deal in securities and commodities conduct, of course, a national business
because their customers live in every part of the country. The
managers of these exchanges have, it is true, often taken steps to
correct certain obvious abuses. We must be certain that abuses
are eliminated and to this end a broad policy of national regulation is required.

It is my belief that exchanges for dealing in securities and commodities are necessary and of definite value to our commercial
and agricultural life. Nevertheless, it should be our national policy to restrict, as far as possible, the use of these exchanges for
purely speculative operations.

I therefore recommend to the Congress the enactment of legislation providing for the regulation by the Federal Government
of the operations of exchanges dealing in securities and commodities for the protection of investors, for the safeguarding of values,
and so far as it may be possible, for the elimination of unnecessary, unwise and destructive speculation.

NOTE: The Democratic National Platform of 1932 stated: "We advocate . . . regulation to the full extent of federal power of . . . exchanges in securities and commodities."

Pursuant to the foregoing message (see also Item 52, this volume), the Congress enacted the Securities Exchange Act of 1934, which I approved on June 6, 1934 (48 Stat. 881; Public No. 291, 73d Congress).

The purposes of this Act in general were threefold:

1. To correct unfair practices in the securities markets. To this end, stock exchanges were placed under the jurisdiction of the Securities and Exchange Commission; manipulation of the prices of securities was prohibited; and trading in securities was made subject to the regulations of the Commission. The Commission was also empowered to set up comparable regulations for securities

traded in over-the-counter markets.

2. To furnish to the public adequate information concerning the management and financial condition of corporations whose securities are traded on the exchanges. For this purpose a registration statement disclosing full information was required for each security listed on an exchange, which is kept up to date through the filing of annual reports.

3. To regulate the use of credit in financing trading in securities. This is accomplished by the regulation of margin requirements and is administered by the Board of Governors of the Federal Reserve System.

As of June 30, 1937, the twenty-two leading stock exchanges of the country were operating under the jurisdiction of the Securities and Exchange Commission, and seven minor exchanges had received exemptions. At the same date there were registered with the Commission approximately 2,850 listed stock issues representing over 2,-500,000,000 shares of stock, and approximately 1500 bond issues representing a par value of over $24,-000,000,000. The Act transferred the administration of the Securities Act of 1933 (see Item 25, Vol. II) from the Federal Trade Commission to the Securities and Exchange Commission. It does not, however, relate to commodities exchanges.

One very important provision of the Act is that which requires every officer, director and principal stockholder in each registered company to make a monthly report of any purchases or sales, gifts or transfers of any of the equity securities of his company. Up to the end of June, 1937, the Commission had established 25,017 files for 23,340 such persons, representing largely the leaders of American business and industry. By the middle of 1937, over 85,000 such reports had been received by the Commission and had been made public.

Preventing the manipulation of security prices is another of the Commission's important functions. Proceedings for this purpose have already been instituted in seven major cases involving nine large firms. In addition, sixty trading investigations were in progress at the end of June, 1937, and thirteen cases involving violations of various trading rules had been referred to the exchanges themselves for action.

The Commission is further constantly engaged in studying and seeking to remedy the excesses of speculation so injurious to the general public, and as a result has caused many requirements to be made in the rules of various exchanges.

The benefits of this statute and of the Securities Act of 1933, depend in great part upon the vigilance of the Commission itself. The past years have shown extreme watchfulness on the part of the Commission, resulting in a much higher standard of securities trading than ever before existed. By June 30, 1937, 270 firms and individuals had been permanently enjoined from violations of this statute or the Securities Act of 1933 (see Vol. II, Item 25); 49 were under temporary injunctions and 33 had stipulated to discontinue their activities. For criminal violation of the two statutes, 375 defendants had been brought to trial or were awaiting trial, of whom 99 had been convicted by the end of June, 1937.

23 ❡ The Army Temporarily Flies the Mail. Executive Order No. 6591. February 9, 1934

WHEREAS by an order of the Postmaster General of the United States all domestic air mail contracts for carrying the mails have been annulled; and

WHEREAS the public interest requires that air mail service continue to be afforded and the cancellation of said contracts has created an emergency in this respect;

Now, THEREFORE, I, Franklin D. Roosevelt, President of the United States, under and by virtue of the authority in me vested, do hereby order and direct that the Postmaster General, Secretary of War, and Secretary of Commerce, together with other officers of their respective Departments, cooperate to the end that necessary air mail service be afforded.

It is further ordered and directed that the Secretary of War place at the disposal of the Postmaster General such airplanes, landing fields, pilots, and other employees and equipment of the Army of the United States needed or required for the transportation of mail, during the present emergency, by air over routes and schedules prescribed by the Postmaster General.

NOTE: On February 6, 1934, the Solicitor for the Post Office Department submitted a brief to Postmaster General Farley, in accordance with the Postmaster General's instructions to make an investigation of air-mail contracts, and to attend hearings held before the special committee of the Senate of the United States then engaged in the investigation of ocean- and air-mail contracts.

The Postmaster General, after reviewing all of the facts and after studying the entire situation, concluded that existing air-mail contracts with the various airplane companies had not been entered into according to law and that the cancellation of them was in order. Accordingly, he annulled them all.

I issued the foregoing Executive Order directing the Secretary of War to furnish the Postmaster General with the necessary airplanes and other facilities for the transportation of air mail. I issued this Order only after assurances were given to me by the Army Air Corps that its flying equipment and personnel could meet the necessary requirements for air-mail service.

On February 20, 1934, the Army Air Corps commenced this temporary assignment. It was realized that familiarity with the routes would have to be established, in order to maintain schedules; and the ten-day interval between my Executive Order and the date the Army actually began to fly the mail was devoted to the establishment of stations and equipment and the making of test flights. This was particularly essential because winter flying presents definite additional hazards.

On February 16, 1934, before the Army Air Corps began its assignment, two planes crashed. These accidents did not occur while mail was being carried, but while the pilots were flying over the routes to familiarize themselves with them. Minute and definite instructions were thereupon issued to all stations to pay particular attention to safeguarding lives, even if it were necessary to sacrifice efficiency in mail service, and detailed instructions were issued to endeavor to obtain the safest equipment and to provide the utmost precautions for flights.

However, weather conditions were extremely bad throughout the country for flying; and accidents continued to occur. On March 10, 1934, I sent a letter to the Secretary of War, ordering temporary curtailment of the air-mail service by the Army (see Items 40 and 41 of this volume).

24 ⟨ Radio Address to the Boy Scouts of America. February 10, 1934

Fellow Scouts:

I AM happy to participate in the 24th Anniversary Celebration of our organization, the Boy Scouts of America. Nearly a million of us are mobilized at this time in all parts of the country as a part of the program for this week of celebration. Home and farm patrols and troops of farm boys are joining with their brother scouts in the big cities.

To the Boy Scouts of America

In front of the City Hall in San Francisco — and it is nine o'clock in the morning there — thousands of scouts join with other thousands in the Hippodrome in New York in carrying on the cause of world-wide brotherhood in Scouting.

As most of you know, Scouting has been one of my active interests for many years. I have visited hundreds of Troops in their home towns and in their camps. I know therefore from personal experience the things we do and stand for as Scouts. We have ideals. We are a growing organization. We believe that we are accomplishing fine American results not only for our own membership, but also for our families, our communities and our Nation.

Summed up in one sentence, the aim of Scouting is to build up better citizenship. I believe that we are contributing greatly to that objective.

I am especially happy today to extend personal greetings and congratulations to the Scouts and Leaders who have earned the President's award for progress in the year 1933, as a part of the Ten-Year Program. It is appropriate that we are planning for a celebration of our Silver Jubilee, the Twenty-fifth Anniversary of the Boy Scouts of America, which will culminate in a great national Jamboree here in the Nation's capital in the summer of 1935. Of course it would be physically impossible for us to have the whole membership of the Boy Scouts of America, a million strong, come to Washington at one time, but I much hope that it will be possible to have every nook and cranny of our Nation represented.

As a preliminary to our Silver Jubilee, and in line with the emphasis of service for others which we have always stressed, I suggest to you that it is time once more for us to do a National Good Turn.

As many of you know, we are doing everything possible in this emergency to help suffering humanity. I called upon the Federal Emergency Relief Administrator, Mr. Harry L. Hopkins, to tell me what kind of National Good Turn would be of the greatest service. He has recommended that during the balance of the month of February every troop and every Scout do everything

95

possible in their separate localities to collect such household furnishings, bedding and clothes as people may be able to share as gifts to those who greatly need them.

Therefore, I ask you, under the direction of your own local officers, and in conference with the representatives of the Federal Relief Administration and other local social agencies, to gather up such of this material as may be available for distribution.

I am confident that the American people will generously cooperate and respond. Indeed, I am hoping that in many cases they will telephone or send letters to the local Scout offices to offer their help to carry through this National Good Turn.

I have already received offers of cooperation from Governors of States, from mayors and other community leaders. May you carry out this new service and rededicate yourselves to the Scout Oath.

I ask you to join with me and the Eagle Scouts and our President and Chief Scout Executive who are here with me in the White House in giving again the Scout Oath.

All stand!

Give the Scout sign!

Repeat with me the Scout Oath!

"On my honor I will do my best:

To do my duty to God and my country and to obey the Scout Law;

To help other people at all times;

To keep myself physically strong, mentally awake, and morally straight."

25 ❪ A Letter to the Chaplains of the Military and Naval Services. February 13, 1934

My dear Colonel Brasted:

THE Great Teacher said: "I come that ye may have life and that ye may have it more abundantly." The object of all our striving should be to realize that "abundant life."

The supreme values are spiritual. The hope of the world is that character which, built upon the solid rock, withstands triumphantly all the storms of life.

To build this exemplary character is our great task. Without it the abundant life cannot be realized, and the best citizens and best soldiers of a country are those who have put on the armor of righteousness.

Chaplains of the military and naval services and clergymen everywhere who by word and life are advancing the cause of idealism and true religion are doing a commendable work, one that is absolutely essential to the life of the Nation.

Very sincerely yours,

Colonel Alva J. Brasted,
Chief of Chaplains, U. S. A.,
War Department,
Washington, D. C.

26 ❡ An Appeal to Railroad Executives and Employees to Extend Their Wage Agreement. February 14, 1934

Gentlemen:

ON JUNE 21, 1933, the railroad managers and the railroad labor executives entered into an agreement under which the arrangement by which 10 percent is being deducted from the pay checks of railroad employees was extended from October 31, 1933, until June 30, 1934, and under which the date on which either party could submit a notice in accordance with the provisions of the Railway Labor Act, indicating a desire to change the basic rates of pay, was extended from June 15, 1933, to February 15, 1934.

It was stated that this agreement had been reached because both the railroads and the employees wished to do nothing which would in any way embarrass or threaten the policy of the Administration; that they realized that the Government had embarked upon a wholly new policy designed to promote business and industrial activity and to further the general welfare; that they appreciated that until the results of this policy could be more clearly determined, it would be difficult to deal wisely with the wage controversy; and that the active prosecution of such a controversy at that time might have a most disturbing and unsettling effect. Neither side relinquished in any way its views as to what the wages should be, but they agreed to a postponement of the controversy out of deference to what they believed to be the desire and policy of the Administration and in the general public interest.

The advent of February 15 makes it necessary again to give consideration to this wage matter. Marked progress toward national recovery has been made since last June, and I am sure that the goal will be reached. Nevertheless much remains to be accomplished; the emergency still exists, and the country has not yet attained conditions of stability. There has been comparatively little change in the cost of living, but prices are unsettled and I am hopeful that they will in general rise to higher levels. The traffic of the railroads is improving, but their financial condition is still impaired and their credit has not yet been restored so far as private capital is concerned. Under present conditions the prosecution of a bitter controversy between the railroads and their employees over wages would have a most disturbing influence, and I am further convinced that conditions are not yet sufficiently stable to permit of a wise determination of what the wages should be for the future.

In the circumstances I venture to express the hope that the railroads and their employees may be able to agree upon an extension of the present agreement for at least six months. I am confident that such an extension would be of advantage to those directly concerned, and also to the entire country.

Very sincerely yours,

To the Conference Committee of Managers
(representing the Class I Railroads), and
the Railway Labor Executives Association.

NOTE: On June 15, 1933, the railroads, pursuant to the provisions of the Railway Labor Act and the then existing Chicago wage agreement dated December 21, 1932, notified their employees that they intended to reduce basic rates of pay by 22½ percent for all railroad employees. At that time the Government was engaged in a united effort to raise wages and prices and to protect employees. This proposed reduction of wages by the railroads was therefore directly opposed to Government policy.

In this situation I requested the Federal Coordinator of Transportation to confer with the representatives of the managers and labor executives. He asked them to confer with him on June 20, 1933. As a result of his efforts an agreement was reached, whereby the notice of reduction of pay was revoked, the then prevailing arrangement of deducting 10 percent from the pay checks of the employees was extended to June 30, 1934, and the right to submit further notice of change of pay was extended to February 15, 1934.

This agreement was reached solely because the railroads and employees were willing to forego any action which would embarrass or jeopardize the efforts of the Administration to promote business and industrial recovery. It was an agreement which in no way relinquished the respective views as to what the wages should be, but one which merely postponed the controversy in the general public interest until the results of the efforts of the Administration could be more clearly determined.

Before February 15, 1934, arrived, the railroads had indicated an intention again to serve notice of a demand for a 15 percent reduction, instead of the then pending deduction of 10 percent from pay checks. Again, the managers and the employees came to an impasse. Accordingly, on the day before, February 14, 1934, I addressed the foregoing joint communication to the managers and to the labor executives. On February 15th, the managers served the 15 percent reduction notice.

The parties were unable to agree, although they did meet in joint conference, and on March 20th I addressed another joint communication to the managers and to the employees, which is printed as Item 45, this volume.

27 ❡ The President Urges Crop Control of Cotton. February 16, 1934

My dear Mr. Chairman:

As you know, I have watched the cotton problem with the deepest attention during all these months. I believe that the gains which have been made — and they are very substantial — must be consolidated and, insofar as possible, made permanent. To do this, however, reasonable assurance of crop limitation must be obtained.

In this objective, the great majority of cotton farmers are in agreement. I am told that the recent poll by the Department of Agriculture shows that at least 95 percent of the replies are in favor of some form of control.

My study of the various methods suggested leads me to believe that the Bankhead bills in principle best cover the situation. I hope that in the continuing emergency your Committee can take action.

Very sincerely yours,

Hon. Marvin Jones,
Committee on Agriculture,
The Capitol,
Washington, D. C.

NOTE: The 1933 voluntary cotton reduction program under A.A.A. had been a complete success (see Vol. II, Items 83, 92).

When the cotton farmers began to sign their contracts for 1934 cotton reduction, a strong sentiment grew up in favor of a supplementary kind of production control, which would prevent non-cooperating farmers from increasing their individual planting in order to take advantage of the price advances which had resulted from the 1933 reduction in production and from the revaluation of the dollar.

The increase in farm population through the migration of city people to farms in the South, the tendency toward more intensive cultivation, and the temptation for entering the cotton-production business arising from increased prices — all led to a growing belief that the efforts of A.A.A. were going to be impeded during the coming year.

Accordingly, there was introduced in Congress a bill, later commonly known as the Bankhead Act, designed to use the taxing powers of the Federal Government to keep total cotton production within the limits of a fixed national quota.

While this bill was pending, the Secretary of Agriculture in January, 1934, sent out more than 40,000 questionnaires to representative cotton producers and farm leaders to obtain their views as to the compulsory features of this legislation.

Twenty-four thousand seven hundred eighty-nine questionnaires were returned, indicating an overwhelming desire on the part of cotton producers for some form of compulsory control to supplement the effect of voluntary agreements made under the Agricultural Adjustment Act.

The bill was passed and approved by me on April 21, 1934, with a statement printed as Item 62, this volume.

28 ❡ The Beginnings of a Comprehensive Plan for the Social and Economic Advancement of the Virgin Islands. White House Statement. February 23, 1934

THE President today formed an Advisory Council to assist in the formulation of a comprehensive plan for the social and economic advancement of the people of the Virgin Islands, to be financed from public works funds.

The Advisory Council will consist of seven members, including the Secretaries of Interior and Agriculture.

The letter to the Secretary of the Interior read:

Dear Mr. Secretary:

THE Administration has formulated a comprehensive plan for the social and economic advancement of the people of the Virgin Islands which is being financed from public works funds. For the first time, sufficient capital is available to develop a well-rounded program which I believe will bring a permanent benefit to the

Islands if properly executed. The economic phases will be conducted on a non-profit-sharing basis and will include the development of cane lands and the operation of sugar mills and a rum distillery. Coincidently, the social aspects will be cared for through adult education, nursery schools, homesteading and improved housing conditions. Cooperative methods will be used wherever practicable, which will enable these people to help themselves toward an improved standard of living.

I desire to form an advisory council of seven members to assist in the program, and I would like you to serve with the Secretary of Agriculture, business and professional men, and others interested in the economic condition of the Negro. As you know, the active functions of management will be assumed by the Governor and his staff and by men who will be engaged for the purpose, under the general supervision of the Department of the Interior. I believe your support will be helpful in this unique movement and that you will have an opportunity for accomplishment in a field in which I am sure you are interested. Will you please advise me whether you would accept an appointment to the council?

Sincerely yours,

Hon. Harold L. Ickes,
Secretary of the Interior,
Washington, D. C.

NOTE: In the years preceding 1933, there had been a gradual and serious decline in the economic well-being of the Virgin Islands. While this condition was in large measure the result of the general world depression, it was aggravated by certain special circumstances peculiar to the Virgin Islands. The gradual retirement of Danish capital after 1917, and the failure to attract American capital, left many of the population stranded. In 1933, shipping had sunk to its lowest ebb; cane cultivation had reached the lowest acreage; municipal revenues had touched the bottom; unemployment was so widespread that over 60 percent of the population was found to be eligible for relief; municipal services, such as health and education, were seriously crippled by the lack of funds.

As soon as possible, we undertook to formulate a general program of economic rehabilitation, as outlined in the foregoing letter. A comprehensive homestead program was adopted, under which 380 homestead families have been established through advancement of credit payable on easy long-term plans. A program for the development of St. Thomas, V. I., as a tourist center has been substantially furthered by the construction of the Bluebeard Castle Hotel operated directly by the Federal Government through the Department of the Interior.

The major industry in the Virgin Islands has always been the sugar business, centered chiefly in the Island of St. Croix. In 1930, the West India Sugar Factory, Inc., which controlled 75 percent of the sugar business in St. Croix, discontinued operations. Efforts to organize a successor company were unsuccessful. All of the people who had worked in the industry, and in the cultivation of sugar cane for it, were thrown out of employment.

While the great relief problem which resulted from the shut-down of the plant was met temporarily and in part by large C.W.A. and similar projects, it was obvious that the relief problem would continue indefinitely unless steps were taken to rehabilitate the basic industry of the island.

Accordingly, plans were prepared and carried through for the establishment of The Virgin Islands Company, a Federal Government Agency, to take over the sugar mills and a number of the plantations which had been previously operated by the West India Sugar Factory, Inc. A distillery was purchased at the same time. Additional land was acquired by the United States, so that now a total of 5,000 acres of land has been acquired by the Federal Government and turned over to The Virgin Islands Company. Three thousand acres have been put into cultivation in sugar cane. The Virgin Islands Company now manufactures raw sugar and a substantial amount of rum, and has been engaged in restoring waste lands to sugar-cane cultivation. During the development of the physical equipment of the company, employment was given to approximately 1,500 people, a very large percentage of the unemployed of the island of St. Croix. In fact, during this period of development there was practically no unemployment whatsoever in that island.

With the completion of construction, the employment rolls of The Virgin Islands Company have decreased; but it is anticipated that a thousand persons will be constantly employed by that company as long as it continues. It is generally believed that the operations of the company have solved the major economic problems of the island of St. Croix.

Substantial improvements have been made to the road systems of the Islands since 1933; and much important work has been accomplished in improving the sanitation facilities. Thirteen school buildings have been constructed or reconstructed under P.W.A. grants, as have many other public buildings. Several grants of relief funds were made in 1934 for the establishment of cooperatives in the Virgin Islands. The Civilian Conservation Corps has set up three camps in the Islands. Three urban housing projects, located in each of the towns, were undertaken by the P.W.A. Housing Division in 1935; and all of these projects are now completed.

By an Act approved June 22, 1936 (Public No. 749, 74th Congress), a civil government was provided for the Virgin Islands of the United States, replacing the Act of March 3, 1917. This new Organic Act, as it is called, has established a considerable measure of local autonomy and democracy.

To obtain first-hand knowledge of the conditions and recent developments in the Virgin Islands, as well as in other outlying parts of the United States, I made a personal visit and tour of the Islands in July of 1934. Some of my remarks on that occasion will be found in Items 130 and 131 of this volume.

29 ⟨The One Hundredth Press Conference (Excerpts). February 23, 1934

(Crop-production loans — Cotton crop reduction — National Committeemen bidding for Government contracts.)

THE PRESIDENT: On the forty-million-dollar emergency crop-production loan bill, I am signing it this afternoon. I haven't done it yet, but will do it in the next five minutes. I am going to sign it with the explanation that in signing this bill I do so only on the theory that it is proper to taper off the crop-loan system rather than to cut it off abruptly. This year they got something like eighty million dollars, and it is forty for the coming year.

A useful purpose will be served by aiding certain farmers who cannot qualify yet for crop-production loans from the newly established production credit associations. Such credit associations have been formed to take care of these crop loans. Where farmers have security to offer this year, they should be required to obtain their loans from the associations which have been established to give farmers a permanent source of production credit.

The record of these crop-production loans in the past is very bad. Unfortunately, previous crop loans show a large loss to the Government. In prior years, the rate of repayment of the loans runs 60 and 70 and 75 percent. In other words, the returns show a big loss; and in prior years the administrative costs have also actually exceeded the interest collected. That is bad business.

The amount appropriated this year is far below the appropriations of previous years. I think it is less than half of what it was last year; but this 1934 loan by the Government ought to be considered as a tapering-off loan, and should be the last of its kind. In other words, I do not want any more bills along this line next year.

I was rather horrified by the returns that came in. For instance, in loans made in 1933 so far, up to the first of the year, only 73 percent have been repaid. . . .

Q. Would you care to state whether or not the crop-reduction plans have anything to do with cutting of production loans?

THE PRESIDENT: No, it is an entirely different thing. The new associations being formed are intended to take care of crop loans.

Q. Have you had a return on the fifty thousand questionnaires that went out in reference to the advisability of making compulsory or voluntary reductions?

THE PRESIDENT: The last I heard from the Department of Agriculture was 95 percent in favor.

Q. That was on cotton, was it not?

Q. Was that in favor of the tax idea?

THE PRESIDENT: No. It was put out in three different ways and split roughly three different ways. The 95 percent was split three different ways, but the whole of the 95 percent was in favor of some kind of more compulsory system than the old method. I thought those figures were given out. I thought that they had been given out by the Department of Agriculture. . . .

Q. You recently told us, or did you, about National Committeemen practicing as lawyers? I have an inquiry from Chicago asking if that applies to National Committeemen who bid on municipal contracts where P.W.A. funds are involved.

THE PRESIDENT: If you just leave it in general form and do not talk about the gentleman himself, just leave it as a matter of broad general principle, I am inclined to think that a National Committeeman within any State ought to make a choice. If he wants to bid on public contracts that have any relationship at all with the national Government and if he is the low bidder, he should get it; but I don't think he should continue to be National Committeeman at the same time. It is a question of ethics. He ought to choose between them.

Q. There seems to be a little distinction there. Do you mean, holding his job, it would be suitable for him to make a bid and then if he does get the project itself . . .

THE PRESIDENT: No, I don't think he should engage in that work.

NOTE: As appears from the foregoing Press Conference, I approved the 1934 Emergency Crop and Feed Loan (Public No. 97, 73d Congress; 48 Stat. 354) with the idea that crop loans of this kind would be tapered off. That part of the conference which dealt with these loans was made public as a direct statement by me.

The Emergency Crop and Feed Loan, authorized by the Act of the previous Congress (Public No. 327, 72d Congress, approved February 4, 1933) had appropriated $90,000,-000 for that purpose. The total amount loaned out of that $90,000-000 was about $57,376,000 distributed among 633,586 loans of an average size of $90. Up to October 31st, of 1937, only approximately $47,417,000 had been collected on account of this principal. This means that on the average loan of $90 there has been a loss even up to date of $15.70 per loan. That is one of the chief reasons for my reluctance to approve the new bill.

However, the Act which was signed by me with the foregoing statement was made very necessary by the fact that there were a substantial number of farmers whose financial condition precluded them from receiving short term agricultural credit from existing sources.

Pursuant to this Act authorizing $40,000,000 of loans, approximately

$37,890,000 was loaned, of which the sum of $23,400,000 was loaned to farmers in States affected by the 1934 drought (see Items 81, 103, 147 of this volume). The total principal collections on all the loans under this Act up to October 31, 1937, amounted to approximately only $23,413,000. The number of loans made was 445,188, of an average size of $85. The average loss per loan to date has been $32.50.

For further loans of this character, see Item 18 of Vol. IV and Item 25 of Vol. V.

30 ❨ A Recommendation for the Creation of the Federal Communications Commission. February 26, 1934

To the Congress:

I HAVE long felt that for the sake of clarity and effectiveness the relationship of the Federal Government to certain services known as utilities should be divided into three fields — transportation, power and communications. The problems of transportation are vested in the Interstate Commerce Commission, and the problems of power, its development, transmission and distribution, in the Federal Power Commission.

In the field of communications, however, there is today no single Government agency charged with broad authority.

The Congress has vested certain authority over certain forms of communications in the Interstate Commerce Commission and there is in addition the agency known as the Federal Radio Commission.

I recommend that the Congress create a new agency to be known as the Federal Communications Commission, such agency to be vested with the authority now lying in the Federal Radio Commission and with such authority over communications as now lies with the Interstate Commerce Commission — the services affected to be all of those which rely on wires, cables or radio as a medium of transmission.

It is my thought that a new Commission such as I suggest

might well be organized this year by transferring the present authority of the Radio Commission and the Interstate Commerce Commission for the control of communications. The new body should, in addition, be given full power to investigate and study the business of existing companies and make recommendations to the Congress for additional legislation at the next session.

NOTE: The foregoing message was based upon recommendations made to me on January 23, 1934, by an Inter-departmental Committee which I had appointed in 1933. The message sought legislation unifying Federal control over various types of communication in one Federal agency, instead of being divided between the Federal Radio Commission, the Interstate Commerce Commission and other agencies. Pursuant to the foregoing recommendation, the Communications Act of 1934 was passed by the Congress and approved by me on June 19, 1934 (Public No. 416, 73d Congress; 48 Stat. 1064).

31 ⟨ "Unemployment Must Be Faced on More Than One Front"—White House Statement on a Plan for Relief. February 28, 1934

THE experience of the past nine months has shown that the problem of unemployment must be faced on more than one front.

Coincident with the plans for the demobilization of Civil Works has been the development of a program to meet the peculiar needs of three separate and distinct groups in want through no fault of their own.

It has been found that these three groups fall into the following classifications:

(1) Distressed families in rural areas.

(2) Those composing "stranded populations," i.e., living in single-industry communities in which there is no hope of future reemployment, such as miners in worked-out fields.

(3) The unemployed in large cities.

A Plan for Relief

The Administration will be guided by these groupings in expending the $950,000,000 recently appropriated by Congress.

The care of needy persons in rural areas is a problem quite distinct and apart from that of the industrial unemployed. Their security must be identified with agriculture. They must be placed in positions of self-support. In many parts of the country this calls for a change from commercial farming and dependence upon a single cash crop, to the raising of the various commodities needed to maintain the family.

Relief funds, therefore, will be expended on behalf of rural families in a manner and to an extent that will enable them to achieve self-support. Work for wages from relief funds is not an essential part of this phase of the program and will be provided only insofar as it is necessary to accomplish the primary objective. No encouragement of an extension of competitive farming is contemplated, but rather the placing of thousands of persons, who have made their living from agriculture, into a relationship with the soil that will provide them a security they do not now enjoy.

Some of the methods to be employed include building, or rebuilding, to provide adequate farm homes; providing seed and stock for other than commercial purposes, and furnishing opportunities to these workers to earn modest cash incomes through part-time or seasonal employment in small industrial enterprises. There should also be a planned distribution of the regular jobs on highways; in the national and State parks and forests, and other public work prosecuted in agricultural communities.

The plan calls for complete cooperation with the Department of Agriculture, and with the State and county agricultural departments throughout the country. It substitutes for direct relief an opportunity to obtain and maintain self-support in an accustomed environment, and completely divorces relief activities in rural areas from those in the cities.

Only a careful survey can determine the number of families included in "stranded populations," but there are sufficient data already collected to indicate a situation of substantial proportions. The solution of the problem of these families involves their physical transplanting, in a large majority of cases, since the areas in which they are concentrated offer neither future employment at wages nor opportunities for self-support through agriculture.

It is planned to explore this difficult situation and, in collaboration with the Subsistence Homesteads Division of the Department of the Interior, and with other Federal and local agencies, to devise and apply definite remedial measures which will affect an appreciable number of these families. These measures will be directed, first, at maintenance on small tracts of land and, then, at the development of supplemental industrial opportunities to provide for a normal standard of living.

The needy unemployed living in cities and towns and who, in the course of coming months, may reasonably look forward to regular jobs, are entitled to, and should receive, insofar as possible, adequate assurance of means to maintain themselves during the balance of the period of their enforced idleness. The Federal Government, both in its relief measures and in its Civil Works program, now nearing completion, has been meeting an emergency situation.

Direct relief as such, whether in the form of cash or relief in kind, is not an adequate way of meeting the needs of able-bodied workers. They very properly insist upon an opportunity to give to the community their services in the form of labor in return for unemployment benefits. The Federal Government has no intention or desire to force either upon the country or the unemployed themselves a system of relief which is repugnant to American ideals of individual self-reliance. Therefore, work programs which would not normally be undertaken by public bodies, but which are at the same time outside of the field of private industry, will be projected and prosecuted in and near industrial communities. Labor on those projects will not be expected of dependent members of the community who are unable to work, but will be confined to those needy unemployed who can give adequate return for the unemployment benefits which they receive.

Work will be given to an individual for a period not to exceed six months. This is in order that it may not be considered, or utilized, as a permanent method of support. It will be administered by and under the direction of those responsible for the unemployment relief activities in industrial communities.

Every effort will be made to continue opportunities for work for the professional groups in need — teachers, engineers, architects, artists, nurses, and others.

This program expresses a conviction that industrial workers who are unemployed and in need of relief should be given an opportunity for livelihood by the prosecution of a flexible program of public works. The several States will be aided, as the Federal relief law provides, in the financing of this enterprise.

NOTE: The foregoing statement outlined the general future plans and objectives for the relief of the unemployed of the Nation.

While the Civil Works Administration (see Item 155A, Vol. II) was carrying on its work relief program during the winter of 1933-1934, F.E.R.A. funds granted to the States were being used chiefly for direct relief.

On January 27, 1934, I sent a special message to the Congress requesting additional appropriations of $950,000,000 for F.E.R.A. and to continue C.W.A. until the date set for its termination. This sum was appropriated February 15, 1934. (Pub. No. 93, 73d Congress; 48 Stat. 351.)

Upon the dissolution of the C.W.A. (see Item 155A, Vol. II) the F.E.R.A. again fostered large-scale work relief. Its operation was called the Emergency Work Relief Program, to which a large number of C.W.A. projects and employees were transferred. By April, 1934, more than a million persons were employed by it, and by January, 1935, its employment peak of 2,500,000 was reached. However, during this period, more cases were receiving direct relief than work relief.

By this time a real effort was being made to adapt work relief to the occupational skills and varying characteristics of the unemployed to whom assistance was being given. Special groups of persons were given specific activities which fitted in with their past training and qualifications, such as the Emergency Education Program and the Student Aid Program. Individual effort was being made to reach such diversified classes as drought-stricken farmers, and other rural groups, the great numbers of transients, unemployed teachers, artists, musicians and other white collar classes.

The next great step in the program of relief was taken by the organization, in 1935, of the Works Progress Administration (see Vol. IV, Items 54, 79, 85).

32 ❨A Recommendation for Legislation to Guarantee Principal on Home Owners Loan Bonds. March 1, 1934

To the Congress:

ON JANUARY 10th I recommended to the Congress the passage of legislation guaranteeing the principal as well as the interest of the $2,000,000,000 of bonds authorized for the refinancing of agricultural indebtedness.

I now recommend that the Home Owners Loan Act be similarly amended. The purpose of such legislation, as in the case of farm financing, will be to assure the continued progress on a self-sustaining basis of the making of loans for the purpose of refinancing home mortgages without interruption. There is the same reason for acknowledging publicly what already amounts to a moral obligation in respect to these bonds as there was in the case of bonds authorized to be issued through the Farm Credit Administration.

By making provision for an exchange of the new type of bonds guaranteed as to principal as well as interest for those already issued, those mortgagees who have shown their willingness to cooperate with the Government's program by accepting the original bonds will be placed on an equal footing with mortgagees who will hereafter obtain the fully guaranteed obligations proposed by this legislation.

Out of the funds which may be made available as a result of the proposed guarantee of principal of these bonds, the Home Owners Loan Corporation should be enabled to extend further assistance for the modernization of homes as well as for the making of repairs. Authority should also be given to the Home Owners Loan Corporation to purchase bonds of the Federal Home Loan Banks, thus enabling the Corporation to make funds available to those banks and to Building and Loan Associations which are in need of financing in order to encourage private building.

NOTE: The recommendations which I made in the foregoing message for legislation to guarantee principal on Home Owners Loan Corporation bonds (see Items 39 and 74 of Volume II) were adopted by an act approved April 27, 1934 (Public No. 178, 73d Congress; 48 Stat. 643).

33 ❡ Request for Authority to Consummate Reciprocal Trade Agreement for the Revival of Foreign Trade. March 2, 1934

To the Congress:

I AM REQUESTING the Congress to authorize the Executive to enter into executive commercial agreements with foreign Nations; and in pursuance thereof, within carefully guarded limits, to modify existing duties and import restrictions in such a way as will benefit American agriculture and industry. This action seems opportune and necessary at this time for several reasons.

First, world trade has declined with startling rapidity. Measured in terms of the volume of goods in 1933, it has been reduced to approximately 70 percent of its 1929 volume; measured in terms of dollars, it has fallen to 35 percent. The drop in the foreign trade of the United States has been even sharper. Our exports in 1933 were but 52 percent of the 1929 volume, and 32 percent of the 1929 value.

This has meant idle hands, still machines, ships tied to their docks, despairing farm households, and hungry industrial families. It has made infinitely more difficult the planning for economic readjustment in which the Government is now engaged.

You and I know that the world does not stand still; that trade movements and relations once interrupted can with the utmost difficulty be restored; that even in tranquil and prosperous times there is a constant shifting of trade channels.

How much greater, how much more violent is the shifting in these times of change and of stress is clear from the record of current history. Every Nation must at all times be in a position quickly to adjust its taxes and tariffs to meet sudden changes and avoid severe fluctuations in both its exports and its imports.

You and I know, too, that it is important that the country possess within its borders a necessary diversity and balance to maintain a rounded national life, that it must sustain activities vital to national defense and that such interests cannot be sacrificed for passing advantage. Equally clear is the fact that a full and permanent domestic recovery depends in part upon a revived and strengthened international trade and that American exports cannot be permanently increased without a corresponding increase in imports.

Second, other Governments are to an ever-increasing extent winning their share of international trade by negotiated reciprocal trade agreements. If American agricultural and industrial interests are to retain their deserved place in this trade, the American Government must be in a position to bargain for that place with other Governments by rapid and decisive negotiation based upon a carefully considered program, and to grant with discernment corresponding opportunities in the American market for foreign products supplementary to our own.

If the American Government is not in a position to make fair offers for fair opportunities, its trade will be superseded. If it is not in a position at a given moment rapidly to alter the terms on which it is willing to deal with other countries, it cannot adequately protect its trade against discriminations and against bargains injurious to its interests. Furthermore a promise to which prompt effect cannot be given is not an inducement which can pass current at par in commercial negotiations.

For this reason, any smaller degree of authority in the hands of the Executive would be ineffective. The executive branches of virtually all other important trading countries already possess some such power.

I would emphasize that quick results are not to be expected. The successful building up of trade without injury to American producers depends upon a cautious and gradual evolution of plans.

The disposition of other countries to grant an improved place to American products should be carefully sounded and considered; upon the attitude of each must somewhat depend our future course of action. With countries which are unwilling to abandon purely restrictive national programs, or to make concessions toward the reestablishment of international trade, no headway will be possible.

The exercise of the authority which I propose must be carefully weighed in the light of the latest information so as to give assurance that no sound and important American interest will be injuriously disturbed. The adjustment of our foreign trade relations must rest on the premise of undertaking to benefit and not to injure such interests. In a time of difficulty and unemployment such as this, the highest consideration of the position of the different branches of American production is required.

From the policy of reciprocal negotiation which is in prospect, I hope in time that definite gains will result to American agriculture and industry.

Important branches of our agriculture, such as cotton, tobacco, hog products, rice, cereal and fruit-raising, and those branches of American industry whose mass production methods have led the world, will find expanded opportunities and productive capacity in foreign markets, and will thereby be spared in part, at least, the heartbreaking readjustments that must be necessary if the shrinkage of American foreign commerce remains permanent.

A resumption of international trade cannot but improve the general situation of other countries, and thus increase their purchasing power. Let us well remember that this in turn spells increased opportunity for American sales.

Legislation such as this is an essential step in the program of national economic recovery which the Congress has elaborated during the past year. It is part of an emergency program necessitated by the economic crisis through which we are passing. It should provide that the trade agreements shall be terminable within a period not to exceed three years; a shorter period probably would not suffice for putting the program into effect. In its execution, the Executive must, of course, pay due heed to the requirements of other branches of our recovery program, such as the National Industrial Recovery Act.

I hope for early action. The many immediate situations in the field of international trade that today await our attention can thus be met effectively and with the least possible delay.

NOTE: The Democratic National Platform of 1932 stated: "We advocate . . . reciprocal tariff agreements with other Nations, . . ."

Pursuant to the foregoing message, an act entitled "An act to amend the tariff act of 1930" (Public No. 316, 73d Congress) was passed by the Congress and approved by me on June 12, 1934, which is commonly referred to as the "Trade Agreements Act."

It authorized the President, for a period of three years, to enter into trade agreements with foreign Nations, in order to secure outlets for American products. In order to bring about this result, the President was authorized to proclaim modifications of duties and other import restrictions, up to 50 percent of existing rates. The President was also authorized to deny the benefits of such lower rates to the products of those countries which discriminated against the commerce of the United States.

The program of negotiating trade agreements has been carried out since this date under the general supervision of the Secretary of State. Questions of general policy are considered by the Executive Committee on Commercial Policy. (See Vol. II, Item 160.)

The Executive Committee on Commercial Policy established as a sub-committee the Interdepartmental Committee on Trade Agreements, on which are representatives of the Departments of State, Commerce, Agriculture, Treasury, the Tariff Commission, and originally the Special Adviser to the President on Foreign Trade.

This Committee on Trade Agreements is the central operating agency in preparing for and negotiating trade agreements.

Pursuant to the provisions of the statute, public notice of the intention to enter into a reciprocal trade agreement with any foreign country is given so as to allow all interested parties an opportunity to present their objections or suggestions or general views with respect to any proposed agreement.

The procedure as to such notice and presentation of views is set forth in Executive Order No. 6750, June 27, 1934, printed as Item 111, this volume. For the purpose of receiving the presentation of such views a separate Committee for Reciprocity Information was established on July 3, 1934.

The first public notice of intention to negotiate an agreement was given on July 3, 1934, for Cuba. That treaty was proclaimed on August 24, 1934. Between that first treaty and the expiration date of the original Act, June 12, 1937, public notices of intention to negotiate trade agreements were given for nineteen countries. As of July 15, 1937, agreements have finally been concluded with sixteen countries, all of which were effective by August 2, 1937. The order in which the agreements were signed was: Cuba, Brazil, Belgium, Haiti, Sweden, Colombia, Canada, Honduras, The Netherlands, Switzerland, Nicaragua, Guatemala, France and its colonies, Finland, Costa Rica and El Salvador.

Our trade with these sixteen countries in 1934 constituted almost 38 percent of our total foreign trade. In 1929 our trade with these countries aggregated $3,600,000,000; by 1934 it had dropped to $1,400,000,000.

The increase in our exports from 1935 to 1936 was about $170,000,000. It is of course impossible to state how much of that increase was due to reciprocal trade agreements. There is no question, however, that these agreements have substantially increased our foreign trade.

For instance, our exports to the twelve countries with which agreements were in force for the last six months of 1936 were almost 14 percent greater during 1936 than during 1935; whereas, our exports to other countries during the same periods increased only 4.3 percent. Our exports to Belgium increased by over $11,000,000, or 24 percent during the first year under the Belgian agreement, as compared with the preceding year. During 1936, the first year of the Canadian Trade Agreement, our exports to that country increased by nearly $61,000,000.

These examples indicate the tangible results of these trade agreements in dollars and cents. But there have been even greater and more far-reaching intangible effects which are measured in terms of the spirit of peace and of more friendly relations between Nations.

34 ❲A Promise Fulfilled—The First Step toward Independence for the Philippine Islands. March 2, 1934

To the Congress:

OVER a third of a century ago the United States as a result of a war which had its origin in the Caribbean Sea acquired sovereignty over the Philippine Islands, which lie many thousands of miles from our shores across the widest of oceans. Our Nation covets no territory; it desires to hold no people against their will over whom it has gained sovereignty through war.

In keeping with the principles of justice and in keeping with our traditions and aims, our Government for many years has been committed by law to ultimate independence for the people of the Philippine Islands whenever they should establish a suitable Government capable of maintaining that independence among the Nations of the world. We believe that the time for such independence is at hand.

A law passed by the Seventy-second Congress over a year ago was the initial step, providing the methods, conditions and circumstances under which our promise was to be fulfilled. That Act provided that the United States would retain the option of keeping certain military and naval bases in the Islands after actual independence had been accomplished.

As to the military bases, I recommend that this provision be eliminated from the law and that these bases be relinquished simultaneously with the accomplishment of final Philippine independence.

As to the naval bases, I recommend that the law be so amended as to provide for the ultimate settlement of this matter on terms satisfactory to our own Government and that of the Philippine Islands.

I do not believe that other provisions of the original law need be changed at this time. Where imperfections or inequalities exist, I am confident that they can be corrected after proper hearing and in fairness to both peoples.

May I emphasize that while we desire to grant complete independence at the earliest proper moment, to effect this result without allowing sufficient time for necessary political and economic adjustments would be a definite injustice to the people of the Philippine Islands themselves little short of a denial of independence itself? To change, at this time, the economic provisions of the previous law would reflect discredit on ourselves.

In view of the fact that the time element is involved, I suggest that the law be amended as I have above suggested and that the time limit for the acceptance of the law by the proper authorities and by the people of the Philippine Islands be sufficiently extended to permit them to reconsider it.

For thirty-six years the relations between the people of the Philippine Islands and the people of the United States have been friendly and of great mutual benefit. I am confident that if this legislation is passed by the Congress and accepted by the Philippines we shall increase the mutual regard between the two peoples during the transition period. After the attainment of actual independence by them, friendship and trust will live.

NOTE: On October 17, 1933, the Philippine Legislature declined to accept the Hawes-Cutting Act (Pub. No. 311, 72d Congress) which had been passed by the Congress over President Hoover's veto on January 17, 1933. In a message dated January 8, 1934, I transmitted this Concurrent Resolution of refusal to the Congress.

On March 2, 1934, I sent the foregoing message to the Congress, recommending that legislation be enacted to grant the Philippine Islands their independence. In this message I recommended certain changes in the provisions of the Hawes-Cutting Act, with regard to military and naval bases.

In conformity with my recommendations the Tydings-McDuffie Act (Public No. 127, 73d Congress; 48 Stat. 456) was passed by the Congress and signed by me March 24, 1934, providing for a Commonwealth Government, to be followed by complete independence in ten years.

The Tydings-McDuffie Act was adopted by the Philippine Legislature by concurrent resolution on May 1, 1934. On the same date I sent a message of congratulation through the Governor General to the Filipino people and transmitted the Concurrent Resolution to the Congress on May 4, 1934.

On May 10, 1934, I transmitted to the Congress a copy of the radio-gram from the Governor General of the Philippine Islands, quoting the text of an Act of the Philippine Legislature providing for an election of delegates to a Constitutional Convention, as authorized by the act of the Congress to prepare a Constitution for the Philippines.

On March 23, 1935, I certified to the Governor General of the Philippine Islands and to the Congress, that the proposed Constitution of the Philippines as adopted by the Philippine Constitutional Convention on February 8, 1935, conformed substantially with the provisions of the Tydings-McDuffie Act. I issued a public statement at that time, printed as Item 34 of Vol. IV.

35 ❲ A Letter to the National Federation of Business and Professional Women's Clubs. March 3, 1934

My dear Miss Kneubuhl:

Because of the widening of women's horizons through recent decades, they have acquired such a knowledge and understanding of human needs that they are qualified to make a valuable contribution to our program of national planning for social justice.

Women already can point to some fine achievements along this line. They can rejoice in the success of the representatives of their sex in public positions and particularly in the constructive contributions that these women leaders are making to the whole program of progress. Women also can take justifiable pride in the widespread accomplishments of their own organizations, the indefatigable efforts of which have been largely responsible for much of the social legislation already achieved in State and Federal Government, in the way both of permanent statutes and of emergency measures.

I appeal to you, therefore, to continue to show even in the face of uncertainties the courage, the vision, the initiative and the co-

operation that you have displayed in the first months of our new
era.

Very sincerely yours,

Miss Emily R. Kneubuhl,
The National Federation of
Business and Professional Women's Clubs,
New York, N. Y.

36 ❡ "We Need a Trained Personnel in Government" — Extemporaneous Address Before American University, Washington, D. C., on Receiving an Honorary Degree. March 3, 1934

I T IS very delightful to me to become today an alumnus of American University. I am honored also in the association with your new Chancellor which it affords.

It is a good thing for our American life that this university should be situated in the capital of the country. It is good in the opportunity which it gives to higher education to come into a more intimate understanding of the problems of what we call government; it is good for government to expand its associations with the teachers and pupils of a liberal institution.

It is, of course, natural that I should take special interest in the announcement of the creation of a School of Public Affairs by American University. Many articles have been written; many speeches are being made which seek to review and to estimate the history of the United States during the past year. I am willing to hazard the guess that few of these epitomes will stress what to me stands out as one of the most salient features of a salient year in our American life.

I speak of the amazing and universal increase in the intelligent interest which the people of the United States are taking in the whole subject of government. In cities, in hamlets and on farms men and women in their daily contacts are discussing, as never before except in time of war, the methods by which community and national problems are ordered; and war is not, in the true sense, an exception because in such case there is but a single objective.

In the broader problem of government of all kinds, local and State and Federal and international, we in this country today are thinking not merely in terms of the moment, but in terms that apply to the rest of our lives and to the lives of our children. It is true that the immediate cause of this logical and deep-seated interest was a crisis—an immediate crisis which broke over our heads a year ago. It would have been possible perhaps for all of us to have sought only a temporary cure for the immediate illness of the Nation. We can be thankful that we have studied and are engaged in the process of eradicating the deeper causes of that illness and of many other illnesses of the body politic.

In so doing, we need very definitely practical contacts between the collegiate and educational world and the operations of government. The development of our economic life requires the intelligent understanding of the hundreds of complicated elements in our society. Government needs very definitely not only the sociological and economic points of view, but also the practical assistance of men and women who represent the academic, the business, and the professional elements in the community.

We need a trained personnel in government. We need disinterested, as well as broad-gauged, public officials. This part of our problem we have not yet solved, but it can be solved and it can be accomplished without the creation of a national bureaucracy which would dominate the national life of our governmental system.

That is why I am especially happy in the announcement of the establishment of this School of Public Affairs. I can assure you of the hearty cooperation of the Administration. In the conduct of this school the more widely you can draw on every part of the Nation for the membership of its student body, the greater will be its influence in the dissemination of knowledge of government throughout the country.

Among our universities, you are young; you have a great future — a great opportunity for initiative, for constructive thinking, for practical idealism and for national service.

37 ❡ A Survey of the Purposes, Accomplishments and Failings of N.R.A. Extemporaneous Address Before the Code Authorities of Six Hundred Industries. March 5, 1934

Eight and a half months ago when I signed the bill of the Congress creating the National Industrial Recovery Commission, I said this: "Must we go on in many groping, disorganized, separate units to defeat or shall we move as one great team to victory?"

That team is before me this morning, four or five thousand strong, leaders of six hundred or more organized industries representing, as measured by employment, more than 90 percent of the industrial field which is covered by the N.R.A. Naturally I am deeply gratified that the faith which I expressed last June is so well justified in March.

I do not undertake today to present either a broad review of all the manifold causes which led up to the distressful situation from which the Nation is emerging or a recapitulation of the events, the measures and the results of this past year. You are here as the direct representatives of only one element in our complex modern life, but at the same time because of the fine spirit you have shown I can congratulate you on an approach to your own problems which shows an understanding of the many other problems which criss-cross and dovetail into each other to make up the broad objective of the American people.

It is sufficient for me to point out once more that the difficult and dangerous situation into which the United States had got itself was due to the general attitude, "Every man for himself; the devil take the hindmost." Individuals were seeking quick riches at the expense of other individuals. Geographical sections were seeking economic preference for themselves to the disadvantage of other sections. Cities were recklessly offering inducements to manufacturing plants to move away from other cities. Within given industries unfair competition went on unheeded or resulted in vast consolidations whose securities were peddled to the public at dishonest prices. There was little consideration for the social point of view, and no planning whatsoever to avoid the pitfalls of overproduction or of selling methods which foisted articles on a gullible public, which the family budget could not afford.

That is a strong picture but you and I, in the bottom of our hearts, know that it is a true picture. Most of us participated in the making of that picture. We did not know as much then as we know now and because our eyes have been opened it is possible that future history will call that crazy decade of 1919 to 1929 one of the greatest blessings that ever came to the American people.

It was because the situation in March, 1933, was so serious all along the line that remedies had to be applied to every phase of the illness. The objective was, as you know, to apply these remedies in the American way and not to copy those which are being tried in other countries which do not live under the same form of democratic government as ours. I am always a little amused and perhaps at times a little saddened — and I think the American people feel the same way — by those few writers and speakers who proclaim tearfully either that we are now committed to Communism and collectivism or that we have adopted Fascism and a dictatorship. The real truth of the matter is that for a number of years in our country the machinery of democracy had failed to function. Through inertia on the part of leaders and on the part of the people themselves the operations of government had fallen into the hands of special groups, some of them vociferously led by people who undertook to obtain special advantages for special classes and others led by a handful of individuals who believed in their superhuman ability to retain in their own hands the entire business and financial control over the economic and social structure of the Nation.

The fine response given by the overwhelming majority of the component parts of industry as represented here today proves to me that you have the same understanding of our broad purpose as is held by the average of the workers of the United States — and that word "workers" means almost all of the American people. You have shown sincere desire for real cooperation; you have shown prompt response to the governmental request for national unity. For this support I give you my thanks.

The National Industrial Recovery Act was drawn with the greatest good of the greatest number in mind. Its aim was to increase the buying power of wage earners and farmers so that industry, labor and the public might benefit through building up the market for farm and factory goods. Employer, wage earner and consumer groups are all represented on its boards with the Government. All three groups with the Government must have the interests of all the people as their main responsibility.

What we seek is balance in our economic system — balance between agriculture and industry, and balance between the wage earner, the employer and the consumer. We seek also balance that our internal markets be kept rich and large, and that our trade with other Nations be increased on both sides of the ledger.

You and I are now conducting a great test to find out how the business leaders in all groups of industry can develop capacity to operate for the general welfare. Personally I am convinced that with your help the test is succeeding.

The very conception of N.R.A. follows the democratic procedure of our Government itself. Its theory of self-regulation follows the American method rather than any of the experiments being tried in other Nations. The very fact that you have been in Washington to criticize and to discuss the way N.R.A. is working out is sufficient proof of this point.

There are some people, of course, who do not think things through; as, for example, the man who complained in one of yesterday morning's papers that criticism was held to be unpatriotic. Let me put the case so clearly that even his type will understand. If we admit that the Government has a specific problem to solve and undertakes to do it in a specific way, the critic is un-patriotic who contents himself with loudly proclaiming that that way, that method is no good; that it will not work; that it is wrong to do this. This critic contributes nothing; he is not constructive; he is unpatriotic because he attempts to destroy without even suggesting a way to build.

On the other hand, the critic is patriotic whether he be a business man, a worker, a farmer or a politician if he says, "I do not like the methods you are using to solve the problem; I believe it would be far better if we were to use the following alternate method," and if he thereupon outlines a helpful proposal for the benefit of his neighbor and his Government.

In this great evolution through which we are passing, the average American is doing splendid service by coming back at the captious critic and saying to him, "Well, old man, and what do *you* suggest?" One thing is very certain — we are not going back either to the old conditions or to the old methods.

And now to be more specific in regard to N.R.A. itself. You have set up representative government in industry. You are carrying it on without violation of the constitutional or the parliamentary system to which the United States has been accustomed. Your industrial groups are composed of two parts — labor and management; and the Government is a participant in this organization in order to carry out this mandate of the law, "To promote organization in industry for the purpose of cooperative action in trade groups and to induce and maintain united action of labor and management under adequate Government sanction and supervision." Somebody, of course, must strike the equitable balance between conflicting interests and especially must protect the third group — the consumer. And that word "consumer" means the whole American people.

That group has also been in Washington, invited to come here and to make known publicly any complaint as to the effects of any of the codes. I am sure it will hearten you to know that the great majority of the complaints were directed not at the codes but at errors and omissions in what has been done under codes.

A Survey of N.R.A.

The great bulk of complaint or criticism of the Recovery Act does not go to the Act itself or to its basic principles, but rather to the details of mere method. In this we should feel encouraged and heartened that we are on the right track and can go forward.

In working out the balance on a national scale, of which I have spoken before, we can list certain immediate objectives. I spoke last June of the fact that wage increases will eventually raise costs, but I asked that management give first consideration to increasing the purchasing power of the public. I said, "That is good economics and good business. The aim of this whole effort is to restore our rich domestic market by raising its vast consuming capacity." Complaint has been made of a few industries and of some companies that they have not followed this suggestion, and evidence brought forward shows that in some cases these complaints are justified. What I said was true in June and it is true now. The first task of industry today, as it was then, is to create consuming power.

We must remember that the bulk of the market for American industry is among the 90 percent of our people who live on wages and salaries, and only 10 percent of that market is among people who live on profits alone. No one is opposed to sensible and reasonable profits, but the morality of the case is that a great segment of our people is in actual distress, and that as between profits first and humanity afterwards and humanity first and profits afterwards we have no room for hesitation. With millions still unemployed the power of our people to purchase and use the products of industry is still greatly curtailed. It can be increased and sustained only by striving for the lowest schedule of prices on which higher wages and increasing employment can be maintained.

Therefore, I give to industry today this challenge: It is the immediate task of industry to reemploy more people at purchasing wages and to do it now. Only thus can we continue recovery and restore the balance we seek. It is worth while keeping in the front of our heads the thought that the people in this country whose incomes are less than $2,000 a year buy more than two-thirds of

127

all the goods sold here. It is logical that if the total amount that goes in wages to this group of human beings is steadily increased, merchants, employers and investors will in the long run get more income from the increased volume of sales.

I want to speak for a moment directly to the public. In my initial statement of policy, I said:

"Finally, this law is a challenge to our whole people. There is no power in America that can force against the public will such action as we require. But there is no group in America that can withstand the force of an aroused public opinion. This great cooperation can succeed only if those who bravely go forward to restore jobs have aggressive public support and those who lag are made to feel the full weight of public disapproval."

You all know what happened. We gave you the Blue Eagle as a symbol of cooperation. Its display in a shop or factory window, or upon a garment, or product, or delivery wagon, informed you that the firm with which you were dealing was doing its part in this great national cooperation to defeat depression. For the first time — so far as I know — all of the people in this country were given a part in making a law effective.

This is a law for the public benefit. Obviously an employer who pays Blue Eagle or code wages cannot compete with an employer who does not. It is, therefore, common sense for the consuming public in their own interest, as well as for labor and for industry, to join in seeing to it that the few who think only of selfish gain be made to play the game with the overwhelming majority.

Every examination I make, and all the information I receive, lead me to the inescapable conclusion that we must now consider immediate cooperation to secure increase in wages and shortening of hours. I am confident that your deliberations will lead you also to this conclusion. Reduction in hours coupled with a decrease in weekly wages will do no good at all, for it amounts merely to a forced contribution to unemployment relief by the class least able to bear it. I have never believed that we should violently impose flat, arbitrary and abrupt changes on the economic structure, but we can nevertheless work together in arriving at a common objective. The Government cannot forever continue to absorb the whole burden of unemployment. The thing to do now is to get more people to work. Your self-governing groups are not here to devise ingenious plans to circumvent the purposes of the Act. You are here in a patriotic spirit to effect these purposes. With few exceptions industry will give wholehearted compliance. It is only in the case of rare exceptions where industrial self-government may fail, that the Government itself must and will, under the law, move firmly and promptly to prevent failure.

Under the code system you and I are aware that experience must be the guide for the working out of difficulties and the prevention of abuses. For example, you on code authorities are your industrial brother's keeper, and especially are you the keeper of your small industrial brother. We must set up every safeguard against erasing the small operator from the economic scene. Many years ago anti-trust laws were passed and one of the primary reasons for their enactment was the protection of the little fellow against the big fellow. In many cases these laws failed to protect the little fellow. We do not want to maintain that condition. The essential provisions of the codes should check or reverse competitive methods by which the small business man was or is being squeezed out.

These same anti-trust laws must continue in their major purpose of retaining competition and preventing monopoly; it is only where these laws have prevented the cooperation to eliminate things like child labor and sweat shops, starvation wages and other unfair practices that there is justification in modifying them.

One more subject I call to your special attention. The law itself has provided for free choice of their own representatives by employees. Those two words "free choice" mean just what they say. It is obvious that the Government itself not only has the right but also the duty to see, first, that employees may make a choice and, secondly, that in the making of it they shall be wholly free. I ask that the letter and the spirit of free choice be accorded to its workers by every corporation in the United States.

We have been seeking experience in our first eight months of code making; for that same reason we have been tolerant of certain misunderstandings even when they resulted in evasions of the spirit if not of the letter of the law. Now we are moving into a period of administration when that which is law must be made certain and the letter and the spirit must be fulfilled. We cannot tolerate actions which are clearly monopolistic, which wink at unfair trade practices, which fail to give to labor free choice of their representatives or which are otherwise hostile to the public interest.

In a word, we cannot tolerate abuses of economic power — abuses against labor, abuses against employers or abuses against the consuming public — whether they persist either with the aid of codes or despite their prohibitions. This does not mean that we can at once make perfect many hundred codes covering the major trades and industries of the Nation, or that we can get a mark of perfection in a day or a month. It does mean that we have arrived at the time for taking stock for correcting manifest errors, for rooting out demonstrated evils.

One year ago we were suffering and shrinking under economic pressures so intolerable that collapse was at hand. We had arrived at the day to make our choice. We made that choice. The American people responded to the call for action with eager enlistment — enlistment in the struggle against ruthless self-seeking, reckless greed and economic anarchy. We undertook by lawful, constitutional processes to reorganize a disintegrating system of production and exchange.

The methods and details of that reorganization may and will change from year to year, but it is very certain that the American people understand that the purpose of the reorganization was not only to bring back prosperity. It was far deeper than that. The reorganization must be permanent for all the rest of our lives in that never again will we permit the social conditions which allowed the vast sections of our population to exist in an un-American way, which allowed a maldistribution of wealth and of power.

The willingness of all elements to enter into the spirit of the New Deal becomes more and not less evident as it goes on. As an example, I have just received a telegram from Mr. Francis M. Law, the President of the American Bankers Association. In it he said: "On this your first anniversary please allow me in behalf of the country's banks to express our full confidence and our sincere desire to cooperate in your courageous efforts to bring about recovery. . . . The Banking structure of the country is sound and liquid, and banks have never been in stronger position to function effectively. Conditions have improved to the point where it is no longer necessary for banks to be super-liquid. . . . There is a definite call now for banks not to extend loose credits or to make improper loans but for a most sympathetic attitude toward legitimate credit needs and for a recognition of responsibility for their proper and vital part in the program of recovery."

If the banks go along, my friends, we shall have three great elements of American life working together: industry, agriculture, and banking; and then we cannot stop.

Think back to exactly one year ago today. You know where the banks stood at that time; you know where your own business stood. That telegram from the American Banking Association is a living illustration of the progress we have made in that year. Let us consolidate our gains and let us resolve that that consolidation shall be for the continued progress and especially for the greater happiness and well being of the American people.

NOTE: In March, 1934, a general code conference was called for a review of N.R.A. efforts, to provide a forum for criticism and constructive recommendations. This conference began March 5th, with the foregoing speech by me.

It was the largest, most representative conference of American business ever held. There were so many present that an overflow meeting was held in another hall in the same building connected by a loud speaker with the hall in which I was speaking. I later made a short talk to this overflow meeting.

The conference provided a liberal education for all in attendance, and in the resulting discussion throughout trade and industry it produced a better understanding of the complexity and interrelation of business activities than could have been obtained in any other way.

As I said, the period had arrived for stock-taking, for consolidating gains and advantages, and for eliminating mistakes. Perhaps the most consistent thought which emerged from the conference was that the N.R.A. had undertaken a monumental task, and that the great problem which lay ahead was not the expansion of the N.R.A., but rather the concentration of its efforts in those directions most promising of permanent gain, the elimination of many policies and practices shown to be of dubious value, and the imperative need for defining fundamental principles and policies and for improving the machinery of code compliance.

It had become evident by the time of this conference that the N.R.A. lacked any general agreement, either among leaders in industry or in the Government, upon the fundamental economic policies which the N.R.A. would seek in the future to advance, as well as any underlying policies for administering an economic program. We had been obliged to plunge into a tremendous reconstruction and integration of business activities, with very clearly established convictions only as to general objectives, and without the necessary information and planning which haste and emergency made it impossible to formulate. The N.R.A. had been proceeding along the line of establishing policies by pronouncement and precedent, without any great assurance that such policies would meet with the general business support necessary for their success.

On May 9, 1934, the N.R.A. established, for the first time, a Policy Board charged with working out acceptable, desirable policies as to code provisions — a Board relieved in part of administrative duties so that it would have the opportunity to discuss, to confer and to think out these basic problems.

In the second phase of the N.R.A. when the National Industrial Recovery Board was established on September 27, 1934, I emphasized that the formative period of code-making was at an end, and that it was now necessary to begin to plan for a permanent method of code-making and revision, to conform with settled economic and political policies (see Item 159, this volume).

38 ⟨A Message Transmitting to the Congress a Report on the Inter-American Highway. March 5, 1934

To the Congress:

I TRANSMIT herewith two copies of a report prepared by the Bureau of Public Roads, Department of Agriculture, a letter of transmittal addressed to the Secretary of State by the Secretary of Agriculture, and a letter from the Secretary of State (see Item 38A) concerning a reconnaissance survey for an Inter-American highway.

38A ⟨A Letter from Secretary of State Hull Submitting Inter-American Highway Report for Transmission to the Congress. March 5, 1934

The President:

Pursuant to the Act of Congress approved March 26, 1930 (Public No. 78, 71st Congress), I beg to submit herewith, for transmission to the Congress, two copies of a report of a reconnaissance survey for an Inter-American highway between the Republic of Panama and the United States, together with a letter of transmittal from the Secretary of Agriculture dated January 25, 1934. As shown in that letter, the report was prepared by the Bureau of Public Roads, Department of Agriculture, which Bureau was the agency selected to cooperate with the several Governments, members of the Pan-American Union, which signified a desire to participate in the surveys. A third copy of the report, for your personal use, is also submitted.

The report contains a description of the selected route, with accompanying diagrams of line and profile, and there appears in regard to each country which will be traversed by the highway a general statement of the principal facts of an economic nature related to the proposed enterprise. There is also included in the report a series of airplane photographs, as well as other pertinent information regarding the proposed highway.

In submitting the report, I desire to acknowledge the helpful cooperation which has been received from officials of the several interested Governments.

That of Panama not only collaborated with the representatives of this Government in connection with the survey conducted through that country, but also generously provided, free of rent, office space in which were established the headquarters of the officials conducting the surveys throughout the three-year period during which the work was in progress. Valuable assistance was also received from officials of the Governments of Costa Rica, Nicaragua, Honduras and Guatemala in connection with the reconnaissance surveys made in these countries. While the Governments of El Salvador and Mexico did not make an official request for cooperation through the Pan-American Union as provided for under the Act of Congress, since the route through those countries had already been largely determined and the highway partly constructed, nevertheless officials of both of these Governments furnished important information regarding the route selected and highways completed in their respective countries.

Respectfully submitted,

CORDELL HULL

NOTE: This letter and report were transmitted by me to the Congress on March 5, 1934 (see Item 38).

The building of the Inter-American Highway is important socially and economically. It will help cement the friendship between the United States and the Central American Republics. With frequent intercourse will come greater knowledge and understanding.

Socially, it will enlighten our people in regard to an ancient civilization and offer acquaintance with different peoples of a tropical zone.

Economically, such a highway through Central America will bring new markets to all. The route passes through a region of varied climate and altitude which is rich in agricultural possibilities, and capable of producing a wide variety of products. The soil will supply many tropical products, including hard rice, tea, spices and other condiments, drugs, rubber, copra, palmnut and other oils, varnish gums, and insecticide and textile plants. The forests contain many different hardwoods, including mahogany. Supplies of minerals and semi-precious stones are also found. Development of these resources, and commerce in them with the United

States and the rest of the world, will come with economical and easily available transportation. With more prosperous neighbors to the south of us, the United States will profit also from the new markets which they will supply with this new purchasing power. The new highway will of course result in continuous and extensive tourist travel.

Because of these mutual advantages, a substantial beginning had already been made with respect to this highway. At the First Inter-American Highway Conference which convened at Panama in 1929, a highway from the United States to Panama City was decided upon as the first and most practical part of a proposed highway through North and South America.

On May 4, 1928, the Congress of the United States passed a resolution that this country take the utmost interest in this proposed Inter-American Highway. On March 4, 1929, and on March 26, 1930, respectively, Congress passed a resolution and appropriated $50,000 for a reconnaissance survey of possible routes through Central America.

On March 6, 1934, I transmitted by the foregoing message a report of the Bureau of Public Roads of the Department of Agriculture submitted to the Secretary of State, giving the results of the reconnaissance survey through Panama, Costa Rica, Nicaragua, Honduras and Guatemala. The routes through Mexico and El Salvador had already been

largely selected and work was in progress thereon.

On June 18, 1934, I approved an act of Congress which authorized $75,000 for continuation of the reconnaissance surveys. (48 Stat. 993; Public No. 393, 73d Congress.)

On June 19, 1934, an appropriation of $1,000,000 in the Emergency Appropriation Act, fiscal year 1935, was made, to be used at the discretion of the President in cooperation with the several Central American Governments, members of the Pan-American Union, for both the survey and actual construction on the highway. It was decided to expend the money largely in the construction of bridges, thus removing primary obstacles along the route. Building materials and machinery were to be supplied by the United States; the Central American States were to cooperate by transporting the materials and supplying labor for construction.

The surveyed route of the Inter-American Highway extends from Nuevo Laredo on the Texas border, down to Panama City in Panama. The Pacific slope was found to be preferable to the Atlantic for several reasons: the Atlantic seaboard is mostly marsh and swampland with twice the rainfall of the western coast. The east side uses shipping ports instead of inland routes. The configuration of the eastern coast, if followed closely, would require a longer route. The denser population is on the western coast, and on a few plateaus that are included in the route. El Salvador would have been left out entirely if the road had taken the eastern route. The western coast includes branches reaching out eventually to all but one capital city, that of Honduras, whose capital is reached by a branch road. And finally, the required policy of using primarily those roads already built demanded that the Pacific coast be chosen. The highway is used as a trunkline, with all maritime ports, east and west, and to all large cities of importance.

From the $1,000,000 appropriation of the United States for highway construction, fourteen bridges have been built or are building: four in Panama over the Chiriqui, Platanar, San Cristobal and Chirigaga Rivers; six in Guatemala over the Tamazulapa, Amatal, Tahuapa, Tiucal and Mongoy Rivers; three in Nicaragua over the Rio Grande, Esteli and Maderas Rivers; and one in Honduras over the Choluteca River. This Government is also assisting in the construction of sections of the highway in Guatemala, Nicaragua, and Costa Rica.

The total length of the highway will be 3,250 miles.

If the policy of the United States with respect to this highway has done nothing else but further and cement cordial relations between the United States and the Central American States, it will have been well worthwhile.

39 ❨ The National Recovery Review Board Is Created to Investigate Monopolistic Codes. Executive Order No. 6632. March 7, 1934

BY VIRTUE of the authority vested in me under the provisions of Title I of the National Industrial Recovery Act of June 16, 1933 (ch. 90, 48 Stat. 195), and in order to effectuate the purposes of said Title, I hereby establish an organization which shall be known as the National Recovery Review Board.

The following persons are hereby appointed to serve as members of the said Board:

Clarence Darrow	Fred P. Mann, Sr.	Samuel C. Henry
W. W. Neal	John F. Sinclair	W. O. Thompson.

The duties and functions of the National Recovery Review Board shall be as follows:

(1) To ascertain and report to the President whether any code

or codes of fair competition approved under the authority of Title I of the National Industrial Recovery Act are designed to promote monopolies or to eliminate or oppress small enterprises or operate to discriminate against them, or will permit monopolies or monopolistic practices, and if it finds in the affirmative to specify in its reports wherein such results follow from the adoption and operation of any such code or codes.

(2) To recommend to the President such changes in any approved code or codes as, in the opinion of the Board, will rectify or eliminate such results.

The facilities and records of the National Recovery Administration shall be available to the Board whenever required in connection with the performance of its duties.

NOTE: In order to have an independent study made of the complaints which were coming in about monopolistic practices resulting from codes under N.I.R.A. (see Item 11, this volume), I set up the National Recovery Review Board by the foregoing Executive Order for the purpose of making a report to me. The Board, by reason of the name of its chairman, became known as the Darrow Board.

Unfortunately, the Board, in its investigation, proceeded rather as a prosecuting agency to prove a case against big business, than as an impartial investigating body to determine how far in fact the control by large business over business conditions had been strengthened by the codes, and how far in fact smaller, independent businesses had been protected by the abolition of unfair competition.

Little evidence was produced of increased monopolistic power. On the other hand, it was established that the N.R.A. on the whole had not interfered with the existence of legitimate competition either within any industry or between different industries, particularly within an industry and between industries. Most of the monopolistic conditions uncovered by the Board were found to be based either on control of certain natural resources or patents, or in the inevitable power inherent in vast industrial organizations to dominate in the price and marketing policies of an industry.

I do not think that it can be proved that the relaxation of the anti-trust laws during the N.R.A., to permit cooperation between business men, did in fact develop any additional monopolistic controls over trade and industry. On the contrary, it was a demonstrated fact that innumerable small and independent business men were greatly helped in their struggle to survive by the establishment of fair competition and the elimination of such monopolistic practices as destructive price cutting.

It is true that many smaller business men, who had been able to survive through sweat-shop practices of long hours and low wages, were handicapped by the labor provisions of their codes. Many of the complaints of monopoly by big business enterprises came from some business men who were thus compelled to pay decent wages for decent hours of labor, and who sought by such complaints to cover up the reasons for their resultant distress.

The Board, having completed the functions for which it was established, was abolished June 30, 1934, by Executive Order No. 6771.

40 ❨ A Recommendation for "Sound, Stable and Permanent Air-Mail" Legislation. March 7, 1934

My dear Mr. Chairman:

OUR domestic air-mail contracts have been canceled. The Army Air Corps is temporarily carrying the air mail. I believe we should make new contracts with commercial air carriers as soon as possible to carry the greater part of our air mail.

To protect the public interest and to provide for new contracts on a basis of honest payment for honest service, I suggest new legislation on this subject.

We must avoid the evils of the past, and at the same time encourage the sound development of the aviation industry.

I suggest that new air-mail contracts be let for a period not exceeding three years on full, open and fair competitive bidding, with a limitation of the rate of compensation above which no contract will be awarded.

Any combinations, agreements, or understandings, intended to prevent free competitive bidding should be prevented and such action should be a basis for cancellation of contracts.

In order that the bidding shall be really competitive, I suggest that in determining the specifications for proper equipment, only speed, useful load capacity, safety factors and safety devices should be considered.

So that all companies desiring to qualify and bid may have an opportunity fully to prepare themselves for actual service I suggest that after the contract is awarded a period of not longer than six months shall be allowed the successful bidder to qualify under the terms of the law and the bid.

It is my judgment that six months before expiration of the contracts made under competitive bidding the Interstate Commerce Commission should pass upon the question of public convenience and necessity of air-mail routes, and thereafter fix a maximum rate of air-mail pay on the routes designated, subject of course to equipment specifications to be laid down.

I suggest that the proposed law prohibit the award of an air-mail contract to any company having connections with subsidiaries, affiliates, associates, or holding companies, directly or indirectly, by stock ownership, interlocking directorates, interlocking officers, or otherwise, if said subsidiaries, affiliates, associates, or holding companies are engaged, directly or indirectly, in the operation of competitive routes or in the manufacturing of aircraft, or other materials or accessories used generally in the aviation industry.

No air-mail contract should be sublet or sold to any other contracting company, nor should a mail contractor be allowed to merge or consolidate with another company holding an air-mail contract. Obviously also, no contract should be made with any companies, old or new, any of whose officers were party to the obtaining of former contracts under circumstances which were clearly contrary to good faith and public policy.

Such safeguards should be provided as will prevent the evil practices of excessive salaries, unearned bonuses, and illegitimate personal expense accounts detrimental to the interests of legitimate stockholders and the public.

Public safety calls for pilots of high character and great skill. The occupation is a hazardous one. Therefore, the law should provide for a method to fix maximum flying hours, minimum pay and a system for retirement or annuity benefits.

Enactment of legislation along the lines suggested will establish a sound, stable and permanent air-mail policy. The knowledge that the Interstate Commerce Commission, a judicial body, will hereafter regulate air-transportation routes and air-mail pay will remove uncertainty as to routes and mail pay.

Such legislation will relieve air transport companies from paralyzing monopolistic control which has heretofore often influenced them to buy planes and other equipment from associates and affiliates.

Real competition between the manufacturing companies will stimulate inventive genius, and should give to our people safer and better equipment both for commercial and military purposes.

I am sending letters similar to this to Representative Mead, Chairman, House Committee on Post Offices and Post Roads, and to Senator Black.

Very sincerely yours,

Honorable Kenneth McKellar,
Chairman, Senate Committee on
Post Offices and Post Roads,
Washington, D. C.

NOTE: At this time the Army was carrying the air mail, for the private air-mail contracts had been canceled (see Item 23, this volume). The legislation which I recommended in the foregoing letter was finally adopted and approved June 12, 1934 (Public No. 308, 73d Congress; 48 Stat. 933).

On March 10, 1934, when I discontinued the flying of the air mail by the Army because of the accidents which were occurring (see Item 41, this volume), I sent a further letter urging the early enactment of the legislation. In the meantime, until legislation was adopted, new air-mail contracts were let for temporary periods by public bidding.

41 ⦗ The Army Stops Flying the Mail.
March 10, 1934

My dear Mr. Secretary:

ON FEBRUARY 9th the Army Air Corps was given the temporary assignment of carrying the air mail and commenced the actual carrying on February 20th. This action was taken on the definite assurance given me that the Army Air Corps could carry the mail.

Since that time ten Army fliers have lost their lives. I appreciate that only four of these were actually flying the mail, but the others were training or were proceeding to the mail route. I appreciate also that almost every part of the country has been visited during this period by fog, snow and storms, and that serious accidents, taking even more lives, have occurred at the same time in passenger and commercial aviation.

Nevertheless, the continuation of deaths in the Army Air Corps must stop.

We all know that flying under the best of conditions is a definite hazard, but the ratio of accidents has been far too high during the past three weeks.

Will you therefore please issue immediate orders to the Army Air Corps stopping all carrying of air mail, except on such routes, under such weather conditions and under such equipment and personnel conditions as will insure, as far as the utmost care can provide, against constant recurrence of fatal accidents?

This exception includes, of course, full authority to change or modify schedules.

As you know, the period of emergency will end as soon as the necessary legislation has been enacted and new contracts can be obtained. I am writing once more to the chairmen of the House and Senate committees urging speed in the enactment of the legislation. Because military lessons have been taught us during the past few weeks, I request that you consult immediately with the Postmaster General and the Secretary of Commerce in order that additional training may be given to Army air pilots through cooperation with private companies who later on will fly the mails. This should include, of course, training in cross-country flying, in night flying, blind flying and instrument flying.

I am sending a copy of this letter to the Postmaster General in order that he may make arrangements with you. He will, of course, modify the instructions given on February 9th to conform with the Army plans.

Very sincerely,

The Secretary of War
Washington, D. C.

NOTE: The Army Air Corps experienced many difficulties during the time that it took over the airmail service (see Items 23 and 40 of this volume). Not only lack of familiarity with the routes, but extremely bad flying weather all over the United States made the flying particularly hazardous. After ten lives had been lost I sent the foregoing letter to the Secretary of War, discontinuing the Army air-mail service temporarily. On March 19th, the Army Air Corps resumed carrying the mail and continued successfully to maintain its schedules until May 8, 1934. Its last scheduled flight was June 1, 1934.

In the meantime, I wrote to the Congressional committees in charge of the new air-mail legislation, requesting them to expedite the passage of it. Pending the adoption of new legislation, advertisements for bids were issued on March 30, 1934, for the transportation of air mail by commercial air companies on the most essential air-mail routes.

The period of these contracts with the private air companies was only three months, with renewal periods of three months. These temporary contracts were awarded to the lowest responsible bidders, and service by commercial companies again began on May 8, 1934.

Permanent air-mail legislation was finally adopted on June 12, 1934 (Public No. 308, 73d Congress).

On July 11, 1934, I issued Executive Order No. 6792, directing the Postmaster General to make an investigation as to the foreign air-mail contracts and ocean air-mail contracts entered into prior to June 16, 1933, to see whether grounds existed for their modification or cancellation, as in the domestic air-mail contracts.

After investigation, it was concluded that the cancellation of these contracts would not be in the public interest, as they would disrupt American service to the Latin-American countries and might result in great harm to our trade relations with those countries. Certain changes in service and reductions in pay, however, were recommended, some of which were adopted.

42 ❧ The Government Does Business Only with Those Complying with N.R.A. Codes. Executive Order No. 6646. March 14, 1934

BY VIRTUE of authority vested in me as President of the United States, it is hereby ordered that:

1. (a) All invitations to bidders hereafter promulgated by or in behalf of any executive department or independent establishment or other agency or instrumentality of the United States, including Government-owned and Government-controlled corporations (all of the foregoing being hereinafter described as agencies of the United States), shall contain a provision to the effect that no bid will be considered unless it includes or is accompanied by a certificate duly executed by the bidder stating that the bidder is complying with and will continue to comply with each approved code of fair competition to which he is subject, and if engaged in any trade or industry for which there is no approved code of fair competition, then stating that as to such trade or industry he has become a party to and is complying with and will continue to comply with an agreement with the President under Section 4(a) of the National Industrial Recovery Act.

(b) No bid which does not comply with the foregoing requirements shall be considered or accepted.

(c) All contracts and purchase orders authorized by any agency of the United States shall contain a provision to the effect that the party or parties awarded any such contract or purchase order shall comply with each approved code of fair competition to which it is subject and if engaged in any trade or industry for which there is no approved code of fair competition, then, as to such trade or industry, with an agreement with the President as aforesaid; and that the United States shall have the right to cancel any contract for failure to comply with such provision and make open market purchases or have the work called for by the contract otherwise performed, at the expense of the contractor.

(d) No agency of the United States and no Government contractor or supplier shall hereafter accept or purchase for the performance of any contract or purchase order or enter into any subcontracts for any articles, materials or supplies, in whole or in part produced or furnished by any person who shall not have certified that he is complying with and will continue to comply with each code of fair competition which relates to such articles, materials, or supplies, or in case there is no approved code for the whole or any portion thereof, then, to that extent, with an agreement with the President as aforesaid.

(e) The foregoing provisions of this order shall likewise apply to all contracts and purchase orders authorized by any State, municipal corporation, local subdivision, person or corporation in connection with projects carried out or to be carried out, wholly or in part, with funds loaned or granted by any agency of the United States, and all contracts and agreements for the making of any such loan or grant shall contain a provision requiring the State, municipal corporation, local subdivision, person or corporation receiving such loan or grant, to comply with the provisions of this order; provided that this paragraph shall not be construed as requiring the restriction of the use of materials to those produced within the United States nor to require price differentials in favor of such materials.

* * *

4. All provisions of approved Codes of Fair Competition shall apply to the making and performance of contracts with or sales to agencies of the United States.

5. The Administrator for Industrial Recovery may make exceptions in specific cases or otherwise under this Order whenever such action shall be recommended to him by an agency of the United States and when in the judgment of the Administrator justice or public interest will best be served thereby.

NOTE: The foregoing Executive Order was an amplification and extension of Executive Order No. 6246, August 10, 1933 (see Volume II, Item 112).

These Orders indicate one of the means to enforce compliance with codes, namely, the refusal to spend Federal funds with concerns violating code provisions.

43 ❬ The One Hundred and Fifth Press Conference (Excerpts). March 14, 1934

(General aviation policy — Treaty for development of St. Lawrence River — Soldiers' bonus — Income-tax prosecutions.)

Q. Mr. President, yesterday Senator Robinson of Arkansas said that he was for a unified air force. I was wondering whether that is a reflection of the Administration's viewpoint or just his own. Can you tell us anything about that?

THE PRESIDENT: Only this, for background. We have by no means solved permanently the general aviation policy of the Government. It has been kicking around, as you all know — you have to use this as background — and the present board that has been reconstituted will take it up from the point of view of the Army Air Service. It is primarily limited to that. Now, of course, that covers only a part of the story. You still have all the other relationships of Government to aviation. You have the Customs Service, the Internal Revenue Service, and the Department of Commerce and its relationship to civilian aviation. You have the Navy and the Marine Corps. There has never yet been worked out a satisfactory complete Government policy. It is a thing you cannot work out immediately. The only thing you can say is that we are all studying it and hope to work out a complete Government policy. That will be the objective. The appointment of the Board is only in relation to the Army Air Service. I think we shall be able to work something out. We may eventually appoint a board or an individual, but the object will be to get a complete Government policy. . . .

Q. Mr. President, they are about to vote today on the St. Lawrence Treaty, and it looks like the vote is against you. I was wondering if you would care to offer any comment on that.

THE PRESIDENT: No. However, there is one phase of it — in fact, two phases of it. One is perfectly simple to mention and the other is a bit more difficult.

The first phase of it is that whether the thing goes through this afternoon or not makes little difference, because the St. Lawrence Seaway will ultimately be built. That is perfectly obvious. And it will be built at a very, very low cost as things go today. There are left only the International Rapids Section and the Lachine Rapids Section. You can visualize the whole navigation problem; it is obvious that man is going to follow the lead of Nature. Whether the thing goes through today or next year makes, on the whole, very little difference — it is going through.

You see, you have got today a seaway practically from the top end of Lake Superior down through the Sault Ste. Marie locks, which are big locks, down through Lake Michigan and Lake Huron, then through the Detroit River into Lake Erie, through the Welland locks, which are big locks, and then through Lake Ontario to the St. Lawrence River. And of course the St. Lawrence River runs to the sea.

Now, there are three waterfalls — rapids. One of them, the middle one, at Beauharnois, has already been built or they are nearly finished with it. Some of you were up there with me about three years ago. They have already practically completed the power development and, as a part of that power development, they can add locks for just a very small sum.

The Canadian Government is also proceeding with plans for the last waterfall, the Lachine. There they can do one of two things: They can either build a dam and put locks in the dam, or they can deepen the old Lachine Canal from twelve to thirty feet without building a dam. That leaves only the top or western waterfall, called the International Rapids. Canada already has a twelve-foot canal around the International Rapids.

It is not the least bit necessary to develop power which, of course, calls for a dam. It would be a perfectly proper thing and a perfectly possible thing for Canada to enlarge the International Rapids Canal on the Canadian side of the river without ever building a dam. Canada isn't so crazy to have water power; they have an awful lot of it. If Canada were to do that on the Canadian side of the river, there would be a Canadian seaway. Mind you, the amount necessary to do that canal over would be less than one hundred million dollars, so you see what a small amount it is. There would then be a Canadian seaway from salt water up the St. Lawrence River, past the Lachine, Beauharnois and the International sections, and then you would be in the lake. That seaway would be 100 percent under the control of Canada. . . .

Now, one other phase of it — and I will tell you a story. A certain Senator said that he was going to vote against the treaty because of the Mississippi and the taking of water out of Lake Michigan. I asked him if he thought we had any right to divert water over and above the need for drinking and health purposes from one watershed into another. Then I told him a story about an old case in up-State New York. A fellow had a piece of property on a river, but, at that particular point, there was practically no drop in the river — it was practically a flat river. He was most anxious to put up a grist mill and he didn't have any water power. People down in the stream below him had grist mills. Suddenly he had a bright thought one night. He said to himself, "By cutting a little ditch through a little hill on my property I can run this water over into the watershed of another little river and I can get a fifty-foot drop. I can take the water out of this river and carry it through the ditch, drop it down over a wheel and put it into another river." Of course, it was a grand idea. But, unfortunately, he ran up against what is known in the common law as the riparian right of the man farther down the stream. . . .

The Government of the United States believes in the common law and believes that we have no right to injure our neighbor, Canada, by diverting water out of the Great Lakes into another watershed, any more than the fellow upstream a hundred years ago in New York had a right to divert water from one creek into another. Canada is absolutely entitled, under the common law and under common decency, to all the water it wants to drink, to all the water it needs for sewage purposes. Canada has even gone further — it has given up enough water by treaty to provide, in all probability, pretty decent navigation down to the Mississippi and down from there to the Gulf — of course, not for ocean-going steamers, but probably a nine-foot draft, which is the same as the upper Mississippi.

The thing is going through; perhaps not today, but the St. Lawrence Seaway is going to be built just as sure as God made little apples. The only difference is that I would like to see it done by joint action of two neighboring Nations. If we don't go along, Canada has a perfect right to build an all-Canadian seaway and discriminate against us, if it so desires.

Q. In other words, this treaty will go back again?

THE PRESIDENT: It will go back in some form. How soon, I don't know, but it will go back as soon as it can.

Q. Can we use this?

THE PRESIDENT: As background, I think it is all right.

Q. What did the Senate leaders tell you about the bonus?

THE PRESIDENT: I haven't talked to them about the bonus at all.

Q. Will you say anything on the House action on the bonus?

THE PRESIDENT: No. I never comment on that. There is an article in this morning's *Wall Street Journal* by Bernard Kilgore that really anybody who writes about finances and bonuses and currency issues and so forth ought to read, because it is pretty good. I don't agree with the story all the way through; but it is a good story. It is an analytical story on an exceedingly difficult subject — on the question of issuing currency to meet Government obligations. I think that Kilgore could have gone just a little bit further than he did. Of course this is all background.

It was along the general line that almost everybody who has studied — well, I will tell you a story: A good many years ago, ten years ago, Paul Warburg, who had a very great mind, talked over with me one day the proposition of issuing Government currency to retire Government debts. In other words, they were what might be called baby bonds to retire outstanding Government debts. As he put it, there is nothing wrong about it except the opportunity that it gives to a legislative body in the future to pay the running expenses of Government by printing paper. Now, there is all the difference in the world between paying the running expenses of the Government by issuing paper and retiring the outstanding interest-bearing obligations by the issuance of paper, provided always that the paper is amortized and retired year by year as the bonds would have been.

But the one fear is that, if a legislative body gets into the habit of it, they will just run wild year after year. And if they once started to run wild, they would pay off the veterans this year, and then next year they would say to the people who in 1917 and 1918 worked on munitions in this country, who had rather unhealthful conditions, long hours and not much sanitation — good, patriotic men and women who probably came out of the war physically rather worse off than they went in, certainly far worse off than the men in uniforms who spent their time in camps a few miles away from them — they would say, "Why shouldn't you come in for a bonus on the ground that you have worked overtime and under difficult conditions for two horrible years?" And then, if you paid them, you would find some other class in the community entitled to the same treatment. "Take Government employees, for example, why shouldn't they get better treatment, get 25 percent more than anybody else?"

And so you would start paying with paper and you would keep on paying with paper. In other words, this bonus bill comes down to a fundamental — you might say two fundamentals: One is the method of payment, and the other is whether the Government is going back on its contract. The Government has a contract. Kilgore's article is well worth reading.

Q. The other day the Department of Justice gave notice that

they were going to seek proceedings against Mellon and others on tax evasion. Can we look for others on that?

THE PRESIDENT: I will give you something off the record on that, if you wish.

Q. Yes.

THE PRESIDENT: The income-tax prosecutions are not exactly prosecutions. Here is the real problem that was put up; and, frankly, it is a problem in government. I think the reason there was an announcement of names the other day—and of course there are a great many other names—was because if there had not been an announcement from here, the story about these particular names would have broken in each of the districts very shortly. Therefore it was easier to announce them from here. Now, these actions are by no means confined to the names announced. There are several hundred cases in exactly the same category.

Here is the Government problem, and I will put it up to you. The Government finds, in going over income-tax records, that there are a certain number of people who have failed to include certain income. Putting it the simplest way, they have either done that, or in working out their returns they have made the amount owing to the Government a great deal less than the Government thinks it ought to get. Immediately there arises the question of motive. If the motive was to cheat the Government, it is a criminal offense. If, however, the motive was perfectly honest, if there was a *bona-fide* mistake, it is not a criminal offense and the Government has only a civil suit to recover the legal tax. Now, who is going to determine what the motive was in filing a return that lacked either the proper amount or the inclusion of certain income? Who is going to determine whether the motive was to cheat the Government or not?

If you leave that determination to some individual in the Department of Justice or in the Internal Revenue Bureau, and if he lets off a very prominent man, you know what the people of this country will say. If he decides to prosecute the little fellow and let the big fellow off, you know what the country will say. On the other hand, if he decides to prosecute the big fellow, you know what some people will say. They will say that it is persecution and not prosecution.

It puts Government action up to some Government individual in Washington. Well, they are human; and it is a mighty difficult thing to put up to them. We have, in our laws, an organization for determining motive. It is called a grand jury. Now, the policy that has been adopted is based not only on law as we have it, but on common sense. If we were to determine these matters here and say, "Why, no; Mr. Jones did not intend to cheat the Government; he merely followed his highly paid lawyer's advice," every other Mr. Jones in the country would thereupon go to his high-priced lawyer for similar advice. He would be open to the temptation of putting in a return that was, in effect, cheating the Government, with the assurance, mind you, that two or three years later all he would have to do would be to go to Washington and say, "I did not intend to cheat the Government; I merely took the advice of my lawyer." And he, too, would ask for a clean bill of health.

In other words, it is a definite invitation to people to cheat the Government, and then afterwards say, "I did not cheat the Government; I did not intend to." Therefore, what we are doing is taking all of these cases, sending them to the District Attorneys of the respective districts and saying to them: "Put these up to the grand jury. If the grand jury does not think that the man or his lawyer was trying to cheat the Government, it is perfectly all right. In that case we will bring a civil suit and recover our money. If the grand jury does think there was a motive there to cheat and avoid the payment of taxes, then the grand jury will indict." And so, you have a panel of twenty-three men who determine the question of motive. Now, that is all there is to any of these income-tax cases. They catch the big fellow and the little fellow; and we apply the same rule to the big fellow and the little fellow. We are going to put them all up to the grand jury.

Q. Is that off the record, Mr. President?

THE PRESIDENT: You can make it background. Don't write the story around the Mellon case because the rule applies just as much to the man with an income of $3,000 a year as it does to the man whose income is very high, or to Mr. Mellon. It is a matter of principle.

(As to the subject of the St. Lawrence Treaty, see Item 7, this volume and Item 34 of Volume V.

As to the Soldiers' Bonus, see Item 62, Vol. IV and Item 12, Vol. V.)

44 ❦ A Request for Credit Facilities for Small Industries. March 19, 1934

Dear Senator:

MAY I suggest to your Committee legislation to create twelve Credit Banks for Industry.

I have been deeply concerned with the situation in our small industries. In numberless cases their working capital has been lost or seriously depleted. This condition should be remedied.

We have afforded much aid in the recovery of agriculture, commerce, our larger industries and our financial institutions, and our improved condition nationally furnishes full justification for these efforts. We must continue in behalf of the medium-size man in industry and commerce.

With this purpose in mind I have discussed with the Treasury, the Federal Reserve Board, and the Reconstruction Finance Corporation a comprehensive study of the situation in the smaller industries and the presentation of a plan which would show their condition and furnish relief for it.

A nationwide survey has been made by them. Information has been obtained from 4,958 banks and 1,066 Chambers of Commerce covering three points: first, the probable amount of working capital required now by smaller industries; second, the number of employees who would be retained by these industries if working capital is afforded them; and third, the number of new employees that can be taken on by them through such supply of working capital.

Estimates based on this survey indicate that approximately $700,000,000 of such working capital is required; that such working capital may continue in employment some 346,000 employees and may furnish new employment to some 378,000 men and women.

While these estimates in their nature cannot be definite and must be considered as estimates only, they indicate the urgent need of these small industries for working capital.

The Administration will be glad to furnish you such information and assistance as you may desire in order to set up the machinery to supply this need.

The details will be presented to you, but I desire to call attention to two prominent features: first, the matter of caring for the small or medium-size industrialist; second, the control of the proposed banks by directorates, a majority of which will themselves be industrialists.

I shall appreciate early consideration by your Committee and by the Congress, as I feel that the situation disclosed calls for immediate relief and that such situations as can be relieved through the medium of working capital should have our earnest support.

Very sincerely yours,

Senator Henry P. Fletcher
Chairman, Senate Banking and Currency Committee
Washington, D. C.

NOTE: On March 19, 1934, I addressed the foregoing letter to the Banking and Currency Committees of both Houses in the Congress, pointing out that in numerous cases the working capital of small industries had been lost or seriously depleted, and that the absence of adequate credit facilities for such enterprises called for some remedial action. It was almost impossible for that type of business to obtain its requirements of working capital through the open capital market; and commercial banks and other financial institutions, in many cases, refused to undertake the risks involved in making relatively long-time loans for working-capital purposes. I was interested, as appears from the foregoing letter, not only in helping the owners of such business but also in providing employment in them for thousands of people.

By an Act of Congress approved on June 19, 1934 (Pub. No. 417, 73d Congress; 48 Stat. 1105) the Federal Reserve Banks and the Reconstruction Finance Corporation were authorized, within prescribed limitations, to make credit available for the purpose of supplying working capital to established industrial and commercial business. Federal Reserve Banks were given broad powers to enable them to make advances for such working capital, through the medium of financing institutions, provided the financing institution obligated itself for at least 20 percent of any loss sustained. It was also provided that direct loans could be made by the Federal Reserve Banks in exceptional circumstances, when credit was not obtainable on a reasonable basis from the usual sources, and if the loan were made on a reasonable and sound basis.

The law required that the purpose of the loans should be the supplying of working capital to then-established industrial or commercial business, and that the loans mature in not exceeding five years.

The law also provided for the appointment of an industrial advisory committee in each of the twelve Federal Reserve districts. Members of these advisory committees were selected by the third week in July, 1934, and the consideration of applications by the committees and by the Reserve Banks began immediately. The first loan was made as early as August 1, 1934.

The volume of the advances outstanding by the Federal Reserve Banks under this statute reached a peak of approximately $33,000,000 in October and November, 1935, but by December 1, 1937, they had been reduced to $20,000,000. In addition, the Reserve Banks were under commitment for about $13,000,000 of advances made by other financing institutions on December 1, 1937 compared with $28,000,000 in November, 1935. In the entire period, through November, 1937, the Reserve Banks acted upon 8,600 applications for advances or commitments involving $360,000,000. Over 2,350 applications were approved, with or without conditions, amounting to a total of $148,000,000. Most of the other loans applied for were either ineligible under the conditions imposed by the Act or were without a satisfactory credit base.

Industrial advances by the Reconstruction Finance Corporation were made directly or in cooperation with the Federal Reserve Banks and other banks or lending agencies, subject to much the same conditions as those made by the Federal Reserve Banks, except that originally no loan could have a maturity of more than five years or exceed $500,000. On January 31, 1935, the Act was amended permitting the Corporation to make advances with maturities extending to January 31, 1945; and the $500,000 limitation on the amount of loans to any one borrower was removed, as was the provision that the industrial or commercial business be established prior to January 1, 1934. Loans approved by the Reconstruction Finance Corporation were about equal in number to those approved by the Federal Reserve Banks, but somewhat larger in amount. During the period, June 19, 1934, through November, 1937, the Reconstruction Finance Corporation under this Act authorized over 2,500 loans (including commitments and participations with banks in loans) amounting to a total of about $175,000,000. Of this amount approximately $54,700,000 has been withdrawn or canceled, substantially due to the fact that local banks were willing to advance the credit after the corporation authorized the loans.

The total number of loans approved under the statute by the Reconstruction Finance Corporation and the Federal Reserve Banks was about 4,800, amounting to approximately $323,000,000.

45 ❰ Further Efforts to Settle the Railway Wage Dispute. March 20, 1934

Gentlemen:

I HAVE been advised of what has transpired at the conferences between the Conference Committee of Managers, representing the railroads, and the Railway Labor Executives Association, representing the employees, which have been held in response to my communication of February 14, 1934. · · ·

It is a profound disappointment to learn that no progress toward an agreement has been made at the conference. I fear that sight is being lost of the most important factor of all, the good of the country. If no agreement is reached, and in default of arbitration, it may be necessary for me, with due regard to the protection of the general public interest, to appoint a commission to examine thoroughly into the labor controversy, covering all classes of railroad employment, in order that the country may be advised of the merits. . . .

Since I addressed my previous communication to you, however, the fact has been developed that some of the railroad employees are now receiving compensation for their work at rates which are below minimums which have been established in the N.R.A. codes, if not actually below a subsistence basis. . . . To the extent that it exists, it should be corrected, and in this expression of opinion I feel confident that the railroads and the holders of their securities will concur. . . .

I shall be glad to extend to you the services of the Federal Coordinator of Transportation to help in composing your present differences, if that be desired. For the good of the country I strongly urge that further efforts be made to reach an agreement.

Very sincerely yours,

Mr. W. F. Thiehoff,
Chairman, Conference Committee of Managers
     and Mr. A. F. Whitney
Chairman, Railway Labor Executives Ass'n
Washington, D. C.

NOTE: This was the second time I had intervened in this national railroad wage dispute upon my own initiative (see Item 26, this volume). The services of the Federal Coordinator were offered, as I stated in my letter, and were accepted.

At first the conferences with the Coordinator were unproductive of agreement. In fact, while in conference, the employees themselves demanded an increase of 10 percent in the basic rates of pay.

On March 27, 1934, I had a meeting with the labor executives, at which the Federal Coordinator was present. In April, 1934, I had a conference with the railroad managers. Efforts at settlement were, however, unavailing.

Finally the parties again resumed conferences among themselves, and an agreement was entered into on April 26, 1934 (see Items 61 and 66 of this volume).

46 ⟨ White House Statement on President's Efforts to Settle by Negotiation Impending Pacific Coast Longshoremen's Strike. March 22, 1934

THE President has received a telegram from George Creel, State Director, National Emergency Council, San Francisco, advising that the International Longshoremen's Association of the Pacific Coast has voted in ratio of 100 to 1 to strike Friday morning, March 23d.

Mr. Creel's dispatch said 12,000 men "will probably quit work and whole Coast involved from Vancouver to San Diego" and added that the inevitable result "is bound to be industrial war and a crushing blow to revived prosperity of the Pacific States."

The President late today dispatched the following telegram to W. J. Lewis, President, Pacific Coast District, International Longshoremen's Association, San Francisco, California:

"In public interest I am constrained to ask you to suspend strike order effective Friday March 23d until an investigation of all matters in controversy can be made by impartial board which I will name. This Board will be empowered to conduct hearings and make recommendations as a basis for peaceful settlement of differences by negotiation. I earnestly ask your cooperation and will appreciate an immediate reply."

NOTE: The strike of the longshoremen on the Pacific Coast in 1934 was one of the most difficult strikes of that year. The longshoremen had made demands upon their employers for wage increases and improved working conditions. Using the power conferred upon me by Public Resolution No. 44, 73d Congress, approved June 19, 1934, I appointed a National Longshoremen's Board to try to settle the dispute. The strike involved all of the maritime unions in San Francisco, and for a few days most of the other unions in San Francisco went out on a sympathy strike with them.

The National Longshoremen's Board finally brought an end to the strikes on July 31st, but the arbitration work, which the settlement provided for, kept the Board busy until mid-October. The arbitrators' award defined the work of the longshoremen, provided for wage-rate increases, and for labor relations com- mittees in the different ports of the

Pacific Coast to adjust future disputes.

47 ❧ White House Statement on Presidential Policy of "Hands-off" in Local Political Fights. March 23, 1934

IN ANSWER to newspaper reports that the anti-Curry fight in New York City would be discussed with the President by Postmaster General Farley, it was definitely stated today at the White House that the President will take no part whatever in such discussions nor will he in any way allow himself to be drawn into the political controversy between Curry and anti-Curry factions.

Press reports suggesting that Mr. Farley would outline the situation to President Roosevelt and discuss with him the part the National Administration should take in the anti-Curry movement were categorically denied.

It was emphasized that the President will strictly adhere to this "hands-off" policy when and wherever attempts are made to involve him in local political party contests.

NOTE: I have consistently adhered to the policy mentioned in the foregoing statement of keeping "hands off" in all local political party contests. The only exceptions I have made to this rule since March 4, 1933, have been to urge the reelection of Senator George Norris, of Nebraska (see Vol. V, Item 156), and to comment occasionally upon candidates in my own town, county and State.

48 ❧ The Office of Special Adviser to the President on Foreign Trade Is Created. Executive Order No. 6651. March 23, 1934

WHEREAS the guidance of public policy in relation to international commerce has tended, in recent years, to encounter increasingly complex problems, which can be solved only upon the basis of the comprehensive analysis and coordinated utilization of those of our resources which relate to trade with other countries; and

WHEREAS this analysis and utilization require that the powers and duties assigned to various executive establishments and agencies for the purpose of promoting, reinforcing, or protecting the foreign trade of the United States be coordinated and the work of such establishments and agencies be made as effective as possible;

Now, THEREFORE, by virtue of and pursuant to the authority vested in me under Title I of the National Industrial Recovery Act approved June 16, 1933 (ch. 90, 48 Stat. 195), and otherwise, and in order to aid in effectuating the policy of said title and the fulfillment of the purposes hereinbefore set forth —

1. There is hereby established the Office of Special Adviser to the President on Foreign Trade, the head of which shall be the Special Adviser, who shall be appointed by the President and shall receive a salary to be fixed by me. . . .

2. (*a*) The Special Adviser, in order to effectuate the general purposes of this order, and to keep me informed with respect to our foreign trade, is authorized to obtain, review, and coordinate the information, statistics, and data with reference to the foreign trade of the United States collected or prepared by any department or other establishment or agency of the Federal Government (hereinafter referred to as "department or other agency"), or elsewhere.

(*b*) In connection with foreign trade activities, the Special Adviser is authorized to carry on negotiations with respect to specific trade transactions with any individual, corporation, association, group, or business agency interested in obtaining assistance from the Federal Government through (1) financing transactions, (2) barter transactions, or (3) other forms of governmental participation authorized by law.

(*c*) The Special Adviser shall bring such proposals with respect to these transactions as seem meritorious to him before the departments or other agencies affected by or having an interest therein for appropriate action, and shall keep me advised concerning the action taken or proposed by such department or other agency.

(*d*) The authorization herein set forth shall not exclude any department or other agency from carrying on such activities as are now authorized by law. For example, the State Department shall function in its usual way to the extent that any question of foreign policy is involved. . . .

4. For the purposes of this order the sum of $100,000 is hereby allocated to the Office of the Special Adviser to the President on Foreign Trade from the appropriation of $3,300,000,000 authorized by section 220 of the National Industrial Recovery Act and made by the Fourth Deficiency Act, fiscal year 1933, approved June 16, 1933 (ch. 100, 48 Stat. 274).

5. (*a*) The temporary committee created by me as set forth in the public statement of December 11, "to recommend permanent machinery to coordinate all Government relations to American foreign trade," is supplanted by the present arrangement. The Special Adviser, with the approval of the President, is hereby authorized to create such committees as he may deem appropriate or necessary to assist and promote in carrying out the purposes of this order.

(*b*) The formulation of commercial policies with respect to foreign trade and the effecting of general foreign-trade agreements will remain in the department or other agency now charged by law with responsibility therefor.

NOTE: The foregoing Executive Order, which was issued pursuant to the authority vested in me by the National Industrial Recovery Act, enumerates the functions of the Special Adviser on Foreign Trade.

A subsequent Executive Order, No. 6656, dated March 27, 1934, directed the Special Adviser to cooperate with and to supplement the work of the Executive Committee on Commercial Policy which had been appointed November 11, 1933 (see Item 160, Vol. II). Pursuant to that order the Special Adviser on Foreign Trade became a member of the Executive Committee on Commercial Policy.

The office was abolished on June 16, 1935, along with certain other agencies of the N.R.A., which had completed the work for which they had been established. (See Items 68, 78, 78A, 78B of Vol. IV.)

49 ❧ The President Expresses His Approval of the Principle of Unemployment Insurance under State Laws. March 23, 1934

Dear Mr. Congressman:

I HAVE received your inquiry about my opinion on H. R. 7659, a bill levying a Federal excise tax upon large employers, but allowing them to deduct from their tax amounts contributed pursuant to unemployment insurance laws that have been or may be passed by the several States.

I need not tell you that for a long time I have advocated unemployment insurance as an essential part of our program to build a more ample and secure life. The loss of a job brings discouragement and privation to the individual worker and his family. If an insurance or reserve fund has been accumulated, even a small payment from it at such a critical time will tide over the worker and keep up his morale and purchasing power.

The benefits of such a system will not be limited to the individual, however, but will extend throughout our social and financial fabric. We have in the past relied almost entirely upon private charities and public treasuries to sustain the costs of seasonal and intermittent unemployment. This is a practice that necessity will compel us to change to a very substantial degree. There is no reason why they should assume the entire burden of meeting a foreseeable loss, the major cost of which ought to be computed and borne like every other cost of a business.

Of course, unemployment insurance alone will not make unnecessary all relief for all people out of work for the entire period of a major economic depression, but it is my confident belief that such funds will, by maintaining the purchasing power of those temporarily out of work, act as a stabilizing device in our economic structure and as a method of retarding the rapid downward spiral curve and the onset of severe economic crises.

I am interested to see that the bill before your committee seeks to promote unemployment insurance under State rather than national laws. This is an approach with which I agree, and which fulfills the promise of the Democratic Platform for 1932 to favor "unemployment insurance under State laws." The States are peculiarly equipped to administer legislation of this type, and the recent efforts of this Administration in such a closely allied field as the creation of public employment offices have been along this line.

The bill has another advantage in establishing a suitable relation of the national Government to unemployment insurance. Under our system of government the task of caring for the unemployed falls primarily on the States. If a State cannot bear the burden, the United States must be prepared to do so and to collect revenue for that purpose. That is why this bill is properly considered a revenue measure. But if a State, by requiring local industries to contribute to unemployment reserves, has cared for its needy and avoided a strain upon the Federal Treasury, such contributions ought to be deductible from Federal taxes.

The general principles of H. R. 7659 seem to me sound, and the effect sought a necessary one for recovery and prevention of future economic crises; and I hope that the bill will be passed by the Congress at this session.

Sincerely yours,

Hon. Robert L. Doughton,
Chairman, Committee on Ways and Means,
Washington, D. C.

NOTE: It is interesting to note that the policy expressed in the foregoing statement was the one finally adopted in the Social Security Act of 1935 (see Vol. IV, Item 107).

See also Chapter XVII of Vol. I, particularly Items 95, 96, and 99 thereof, for my views and acts as Governor of New York with respect to this subject of unemployment insurance.

50 ❡ The One Hundred and Eighth Press Conference (Excerpts). March 23, 1934

(Open-price posting — Slum clearance and the prohibitive price of land in cities — Naval construction.)

Q. Mr. President, there is a delegation of steel officials at the N.R.A. conferring with General Johnson and there is considerable secrecy around their negotiations. Do you know anything?

THE PRESIDENT: I cannot imagine anything unless it is caused by the report of the Federal Trade Commission. It might have been. It created quite a commotion.

Q. Have you any observations on that report?

THE PRESIDENT: No, except as background. It goes back — I think I talked to you about this before — it goes back to the question of this open-price posting. Of course in practice that almost necessarily results in one-price bidding, because everybody else follows the first one to post, and posts exactly the same price; and then they all bid on exactly the same identical price. Of course that is not free competition and the thing is not working. We have to find some method of restoring competitive bidding, which seems to be pretty well precluded by this open-price posting method that exists. How we are going to go about it we don't know; but we have to do something about it.

Q. Mr. President, are any new slum-clearance plans being considered?

THE PRESIDENT: No. On the slum clearance, as a whole, the general thought is this: Our difficulty in giving Federal aid to the majority of cities that need slum clearance arises out of real-estate values which are very largely fictitious. In fact, in many cases the assessed valuations themselves are fictitious. There are many cases in the slum areas in New York where the city assessment is way above what the owner of the property would be willing to sell the property for. There are a great many tenement-house owners that would be tickled to death if they could get 75 percent of the assessed value in cash. Obviously, just so long as you have to pay exorbitant real-estate prices in clearing slum properties, you cannot put up any new buildings on a sufficiently sound basis so that you will be able to get your money back.

What we would like to see is some method of getting lower real-estate costs; and, if we can get that, it means we would be able to put up buildings in the City of New York that would rent for $6 or $7 instead of $10 or $12 a room a month. We are being held up by the real-estate problem. That is the answer. If we can get around that and purchase real estate at a lower price so that we can put up buildings with low rents, the Federal Government stands ready to increase very greatly its slum clearance allotment out of its next year's appropriation.

Q. Subject to that condition?

THE PRESIDENT: Subject to that condition.

Q. You mentioned New York. Does that hold good elsewhere?

THE PRESIDENT: Yes, except that in other places the scale of real-estate prices is a different one, of course. For example, in a great deal smaller city that has a slum problem, $6 or $7 a month per room is too high. In a city of that kind, you want rentals of $4 or $5 a month per room.

Q. Have you signed the Vinson Bill yet?

THE PRESIDENT: No, it has not come down. It does not come down until tomorrow. If I do sign it and if I have time and do not get taken up too much with automobiles and things like that, I shall file a memorandum with it for your information. Perhaps you had better not break the story at all and make this off the record. It will be a memorandum which will point out the distinction between an appropriation and an authorization. It is time that the public was informed of the difference. It is not the fault of the press, because we have all been using a word that we understand, but the reading public does not understand when they read a story in the newspaper that Congress has authorized the building of one hundred two new ships. The public assumes that they are going to start building those one hundred two new ships right away.

So I have to point out in a memorandum that in its essentials this bill is really nothing more than a resolution that it is still the policy of the United States to build up to the London Naval Treaty limits, and that it depends on the action of future Congresses as to whether the ships will be actually started or not. I have to do that because I have had so many appeals from pacifist organizations which do not understand it.

Q. Are you coming up to the Press Club tomorrow night, Mr. President?

THE PRESIDENT: What happens?

Q. The dinner.

THE PRESIDENT: Do I have to make a speech?

Q. I don't know about that. We will let you off on the speech, if you come.

THE PRESIDENT: All right, if you will do that I will come. . . .

(With respect to the discussion of the Vinson Bill, see Item 54, this volume.)

51 ❡ The Threat of a Serious Automobile Strike Is Averted by Settlement. Presidential Statement. March 25, 1934

AFTER many days of conferring in regard to the principles of employment in the automobile industry the following statement covers the fundamentals:

1. Reduced to plain language Section 7a of N.I.R.A. means —
    (a) Employees have the right to organize into a group or groups.
    (b) When such group or groups are organized they can choose representatives by free choice; and such representatives must be received collectively, in order to

straighten out disputes and improve conditions of employment.

(c) Discrimination against employees because of their labor affiliations, or for any other unfair or unjust reason, is barred.

A settlement and statement of procedure and principles is appended hereto.

It has been offered by me to, and has been accepted by, the representatives of the employees and the employers. It lives up to the principles of collective bargaining. I hope and believe that it opens up a chance for a square deal and fair treatment. It gives promise of sound industrial relations. It provides further for a Board of three of which the Chairman will as a neutral represent the Government.

In actual practice details and machinery will, of course, have to be worked out on the basis of common sense and justice, but the big point is that this broad purpose can develop with a tribunal which can handle practically every problem in an equitable way.

PRINCIPLES OF SETTLEMENT

Settlement of the threatened automobile strike is based on the following principles:

1. The employers agree to bargain collectively with the freely chosen representatives of groups and not to discriminate in any way against any employee on the ground of his union labor affiliations.

2. If there be more than one group each bargaining committee shall have total membership pro rata to the number of men each member represents.

3. N.R.A. is to set up within twenty-four hours a board, responsible to the President of the United States, to sit in Detroit to pass on all questions of representation, discharge and discrimination. Decision of the Board shall be final and binding on employer and employees. Such a board is to have access to all payrolls and to all lists of claimed employee representation and such

board will be composed of, (a) a labor representative, (b) an industry representative, (c) a neutral.

In cases where no lists of employees claiming to be represented have been disclosed to the employer, there shall be no basis for a claim of discrimination. No such disclosure in a particular case shall be made without specific direction of the President.

4. The Government makes it clear that it favors no particular union or particular form of employee organization or representation. The Government's only duty is to secure absolute and uninfluenced freedom of choice without coercion, restraint, or intimidation from any source.

5. The industry understands that in reduction or increases of force, such human considerations as whether a man is married and has a family shall come first and then seniority, individual skill and efficient service. After these factors have been considered no greater proportion of outside union employees similarly situated shall be laid off than of other employees. By outside union employees is understood a paid-up member in good standing, or anyone legally obligated to pay up. An appeal shall lie in case of dispute on principles of paragraph 5 to the Board of three.

In all the hectic experience of N.R.A. I have not seen more earnest and patriotic devotion than has been shown by both employers and employees in the automotive industry. They sat night and day for nearly two weeks without faltering. The result is one of the most encouraging incidents of the recovery program. It is a complete answer to those critics who have asserted that managers and employees cannot cooperate for the public good without domination by selfish interest.

In the settlement there is a frame-work for a new structure of industrial relations—a new basis of understanding between employers and employees. I would like you to know that in the settlement just reached in the automobile industry we have charted a new course in social engineering in the United States. It is my hope that out of this will come a new realization of the opportunities of capital and labor not only to compose their differences at the conference table and to recognize their respective rights and responsibilities, but also to establish a foundation on which they can cooperate in bettering the human relationships involved in any large industrial enterprise.

It is peculiarly fitting that this great step forward should be taken in an industry whose employers and employees have contributed so consistently and so substantially to the industrial and economic development of this country in the last quarter century. Having pioneered in mechanical invention to a point where the whole world marvels at the perfection and economy of American motor cars and their widespread ownership by our citizens in every walk of life, this industry has indicated now its willingness to undertake a pioneer effort in human engineering on a basis never before attempted.

In the settlement just accomplished, two outstanding advances have been achieved. In the first place we have set forth a basis on which, for the first time in any large industry, a more comprehensive, a more adequate and a more equitable system of industrial relations may be built than ever before. It is my hope that this system may develop into a kind of works council in industry in which all groups of employees, whatever may be their choice of organization or form of representation, may participate in joint conferences with their employers and I am assured by the industry that such is also their goal and wish.

In the second place, we have for the first time written into an industrial settlement a definite rule for the equitable handling of reductions and increases of forces. It would be ideal if employment in all occupations could be more generally stabilized, but in the absence of that much desired situation, if we can establish a formula which gives weight to the human factors as well as the economic, social and organizational factors in relieving the hardship of seasonal layoff, we shall have accomplished a great deal. My view, and that of both employees and employers, is that we have measurably done so in this settlement.

This is not a one-sided statute, and organizations of employees seeking to exercise their representative rights cannot at the same time be unmindful of their responsibilities.

Industry's obligations are clearly set forth and its responsibilities are established. It is not too much to expect organizations of employees to observe the same ethical and moral responsibilities even though they are not specifically prescribed by the statute. Only in this way can industry and its workers go forward with a united front in their assault on depression and gain for both the desired benefits of continually better times.

NOTE: The threatened strike in the automobile industry was averted after conferences held by me with the employers and with the partly organized workers. An agreement was finally reached, under which an Automobile Labor Board was created, consisting of one employer, one worker and one impartial person, all three named by me, but the first two on the nomination of the parties concerned. It was the claim of the employers in this dispute that only a portion of the men in their plants desired to be represented by the particular organization which had threatened to call the strike. They desired definite recognition of the right to bargain collectively with those in their employ who did not regard themselves as represented by the union in question.

In the effort to settle this dispute and to make adjustment of the varied and confusing points of view involved in this situation, where the union was admittedly young and not completely expressive, an agreement for proportional representation was used.

5 2 ❰ The President Insists upon Federal Supervision of the Sale of Securities. March 26, 1934

My dear Mr. Chairman:

Before I leave Washington for a few days' holiday, I want to write you about a matter which gives me some concern.

On February 9, 1934, I sent to the Congress a special message asking for Federal supervision of national traffic in securities.

It has come to my attention that a more definite and more highly organized drive is being made against effective legislation to this end than against any similar recommendation made by me during the past year. Letters and telegrams bearing all the earmarks of origin at some common source are pouring in to the White House and the Congress.

The people of this country are, in overwhelming majority, fully aware of the fact that unregulated speculation in securities and in commodities was one of the most important contributing factors in the artificial and unwarranted "boom" which had so much to do with the terrible conditions of the years following 1929.

I have been firmly committed to definite regulation of exchanges which deal in securities and commodities. In my message I stated, "It should be our national policy to restrict, as far as possible, the use of these exchanges for purely speculative operations."

I am certain that the country as a whole will not be satisfied with legislation unless such legislation has teeth in it. The two principal objectives are, as I see it:

First, the requirement of what is known as margins so high that speculation, even as it exists today, will of necessity be drastically curtailed; and

Second, vesting the Government with such definite powers of supervision over exchanges that it will be able itself to correct abuses which may arise in the future.

We must, of course, prevent, in so far as possible, manipulation of prices to the detriment of actual investors, but at the same time we must eliminate unnecessary, unwise and destructive speculation.

The Bill, as shown to me this afternoon by you, seems to meet the minimum requirements. I do not see how any of us could afford to have it weakened in any shape, manner or form.

Very sincerely,

Hon. Duncan U. Fletcher,
Chairman, Banking and Currency Committee,
Hon. Sam Reyburn,
Chairman, Interstate and Foreign Commerce Committee,
Washington, D. C.

NOTE: On February 9, 1934, I had recommended this type of legislation (see Item 22, this volume). A highly organized and expensive campaign of propaganda was directed against the legislation by those who did not wish to have speculation in securities limited to decent standards.

The Securities Exchange Act of 1934, designed to that end, was enacted, however, and approved June 6, 1934 (48 Stat. 881; Public No. 291, 73d Congress). See Item 22, this volume, for a description of this statute.

53 ⟨A Letter on the Critical Plight of Our Schools. March 27, 1934

My dear Dr. Arps:

MAY I congratulate the organizers of the Citizens' Conference on the Crisis in Education for calling together leaders in American thought to consider ways and means of solving some of the critical problems that confront the schools of the Nation?

That our educational institutions have suffered much within the past few years is evident. Because of a lack of funds, thousands of schools have closed early this year and many have eliminated highly essential services.

Although the effects of the present lack of adequate educational opportunities on our national life may not be noticeable today, the time may soon come when dire effects will be apparent. It is, therefore, the responsibility of every American to see that the great strides that we have made in education since Colonial times shall not be lost. It is also his responsibility to see that the schools march forward, that the scope of education become such as to provide educational opportunities for every person from early childhood on into adult life. One group that we need to consider especially are the many youths who are not in school and who are apparently drifting.

I realize the seriousness of the problems that will be discussed at your Conference, but I am confident that after careful deliberation you will be able to formulate a plan of action. My great

regret is that I find it impossible to participate in your deliberations upon so important a subject.

I send you my heartiest wishes for a fruitful and epoch-making
Conference.

Very sincerely yours,

Dr. George F. Arps,
The Ohio State University,
Columbus, Ohio

54 ❨ Presidential Statement Issued upon Sign-
ing the Vinson Navy Bill. March 27, 1934

BECAUSE there is some public misapprehension of fact in relation to the Vinson Bill, it is only right that its main provision
should be made wholly clear.

This is not a law for the construction of a single additional
United States warship.

The general purpose of the Bill is solely a statement by the
Congress that it approves the building of our Navy up to and not
beyond the strength in various types of ships authorized, first, by
the Washington Naval Limitation Treaty of 1922 and, secondly,
by the London Naval Limitation Treaty of 1930.

As has been done on several previous occasions in our history,
the Bill authorizes certain future construction over a period of
years. But the Bill appropriates no money for such construction
and the word "authorization" is, therefore, merely a statement of
the policy of the present Congress. Whether it will be carried out
depends on the action of future Congresses.

It has been and will be the policy of the Administration to
favor continued limitation of Naval armaments. It is my personal
hope that the Naval Conference to be held in 1935 will extend all
existing limitations and agree to further reductions.

NOTE: The Democratic National
Platform of 1932 stated: "We advocate a Navy . . . adequate for
national defense. . . ."

The foregoing statute authorized the construction of vessels and aircraft to bring the Navy to the strength prescribed by the Naval Treaty entered into at London in 1930, and to replace ships as they became over age. The Act also removed the statutory maximum limitation of 1,000 for the number of useful airplanes in the Navy which had been imposed by the Act of June 24, 1926; and it expressly authorized the President "to procure the necessary naval aircraft for vessels and other naval purposes in numbers commensurate with a treaty Navy."

In 1933 funds were made available to commence construction of 37 vessels; in 1934, 24 vessels; in 1935, 24 vessels; and in 1936, 20 vessels.

The following is a summary of the four-year program during the first term of my Administration:

SUMMARY OF FOUR-YEAR PROGRAM

	Private Shipyards	Government Navy Yards
Battleships	0	2
Aircraft carriers ..	3	0
Heavy cruisers	1	1
Light cruisers	5	4
1850-ton destroyers	13	0
1500-ton destroyers	21	31
Submarines	11	11
Gunboats	0	2
	54	51

Total four-year program........ 105

55 ❡ The President Vetoes the Appropriation Bill as Violating the Administration's Policies of Economy. March 27, 1934

To the House of Representatives:

I RETURN herewith without my approval H. R. 6663 entitled "An Act making appropriations for the Executive Office and sundry independent executive bureaus, boards, commissions, and offices, for the fiscal year ending June 30, 1935, and for other purposes." I am impelled to do this on a number of grounds, any one of them sufficient to require disapproval of the Bill.

In March, 1933, the Congress passed, and I signed "An Act to maintain the credit of the United States Government." This law became one of the principal pillars of national recovery for the clear reason that for the first time in many years the recurring annual expenses for the maintenance of the Government were brought within the current revenues of the Government. It is

173

true that very large but wholly distinct funds are being dispensed daily for emergency purposes, but these funds are going directly to the purpose of saving farms, saving homes and giving relief and employment to millions of our fellow citizens. They are non-recurring in nature, while the increases contemplated in this Bill are continuous and permanent.

Furthermore, the Budget submitted by me to the Congress on January 4, 1934, laid down a definite program of expenditures and a definite estimate of receipts. Because of the emergency expenditures for relief and unemployment, the expected total deficits this year and in 1935 are necessarily large; but at the same time a program for a completely balanced budget by June 30, 1936, was determined upon as a definite objective.

This Bill exceeds the estimates submitted by me in the sum of $228,000,000. I am compelled to take note of the fact that in creating this excess the Congress has failed at the same time to provide a similar sum by additional taxation. Moreover, to the extent that the amount of money appropriated by the Congress is in excess of my Budget estimates, and in the absence of provision for additional revenues, there must be a decrease in the funds available for essential relief work.

This Bill increases the compensation for employees of the United States Government $125,000,000 over my Budget estimates for this purpose. I have great sympathy for the employees, but I cannot forget that millions of American citizens are today still without employment, and reduction in the compensation of Federal employees has been and still is on the average less than the reduction in compensation that has been patiently endured by those citizens not in the employ of the United States Government.

Let me be specific. This Bill makes a portion of the restored compensation retroactive to February 1, 1934. I believe it unwise to establish this precedent, and I cannot overlook the serious administrative difficulties involved in paying back pay to individuals, many of whom are no longer in the employ of the Government.

The Bill also contains several discriminatory provisions, such as paying employees in some departments of the Government 48 hours' pay for 40 hours' work.

In submitting the Budget estimates last December, I recommended compensation restoration of 5 percent for the next fiscal year. The cost of living seems to be rising slowly. The present authority is not responsive enough to changing conditions. I therefore shall be glad to confer with the Congress on improving the methods of restoring Federal pay so that in actual practice the pay will keep ahead of the cost of living increases instead of lagging behind. Adjustments can well be made immediately on the passage of appropriate legislation followed by more frequent adjustments in the future.

I come now to the provisions in this Act relating to World War veterans. First let me speak of principles. Last October I said this to the American Legion Convention:

"The first principle, following inevitably from the obligation of citizens to bear arms, is that the Government has a responsibility for and toward those who suffered injury or contracted disease while serving in its defense.

"The second principle is that no person, because he wore a uniform, must thereafter be placed in a special class of beneficiaries over and above all other citizens. The fact of wearing a uniform does not mean that he can demand and receive from his Government a benefit which no other citizen receives. It does not mean that because a person served in the defense of his country, performed a basic obligation of citizenship, he should receive a pension from his Government because of a disability incurred after his service had terminated, and not connected with that service.

"It does mean, however, that those who were injured in or as a result of their service are entitled to receive adequate and generous compensation for their disabilities. It does mean that generous care shall be extended to the dependents of those who died in or as a result of service to their country."

175

I am very confident that the American people, including the overwhelming majority of veterans themselves, approve these principles and in the last analysis will support them.

Applying them to the provisions of this Bill I cannot give it my approval.

Last year it was determined — and I had hoped permanently — that a service-connected disability is a question of fact rather than a question of law. In other words, each individual case should and must be considered on its merits and there is no justification for legislative dicta which, contrary to fact, provide that thousands of individual cases of sickness which commenced four, five or six years after the termination of the War are caused by war service. Therefore local boards were established — boards on which three out of the five members were in no way connected with the Veterans Administration and on which two-thirds of those serving were ex-service men. These local boards approved disallowances in the case of 29,000 veterans and these decisions were unanimous in 94 percent of the cases. Not content with that, I created a Board of Appeals the majority of which again are in no way connected with the Veterans Administration and a majority of which are ex-service men. This Board is now engaged in hearing appeals of those cases disallowed by the local boards.

A few weeks ago I gave approval to an amendment the purpose of which was, pending the determination of their appeals, to restore to the rolls at 75 percent of their compensation, those veterans in whose cases the presumption of service connection was disallowed by the local boards. This, however, was rejected in the Congress. I intend now by regulation forthwith to direct an appeal by the Administrator of Veterans' Affairs in each and every one of these disallowed 29,000 cases with the further direction that in the final determination of these cases every reasonable doubt be resolved in favor of the veteran, and every assistance be rendered in the preparation and presentation of these cases. While these cases are pending, the veterans will be paid 75 percent of the compensation they received prior to the time they were removed from the rolls. If the appeal is allowed they will receive back compensation. Only in cases disallowed by the Board of Appeals will the veteran thereafter be permanently removed from the rolls. This regulation will be put into effect at once.

By reason of the fact that many totally and permanently disabled veterans have been the recipients of benefits from their Government for a long period of time, it is difficult in the event of a disallowance of service connection by the final Board of Appeals to remove them completely from the rolls. Existing regulations therefore provide that if their cases are disallowed and if they are found to be totally and permanently disabled they shall, notwithstanding fundamental principles enunciated, if in need, receive $30.00 a month and domiciliary care and hospitalization.

It is a simple and undeniable fact that the United States, in terms of compensation and in terms of hospitalization, has done and is doing infinitely more for our veterans and their dependents than any other Government.

I come now to the provisions of the Bill relating to Spanish-American War veterans. To this group of ex-service men I have devoted much thought. Because of their age, they command sympathy. Nevertheless, we must recognize also that many abuses have crept into the laws granting them benefits.

The Spanish-American War Veterans' Amendment to this Act provides for service pensions. This violates the principles upon which benefits to veterans should be paid and the principles to which I have referred in this message. Moreover, if that principle should in the future be applied to the World War veterans at the same rate as contemplated for Spanish-American War veterans by this Bill, the annual and continuing charge upon the people of this country by 1949 will amount to more than $830,-000,000 for that item alone. This would be in addition to the large cost of all existing veterans' benefits and future hospitalization. This I cannot approve.

However, I am today directing the restoration to the rolls of those Spanish-American War veterans who in 1920 were receiving pensions as a result of having sustained an injury or incurred a disease arising out of their war service.

By Regulation 12 a presumption of service origin was extended to Spanish-American War veterans on the rolls on March 19, 1933. In order to take the same action which I am taking in regard to World War veterans, I am directing the restoration to the rolls, as of this date, at 75 percent of the amount they were receiving on March 19, 1933, all Spanish-American War veterans pending a final determination of their cases before the Board of Appeals.

Without going further into all of the details relating to the treatment — past, present and future — of Spanish-American War veterans, it seems sufficient to repeat that I am wholly and irrevocably opposed to the principle of the general service pension, but I do seek to provide with liberality for all those who suffered because of their service in that War. As in the case of World War veterans, I shall not hesitate further to alter or modify the regulations in order that substantial justice may be done in every individual case.

What you and I are seeking is justice and fairness in the individual case. I call your specific attention to the fact that since the original regulations were established a year ago actual experience has shown many cases where these regulations required modification. I have not hesitated to take the necessary action and have issued regulations which have made many changes. These changes based on principles of justice to the individual veteran involve additional expenditures of approximately $117,000,000. It goes without saying that I shall not hesitate to make further changes if the principles of justice demand them.

On the basis of the original regulations following the Economy Act, the annual cost to the United States of veterans' relief was $486,000,000. Since that time by Executive Order the addition of $117,000,000 increases to $603,000,000 the total cost for veterans' relief for the fiscal year 1935.

My disapproval of this Bill is not based solely on the consideration of dollars and cents. There is a deeper consideration. You and I are concerned with the principles herein enunciated. I trust that the Congress will continue to cooperate with me in our common effort to restore general prosperity and relieve distress.

NOTE: The reasons for my veto of the Independent Offices Appropriation Act for the fiscal year 1935 are set forth in the foregoing veto message. They are briefly: (1) the Congressional appropriations exceeded by $228,000,000 the estimates submitted by me in my budget, without making provision to raise this excess by taxation; (2) the amount of my budget estimate for compensation of employees of the Federal Government pursuant to the Economy Act of March 20, 1933, was raised by $125,000,000; (3) restoration was made of portions of salary reductions of Federal employees retroactively to February 1, 1934; (4) discriminatory provisions were made between employees of different departments of the Government; (5) provisions of the bill relating to World War veterans restored a great many of the reductions which I had made pursuant to the Economy Act of 1933; (6) provisions of the bill relating to Spanish-American War veterans also restored a great many of the reductions which I had made pursuant to the Economy Act of 1933.

Between the date of the last veterans' regulations of January 19, 1934, and the passage of Public No. 141; 73d Congress (48 Stat. 509) which became law on March 28, 1934, over my foregoing veto message, several clarifying and liberalizing Executive Orders were issued

by me, two of which, proposing increased benefits of $22,000,000, annually, were canceled in view of the passage of Public No. 141.

The effect of Public No. 141 was to restore under certain conditions the full rates of compensation being paid on March 19, 1933, to World War veterans who had directly service-connected disabilities. This Act also restored to the rolls presumptively service-connected cases at 75 percent of the prior rates, and liberalized hospital and domiciliary provisions relating particularly to non-service-connected cases where the veteran was unable to defray his own hospital expense.

On March 19, 1935, I promulgated further Executive Orders (known as Nos. 6989 to 6992, inclusive) granting increased benefits to Spanish-American War and World War widows and children, as well as liberalizing certain provisions having to do with proof and evidence pertaining to claims as to dependency of parents in service-connected cases.

Following the termination on March 19, 1935, of the two-year period during which I was authorized by the terms of Public No. 2, 73d Congress (see Items 12 and 28 of Vol. II) to promulgate regulations relating to veterans' relief, important legislation pertaining to veterans was enacted by the Congress. The first was that contained in the Second Deficiency Appropriation Act of 1935 (Public No. 260, 74th Congress) which was approved by me on August 12, 1935, and which made provision for a total expenditure of $21,250,000 for the purpose of extending and increasing hospital facilities for veterans of all wars.

The next Act of the 74th Congress with respect to veterans (Public No. 262, August 12, 1935) related to the safeguarding of estates of veterans derived from payment of pensions, compensation, emergency officers' retirement pay, etc., and authorized the Administrator of Veterans' Affairs to exercise closer supervision over the estates of insane veterans and minor and incompetent dependents.

On August 13, 1935, I approved Public No. 269, 74th Congress, which restored to the Spanish-American War veterans, including the Boxer Rebellion and Philippine Insurrection, and their widows and dependents, full pensions which were in effect prior to March 19, 1933. The effect of this measure was estimated to increase the annual cost of veterans' relief by $45,500,-000.

Several other measures having to do with veterans' relief of a minor nature were passed during the 74th Congress; but the Act of major importance was Public No. 425, enacted on January 27, 1936, known as the Adjusted Compensation Payment Act, 1936 (Bonus Bill). This measure was passed over my veto (see Vol. V, Item 12), and provided for the payment of Adjusted Service Certificates. It required an appropriation of $1,730,000,000, together with an appropriation of an amount approximating $500,000,000, to cover bonds required to be issued to the United States Government Life Insurance Fund or an appropriation aggregating over $2,230,-000,000, and in addition $5,500,000 for administrative expenses of the Veterans Administration.

Public No. 788 of the 74th Congress, approved by me on June 24, 1936, restored to peace-time veterans 75 percent of the pension being paid prior to the Economy Act, which increased expenditures in this regard in excess of $1,900,000 annually.

The final Act of importance affecting veterans' benefits during the 74th Congress was Public No. 844, approved by me on June 29, 1936. This Act covered three primary purposes: first, the enlargement of the group of widows and children of World War veterans to whom benefits are payable; second, the codification of certain laws relating to the administration of benefits under the Veterans Administration; and third, the extension of time for filing suits in claims arising under insurance laws relating to veterans.

In spite of all the liberalizing Executive Orders issued by me since the original cuts under Public No. 2

of the 73d Congress, and in spite of all the liberalizing acts of the Congress since that date, including the Act passed over my veto (Public No. 141, 73d Congress), there is still an annual saving of about $200,000,000 in veterans' and dependents' compensation and pensions over what they would have cost in 1934 (exclusive, of course, of the Adjusted Compensation Payment Act, 1936) had the laws been allowed to remain as they were prior to the Economy Act of 1933.

56 ❡ A Letter Reaffirming the Freedom of the Press. April 13, 1934

My dear Mr. Connolly:

A press association, collecting and disseminating news, enjoys a prominent place and exercises a tremendous influence in its field of operations. That it has functioned always without fear or favor, exercising the responsibilities for clean, factual and intelligent reporting, should be a matter of great pride to its builders, and its world-wide staff of workers.

I do not believe it would be amiss here for me to say that I personally find high satisfaction in the knowledge that it is possible in this land of ours for anyone to establish a newspaper or a news service and to enjoy the freedom of operation guaranteed by our fathers and which, I am glad to say, still prevails. I am glad, too, that our Government never has seen fit to subsidize a newspaper or a news service and I dare to make the prediction that it never will.

Very sincerely yours,

Mr. Joseph V. Connolly,
President, International News Service, Inc.,
New York, N. Y.

57 ❲ "I Am a Tough Guy" — Informal Remarks to a Congressional Delegation. April 13, 1934

I AM very glad to see you all and it is mighty good of you to come down here. I can't be truthful and say I am glad to get back — I am awfully sorry to get back, but while I have been having a wonderful time, I gather also that both houses of Congress have been having a wonderful time in my absence. Furthermore, I expected on this trip to get some good publicity about the fish I was catching, but couldn't in view of the fact that here in Washington apparently you good people have been going from Wirt to Wirt.

The newspapermen on the train have been trying to make me say that I hope that Congress would go home very soon. I wouldn't say it because I hope you will stay here just as long as you like to. For you younger members of both Houses — speaking from an experience of many years in Washington — I want to point out to you the advantages of the Washington climate in July and August. It rarely gets over 110° here; there is no humidity and I don't mind if I stay here all summer.

Well, anyway, I wish you had had the chance I had to get away for two weeks because I did have a wonderful holiday and I have come back with all sorts of new lessons which I learned from barracuda and sharks. I am a tough guy. So, if you will come down and see me as often as you possibly can, I will teach you some of the stunts I learned.

It's fine to see you; many thanks; and I will see you all soon.

NOTE: The occasion for these remarks from the train platform was the surprise appearance of a large delegation of members of the Senate and House who came to welcome me on my return from a two weeks' fishing trip in the Bahamas. Prior to this time it had been customary for Presidents to remain in Washington during the sessions of the Congress, except for occasional absences of two or three days to attend special functions.

From my earlier experience in the Navy Department I had long felt that any President would be greatly benefited by a complete change of scene and thought for a week or two during long Congressional sessions.

On this fishing trip which began on March 27th, and ended on the occasion of the foregoing remarks, temporary executive offices were set up in Miami, Fla., under the direction of Marvin H. McIntyre, Secretary to the President, with a small White House staff. Several newspaper reporters and photographers accompanied us to cover the trip.

Contact between the temporary office at Miami and the fishing boat was maintained by radio communication through the escort destroyer. Mail was delivered to those in the fishing party by airplane. Communication with the press was maintained through the temporary offices; and on this particular occasion the members of the press actually arranged to meet me out at sea for a short time.

Mr. McIntyre has generally been in charge of temporary White House Offices set up on trips such as these; also during visits by me to my home at Hyde Park, New York, or to Warm Springs, Ga. He has been in charge of office arrangements and appointments on nearly all the extended railroad trips during my term as President.

In addition to this work, Mr. McIntyre has been in charge of appointments and similar duties at the White House proper and has been of great service to me in that and in many other capacities.

The reference in the above remarks to "going from Wirt to Wirt" is a poor pun brought to mind by the charges made by a western professor by the name of Dr. William A. Wirt, alleging, as I recall, that the Nation was about to fall apart in complete chaos.

58 ❡ White House Statement on a Study of a Governmental Aviation Policy. April 16, 1934

IN CONVERSATION with Senators McKellar and Black and Congressman Mead, the President suggested that in connection with pending aviation legislation, it should be borne in mind that the United States has had no broad aviation policy; that a large number of inter-related factors enter into the general subjects of civilian and military flying and their subdivisions into material, personnel, manufacturing and experimentation.

The President suggested that in view of the lack of, and the need for, a national policy the Congress might well authorize the appointment of a commission to make immediate study and recommend to the next Congress a broad policy covering all phases of aviation and the relationship of government thereto.

Insofar as that part of aviation which relates to carrying U. S. mails is concerned, contracts could well be let on competitive bidding for one year or until such time as a broad policy relating to aviation as a whole is adopted.

59 ⟨ Joint Statement by the President and President Vincent on the Relations Between the United States and Haiti. April 17, 1934

WE HAVE had an opportunity to discuss in the most friendly and cordial manner the different problems arising in the relations between the Governments of the United States and of Haiti.

In connection with the departure of the United States Marines from Haiti during the month of October, next, as already provided in the Agreement of August 7, 1933, President Roosevelt intends to request authority from the Congress of the United States to make a gift to Haiti of a portion of the Marine Corps material which the Haitian Government feels would be useful to it.

We have exchanged views regarding the possibility of a commercial agreement which would increase the flow of goods between the two countries; and finally we have discussed a new form of financial administration which is satisfactory to our two Governments and which should be equally satisfactory to the holders of the bonds of the 1922 loan.

We are both inclined to the belief that the policy of the good neighbor which the Government of the United States is endeavoring to apply in its relations with the other American Republics will be signally manifested in the results which will be obtained from this exchange of views and from negotiations which are now taking place with a view to the practical application of the decisions reached in principle during our present conversations.

Certainly Haiti will now be in a position to look forward to her future with the greatest confidence.

NOTE: In the Accord of August 7, 1933, the Government of the United States had agreed to accelerate the Haitianization of the Garde d'Haiti, to turn over the Garde entirely to Haitian officers by October 1, 1934, to withdraw the Marine Brigade and the American Scientific Mission not later than October 31, 1934, and to make various modifications reducing the powers of the Financial Adviser-General Receiver, the name of which office was changed to that of Fiscal Representative beginning January 1, 1934. The Haitian Government was still anxious to obtain further modifications with respect to financial control in Haiti (see Item 172, Vol. II).

During the Pan-American Conference at Montevideo early in December of 1933, the Haitian delegation approached the Secretary of State with a suggestion from the Haitian Government that the existing financial control be withdrawn through the designation by the Government of the United States of the National Bank of Haiti to supervise and carry out the service of the Haitian debt.

At the same time the Haitian Government, desirous of contracting a small loan for the financing of certain public works, was exploring with certain American issue houses the possibilities of obtaining such a loan in the American market.

On March 22, 1934, the President of Haiti, His Excellency Stenio Vincent, accompanied by the Minister of Finance of Haiti, Mr. Lucien Hibbert, sailed from Port-au-Prince for New York City in order to investigate personally the possibilities of obtaining a loan in New York and later to go to Washington to discuss with me and other officials of the Government of the United States the question of certain proposed modifications to the existing American financial control.

In the meantime the Haitian Minister of Finance, with the assistance of Mr. Sidney de la Rue, the Fiscal Representative, had worked out a tentative plan with Mr. Norman Armour, the American Minister to Haiti, which substituted the National Bank of the Republic of Haiti for the office of the Fiscal Representative. The Bank was to be purchased by the Haitian Government and was to have a Board of Directors of six members, four of whom were to represent the Fiscal Agent and the bondholders.

Although this plan had not reached final form by the time that President Vincent reached Washington on April 16th, our two Governments were in such general agreement as to the basis for this plan that it was possible for us to refer to it in our foregoing joint statement of April 17, 1934. Moreover, at the time when the statement was issued, negotiations for a trade agreement between the two countries were so well advanced that it, too, was included in the statement. Contemplating the departure of the United States Marines late in 1934, I was able to inform President Vincent that I would request authority of the United States Congress to make a gift to the Haitian Government of a large part of the Marine Corps material then in Haiti. (See Vol. III, Item 100.)

In July of 1934 I personally visited Haiti (see Item 127, this volume), and there concluded the final arrangements which led to the withdrawal of the American forces of occupation in August, 1934, over two months prior to the original date set for the withdrawal of the Marines.

The trade agreement between the United States and Haiti was later signed in Washington on March 28, 1935.

Due to certain Haitian domestic considerations, the purchase of the National Bank of the Republic of Haiti could not be consummated in 1934 as planned, but was deferred until 1935. Other considerations have since intervened to delay the conclusion of a new form of financial cooperation based upon the purchase of the Bank.

60 ⟨ Letter to the National Conference of Jews and Christians on Brotherhood Day. April 18, 1934

My dear Dr. Ashworth:

I HAVE just learned of the proposed observance of Brotherhood Day by the National Conference of Jews and Christians and I am deeply interested in its possibilities.

This occasion presents an opportunity for concerted thinking on a vital problem of national welfare; it should help us all in our efforts to rise above ancient and harmful suspicions and prejudices and to work together as citizens of American democracy. Good neighborliness, good citizenship and plain common sense in everyday relationships are potential fruits of such a nationwide observance.

Very sincerely yours,

Dr. Robert A. Ashworth,
New York, N. Y.

NOTE: I have made several speeches and written several letters of greeting to the National Conference of Jews and Christians during my term as President. Because of lack of space not all of them have been included in these volumes. This particular letter was sent on the occasion of Brotherhood Day, sponsored by the Conference.

61 ⟨ Further Efforts to Settle the Railway Wage Controversy. April 20, 1934

Dear Mr. Eastman:

As you know, I have recently conferred with representatives of both the railroad managements and the railroad employees in regard to the wage controversy, and have given this matter further consideration. No one who knows the facts can fail to be moved by the suffering which the depression, in combination with the great increase in competition from other forms of transportation, has inflicted on the employees. The 10 percent deduction from basic wage rates, which the employees voluntarily conceded in 1932 for the good of the industry, has not been the major cause of this suffering. Furloughs, part-time employment, demotions, and pay below a reasonable minimum have been more important factors. Wage rates tell only a part of the story; the whole story is told by what a man has in his pay envelope at the end of the week or month.

Realizing this suffering as I do, I have felt that the welfare of the employees, and particularly the welfare of those at the bottom of the heap, is the vital thing to have in mind in this wage controversy. . . . I cannot avoid the conclusion that during the remainder of this year, it is very important that increased earnings should be used in the rehabilitation of the properties and in providing such added and improved service as the increased traffic may demand. This will not only decrease part-time employment but it will add materially to the total number of men employed. An increase in wages will help men now at work, but it will be of considerably less advantage to the employees as a whole, and it will also operate to defer the rehabilitation of the properties and the provision of good service which are essential to the good health of the railroad industry. The employees are part of the railroad industry and are tied to its future. . . .

After careful consideration of existing conditions, therefore, I am fully persuaded that the position which I took in my letters of February 14th and March 20th, addressed jointly to the railroad managements and the labor executives, was sound, and that an extension of the present wage status for at least six months is what the welfare of the railroads, of their employees, and of the entire country demands as the immediate and temporary disposition of this matter. This includes, of course, the recommendation in my letter of March 20th that the minimum wages of railroad employees should be brought into conformity with the standards followed by the National Recovery Administration.

I shall be glad, therefore, if you will undertake to effect a settlement between the employees and the managements along these lines. In that connection, however, I desire to emphasize three things:

(1) Everything practicable should be done to see to it that increased earnings of the carriers during the period of the extension are used to help the more unfortunate employees who have suffered from unreasonably low minimum pay, furloughs, part time, and demotions. . . .

(2) Provision should be made, so far as practicable, to avoid the renewal of the controversy next August or at any other time during the period of the extension. . . .

(3) Negotiations should be brought to an end, one way or the other, without delay, so that if a present settlement should prove impossible, which I sincerely trust will not be the case, there will be opportunity for a thorough investigation by a fact-finding commission prior to July 1st. . . . Such a commission would, I presume, examine into the merits of the wage rates of the different classes of employees, a subject which I have not considered. I have

considered only the wise disposition of the immediate issue for a temporary period.

Very sincerely yours,

Honorable Joseph B. Eastman,
Federal Coordinator of Transportation,
Washington, D. C.

NOTE: The foregoing letter was a continuation of the efforts of the Administration to settle the long-pending railroad wage dispute, which had begun on June 15, 1933, and which was not finally settled until April 26, 1934 (see Items 26, 45 and 66 of this volume).

62 ⟪ Presidential Statement on the Merits of the Bankhead Bill to Aid the Cotton-Growing Industry. April 21, 1934

I AM advised that the overwhelming majority of the South's cotton producers desire the enactment of legislation now embodied in the Bankhead Bill. It aims to prevent that very small minority which has refused to cooperate with their neighbors and the Government from impairing the effectiveness of the current cotton program which now includes 92 percent of the cotton acreage.

There is nothing new in the sentiment which has resulted in the passage of the Bankhead Bill. During the days of the Confederacy methods to adjust cotton production were advocated. Again in 1905, 1915, 1921 and 1927, widespread sentiment was developed for some plan that would prevent the recurring accumulation of cotton surpluses from dragging prices to starvation levels.

The Cotton States have found it impossible to act independently or in unison to achieve this end. They have asked for the use of Federal powers. A democratic government has consented. The sponsors of the Bankhead Bill say it will not supplant but will supplement and make even more effective the present adjustment program. It is the purpose to make certain that the splendid progress already made is consolidated into enduring benefits. The objective of the Bill is to place the cotton-growing industry on a sound financial and economic basis. I hope our progress already made toward this objective will be facilitated by this legislation.

NOTE: The Bankhead Act (Pub. No. 169, 73d Congress; 48 Stat. 598) resulted from a desire of a majority of cotton farmers to safeguard the voluntary A.A.A. program by some method of compulsory control over non-cooperators. Its effective period was to be one crop year, namely, June 1, 1934, to May 31, 1935, unless the President should find that it was necessary to meet the emergency in cotton production and marketing for another year and that two-thirds of the cotton producers favored continuing the provisions of the Act.

The Act set a national maximum quota of cotton for the 1934-35 season of 10,000,000 bales of 500 pounds of lint cotton each (equivalent to 10,460,251 bales of 478 pounds). It levied a tax which was fixed at 5.67 cents per pound of lint on all cotton produced in excess of that maximum.

The national quota was divided among the cotton-producing States on the basis of their production during the period 1928-1932. The State quotas were then allocated among counties on the same basis; and the county allocations were divided among individual farms by the same formula.

The Act was administered in the same decentralized fashion as the voluntary program of crop reduction by farmers under A.A.A. (see Vol. II, Items 20 and 54). In each State, a State allotment board of at least three members was appointed by the State Director of Cooperative Extension Service with the approval of the A.A.A. Within the counties the Act was administered by the cotton-production control associations organized under the program of A.A.A.

Each farmer received a tax exemption certificate for his quota, which entitled him to have his quota ginned without tax. In order to avoid the inequitable results which might have resulted from dividing the national quota strictly upon the basis of the five-year period of production, there was reserved for farmers without such a representative base period not more than 10 percent of the allotment for each State. This 10 percent was distributed among farmers, for example, who had not planned cotton previously; or who, because of uncontrollable natural causes, had subnormal production during the base period; or who for the preceding three years had voluntarily reduced their acreage beyond the reduction made by other farmers; or who for the preceding three years had planted less than one-third of their cultivated land to cotton.

Tax exemption certificates could

be sold by one farmer who did not raise his full allotment to another farmer who had raised more than his allotment. The sale of these certificates provided income to farmers who had suffered a partial failure of crop; and in this way provided an effective form of crop insurance. On the other hand, the price of certificates was not high enough to make them a profitable commodity so as to influence producers to plan to sell certificates rather than cotton.

By the terms of the original Act, when the crop year 1934-35 was over, the compulsory control features could be renewed only if the President found that the economic emergency with respect to cotton production and marketing continued and if two-thirds of the cotton producers were in favor of such renewal. A referendum was held by secret ballot at more than 8,000 polling places to determine farmer sentiment. About 90 percent of the votes cast were in favor of continuation for another year.

By Proclamation No. 2118, February 28, 1935, I declared that the emergency continued and that the provisions of the Act would, therefore, remain in force for another year.

The quota for the following year, 1935-36, was fixed by the Secretary at 10,500,000 bales of 500 pounds each, the equivalent of which was 10,983,264 bales of 478 pounds. The tax was fixed at 6 cents per pound on June 12, 1935, but was later changed to 5.45 cents per pound.

After the decision of the Supreme Court of the United States, January 6, 1936, in *United States v. Butler*, 297 U.S. 1, declaring the production control features of A.A.A. unconstitutional, I recommended, in a Message to the Congress dated February 3, 1936, the repeal of the Bankhead Act because of the invalidity of the voluntary A.A.A. program to which it was supplementary.

The Bankhead Act was only one of several contemporary measures taken to improve the condition of the cotton farmers specially. The voluntary crop-reduction agreements and benefit payments under A.A.A., and the Government cotton loans were all directed toward the same general objectives. The success of the program, as a whole, may be illustrated by the following tabulation:

Years	Total production of American cotton	World carryover of American cotton at beginning of season	Farm price of cotton lint per pound	Cash income from cotton (including benefit payments)
	(*Bales*)	(*Bales*)	(*Cents*)	(*Dollars*)
1932	13,003,000	13,263,000	6.5	464,000,000
1933	13,049,000	11,809,000	10.2	862,000,000
1934	9,636,000	10,701,000	12.4	822,000,000
1935	10,638,000	9,041,000	11.1	861,000,000
1936	12,399,000	6,962,000	12.3*	915,000,000*

* Preliminary

63 (Letter to the National League of Women Voters. April 23, 1934

I WISH to extend my cordial greetings to the Eleventh National Convention of the National League of Women Voters. The splendid work of your organization in promoting the ideals of intelligent citizenship and study of national affairs has helped in no small degree not only to further the successful participation of women in public life, but also to extend knowledge of national, State, and local problems throughout the community.

This type of educational work is of vital importance in our national life, and is more needed today than ever before when the solution of new and baffling problems challenges the cooperation of all our people.

It gives me great satisfaction to send to your members assembled in Boston my appreciation for their contributions to enlightened citizenship and my sincere good wishes for the success not only of their present deliberations but of their continued efforts in behalf of the public welfare.

May I take this occasion to say how much I appreciate the fine work of your President, Miss Belle Sherwin, in the interests of humanity, and to compliment you in having had her understanding and intelligent leadership for so many years?

Very sincerely,

National League of Women Voters,
Boston, Mass.

64 ❨ Extemporaneous Speech at the Subsistence Homes Exhibition. April 24, 1934

Ladies and gentlemen:

THE particular subject that we are here to talk about and to visualize happens to be one of my own pet children. It goes back in my own life a great many years. I think it goes back, so far as I am concerned, to a privilege that I once had. It was the privilege of running for Vice President and being defeated.

It is a privilege for this reason: During three months in the year 1920 I think I spent eighty-nine out of ninety-two days on a sleeping car. I went to forty-two States in the Union. I drove literally thousands of miles by automobile and I got to know the country as only a candidate for national office or a traveling salesman can get to know it.

In that trip, the one great impression I got of our country was that it had grown up like Topsy without any particular planning. People over a period of three hundred years had been wandering around from one section to another, opening up new territory, starting new industries, haphazardly.

And because the country was so vast, during nearly all of those three hundred years nobody seemed to suffer very much because there were plenty of new opportunities in the way of new land and new industries available for generation after generation of our forebears. But as I went over the country I became impressed with the fact that in these latter days we had come, to a certain extent, to the end of that limitless opportunity of new places to go to and new sources of wealth to tap, of new industries to start almost anywhere, and new land to take up. I realized that the

193

time was ripe, even overripe, for the beginning of planning —
planning to prevent in the future the errors of the past, and planning to meet in the future certain perfectly obvious economic
and social needs that were new to the Nation.

Then, later on, eight years later, I had the opportunity to do
something about it in the most populous State of the Union — a
State which we think of sometimes as the site of the largest city
in the country, but which at the same time ranks about fifth
among all the forty-eight States in its agricultural wealth. We
found in the State of New York also that there was no planning;
and we began to visualize the fact that every acre of the thirty
million acres within its borders was fit for something, that every
acre ought to be used for some definite purpose and that it ought
not to be used for a wrong purpose.

So, after somewhat of a tussle with a Legislature that did not
understand what it was all about, after two years, we persuaded
the Legislature to initiate a survey of every one of the thirty
million acres in the State. As a result of that survey, which is still
in progress and will take another four or five years to complete,
we shall know in at least one State of the Union what every acre
in that State is most suited for.

At the same time, in making this survey, it was just as easy to
make it a survey of human and social needs as it was to make it a
survey of merely soil and trees and streams.

And we found, as you will find in every State of the Union,
little pockets of humanity, where the people came from good,
sound stock, but had never had the opportunity of making good,
the opportunity that their brothers and sisters in other communities more on the highways of commerce had had and were
using to the utmost.

And then we came to another class of people, people in communities that were on the highways of traffic and of commerce,
but who had, for one reason or another, become stranded. They
were in communities that had been prosperous a generation ago
because of some specialty, because of some factory or industry
which had either gone out of business or had been put out of the

running through increased competition. There were hundreds and thousands of families in these stranded communities that had no opportunity again of living the right kind of modern, American life.

Now, that is just the story of one State, and there are forty-eight of them. While we, as good Democrats, believe in the development of things by States, nevertheless it is sometimes a very good thing to have some father and mother for all the forty-eight States who will be able to tie in various suggestions, find the facts and lead in the development that is so necessary in our social and economic progress. That is why I am so very glad to see a number of the ladies and gentlemen from the Hill, as we call it here, because I am very certain that they appreciate that these great problems go beyond State lines and that national planning must be carried out.

I was told a few minutes ago that Henry Ford was asked what he thought of this great movement for what we call subsistence homesteads, and he said, "I am cocksure this thing is right because I myself have found it so difficult to do." And that is perfectly true. We are starting something absolutely new, something in which we have very little experience to fall back on, something that has to be developed through what I call evolution. When people talk to you about the word "revolution" in this country, you tell them that they have one letter too many in that word.

I say it is evolution because of this simple fact: I live in two States, in the country in New York and the country in Georgia. You cannot possibly make a plan and seek to attain big objectives for the State of New York that would apply in Georgia, or vice versa. There are all kinds of planning, not just forty-eight plans, but probably a hundred of them, all of which should be tried out, some of which will succeed and others of which will fail.

By this system of trial and error we shall evolve in this country, without any question, a half dozen or a dozen methods of taking care of our stranded, underprivileged families and of giving them a chance to make good in a new environment. We shall be able

195

undoubtedly, by using a little gray matter — brain trust or otherwise — to discover a whole lot of new things that communities can do. Dr. Morgan, the Chairman of the Tennessee Valley Authority, was talking to me this morning, and he said, "Let me give you an example. This does not apply to the Tennessee Valley Authority any more than it does to a great many other parts of the country over which we have no jurisdiction. There are certain sections in that Tennessee Valley where we can grow sweet potatoes which would be the finest in the world. But there is a limit to the sweet potatoes that people can eat. You cannot eat them three meals a day every day in the year and continue to be healthy, so there is a limit to the amount that can be produced for that purpose. But we are seeking things to make that we can sell; we are seeking a greater business; we are seeking things that will bring in cash.

"Somebody, the other day, put his mind to work on this subject and discovered that laundry starch, made out of the sweet potato, is the best starch in the world; and in spite of that, we are actually importing today the major part of our laundry starch from other countries."

Now, I am very much in favor of increasing both our exports and our imports; but if we can develop a laundry starch business through the use of sweet potatoes and in that way help those people and a great many others throughout the country where sweet potatoes are grown, it will be well worth while to make our own laundry starch instead of importing it from the outside.

We have been talking about a tremendous development of our forests; and we are going to buy — we are in the process of buying — twenty-five million dollars' worth of forest areas to add to this great Government domain in national parks and forests. What are we going to do with it? There are a great many people who live on this land that the Government is going to buy. Are we just going to move them out and add to the congestion in other communities? Not at all.

Forestry is not merely the acquisition of land that has trees on it and the maintenance of that land in a state of nature for a thousand years to come. The land ought to be used. The trees ought to be used. Certain areas, of course, should be applied to public recreational purposes, but other areas having tree crops should be used just as much as land having crops of corn or wheat. A tree crop takes longer to grow, but that is the only difference.

There are other countries in the world that have scientific forestry in actual operation—countries whose civilizations go back three thousand instead of three hundred years. Every year they know that they have a perfectly definite yield of timber, an annual crop. Well, what do they do in their forest areas? In a great many of those forest areas in Europe, populations are maintained who use the bottom land for the growing of their food supplies and who are guaranteed a certain number of months of work in those forests by the State which owns the forest. Now, that is not driving people out of the forests; it is keeping people in the forests in an orderly way with an assurance of making an honest livelihood and of having the opportunities of modern civilization.

I have said that this was evolutionary and experimental; and I hope you people from the Congress who are here will realize that in these many, many experiments that we are going to try, in several hundred of them all over the United States, some are going to work—most of them, we hope—but some are not going to work because we have to learn which is the right way and which is the wrong way as we go along. But, taking it by and large, it is going to be an experiment which is going to be far less costly to the taxpayer of the United States from the dollars-and-cents point of view over a period of years than merely handing out money for relief purposes.

If, for example, we have in a city a family that is unemployed, that requires relief in one form or another, for rent, for food and for clothes—say a bare minimum of five or six hundred dollars a year—and that family does not stand any chance of getting employment in the next five years or ten years, is it not much cheaper for us to pay twelve hundred dollars or fifteen hundred dollars

197

and make that family self-sustaining somewhere at the cost of two years of relief money? In other words, in one case you are furnishing a permanent solution for that family's problem and in another case you are just carrying out the obligations of the Government year after year to see to it that the family does not starve.

I do not see why there is not greater enthusiasm for planning, except perhaps for this reason: that the word planning does not signify anything very spectacular about it and it takes a good many years to see results from it. We are all very apt in this life to go after the things that we can throw up our hats and cheer about. We are very apt to favor the panaceas, suggested legislation which would cure all of our troubles in thirty days. We do not like to think ahead. And yet, that is the only solution!

Now, lest some of our friends cry "regimentation," let me make it perfectly clear that we are not going to take people by force, against their will, out of one occupation and put them in another, or take them out of one community and transplant them to another. We believe we can make this whole program so attractive and practical that we are going to find a great many more volunteers than we can possibly take care of.

Just a year and a month ago we started an experiment called the Civilian Conservation Corps; and there were a lot of Doubting Thomases. They said, "These boys from the cities do not want to go to camp. They do not want to go and live in tents. They never saw an ax. They don't know anything about woods. What is more, they don't care anything about it. Three hundred thousand boys, why, it is absurd! You cannot get them to go, and if you do, they will run away the first night they are in camp." I said, "All right, let us try it." So we tried it. Well, what is the answer? Today, if we had the money in this country and if Congress would appropriate it, we would get a million boys to respond tomorrow to go to the Civilian Conservation Camps.

There is only one objection I have to this whole program, and that is the name, "subsistence." A great many years ago, during the War, I was in England and Lloyd George was asking me how this country was getting on, and I said, "We are learning the meaning of the word 'cooperation,'" and he said, "Mr. Secretary, I wish that in addition to learning the meaning of that word, I wish you inventive Americans would invent a new word for 'co-operation.'" In the same way, I wish we could invent a new term to take the place of "subsistence." This work we are doing is not a matter of mere subsistence. Subsistence is just the fact of being alive and we want something more for these families than that. And so I am going to put it up to you good people; and if you have any ideas or any thoughts of new language to take the place of the words "subsistence farm" or "subsistence homestead," I am quite certain that the Secretary of the Interior or the Secretary of Agriculture or the Administrator of Emergency Relief would be delighted to offer a prize for the winning name.

"Subsistence" does not connote the thought that any of us have in mind. It is not a question of keeping people from starvation. It is a matter that affects education, social contacts, a chance to live. It is the thing that we have called "the more abundant life," and even if it costs a little more money to see that these communities have American facilities in them, this Government is rich enough to provide the additional funds.

I had not meant to speak for more than three minutes, but this is, as I said before, one of my pet children. I hope very much that you will act not merely as personally interested parties, but that you, who are gathered here today, will go to every section of the United States, every State, every Congressional district, and explain what this is all about. The great advantage of this plan from the political point of view is the fact that it affects every Congressional district, the rural Congressional districts and the city Congressional districts. If we look at this from the broad national point of view, I believe we are going to make it a practical national policy of our Government that will take fifty years to complete.

And so, my friends, I am going around now to look at some of the exhibits. I am already familiar with most of them. Everything that is done along these lines not only has my official interest, but my very deep personal interest as well; and I hope you will keep me in touch with the actual progress of the work we are undertaking.

(With respect to subsistence homesteads see Chapter XIX, Vol. I and Item 100, Vol. II.)

65 ❪ A Letter to the United Parents Associations. April 25, 1934

My dear Mr. Simon:

PARENTS and parents' associations occupy a unique position in the evolution and stabilization of our democratic form of government, and in the economic and social development of our country.

The school has been called upon to assume many of the responsibilities which were formerly undertaken by the home. It cannot supplant the home in understanding and bringing out the best in the individual child. It is therefore, as I see it, through these group conferences and meetings of parents that parents may discuss how to preserve the essentials of the home, clarify its functions, and adapt them to changing conditions.

The parents of our children are the guardians of our future citizens. They cannot evade the responsibility which is theirs through example and intelligent understanding to inspire and lay the ground work for that type of character which does what is right under any given circumstance, and is able to withstand temptation.

Parents as citizens might well set up standards for themselves as well as for their children. No group of parents can set itself up as immune from the problems of home and society which confront others. The soundness of our governmental institutions and of our economic system depends largely upon the standards which the majority of our citizens set up, and their desire to achieve them even at the cost of personal sacrifice.

I see great hope for the future in the formation, encouragement and support of parents' associations throughout the land.

Very sincerely yours,

Mr. Robert E. Simon,

Education Chairman of United Parents Associations,

New York City

(This letter was read at the Thirteenth Annual Dinner of the Association on April 30, 1934.)

66 ⟨ The Railway Wage Dispute Is Finally Settled. April 26, 1934

I AM very glad that the railroads and their employees have been able to settle their wage dispute by mutual agreement. The country should be, and will be, grateful to them for this disposition of what might have developed into a troublesome controversy. I congratulate both sides on the wisdom and restraint which they have exhibited. They have set a good example.

NOTE: This agreement marked the end of the railroad wage dispute which began on June 15, 1933 (see Items 26, 45 and 61 of this volume).

The agreement finally entered into reduced the prevailing 10 percent wage deduction to 7½ percent from August 1, 1934, to December 31, 1934, then to 5 percent up to March 31, 1935, and provided for a final cancellation of the entire deduction thereafter. The agreement also provided that the managers would recommend that further wage questions be inaugurated and conducted pursuant to the Railway Labor Act.

67 ❡ Presidential Statement Endorsing the Wheeler-Howard Bill to Aid the Indians.
April 28, 1934

Dear Mr. Chairman:

THE Wheeler-Howard Bill embodies the basic and broad principles of the Administration for a new standard of dealing between the Federal Government and its Indian wards.

It is, in the main, a measure of justice that is long overdue.

We can and should, without further delay, extend to the Indian the fundamental rights of political liberty and local self-government and the opportunities of education and economic assistance that they require in order to attain a wholesome American life. This is but the obligation of honor of a powerful Nation toward a people living among us and dependent upon our protection.

Certainly the continuance of autocratic rule, by a Federal Department, over the lives of more than two hundred thousand citizens of this Nation is incompatible with American ideals of liberty. It also is destructive of the character and self-respect of a great race.

The continued application of the allotment laws, under which Indian wards have lost more than two-thirds of their reservation lands, while the costs of Federal administration of these lands have steadily mounted, must be terminated.

Indians throughout the country have been stirred to a new hope. They say they stand at the end of the old trail. Certainly, the figures of impoverishment and disease point to their impending extinction, as a race, unless basic changes in their conditions of life are effected.

I do not think such changes can be devised and carried out without the active cooperation of the Indians themselves.

The Wheeler-Howard Bill offers the basis for such cooperation. It allows the Indian people to take an active and responsible part in the solution of their own problems.

Endorsement of the Wheeler-Howard Bill

I hope the principles enunciated by the Wheeler-Howard Bill will be approved by the present session of the Congress.

Sincerely yours,

Hon. Burton K. Wheeler,
Chairman, Senate Committee on Indian Affairs,
Hon. Edgar Howard,
Chairman, House Committee on Indian Affairs,
Washington, D. C.

NOTE: In its early history, the United States recognized various Indian tribes as quasi-sovereign Nations in making land treaties with them. As our frontier moved westward, treaties were continuously made with the respective tribes for the cession of their lands to the United States. The first treaty with Indians was with the Delawares, September 2, 1778. The practice soon developed that when a cession of claimed territory was made to the United States, a certain area in exchange would be set aside and reserved exclusively for Indian use. This was the beginning of the reservation system.

By 1840, the Indians had surrendered practically all the territory east of the Mississippi. Historically the procedure of Indian land liquidation was practically always the same: a cession would be made and a reservation set aside; almost immediately thereafter the reservations would begin to be progressively diminished and many of them completely extinguished. The tribes were reduced to a condition where they were constantly on the move from one home to another, and always in a westward direction.

The armed conflicts between Indians and white men after the Civil War show the precarious economic position into which the Indians had finally been forced. When the last great herds of buffalo were wiped out altogether, the chief means of livelihood for the Plains tribes was gone, and the Government was driven to the necessity of actually rationing the Indians, a practice which of course had a permanently deteriorating effect upon the Indian character. By 1871 the Congress felt that the Indians were so impotent that it enacted a statute providing that no further treaties would be negotiated with any tribe as an independent Nation; and thereafter the Indians were dealt with simply by administrative action or by act of the Congress. However, except for the extraordinary emergency of the period when the Plains Indians were facing starvation, due to the extinction of the buffalo herds, the Federal Government has not undertaken actually to support ablebodied members of the Indian racial group or their dependents. The gen-

203

eral impression to the contrary is wholly erroneous.

After the Congress had determined that no further treaties would be negotiated, the number of reservations naturally increased. Until March 4, 1933, the foundation of Indian law and policy had been the General Allotment Act of 1887. This statute provided in effect that every Indian would be given a piece of his reservation for himself individually in fee simple, with all the property rights and responsibilities of a white man with respect to that parcel. In order not to make the transition to private ownership and responsibility too abrupt, it was provided that for twenty-five years the Indian would own his land only in trust, with the Government as guardian. During this period of time he did not have to pay taxes; but he could not sell his land without the Government's consent. After the expiration of the twenty-five years, he received a fee patent and his ownership became as complete and unlimited as any white man's.

Between the date of the General Allotment Act and the date of the beginning of my Administration, the amount of land owned by Indians had shrunk from 136,000,000 to less than 50,000,000 acres.

The principal methods by which the Indians were thus separated from approximately 86,000,000 acres of land in forty-seven years were as follows:

1. The practice was followed whereby after each individual obtained his allotment the remaining land would be ceded away at so much per acre. At least 38,000,000 acres of land were disposed of in this way.

2. The practice had grown up to throw open surplus land left over, after allotments were completed, to settlement by white people. At least 22,000,000 acres of land were thus lost.

3. Removal of sale restrictions at the end of the twenty-five-year trust period encouraged Indians improvidently to dispose of their land. Twenty-three million acres of land were thus lost.

4. The Act of March 7, 1902, permitted the Secretary of the Interior to authorize heirs to sell their lands instead of partitioning them physically; and another Act of March 1, 1907, permitted the Secretary to authorize the original allottees to dispose of their lands. Under these two statutes a total of 3,370,000 acres of the best Indian land was alienated.

Furthermore, the development of a system whereby Indians would lease their allotted lands to white people for farming or grazing diverted huge acreages to white use rather than Indian use. Inadequate capital and lack of agricultural education of the Indians totally handicapped them from using effectively the lands which they owned, and encouraged them to lease the lands away.

Of these 50,000,000 acres of land

which were left to the Indians, 20,-000,000 were sterile desert or semi-desert lands, and 7,000,000 were tied up in an heirship status so complicated that little direct use could be made of the land by heirs. Approximately 100,000 Indians were completely landless.

Another result of the allotment system was the gradual loss of Indian forests and grazing ranges. Each individual found it necessary to sell timber as rapidly as possible and overburden grazing lands with more stock than they could support. Early emphasis upon larger projects with respect to irrigation development created an agricultural economy to which the Indian was not fitted either by heritage or inclination. The result was that most of the irrigated lands in Indian ownership had to be leased.

In addition to lack of material security, the tribal life of the Indian was rapidly disintegrating. Native religions, native languages, native ways of life were being discouraged. The backbone of the education of Indian children was the boarding school which largely imitated the white grammar school and high school curriculum, without embodying any Indian traditional experience or local environmental factors. Education was pointed chiefly toward technological employment and white-collar jobs — chiefly in the city. The Indian Service itself, as the result of Government policy and of civil service limitations, was run almost entirely by whites rather than by Indians.

To deal with the many problems which the Indian presented in addition to the normal general depression problems, my Administration began very early the construction of an Indian program seeking to salvage both Indian property and Indian morale. Just as our farm program was evolved in conference with farm groups and farm leaders, our Indian program was begun in conference with the Indians themselves. This was the first time in the history of the Government treatment of Indians since the discontinuance of treaties that the Indians themselves were ever really consulted about Indian policy. A series of nine regional conferences were held throughout the various States where the Indian population was greatest.

From this expression of Indian opinion was evolved the program which was originally written into the Wheeler-Howard Bill.

The foregoing message by me indicates the objectives and goal toward which the Administration was aiming in this new policy toward the Indian.

Although many amendments were inserted in it, the bill was eventually enacted into law and approved June 18, 1934 (Public No. 383, 73d Congress; 48 Stat. 984). It is known as the Indian Reorganization Act.

The statute seeks to protect the

remaining lands of the Indians, both individually and tribally. It prohibits the further allotment of any land of any reservation created or set apart by treaty, agreement, purchase or otherwise. Instead, title is to remain in the United States in trust for the tribe, which itself is to assign the land for the use and occupancy of its members who are without land. Existing trust periods upon any Indian lands are automatically extended until otherwise directed by the Congress; this provision removes the necessity for tribes to pay lawyers or lobbying delegations to obtain extensions of trust periods. The statute takes away the power to approve sales of restricted lands to any persons other than members of the tribe or tribal corporation in the territory in which the land is located; and directs that restricted lands must be sold or transferred only to the Indian tribe or tribal corporation from which the land was derived. Similar restrictions are placed upon transfers of shares in the tribal corporation. Section V authorizes the Congress to make an annual appropriation of two million dollars for the purchase of land for landless Indians or for Indians whose holdings are too small or too poor in quality to furnish a decent living. The title to such land is to remain in the United States in trust, and may be added to existing reservations.

Common sense management of Indian forests and grazing lands is prescribed in the Act, with due regard for principles of conservation.

A revolving fund of ten million dollars is set up, for the purpose of lending money to Indians in need of capital for development of their resources. The credit is available to individuals and groups to start and operate not only farms but all kinds of industrial enterprises.

Specific authority is given in the statute to Indian tribes to organize for the promotion of the common welfare of their members and to exercise existing and new powers of self-government. Once erected and approved, such self-government machinery can be altered or changed only by the tribe or by the Congress.

Since the date of this statute over 246,000 acres of land have been purchased for the Indians. One million dollars of the authorized annual appropriation of two million dollars was appropriated for the fiscal year 1936 and another million dollars for the fiscal year 1937.

The lands purchased to date have been in seventeen different States. It is estimated by the National Resources Board that the Indians will ultimately require 9,700,000 acres of land. While the amount purchased to date is small as compared with such total estimated requirements, it is at least a decent beginning.

The Indian Reorganization Act was made applicable to all Indian tribes unless a tribe specifically voted to exclude itself from the Act. Elections were had for this purpose, and 181 reservations with a total of 133,000 Indians voted to adopt the provisions of the Act. By later additions through later Congressional action the total was raised to 242,211 Indians. By July, 1937, 66 reservations had adopted constitutions and by-laws by popular vote, and 33 had taken the final step of adopting charters of incorporation under the Act.

The purposes of the revolving credit fund may be briefly stated as: (1) to establish Indians in self-supporting enterprises by supplying credit to individuals and to cooperatives and tribal groups; (2) to teach sound business methods and principles by providing advisory technical and supervisory assistance. By July 1, 1937, $2,719,000 had been committed and $411,000 actually advanced. The loans have been largely for industrial purposes, and definite plans are required showing how repayments are expected to be made.

Between 1933 and 1937, Indian holdings have increased by about 2,774,000 acres.

Efforts have been exercised by the Extension Division to build up the Indians' livestock industry by encouraging them to use their own range through the use of credit and by developing livestock associations. Indians are also being encouraged and induced to return to farming and sheep breeding. The new activities of the Irrigation Division have been directed into small subsistence projects of from two to ten acres each for community operation. As a result, the Indians' use of their own land is rapidly increasing. Indian forest and range resources are beginning to be managed on a perpetual yield basis, rather than on immediate returns from practices of overgrazing and excessive lumbering which result in acute conditions of soil erosion and depletion of resources. New timbering and grazing regulations have been issued, designed to conserve the natural resources of forest and soil and at the same time to provide a reasonable annual return.

Civilian Conservation Corps work was particularly helpful on Indian reservations in providing wage work where relief was desperately needed; but it was also important in making possible systematic conservation and building up of reservation resources. The regulations of the C.C.C. were modified with respect to Indian participation in the program. The enrollees have been all Indians, and the percentage of Indians in supervisory positions has steadily increased. Varied work projects have been undertaken on seventy-four reservations in twenty-three States. A definite program of soil conservation practices has been begun on Indian lands; and land-use planning has been instituted on several of the reservations.

Early in the Administration a partial survey of the housing and economic conditions of Indians, preparatory to commencing a program of rehabilitation, showed the desperate straits into which they had fallen. Many of them were without land or other means of support and their housing conditions did not meet any reasonable standards of space or sanitation.

The problem of rehabilitation for these people was complicated by the fact that their only hope for survival was in developing an agricultural economy. The Indian Service was allotted funds on January 11, 1936, by me to be used, as stated in my letter of that date: "to finance the rehabilitation of Indians in stricken rural agricultural areas, by means of loans or grants or both; to enable them to construct or repair houses, barns, outbuildings and root cellars; to develop wells and springs for domestic water; to clear and improve lands for gardens and small farms and to purchase land for such purposes when necessary; to make furniture and other handicraft products; and to establish, maintain and operate other small self-help projects." Under this program, total allotments of $1,858,000 have been spent in twenty-three States, resulting in considerable accomplishments along the lines suggested in my letter. The rehabilitation program has been of the utmost importance in restoring lost initiative and morale and in improving conditions of family and community living.

The development of a road program also has improved reservation conditions and has provided employment for Indians in the process.

The policy of education of children has changed. There is being effected a gradual substitution of public or Federal day schools near the homes of the Indian children in place of the old reservation and non-reservation boarding schools. The educational program has been broadened and liberalized, and general vocational education is being emphasized. It is being helped by an increase in library service and by educational loans.

Encouragement has been given to the development of Indian arts and crafts by establishment of the Indian Arts and Crafts Board (49 Stat. 891; Pub. No. 355, 74th Congress), approved August 27, 1935, which is charged with the responsibility of seeking markets for products of Indian handiwork and promoting a more profitable commerce in Indian arts and crafts by instruction and by help in obtaining loans.

Public health work among the Indians, too long inadequately carried on, has now also become a subject of major consideration and activity.

Indian lands now include approximately 82,700 square miles, or more than the combined areas of Kentucky and Tennessee. The Indian population is approximately equal to that of the State of Vermont and is three times the population of Nevada. These Indian lands, and the

Indian population which retains tribal affiliations, are all scattered through twenty-seven States and the Territory of Alaska.

68 ❧ The President Vetoes Postal Substitutes' Bill as Contrary to Efficient Administration of Post Office. April 30, 1934

To the House of Representatives:

I RETURN herewith, without my approval, H. R. 7483 entitled, An Act to Provide Minimum Pay for Postal Substitutes. The bill is contrary to public policy in that it provides compensation to a certain class of employees regardless of the need for their services. It is discriminatory and establishes a precedent which, if followed, would undoubtedly lead to many abuses.

As a result of the depression, the postal business decreased to such an extent that the Department had no need for the services of thousands of its employees. By orderly processes, this surplus is being reduced without injustice to the personnel. During the period of declining business and with a surplus of regular employees, the Post Office Department had little or no need for the services of the substitutes, who are carried on the rolls for replacement purposes and to augment the regular forces in emergencies. However, at this time, the postal revenues are increasing and more work is being provided for the substitutes. Therefore, from a humanitarian standpoint, there appears to be no need for legislation of this character.

Aside from any consideration of conditions in the postal service with respect to its personnel, this appears to be a relief measure for a particular class of our citizens, and as such is clearly discriminatory.

This bill prohibits the Postmaster General from determining the needs of the postal service as to personnel in that it requires the Post Office Department to retain on its rolls all substitutes of record at this time. It fixes definitely the maximum number of substitutes that may be carried in certain groups, regardless of conditions, and is, therefore, not in the interest of good administration of the public business.

There is attached, the Postmaster General's statement which sets forth in detail the objections to this bill.

My disapproval of this measure is not based on the consideration of the additional expenditures it would require but on the deeper consideration of public policy. I trust that the Congress will continue to cooperate with me in our common effort to establish and follow policies that will be best for all of our people.

68A ❧ White House Statement Explaining Foregoing Veto. May 1, 1934

IN DISAPPROVING H. R. 7483 entitled "An Act to Provide Minimum Pay for Postal Substitutes," the President wants it made perfectly clear that the disapproval is based not so much on the consideration of the additional expense involved should the bill become a law as on the broad consideration of public policy and the management of the postal service, the largest of the governmental functions.

Last year postal revenues had fallen off to such an extent and the volume of business transacted had reached such a low ebb, that the Postmaster General found it necessary in the interest of the taxpayers to curtail expenditures in every way possible. The reduced volume so affected the situation that it was obviously in the public interest to reduce deliveries in cities, to curtail some transportation services and to furlough regular employees for the reason that such employees could not be fully occupied. It necessarily followed that the thousands of substitute or emergency employees were not needed for actual duty. Therefore, allowances for the employment of substitutes were drastically curtailed.

However, within the past few weeks, as has been publicly announced by the Postmaster General, the revenues of the postal service have shown a marked increase and the volume of business has improved to such an extent that the Post Office Department has found it proper to restore much of the service that was curtailed, to eliminate the furloughs of regular employees and again to make it possible for such employees to enjoy their annual vacations with pay during the remainder of this fiscal year. The service increases and the restoration of the vacations have resulted in additional expenditures of approximately $6,000,000 over and above what had been previously authorized for the months of April, May and June. Allowances have been granted which will enable postmasters throughout the country to expend in excess of $3,500,000 additional for the employment of substitutes. There is no doubt that substitute employees in all of the larger cities, and indeed, in practically all of the first class offices, will be employed for more than a hundred hours a month as a result of the service restorations. This provides definite relief for this group of employees and there is every indication that their employment, as above indicated, will be continued.

This bill contains so many provisions that would hamper the administration of the postal service in determining its personnel needs, that as a matter of public policy and in the interest of good business management of the postal service of the United States, the President is impelled to disapprove the bill as presented.

69 ⟨ A Mother's Day Proclamation. May 3, 1934

WHEREAS by House Joint Resolution 263, approved and signed by President Wilson on May 8, 1914, the second Sunday in May of each year has been designated as Mother's Day for the expression of our love and reverence for the mothers of our country; and

WHEREAS Senate Resolution 218, adopted April 26, 1934, states that "there are throughout our land today an unprecedentedly large number of mothers and dependent children who, because of unemployment or loss of their bread-earners, are lacking many of the necessities of life," and the President of the

United States is therein authorized and requested to issue a proclamation calling for the observance of Mother's Day this year;

Now, THEREFORE, I, Franklin D. Roosevelt, President of the United States of América, do hereby call upon our citizens to express on Mother's Day, Sunday, May 13, 1934, our love and reverence for motherhood:

(a) By the customary display of the United States flag on all Government buildings, homes, and other suitable places;

(b) By the usual tokens and messages of affection to our mothers; and

(c) By doing all that we can through our churches, fraternal and welfare agencies for the relief and welfare of mothers and children who may be in need of the necessities of life.

NOTE: A similar Proclamation has been issued by me during each year. However, for lack of space, not all of them have been included.

70 ⟨ On the Death of Secretary of the Treasury William H. Woodin. May 3, 1934

THE PRESIDENT learned of Secretary Woodin's death shortly after 8 o'clock on the evening of May 3, 1934. He was at dinner when the news reached him. He announced the death to his dinner guests and said:

"I am very deeply shocked and distressed by the passing of my dear friend."

This statement was immediately given to the press for publication and a short time later the following statement was issued by the President's direction at the White House Executive Offices:

"It is known that both Mrs. Roosevelt and I have felt deep concern for Mr. Woodin's health ever since the days in the spring of 1933 when he declined to take adequate care of an ulcerated throat and insisted upon working day and night during the financial crisis of the Nation and on the many other problems which had to be solved. No man in time of war showed greater devotion or gave greater sacrifice than Secretary Woodin. He made a great place for himself in the hearts of all Americans and especially among those who, knowing him, loved him for himself."

The following personal telegram was sent to Mrs. William H. Woodin:

"It is impossible for us to tell you how deeply grieved we are at the news of Will's death. For several days we have been hoping against hope that he would rally. Eleanor and I want you to know, as you must know, that our hearts are with you in the loss of your dear husband and our dear friend.

"Franklin and Eleanor Roosevelt"

Mrs. William H. Woodin,
2 East 67th Street,
New York City

71 (Address at Memorial to William Jennings Bryan. May 3, 1934

THIS memorial to William Jennings Bryan, erected pursuant to authorization by a joint resolution of the Congress, I gladly accept on behalf of the United States.

Our Nation thus recognizes through its Government the essential qualities and the high services of a great American.

No selfish motive touched his public life; he held important office only as a sacred trust of honor from his country; and when he sought a mandate from his fellow citizens the soul of his inspiration was the furtherance of their interests, not his own, not of a group, but of all. No man of his time was or could have been more constantly in the limelight than he; yet we can look back and scan his record without being able to point to any instance where he took a position that did not accord with his conscience or his belief.

To Secretary Bryan political courage was not a virtue to be

sought or attained, for it was an inherent part of the man. He chose his path not to win acclaim but rather because that path appeared clear to him from his inmost beliefs. He did not have to dare to do what to him seemed right; he could not do otherwise.

It was my privilege to know William Jennings Bryan when I was a very young man. Years later both of us came to the Nation's capital to serve under the leadership of Woodrow Wilson. Through this service and the intimate relations which ensued, I learned to know and to love him.

As we look back on those days—the many of us who are gathered here together who were his friends and associates in the Wilson Administration—I think that we would choose the word "sincerity" as fitting him most of all. It was that sincerity which brought to him the millions of devoted followers; it was that sincerity which served him so well in his life-long fight against sham and privilege and wrong. It was that sincerity which made him a force for good in his own generation and has kept alive many of the ancient faiths on which we are building today.

It was Mr. Bryan who said:

> "I respect the aristrocacy of learning, I deplore the plutocracy of wealth but I thank God for the democracy of the heart."

Many years ago he also said:

> "You may dispute over whether I have fought a good fight; you may dispute over whether I have finished my course; but you cannot deny that I have kept the faith."

We who are assembled here today to accept this memorial in the capital of the Republic can well agree that he fought a good fight; that he finished his course; and that he kept the faith.

72 (A Request for Authority to Return to Canada the Mace Taken in Battle by the United States. May 4, 1934

To the Congress:

DURING the War of 1812 the Mace of the Parliament of Upper Canada, or Ontario, was taken by United States Forces at the time of the battle of York, April 27, 1813. That Mace, which had been the symbol of legislative authority at York (now Toronto) since 1792, has been preserved in the United States Naval Academy at Annapolis.

On July 4, 1934, there is to be unveiled in Toronto a memorial tablet erected by the United States Daughters of 1812 to the memory of General Pike and others of the United States Forces who were killed in action. The Mayor and Council of Toronto are providing the site for the memorial.

The suggestion has been made that it would be a gracious act for the United States to return this historic Mace to Canada at the time of the unveiling of the tablet.

The Mace is a token of representative government, established at York nearly a century and a half ago. It symbolizes the orderly rule of such government in Canada, continuing from that day to this.

Since the agreement of 1817, the two countries have by common accord maintained no hostile armaments on either side of their boundary; and every passing year cements the peace and friendship between the peoples of Canada and the United States.

I heartily recommend to the favorable consideration of the Congress the enactment of a joint resolution authorizing the return of the Mace to the Canadian Government.

NOTE: The foregoing recommendation was adopted by Senate Joint Resolution 121, 73d Congress, on June 16, 1934 (48 Stat. 978).

73 ⟨White House Statement Following a Conference on Silver Policy. May 8, 1934

At a conference between a number of Senators, the Secretary of the Treasury and the President, there was further discussion of two points relating to the further use of silver as a metallic reserve for the United States.

More specifically, the possibility of nationalizing silver in the same manner in which gold has already been nationalized through the purchase of existing free stocks at a limited price was explored.

The meeting also explored the ultimate objective or national policy of having 25 percent of the monetary value of the metallic reserves of the country in the form of silver.

(See Items 89 and 146, this volume.)

74 ⟨Letter to the American Law Institute on the Modernization of the Criminal Law. May 8, 1934

My dear Mr. Lewis:

IT AFFORDS me a great deal of pleasure to send this word of greeting to the members of the American Law Institute upon the occasion of your twelfth annual meeting.

In 1923 you undertook a great public service; namely, the Restatement of the American Common Law. For eleven years you have been engaged upon this important undertaking, and your labors have been fruitful indeed.

With the generous cooperation of one of our leading public Foundations, you have performed and are performing your task in such manner as to merit and to secure public and professional confidence. The success which has attended your efforts has been due in large measure to the fact that you have succeeded in uniting, in the conduct of a great public undertaking in the field of the law, the expert knowledge of the legal scholar and the practical wisdom of the judge and practicing attorney.

The Restatement of the Law has not yet been completed. You have, however, already published the results of your work on Contracts and Agency, and I understand that the completion of other principal subjects of the common law, such as Trusts, Conflict of Laws, Torts and Property, is in sight.

I wish, therefore, to take the liberty of suggesting that, while you continue to carry forward the clarification and simplification of what we lawyers call the private civil law, serious consideration should be given to the question of whether you should not now begin an undertaking of equal importance in the field of the substantive criminal law. There is an urgent need for intelligent, painstaking and patriotic work in this field. There is no organization better fitted for this great task than the American Law Institute.

We all realize, of course, that the problems of our criminal law and its administration cannot be solved by any one agency. Much of the necessary work can be effectively done only by public commissions charged with the duty of making special investigations and recommendations. However, such an organization as yours is peculiarly well fitted for the task of carrying on those intensive and scholarly investigations which educate the public and furnish essential material and suggestions to public commissions and legislative bodies.

I need not point out to you that the adaptation of our criminal law and its administration to meet the needs of a modern, complex civilization is one of our major problems. I believe the American Law Institute is in a position to make important contributions to the solution of this perplexing problem.

Very sincerely yours,

Mr. William Draper Lewis,
Director, The American Law Institute,
Washington, D. C.

75 ❲ Letter to the American Judicature Society. May 9, 1934

My dear Mr. Baker:

I REGRET very much that the press of official business prevents me from accepting your invitation to attend the annual dinner of the American Judicature Society.

I have followed with interest and approbation the efforts of your Society during the past twenty-one years "to promote the efficient administration of justice." The attainment of that object is vital to the welfare of our country. The Preamble to our Constitution names the establishment of justice as one of the objects for which the Constitution was ordained, and it is clear that without an efficient administration of justice the other objects named cannot be attained.

The educational work which has been carried on by the American Judicature Society in its endeavor to make the administration of justice in the American courts more effective and more economical has resulted in improvements in bar organization, court organization, and civil and criminal procedure, and in the development of machinery for the efficient disposition of small claims.

The activities of your Society along these lines have been very timely. During our generation we have had difficulty in adapting our legal and judicial institutions, which were devised to serve the simple needs of a pioneer country, to the complexities which characterize modern social and economic life. The process of transformation and adaptation has been facilitated by the work of the American Judicature Society.

I desire, therefore, to commend the American Judicature Society for its efforts and achievements over a period of more than a score of years, and to extend best wishes for the future success of the Society.

Very sincerely yours,

Hon. Newton D. Baker,
President, The American Judicature Society,
Washington, D. C.

(This letter was read at the concluding session of the Society's Annual Meeting, Washington, D. C., May 9, 1934.)

76 ⟨ Presidential Statement on Signing Statute Aimed to Help the Sugar Industry. May 9, 1934

ON FEBRUARY 8th last, I sent to the Congress a message setting forth certain facts and problems pertaining to the sugar industry. I said then that "the problem is difficult but can be solved if met squarely and if small temporary gains are sacrificed to the ultimate general advantage."

I have today signed H. R. 8861 which I am advised will permit a rapid approach to the solution of the many vexing and difficult problems within the industry. I hope that this Act will contribute to the economic improvement in Hawaii, Puerto Rico, the Virgin Islands, the Philippines, Cuba and among continental sugar producers. These are the objectives outlined in my message to the Congress last February.

Under the terms of the Act, the rate of the processing tax shall not exceed the amount of the reduction on a pound of sugar raw value of the rate of duty in effect on January 1, 1934, as adjusted by our commercial treaty with Cuba.

Acting upon the unanimous recommendations of the United States Tariff Commission, I have today signed a proclamation, under the so-called flexible tariff provisions of the Tariff Act of 1930, reducing the rate of duty on sugar. Using 96 degree Cuban sugar as the unit of measure, this results in a reduction of the duty from 2 cents to 1½ cents a pound on that sugar. The rate of the processing tax must not exceed the amount of the reduction as adjusted to this unit of measure.

This means that the processing or compensatory taxes will not increase, in themselves, the price to be paid by the ultimate consumers and at the same time our own sugar producers will have the opportunity to obtain in the form of benefit payments, a fairer return from their product.

To cooperate with the Secretary of Agriculture in carrying out the provisions of this Act, I have designated an informal committee from the Cabinet. This committee includes the Secretary of Agriculture; the Secretary of the Interior, who is charged with the administration of Hawaii and the Virgin Islands; the Secretary of War, who is charged with the administration of Puerto Rico and the Philippine Islands; and the Secretary of State, who is charged with the conduct of our negotiations with Cuba.

Those engaged in this industry have an opportunity to improve their economic status through operation of this Act. I urge their cooperation in carrying out its provisions.

NOTE: The foregoing statute was enacted pursuant to recommendations made by me to help the sugar industry (see Item 21, this volume). The comprehensive program established under this Act had the following six principal objectives:

1. To assure fair returns to domestic sugar-beet and sugar-cane producers by crop adjustment programs and by benefit payments to be paid from funds derived from a processing tax on sugar.

2. To assure laborers in the sugar-beet and sugar-cane industries a share in the benefits of the program, by making benefit payments conditional upon the elimination of child labor and the payment of fair and equitable wages to field laborers.

3. To stabilize the price of sugar at levels profitable to producers by limiting the marketing of sugar to estimated consumption requirements, and by fixing a quota for each sugar-producing area within the continental United States, its insular possessions, and foreign countries exporting sugar to the United States.

4. To stabilize sugar production in the Philippines, Hawaii, Puerto Rico, and the Virgin Islands at levels in keeping with the consumption requirements of the United States and harmonious with the economic welfare of those insular areas.

5. To arrest the decline in Cu-

ban sugar imports to the United States so as to increase the Cuban market for American exports of other products to Cuba.

6. To enable the Secretary of Agriculture to mediate in disputes between growers and processors, and growers and laborers, with respect to contractual relationships.

The quotas for 1934 for all sugar-producing areas were announced on June 12, 1934. Production adjustment programs also were developed in the sugar-beet and sugar-cane areas of the United States and in the sugar-producing areas in the insular possessions.

The Act authorized the Secretary of Agriculture to purchase surplus beet sugar from proceeds of the sugar-beet processing tax for the relief of the unemployed. The Federal Surplus Relief Corporation, pursuant to this authority, did purchase a great deal of surplus stocks of sugar and used it in processing foods to be distributed among the unemployed.

During the period of approximately eighteen months in which the full sugar program operated under the Jones-Costigan Act, real results were accomplished. The large surplus of sugar was practically entirely eliminated. The income of growers was materially improved with higher prices for sugar-beets and sugar-cane, resulting from marketing stabilization supplemented by benefit payments. Sugar-beet growers, for example, who had received $5.26 per ton in 1932 and $5.13 in 1933, obtained an average return, including benefit payments, of $6.91 per ton in 1934 and $6.90 in 1935. Net returns to processors also increased substantially from the low point of 1933.

The income of field laborers was raised, partly through the increased ability of producers to pay better wages and partly through the establishment of minimum wages by the Secretary. Child labor was practically eliminated in the continental United States as a factor in sugar-cane and sugar-beet production.

In the interests of consumers, the price of sugar was stabilized at levels comparable to prices prior to the depression.

The Cuban income from sugar sales in the United States increased by 125 percent from 1933 to 1935 inclusive. This fact, together with the reduction of Cuban duties on American imports under the reciprocal trade agreement, resulted in an expanded Cuban market for American agricultural and industrial products. In fact, United States exports to Cuba increased 140 percent from 1933 to 1935 inclusive.

The decision of the Supreme Court of the United States in the case of the *United States* vs. *Butler*, 297 U. S. 1, on January 6, 1936 (see Introduction to Vol. IV), invalidating the processing tax and production-control features of A.A.A., brought to an end the sugar program except for the quota provisions. To remove any doubt about the quota provisions, the Congress enacted a statute approved June 19, 1936, reaffirming the quota powers previously granted to the Secretary. (Pub. Res. 109; 49 Stat. 1539.)

Unfortunately, experience since the decision of the Supreme Court has shown that sugar price protection, based only upon a quota system, falls far short of the achievements of the more complete program as it existed under the Jones-Costigan Act. Betterment of laboring conditions became impossible with the removal of the production-adjustment powers; the consumer has not benefited materially in price by the removal of the processing tax; considerable revenue has been lost; and the processor is receiving substantially the same price for sugar without having to advance the amount of the processing tax.

77 (A Typical Veto of a Private Bill. May 9, 1934

To the House of Representatives:

I RETURN herewith, without approval, House Bill No. 507, entitled "An Act for the relief of John Thomas Simpkin."

The bill provides that Simpkin shall hereafter be held and considered to have received a full, honorable discharge from the Naval service of the United States on February 14, 1921, the purpose being to give him, as to the future, the rights, privileges and benefits conferred by any law upon honorably discharged soldiers.

The records of the Navy Department show that this man was enrolled in the Naval Reserve for a period of four years on May 10, 1918, and served until November 26, 1919, when he was transferred to the regular Navy. On March 15, 1920, he was tried and convicted by general court-martial of "absence from station and duty after leave had expired" and was sentenced to six months' confinement and to be dishonorably discharged from the Naval service. The period of confinement was mitigated to restriction to ship and station, and the dishonorable discharge was remitted on condition that he maintain a conduct satisfactory to his commanding officer for a period of six months. On September 28, 1920, Simpkin was again tried and convicted by general court-martial for a similar offense and in accordance with the sentence of the court was dishonorably discharged from the Naval service on February 14, 1921.

Simply because the man, nearly five years after his dishonorable discharge, developed mental incompetency which caused his commitment to a State hospital for the insane for a period of some seventeen months, it is now proposed that he be viewed as having been mentally incompetent at the time of the committing of the offense which caused his dishonorable discharge. It is solely on this presumptive ground that this bill proposes now to change the character of his service from dishonorable to honorable. To this I cannot agree.

Where a man violates the obligations of his enlistment and thereby debars himself from the rights belonging to those who faithfully and honorably served their country according to the terms of their enlistment, I feel that something more definite than the presumption of mental incompetency shown in this case is demanded to support a change in the record.

77A ❨ Another Typical Veto of a Private Bill. ❨
May 9, 1934

To the House of Representatives:

I RETURN herewith, without my approval, House Bill No. 1870 entitled "An Act for the relief of Corinne Blackburn Gale."

This bill authorizes and directs the Secretary of the Treasury to pay to Corinne Blackburn Gale, widow of William Holt Gale, late American Foreign Service officer, retired, the sum of $8,000, being one year's salary of her deceased husband at the rate of pay received by him at the time of his retirement in 1929.

This bill is objectionable because it provides for the payment of a gratuity to the widow of a retired Foreign Service officer who, after his retirement and until his death in April, 1932, received retirement pay at the rate of $3,596.77 yearly from the Government. While Congress has in some instances authorized payment to the widow of a Foreign Service officer who died while in active service of one year's salary of her deceased husband, no payment of this kind has been authorized to the widow of a Foreign Service officer who died after being retired, and I deem it inadvisable to establish a precedent of approving payments of this character.

NOTE: The foregoing two items are typical vetoes of private bills. The number of vetoes by me has been far in excess of other Presidents in recent years. I have had prepared the following table of comparative percentages of vetoes of my three predecessors and myself:

	approved	vetoed	percentage vetoed
HARDING	930	5	.0053+
COOLIDGE	4137	55	.0131+
HOOVER	2364	37	.0154+
ROOSEVELT (First Term)	3122	227	.0677+

78 ❬ Informal Remarks on Reception of Fund Raised by Birthday Ball in Behalf of Crippled Children. May 9, 1934

THE Birthday Ball initiated by your committee for the creation of a fund to further the infantile paralysis work of the Georgia Warm Springs Foundation gave me a most happy anniversary last January. I continue to get much genuine satisfaction from this generous action and the wonderful response which was given to your suggestion. In accepting this million-dollar check, I want again to express my heartfelt appreciation to all who participated.

The trustees of the Foundation naturally have given much thought to the proper discharge of the responsibility which you impose on them through this presentation. They have reviewed the work of the Foundation and considered with me the ways and means by which it can be most useful in the future through the added impetus of the fund which you now make available. The plan for utilizing your gift, which I shall outline to you, is based on a realization of the scope of the problem created by a disease which alone accounts for one-third of those people, children and adults, in our country who are crippled from any cause other than injury in accidents.

There are no complete statistics to show just what infantile paralysis has done to our people, but it seems conservative to estimate from figures that we have, that there are at least two hundred thousand people in the United States who bear the marks of it in degrees ranging from impairment of a few muscles to total physical helplessness. A large proportion of this great number, to which new victims are added annually, need after-treatment and care for long periods of time. Treatment cannot be measured in terms of days and weeks but must be computed in months and years. To take care of this number on a hospital basis would require very large sums of money to be expended through many institutions.

This care following the acute stage of the disease and after the damage has been done falls within a highly specialized branch of medicine — namely, orthopedics — which requires painstaking, accurate work. It is time-consuming effort to such a degree as to make it economically unwise and practically impossible to concentrate really large numbers of infantile paralysis patients in any one place. It is of course clear that no one orthopedic institution can make a dent in the national problem. Only by co-ordinating the efforts of all these institutions can we hope for real progress toward doing the utmost for the many thousands of victims of infantile paralysis.

Let me pause here to say that the communications which have come to us from all parts of the country since the Birthday Ball have made it more than ever apparent that there is a shortage of properly financed orthopedic beds in many, indeed most, sections of the country. They have also indicated to us that as a result of the new interest built up by your suggestion of a Birthday Ball, at least some of these institutions have received greater local assistance. This work is worthy of enthusiastic and sustained local support.

Modern medical science has advanced so far that a very large proportion of those who for one reason or another have become crippled can be restored to useful citizenship. It remains, therefore, only to spread the gospel in every part of the Nation to enable us to make the same relative progress that we have already made in the field of tuberculosis.

Where does the Georgia Warm Springs Foundation fit into this whole fight against infantile paralysis? Seven years ago we started at Warm Springs, Georgia, an institution to devote its energies to the after-treatment of infantile paralysis. As an institution it has done a modest amount of work. Probably other institutions have rendered treatment to an equal or greater number of infantile paralysis patients as a part of their general work. The work at Warm Springs, however, and the interest in it have resulted in welding together a great band of Americans with a new awareness of the medical, social and economic problems created by this dread disease and with an increased willingness to give more of themselves to the support of those agencies through which the crippled may be benefited.

Thus the Foundation has become more than an institution for the treatment of a limited number of patients. It has become also in effect an organization of those interested in lending their influence and support to the reconstructive work which must be done everywhere in the wake of infantile paralysis. I am sure that this good fortune of the Foundation in interesting so many new friends in the general cause is going to be in its final effect of even greater importance than the actual work at Warm Springs. The force of and help from an enlightened opinion is what the professional workers need to win such a widespread battle.

With this larger view in mind the Trustees of the Georgia Warm Springs Foundation will establish on terms and conditions to be defined by them the following funds from the gift which you bring today:

(1) A $100,000 fund to stimulate and further the meritorious

work being done in the field of infantile paralysis. It is the present intention that this fund will be used in connection with work done elsewhere than at Warm Springs so that the greatest encouragement may be given to others interested in this problem.

(2) A $650,000 fund for the furtherance of the present work done by the Foundation's institution at Warm Springs, Georgia, which, as I have indicated, will enable it to help coordinate the efforts of all engaged in this work, the details to be worked out by the trustees. I have no doubt that such coordination and correlation will be of the greatest value. For instance, there can be no doubt that great good will come from any system which permits not only of the exchange of data and information, but also of doctors, physical-therapists, and visiting nurses, to the end that the best types of care developed anywhere will become the common knowledge and practice of all.

(3) A fund of $253,030.08 for building, maintenance and contingencies of the Foundation.

I, therefore, now give to the Georgia Warm Springs Foundation through its treasurer this sum of one million three thousand thirty dollars and eight cents with which to create the three funds just described and totaling this amount, the income or principal of those funds to be used for the purposes indicated. Of course no part of this fund will be used to repay any advances made to the Foundation by any of its officers or trustees.

Once again I thank you and through you all those who have made possible this splendid gift.

(See Item 14, this volume.)

79 ⟨ Letter to the National Editorial Association on the Freedom of the Press. May 11, 1934

Dear Dean Martin:

PLEASE voice to the Missouri newspapermen and delegates of the National Editorial Association, gathered for your Annual Journalism Week Banquet, my sincere regret that because of duties in Washington I cannot be with you tonight. I understand that at your table tonight are assembled some of the foremost representatives of the relatively small but extremely influential newspapers of the country.

Neither the millions and millions of people constituting the reading public nor the hundreds of individuals representing the overwhelming majority of newspaper publishers can, in any way, be concerned with or wrought up over the silly and wholly unjustified conversation on the part of a small minority who suggest that the freedom of the press has been either destroyed or assailed.

Freedom of the press means freedom of expression, both in news columns and editorial columns. Judging by both these columns in papers in every part of the country, this freedom is freer than it ever has been in our history.

There has been no attempt in Washington to "gag" newspapermen or stifle editorial comment. There will be no such attempt.

On the basis of years of personal experiences with newspaper publishers and newspaper workers — and they have been many — I believe the publishers, with few exceptions, agree with me in all that I have said on the subject of freedom of the press and that they, in the great majority, have the interests of their employees close to their hearts.

Very sincerely yours,

Dean Frank L. Martin,
University of Missouri,
Columbia, Missouri.

80 ❧ The One Hundred and Twentieth Press Conference (Excerpts). May 11, 1934

(Drought — Ever normal granary.)

Q. Mr. President, is there any plan to help the drought sufferers out West?

THE PRESIDENT: Yes, we talked all about it in Cabinet. This is something you cannot use yet; it has to be off the record. We have been working on it for a whole year and I think I have talked informally here about the general theory of it. This has to be off the record, because I am a month away from a definite story on it. With crop control in those crops in which there is a surplus of production over consumption and in which we are trying to bring production within the general field of consumption in order to prevent abnormally low-price levels, you always have to recognize the element of chance that you may have a year of bumper crops and that at another time you may have a year of serious crop shortage.

Over a year ago we began discussing the principle of establishing what might be called a reserve granary which would contain a large carryover, a larger carryover than we have been carrying in normal years. That reserve emergency granary could be used to store surpluses in the bounteous years; and then we could draw on that granary in years of drought in order to prevent any starvation or anything like abnormally high prices. In that way, it would work both ways. In other words, in years of plenty it would help prevent abnormally low prices, and in years of drought it would help prevent abnormally high prices.

The thing has been, more or less, in a very tentative study stage for the past year; and we are working on it at the present time. We hope to have something along that line worked out during the course of the next few weeks, not as a message to be presented to this Congress, but as something to be studied as an essential component part of the general agricultural program.

Q. Do you care to tell us what feature of the drought was discussed in the Cabinet meeting?

THE PRESIDENT: Just the localities, the different localities which came out in the report.

Q. Was there any discussion of making funds available for some of the farmers who complain that their crops are going to be ruined?

THE PRESIDENT: No. Of course that would be handled out of the general relief funds if it came to the point of necessity. . . .

With respect to the drought of 1934, see Items 81, 103 and 147 of this volume.

81 ⟨White House Statement Following a Conference on Drought Relief. May 14, 1934

The President today conferred with Mr. Harry Hopkins, Federal Emergency Relief Administrator, Mr. Chester Davis, Agricultural Adjustment Administrator, Mr. W. I. Myers, Governor of the Farm Credit Administration, and Mr. Lawrence Westbrook, Assistant to Mr. Hopkins, who presented a report on conditions in the drought areas of the country and measures being taken by the Government to meet the situation.

The President was told that any apprehension that there will be a shortage of food in this country is, of course, entirely unwarranted. The wheat carryover is more than twice normal. The supply of corn on hand is adequate to make up any probable deficiency on account of the drought.

The committee agreed that new and present activities to meet needs in the drought area will be continued energetically and expanded as necessary. These include the giving of direct relief to needy farmers and their families; the providing of stock feed until new pastures are available, and the providing of seed for emergency forage crops.

Mr. Hopkins reported that the F.E.R.A. would purchase a substantial number of cattle in the drought areas, paying cash to the farmers for their cattle. The F.E.R.A. will have the beef canned and will use it in general relief work.

The A.A.A., Mr. Davis said, will relax its restrictions on farmers under contract so as to permit production of summer forage crops.

Work of the F.E.R.A. in providing funds to deepen wells and sink new wells will be continued in efforts to provide increased water supplies.

A request will be made to the railroads throughout the drought areas to cooperate in further reducing freight rates to permit the moving of cattle out of the drought areas and to move feed in.

The Government agencies will continue to keep in close touch with the situation here and in the field and stand ready to take every necessary step.

The President indicated that in his judgment it will not be necessary to ask the Congress for additional powers or grants to enable the emergency agencies to cope with the situation.

NOTE: The great drought of 1934 made itself felt over nearly three-fourths of the area of the United States and was then without precedent in its effects in the agricultural history of the Nation. There had been recurring downward trends in rainfall in the area centering around the Dakotas and Minnesota for a decade previously. There had also been pronounced deficiency in rainfall in parts of Kansas, Missouri, Iowa, Wisconsin, Michigan, Illinois, Indiana, Ohio and Kentucky during the first four months of 1934.

The drought entered a serious state in April, 1934, and became worse in May, the month when all small grains normally are getting their start. By this time it was evident that even if rainfall were to come later, so much damage had already been done that full recovery would not be possible. As it turned out, the rainfall did not come in sufficient quantity to be of any substantial help.

I decided in May to mobilize the forces of the country to help the stricken areas. It is fortunate that this most damaging drought then on record found the Government better prepared to meet such emergency than it had ever been, by reason of the fact that emergency agencies had been created by the Congress with broad and flexible powers to meet critical situations as they developed.

I called together the representatives of these various agencies including the A.A.A. and other units of the Department of Agriculture, the Farm Credit Administration and the Federal Emergency Relief Administration to start work at once upon relief measures.

While these emergency agencies were getting into action with funds already available to them for rendering first aid, I sent a special message to the Congress asking for additional money with which to carry the relief program for the drought areas to a successful conclusion. This message was sent on June 9, 1934, and is printed as Item 103 of this volume.

82 (Recommendation for Legislation to Provide Assistance for Repairing and Construction of Homes. May 14, 1934

To the Congress:

MAY I draw your attention to some important suggestions for legislation which should tend to improve conditions for those who live in houses, those who repair and construct houses, and those who invest in houses?

Many of our homes are in decadent condition and not fit for human habitation. They need repairing and modernizing to bring them up to the standard of the times. Many new homes now are needed to replace those not worth repairing.

The protection of the health and safety of the people demands that this renovizing and building be done speedily. The Federal Government should take the initiative immediately to cooperate with private capital and industry in this real-property conservation. We must lay the groundwork for this effort before Congress adjourns its present session.

The purpose of the program is twofold: first, to return many of the unemployed to useful and gainful occupation; second, to produce tangible, useful wealth in a form for which there is great social and economic need.

Repairing and Construction of Homes

The program consists of four major, interrelated divisions:

(1) Modernization, repair, and new construction;
(2) Mortgage insurance;
(3) Mortgage associations, and
(4) Building and loan insurance.

The modernization phase of the program will furnish national guidance and support for locally managed renovizing campaigns throughout the country and protection for home owners against unwarranted cost advances. For these purposes and to assure adequate financing at low cost and on moderate terms of repayment, a new governmental agency is required.

Modernization of commercial and industrial structures is envisioned, as well as residential, but the new features providing governmental assistance are confined largely to home improvements.

Loans to individuals will be made by private agencies which will be insured by a governmental agency against loss up to a certain percentage of their advances. This insurance against loss on the rehabilitation loans will be met by the Government and will be confined to advances of credit that meet standards and conditions designed to protect both the home owners and the co-operating agencies.

To make funds available for new home construction and to improve the mortgage market, the second phase of the program is long-term mortgage financing. It provides mutual mortgage insurance under governmental direction to enable private agencies to make first-mortgage loans on newly constructed houses up to 80 percent of the appraised value of the property, and to make new mortgages on existing homes up to 60 percent of the appraised value of the property. The loans will usually carry not more than 5 percent interest and will be amortized by periodic payments over 20 years. Similar insurance arrangements are provided to help finance low-cost residential projects of the slum-replacement type.

The third phase provides for the incorporation of mortgage

associations under strict Federal supervision to increase the amount of mortgage funds available in regions where interest rates are unduly high because sufficient local funds are lacking. The activities of these associations will be limited almost entirely to insured residential mortgages.

Insurance for share and certificate holders in building and loan associations, similar to the insurance provided for bank depositors, is the fourth phase of the program. These institutions are custodians of the funds of small savers, and it is essential that they should be given every reasonable protection. Insurance of this type is necessary in order to arrest any further drain on these institutions and to put them in a position to resume their normal useful functions.

I believe that the initiation of this broad and sound program will do much to alleviate distress and to raise perceptibly the standards of good living for many of our families throughout the land.

NOTE: The general purposes of the Federal Housing Administration (F.H.A.) program are outlined in the foregoing message.

Pursuant to the message, the Congress enacted a National Housing Act, approved June 27, 1934 (Public No. 479, 73d Congress; 48 Stat. 1246). The declared purpose of the Act was to encourage improvement in housing standards and conditions and to create a sound system of home financing.

The Federal Housing Administration set up by the statute does not loan its own money or make any grant of Federal funds. What it does is to insure loans made by banks, building and loan associations, insurance companies and other private lending institutions for refinancing existing houses, for the construction of new homes and for the modernization and repair of all types of structures.

Owing to the continued depression, residential construction in America had sunk to a very low ebb. Not only was there a cessation of new home construction, but because of general lack of funds, homes had been allowed to fall into disrepair. A program of construction of new homes and of repair and renovation would not only provide useful work for the unemployed, but would produce tangible useful wealth in a form socially and economically desirable.

The Federal Housing Administration has made much progress along the lines and objectives laid down by the statute. From the time of its creation to December 1, 1937, the gross business transacted by it totaled nearly $2,000,000,000. Over 250,000 home mortgages, valued at more than a billion dollars, were accepted by it for insurance. The homes securing these mortgages would provide for a city of nearly a million inhabitants; and it is estimated that, each week, over 2,000 additional families are acquiring their own homes under this program.

Modernization and repair notes amounting to over $560,000,000 were insured under the emergency provisions of the Act which have since expired. By this means the Housing Administration has raised the living standards of the millions of persons residing in the 1,250,000 urban dwellings and farm properties so improved; and it has enabled more than 100,000 small business concerns to modernize their plants and equipment. It is also estimated that the better-housing campaigns sponsored by the Housing Administration in more than 8,000 communities throughout the United States have stimulated additional modernization and repair work amounting to several times the value of the insured modernization and repair notes officially recorded.

The Housing Administration is now paying the major portion of its operating expenses. The income of the Housing Administration comes principally from mortgage-insurance premiums and appraisal fees, at the rate of more than $500,000 per month. The soundness of the appraisal methods used by the Federal Housing Administration is shown by the excellent foreclosure record on properties financed under this insured mortgage system. Of the 250,000 homes on which mortgages have been accepted for insurance, only fifty-four have been conveyed to the Administrator after foreclosure.

Fifty-six percent of the total value of mortgages accepted for insurance by the Federal Housing Administration for the past year has been for newly constructed homes. It is estimated that about one-half of the value of all mortgage loans eligible for insurance on newly constructed single-family urban homes is being financed under the Housing Administration plan.

In addition, F.H.A. has undertaken far-reaching reforms in home financing methods. It has helped discourage certain outmoded lending practices, such as the second mortgage, oppressive interest rates, costly commissions and expensive renewal fees. It has encouraged the substitution of a new system, based upon the principle of insurance to spread losses. It has also encouraged conservative standardized appraisals, long-term monthly amortization, reasonable interest rates and careful consideration of the home buyer's ability to pay. Home financing funds, which had almost vanished from the market when the Federal Housing Administration started operations, are now generally available on fairer terms than ever before in the history of the country. The acquisition of a home has been made easier and safer for the family of moderate means.

The records of F.H.A. show that over one-half of the families buying homes under the F.H.A. plan have annual incomes of $2,500 and less; and that most of these are purchasing their homes by payments of $25 a month or less. Nine out of ten of all new home owners under the F.H.A. plan are using less than one-fifth of their incomes to meet their monthly payments on their home.

83 ❡ A Second Message to Congress on the 1935 Budget. May 15, 1934

To the Congress:

IN MY budget message to the Congress of January 3, 1934, I said to you:

> "It is evident to me, as I am sure it is evident to you, that powerful forces for recovery exist. It is by laying a foundation of confidence in the present and faith in the future that the upturn which we have so far seen will become cumulative. The cornerstone of this foundation is the good credit of the Government.
>
> "It is, therefore, not strange nor is it academic that this credit has a profound effect upon the confidence so necessary to permit the new recovery to develop into maturity.
>
> "If we maintain the course I have outlined, we can confidently look forward to cumulative beneficial forces represented by increased volume of business, more general profit, greater employment, a diminution of relief expenditures, larger governmental receipts and repayments, and greater human happiness."

The budget which I submitted to the Congress proposed expenditures for the balance of this fiscal year and for the coming fiscal year which, in the light of expected revenues, called for a definite deficiency on June 30, 1935, but, at the same time, held out the hope that annual deficits would terminate during the following fiscal year.

It is true that actual expenditures since January have proceeded at a slower rate than estimated; nevertheless, it must be borne in mind that, even though the actual deficit for the year ending June 30, 1934, will be below my estimate, appropriations are still in force and the amounts actually to be expended during the following fiscal year will, therefore, be increased over and above my estimate for that fiscal year. In this connection it is relevant to point out that during the fiscal year 1935 it is estimated that there will be actually expended on public works $1,500,000,000 out of appropriations heretofore made.

In my budget message of January 3, 1934, it was pointed out that there could be no abrupt termination of emergency expenditures for recovery purposes, that the necessity for relief would continue, and that appropriations amounting to $3,166,000,000, in addition to the appropriations contained in the budget itself, would be requested for the two fiscal years ending June 30, 1935.

The present Congress has already made appropriations out of which, for the two fiscal years in question, it is estimated there will be expended the following sums:

Relief	$950,000,000
Crop Loans	40,000,000
Farm Mortgages	40,000,000
Reconstruction Finance Corp.	500,000,000
Veterans' Benefits	22,000,000
Army Air Corps	5,000,000
Flood Control, Mississippi River, etc.	29,000,000
Independent Offices Act	228,000,000
Miscellaneous Supplemental Estimates	30,000,000
	$1,844,000,000

This leaves a balance of $1,322,000,000 to be appropriated.

Out of this balance it is necessary first to take the specific items to be appropriated for:

Federal Land Banks —
 Subscription to paid-in surplus $75,000,000
 Reduction in interest payments 7,950,000
Emergency Bank Act and Gold Transfer 3,000,000
Internal Revenue Service 10,000,000
Salaries, Office of the Secretary of the Treasury   100,000
Secret Service 45,000

            ————————
            $96,095,000

This leaves $1,225,905,000 available for the following purposes:

Civilian Conservation Corps Camps,
Public Works, and
 Relief Work, in addition to amounts already appropriated,
  and including aid to the dairy and beef cattle industries.

It is estimated that the minimum requirements for the Civilian Conservation Corps will be $285,000,000 and that the amount available, therefore, for public works and relief will be $940,-905,000. A very simple checkup of these figures shows that they total $3,166,000,000, to which reference was made in my budget message of January 3, 1934.

It was my thought in January, and is my thought now, that this sum should be appropriated to me under fairly broad powers because of the fact that no one could then, or can now, determine the exact needs under hard and fixed appropriation headings. In furtherance of this thought it seems appropriate to provide that any savings which can be effected out of certain appropriations made for emergency purposes shall be available for emergency relief purposes.

In my judgment an appropriation in excess of the above amount would make more difficult if not impossible an actual balance of the budget in the fiscal year 1936, unless greatly increased taxes are provided. The present estimates should be sufficient as a whole to take care of the emergencies of relief and of orderly re-employment at least until the early part of the calendar year 1935. If at that time conditions have not improved as much

as we today hope, the next Congress will be in session and will
have full opportunity to act.

See also Item 3, this volume.

84 ❧ A Message to the Senate on the Menace of Uncontrolled Manufacture of Arms and Munitions. May 18, 1934

To the Senate:

I HAVE been gratified to learn that, pursuant to a Resolution of
the Senate, a Committee has been appointed to investigate the
problems incident to the private manufacture of arms and munitions of war and the international traffic therein. I earnestly recommend that this Committee receive the generous support of
the Senate in order that it may be enabled to pursue the investigation with which it is charged with a degree of thoroughness
commensurate with the high importance of the questions at issue.
The Executive Departments of the Government will be charged
to cooperate with the Committee to the fullest extent in furnishing it with any information in their possession which it may desire to receive, and their views upon the adequacy or inadequacy
of existing legislation and of the treaties to which the United
States is a party for the regulation and control of the manufacture of and traffic in arms.

The private and uncontrolled manufacture of arms and munitions and the traffic therein has become a serious source of international discord and strife. It is not possible, however, effectively
to control such an evil by the isolated action of any one country.
The enlightened opinion of the world has long realized that this
is a field in which international action is necessary. The negotiation of the Convention for the Supervision of the International
Trade in Arms and Ammunition and in Implements of War,
signed at Geneva, June 17, 1925, was an important step in the
right direction. That Convention is still before the Senate. I hope

that the Senate may find it possible to give its advice and consent to its ratification. The ratification of that Convention by this Government, which has been too long delayed, would be a concrete indication of the willingness of the American people to make their contribution toward the suppression of abuses which may have disastrous results for the entire world if they are permitted to continue unchecked.

It is my earnest hope that the representatives of the Nations who will reassemble at Geneva on May 29 will be able to agree upon a Convention containing provisions for the supervision and control of the traffic in arms much more far-reaching than those which were embodied in the Convention of 1925. Some suitable international organization must and will take such action. The peoples of many countries are being taxed to the point of poverty and starvation in order to enable Governments to engage in a mad race in armament which, if permitted to continue, may well result in war. This grave menace to the peace of the world is due in no small measure to the uncontrolled activities of the manufacturers and merchants of engines of destruction, and it must be met by the concerted action of the peoples of all Nations.

NOTE: The foregoing message expressed my hope that the Disarmament Conference at Geneva, which had been holding periodic sessions for two years prior to this date, and which was to assemble on May 29, 1934, would be able to arrive at an international agreement for the supervision and control of the traffic in arms.

At this Conference, Mr. Norman Davis, the American delegate, urged that special attention be devoted to the regulation of this traffic, and read to the Conference excerpts from the foregoing message, declaring that the United States was anxious to join in the supervision of the traffic in munitions by a treaty which would deal drastically with the problem.

The United States delegation presented to this Conference on June 15, 1934, a memorandum setting forth the proposals of the United States: (1) that the manufacture of arms and munitions, and traffic in them, should be subjected in each country to a definite system of national control; (2) that all the operations of that control should be open to inspection by an international body; (3) that even though a general disarmament treaty such as was desired by the United States could not be then negotiated, a separate agreement dealing with the subject of arms traffic alone was strongly urged by this Government.

On this same date, the United States Senate, pursuant to the recommendation in the foregoing message that it ratify the Convention for the Supervision of International Trade in Arms and Ammunition and in Implements of War, signed at Geneva, June 17, 1925, which still in 1934 remained unratified, did give its advice and consent to its ratification. This Convention was a less thorough-going agreement than that which the United States was proposing to the Disarmament Conference in 1934. In view of certain reservations made by the Senate in consenting to the ratification of this old Convention, however, the ratification was not at that time completed.

During the summer of 1934, the American Delegation to the Disarmament Conference, working with the State, War and Navy Departments, prepared a draft of a thorough-going convention for the regulation and control of the manufacture and trade in arms.

This proposed convention provided for (1) the registration and licensing of all manufacturers of arms; (2) the publication of all licenses issued to manufacturers and of all orders for arms received by registered establishments; (3) the annual publication of the quantities of arms to be required by each country and the proposed expenditures for national defense during that year; (4) the licensing of all exports and imports of arms, and the publication of statistics in regard to such exports and imports; and (5) the creation of a permanent disarmament commission and of regional committees of this commission to exercise supervision and control in the territory of each of the high contracting parties.

Due to disagreement on certain fundamental points, the American proposal was not approved and no further action has been taken upon it since that date.

Meanwhile, on June 6, 1935, the United States Senate gave its advice and consent to the ratification of the Arms Traffic Convention of 1925 without repeating the undesirable reservations. It did, however, make a reservation that the Convention should not become effective so far as the United States was concerned until it should have become effective in respect to a number of other specified arms-producing Nations. Since several of these Nations have not ratified the Convention, it has not yet taken effect.

I am firmly convinced that the question of the control of the manufacture of arms and munitions cannot be adequately dealt with by any Nation alone. It requires the united action of the principal Nations of the world; and the United States has shown its desire to cooperate and lead in the adoption of an adequate policy of control.

In the meantime, however, we have enacted domestic legislation establishing a definite system of national control of the traffic in arms, similar to that contemplated by the American proposal at the Disarmament Conference in 1934. This was the Joint Resolution of Congress approved August 31, 1935, which is discussed in Item 117 of Vol. IV.

85 ⟨ Statement on Signing Bill to Help the Federal Government Wage War on Crime and Gangsters. May 18, 1934

THESE laws are a renewed challenge on the part of the Federal Government to interstate crime. They are also complementary to the broader program designed to curb the evil-doer of whatever class.

In enacting them, the Congress has provided additional equipment for the Department of Justice to aid local authorities. Lacking these new weapons, the Department already has tracked down many major outlaws and its vigilance has spread fear in the underworld. With additional resources, I am confident that it will make still greater inroads upon organized crime.

I regard this action today as an event of the first importance. So far as the Federal Government is concerned, there will be no relenting. But there is one thing more. Law enforcement and gangster extermination cannot be made completely effective so long as a substantial part of the public looks with tolerance upon known criminals, permits public officers to be corrupted or intimidated by them or applauds efforts to romanticize crime.

Federal men are constantly facing machine-gun fire in the pursuit of gangsters. I ask citizens, individually and as organized groups, to recognize the facts and meet them with courage and determination.

I stand squarely behind the efforts of the Department of Justice to bring to book every law breaker, big and little.

NOTE: It had become evident by the beginning of my Administration that the Federal legal and administrative machinery for the detection, prosecution and punishment of crime required complete overhauling. Crime control had traditionally, with few exceptions, been left to the various States and localities. New instrumentalities, however, such as the automobile, the airplane, the telephone and telegraph had enabled many crimes to go undetected and unpunished because of the inability of the respective States to cope with criminals who could travel and communicate from State to State with great speed.

Perhaps the one crime which aroused public opinion to a realization of the outworn Federal penal and procedural statutes was the kidnapping of the child of Colonel Charles A. Lindbergh. That incident was responsible for the immediate passage of a bill then pending in the Congress, which before that had little chance of passage — a bill making it a Federal offense to transport a kidnapped person from one State to another. In the summer of 1933 other gangster crimes served further to emphasize the need for reform in legislation. The Congress decided that it would have to take advantage of its constitutional power to enact crime legislation based on the interstate commerce clause, the tax clause and the implied right of the Federal Government to protect its various agencies and instrumentalities. There was drafted in the Department of Justice and submitted to the 73d Congress a comprehensive program of crime legislation, which was adopted with few exceptions, and which has helped the Federal Government in its war on crime.

Among the most important of these are:

1. Amendments to the Federal kidnapping statute to provide for the death penalty in the event of injury to the victim, and creating a presumption that, if the victim was not returned within seven days, the victim had been taken from one State to another.

2. An Act punishing the transmission of extortion threats in any form of interstate communication. Prior to this, only the mailing of extortion notes was punishable.

3. A statute making it a Federal offense for a person to flee from one State to another to avoid prosecution for certain major felonies or to avoid testifying in felony cases. Since the enactment of this statute hundreds of persons not available to interstate rendition proceedings have been returned to States under Federal warrants for prosecution.

4. A statute punishing the transportation and receipt of stolen goods in interstate commerce where the value is $5,000 or more. This statute has been instrumental in breaking up some of the larger gangs which had been engaged in shipping stolen merchandise from one State to another.

5. An Act punishing robbery of national banks with death penalty where any person is killed during the robbery. The statute is applicable not only to national banks, but to members of the Federal Reserve System and to all banks whose funds are insured by the Federal Deposit Insurance Corporation. It

has done much to reduce the epidemic of bank robbery.

6. A statute requiring registration of all machine-guns and sawed-off shotguns and rifles.

7. An Act making it a Federal offense to assault or kill Federal officers.

8. An Act authorizing agents of the Department of Justice to carry firearms.

9. An Act to protect certain types of trade and commerce against intimidation and racketeering.

10. Various statutes for improving the outworn and archaic Federal criminal procedure to make the prosecution of crime in court more effective.

11. A statute granting Congressional consent to any two or more States to enter into agreements or compacts for the prevention of crime and the enforcement of criminal laws. As a result of this statute and of the impetus given by the Attorney General, compact statutes have been enacted among many States covering such things as: fresh pursuit compacts (enacted in 21 States) permitting the police of one State to pursue and capture a fugitive across the boundary lines of another State; a simplified uniform extradition procedure providing for quick return of criminals (enacted by compacts in 16 States); return of important witnesses in criminal proceedings from one State to another (adopted by reciprocal laws in 21 States); arrangements for supervising parolees of other States (adopted in 17 States).

In addition to the legislative method of bringing the Federal Government's anti-crime machinery up to date, the Federal Bureau of Investigation has been equipped with new facilities, men and funds, which have been used to make it as effective an instrumentality of crime detection and punishment as any of the similar agencies of the world. Between 1934 and 1936 some of the country's most notorious criminals were caught, and the major gangs which had been engaged in spectacular crimes of violence were dispersed and their leaders were placed behind bars.

The period of training for new agents was increased, and retraining courses for experienced agents have been conducted in order to keep them up to date on the developments in crime. The technical laboratory of the Bureau has been expanded; the central fingerprint files have been developed and increased, as has the division devoted to the identification of criminals.

The other investigative units of the Government have also been developed and have served to help in the Government's war on crime — the Narcotic Unit, the Customs Unit, the Secret Service, the Coast Guard, the Intelligence Unit of the Treasury Department, the Immigration Border Patrol and the Post Office Inspectors.

In the meantime, attention was being given to the development of the Federal prison system. New penitentiaries, a new classification system, improvements in the parole system, extension of the probation system, education and improvement of personnel in the prisons and penitentiaries, and elimination of all special privileges have brought the Federal penal and correctional system in line with up-to-date standards.

While the Federal machinery for investigation, prosecution and punishment of crime was being improved, it still remained obvious that the problem of crime remained for the most part one with which the individual States must continue to cope. About 90 percent of all crimes, even now, come within the jurisdiction of State and local authorities rather than within the jurisdiction of the Federal Government.

Realizing, however, that the Federal Government can play an important part in crime control through example and encouragement, the Attorney General, in December, 1934, called a National Conference on Crime, to which were invited 600 representatives of Federal, State, Territorial and local governments, as well as more than 75 quasi-public and private agencies whose activities had a definite relation to the crime problem. I made an address at that conference, printed as Item 193, this volume, December 10, 1934.

The subject of parole has during recent years become the object of increased attention by the public, both as to the theory of it and as to its practical administration.

The Attorney General in 1936, with funds provided by W.P.A., undertook a national survey of records throwing light on the theory and practice of parole. The collection of data has been completed, and is now being sorted and analyzed for purposes of a report which is expected in 1938.

86 ❨ Address Delivered on the One Hundredth Anniversary of the Death of Lafayette.

May 20, 1934

MR. PRESIDENT, Mr. Speaker, Mr. Ambassador, Members of the Congress, Gentlemen of the Supreme Court, my friends: A century ago President Andrew Jackson, in communicating the melancholy news of the death of Lafayette to the Congress of the United States, called it "afflicting intelligence." And so it was. It made more than one Nation mourn, none more than our own. The Marquis de Lafayette was referred to in a General Order to our Army and Navy as "the distinguished friend of the United States"; and the Congress, with rare felicity, added to this the phrase, "the friend of Washington, and the friend of liberty."

In this threefold role of friendship we the people of this Nation have enshrined him in our hearts, and today we cherish his memory above that of any citizen of a foreign country. It is as one of our Nation's peerless heroes that we hail him, just as his beloved France enshrined him in the Pantheon of her immortal sons.

Many generations later, more than two million American boys, backed by the solidarity of a great Nation, went to France. Those soldiers and sailors were repaying the debt of gratitude we owe to Lafayette and at the same time they were seeking to preserve those fundamentals of liberty and democracy to which in a previous age he had dedicated his life.

There is no higher tribute we can pay to his memory than this we pay today. In communicating his death to the Nation, President Jackson ordered that "the same honors be rendered him as were observed upon the decease of Washington." Jackson was moved by the tenderness of a personal friendship — moved as he said, "by personal as by public considerations" to direct that every honor be paid "the last Major General of the Revolutionary Army."

We know the exquisite relationship which existed between Washington and Lafayette, and I am indeed pleased that the Ambassador of the French Republic has referred to this friendship. It was that of father and son. For the great Virginian the Frenchman had a veneration and love which approached homage. To him Washington was an ideal — almost more than human.

With Andrew Jackson, the friendship bore perhaps a more personal and intimate cast, because the two were more of an age. Both were mere youngsters at the outbreak of the Revolutionary War. Jackson, a boy of ten in 1777, first saw Lafayette when he landed in Charleston and before he started northward to meet the Congress. The sight of the gallant young Frenchman was so deeply engraved in the heart of Andrew Jackson that half a century later it was as vivid as the day it was etched. Jackson himself, even in boyhood, was to contribute his mite "to shake off the yoke of tyranny, and to build up the fabric of free government." When Lafayette visited our shores again in 1824, Jackson wrote him a paean of welcome, in which he referred to the state of his "own youthful feelings" on the occasion of that first visit. His coming then, he said, "aroused every patriot from a state of despair to that of confidence in our bleeding cause, while the shout of victory or death was sung through the welkin. It inspired an enthusiasm becoming the people who had resolved to be free."

When they met here in Washington, Lafayette said this to the hero of New Orleans, "Had you witnessed my anxiety, when on a sudden all Europe was pacified, and the flower of the British Army were on their way to Louisiana, you would still better judge what I felt of relief, joy and pride on receiving the glorious account of your victory. I have long anticipated the pleasure to take you by the hand, and whatever be your future movements I will not leave the United States before I have seeked and found opportunity to express in person my high regard and sincere friendship."

This first meeting was as simple and genuine as their natures. Jackson had come to Washington for the session of the Congress, as Senator from Tennessee. He put up with his old friend, John Gadsby, at the Franklin House; and immediately learned that Lafayette was a guest in the same inn. The Mayor of Washington had informed the President of the United States that "the friend of the people (Lafayette) must be the guest of the people, and could not stay at the White House."

It was a memorable Congress that year, the last to elect a President of the United States, and Andrew Jackson was in the thick of the storm. The two old soldiers saw much of each other during that long winter, and as a member of the Senate, Jackson took part in all the ceremonies held in honor of the French patriot.

It stands on the record of the day that "Lafayette was the only man who ever was, in his personal capacity, publicly received by the Senate of the United States." The records show that they received him "as a brother, rather than a stranger, as one of a loving family, come from a distant shore, after a long and weary absence, to revisit the friends of his youth."

Senator Barbour of Virginia presented him. The President and the Senators rose from their seats, uncovered, and the General, advancing toward the Chair of the Senate, was invited to take a seat prepared for him on the right of the Chair. The Senate then was adjourned, the while the Senators flocked about their guest and gave him a warm-hearted welcome.

It was given to the House of Representatives to extend the welcome of the Nation. Exactly such an assembly as this now before me met in the Hall of Representatives, every branch of the Government fully in attendance. Henry Clay, the Speaker, in expressing what was in the hearts of the people, said, "The vain wish has sometimes been indulged that Providence would allow the patriot, after death, to return to his country, and to contemplate the immediate changes which had taken place." To Lafayette had come, he said, "the realization of the consoling object of that wish."

"General, you are in the midst of posterity."

"No, Mr. Speaker," replied Lafayette, "posterity has not begun for me since, in the sons of my companions and friends, I find the same public feelings in my behalf which I have had the happiness to experience in their fathers."

I like to remember also the picture of the visit of General Lafayette to General Jackson at the Hermitage. When Lafayette landed at Nashville, the people stood far back and let Jackson go forward alone to greet him and to welcome him as his feet touched the shore.

At the official welcome of the State of Tennessee, a group of Revolutionary soldiers, some thirty or forty officers and men, stepped forward to greet the old patriot. He saluted each of them with animation and affection. Suddenly his eye fell on one whom he had known in France, who had come with him to America and had been at his side during the Revolution. This worn and wearied old soldier had ridden one hundred miles to see his old General, and when they met they fell into each other's arms, kissed each other as only Frenchmen can perform that act of devotion, and sobbed aloud.

The next day Jackson entertained him at the Hermitage. The people seemed to sense that history was being made and left them much to themselves. They talked about the French and American Revolutions, and much about Napoleon. Jackson took pride in showing him over the house he had built for his beloved wife. He produced a box of pistols, and opening it, asked Lafayette if he knew whose pistols they were. "Yes," said Lafayette, "they are the ones I gave to General Washington in 1778, and," he added, "I feel a real satisfaction in finding them in the hands of a man so worthy of such a heritage."

Today I have brought to show to the Congress of the United States another link between Lafayette and our country — a sword which has never yet been shown to the American people.

After the termination of the World War and the reoccupation of Alsace by the French, this sword was rediscovered. Its history is this: Shortly before the death of Washington, his old companions in arms — those gallant Frenchmen who had taken part in our War of the Revolution — joined together and had this sword made by special order to be presented to their former Commander-in-Chief.

Before the presentation could be made, Washington died and, 133 years later, through the fine courtesy and feeling of the present Government of France, the sword was brought to America by a distinguished descendant of General Lafayette and presented to the present President of the United States. This sword rests and will rest for all time below the portrait of President Washington in the White House.

I like to associate Lafayette and Jackson. Lafayette's last letter to Jackson was an appeal for help from the Congress for the family of a brave Frenchman who had served in our Revolutionary War. His last thoughts were of Congress and of Jackson. He instructed his son to send to Jackson, for transmittal to the Congress, "a copper plate on which was inscribed the first engraved copy of the American Declaration of Independence to be deposited in their Library as a last tribute of respect, patriotic love and affection for his adopted country."

It is a singular coincidence that Jackson's mind many years later turned to Lafayette in his last hours. When Jackson's will, signed with his palsied hand, was opened, it was found that he had bequeathed to George Washington Lafayette "the pistols of General Lafayette which were presented by him to General George Washington, and by Colonel William Robertson presented to me." These he desired sent to the son of his old friend, as his will declared, "as a memento of the illustrious personages through whose hands they have passed, his father, and the Father of his country."

Mr. Ambassador, I trust that you will inform our good friend, the President of the French Republic, the Government of France, and through them the people of France that on this Hundredth Anniversary of the death of Gilbert du Motier Marquis de Lafayette we, the representatives of the people of the United States, have assembled once more to do honor to the friend of America.

87 ⟨ A Letter on the Centenary of the Birth of Cardinal Gibbons. May 21, 1934

My dear Archbishop Curley:

IN my radio address last November on the Maryland Tercentenary Celebration, I expressed the hope that the celebration "will also be a reminder to people throughout the United States of the great fight that Lord Baltimore made three centuries ago for religious freedom in America."

Your recent letter brings to my attention that this year Your Excellency will preside over a special celebration of the tercentenary of Maryland, which will, at the same time, commemorate the one hundredth anniversary of the birth of the late James Cardinal Gibbons, Your Excellency's predecessor as Archbishop of Baltimore.

I take this occasion to couple with the hope expressed above concerning Maryland's anniversary, my tribute to Cardinal Gibbons who illustrated the hope itself. Loyal, steadfast to his own religious faith, a foremost leader in its councils, Cardinal Gibbons during his long life ever extended the gift of freedom, which he himself so highly appreciated, unto all of his fellow citizens, no matter what their religious faith might be.

Both the memory and the fruits of his gracious power and his personal charm endure and, I feel, will endure.

With the wish that every success may attend your celebration,

Very sincerely yours,

Most Reverend
Michael J. Curley,
The Archbishop of Baltimore,
Baltimore, Md.

88 ⟨ Telegrams of Congratulation on the Settlement of the Leticia Dispute between Colombia and Peru. May 21, 1934

I desire to send to Your Excellency my heartiest congratulations on the settlement of the Leticia question. In my judgment, this proof that two great Republics of the American Continent can resolve the difficulties which had arisen between them through peaceful adjustment furnishes an example to the entire world, of which my countrymen in common with all the other peoples of the American Republics may be justly proud.

His Excellency, Senor Doctor Don Enrique Olaya Herrera,
President of Colombia, Bogota, Colombia.

Please accept my warmest congratulations on the happy settlement of the Leticia controversy. In my judgment, this proof that two great Republics of the American Continent can resolve the difficulties which had arisen between them through peaceful adjustment furnishes an example to the entire world, of which my countrymen in common with all the other peoples of the American Republics may be justly proud.

His Excellency, General Oscar R. Benavides,
President of Peru, Lima, Peru.

NOTE: Since September 1, 1932, when a group of about 300 Peruvian nationals seized the Colombian town of Leticia, there had been continued dispute and intermittent fighting between Peru and Colombia about the boundary. Efforts at a pacific settlement of the controversy were made by both the League of Nations and the United States.

We cooperated actively and thoroughly in all of the efforts made for a peaceful determination of the controversy. Success finally resulted in the signing of a treaty by the delegates of the two Governments. The agreement recognized and reaffirmed the sanctity of treaties, since it was based upon the validity of a prior boundary treaty between the two Governments in 1922. It also formed a basis of continued cooperation to solve present and future problems in the area, renouncing war as a means of settlement.

This recognition of the obligation of treaties and this establishment of the principle of arbitration of disputes between the two Nations were important steps in the building of machinery for peace on this continent. The peaceful conclusion of the incident was the occasion of the sending of the foregoing messages by me.

89 ❨ Message to the Congress on Silver Policy. May 22, 1934

To the Congress:

ON JANUARY 11, 1934, I recommended to the Congress legislation which was promptly enacted under the title, "The Gold Reserve Act of 1934." This Act vested in the United States Government the custody and control of our stocks of gold as a reserve for our paper currency and as a medium of settling international balances. It set up a stabilization fund for the control of foreign exchange in the interests of our people, and certain amendments were added to facilitate the acquisition of silver.

As stated in my message to the Congress, this legislation was recommended as a step in improving our financial and monetary system. Its enactment has laid a foundation on which we are organizing a currency system that will be both sound and adequate. It is a long step forward, but only a step.

As a part of the larger objective, some things have been clear. One is that we should move forward as rapidly as conditions permit in broadening the metallic base of our monetary system and in stabilizing the purchasing and debt-paying power of our money on a more equitable level. Another is that we should not neglect the value of an increased use of silver in improving our monetary system. Since 1929 that has been obvious.

Some measures for making a greater use of silver in the public interest are appropriate for independent action by us. On others, international cooperation should be sought.

Of the former class is that of increasing the proportion of silver in the abundant metallic reserves back of our paper currency. This policy was initiated by the Proclamation of December 21, 1933, bringing our current domestic production of silver into the Treasury, as well as placing this Nation among the first to carry out the agreement on silver which we sought and secured at the London Conference. We have since acquired other silver in the interest of stabilization of foreign exchange and the development of a broader metallic base for our currency. We seek to remedy a maladjustment of our currency.

In further aid of this policy, it would be helpful to have legislation broadening the authority for the further acquisition and monetary use of silver.

I, therefore, recommend legislation at the present session, declaring it to be the policy of the United States to increase the amount of silver in our monetary stocks with the ultimate objective of having and maintaining one-fourth of their monetary value in silver and three-fourths in gold.

The Executive Authority should be authorized and directed to make the purchases of silver necessary to attain this ultimate objective.

The authority to purchase present accumulations of silver in this country should be limited to purchases at not in excess of fifty cents per ounce.

The Executive Authority should be enabled, should circumstances require, to take over present surpluses of silver in this country not required for industrial uses on payment of just compensation, and to regulate imports, exports and other dealings in monetary silver.

There should be a tax of at least 50 percent on the profits accruing from dealing in silver.

We can proceed with this program of increasing our store of silver for use as a part of the metallic reserves for our paper currency without seriously disturbing adjustments in world trade. However, because of the great world supply of silver and its use in varying forms by the world's population, concerted action by all Nations, or at least a large group of Nations, is necessary if a permanent measure of value, including both gold and silver, is eventually to be made a world standard. To arrive at that point, we must seek every possibility for world agreement, although it may turn out that this Nation will ultimately have to take such independent action on this phase of the matter as its interests require.

The success of the London Conference in consummating an international agreement on silver, which has now been ratified by all the Governments concerned, makes such further agreement worth seeking. The ebb and flow of values in almost all parts of the world have created many points of pressure for readjustments of internal and international standards. At no time since the efforts of this Nation to secure international agreement on silver began in 1878, have conditions been more favorable for making progress along this line.

Accordingly, I have begun to confer with some of our neighbors in regard to the use of both silver and gold, preferably on a coordinated basis, as a standard of monetary value. Such an agreement would constitute an important step forward toward a monetary unit of value more equitable and stable in its purchasing and debt-paying power.

NOTE: The foregoing message stated the policy of the Administration with reference to the role of silver in our monetary system: (a) to broaden the metallic base of the system; (b) to use silver increasingly in improving the system; (c) to seek international action for making a greater use of silver.

Pursuant to this message, the Silver Purchase Act of 1934 was passed and approved by me June 19, 1934 (Pub. No. 438, 73d Congress; 48 Stat. 1178). Among other things, the Act declared it "to be the policy of the United States that the proportion of silver to gold in the monetary stocks of the United States should be increased, with the ultimate objective of having and maintaining one-fourth of the monetary value of such stocks in silver."

Whenever and so long as the proportion of silver in the stocks of gold and silver of the United States was less than one-fourth of the monetary value of such stocks, the Secretary of the Treasury was authorized and directed by the statute, subject to certain conditions, to purchase silver on rates and terms and conditions most advantageous to the public interest. The statute also made provision for the sale of silver under certain conditions, the issuance of silver certificates, the regulation of the acquisition, importation, exportation or transportation of silver, and the "nationalization" of silver. A tax was imposed of 50 percent of any profits made on certain transfers of silver. Regulations relating to the tax on transfers of silver were issued on June 19, 1934, and amended from time to time.

The legislation was designed to carry out the policy of stabilizing foreign exchange and the purchasing and debt-paying power of the dollar; and of encouraging the ultimate adoption of a permanent measure of value, including both gold and silver as a world standard.

(See note to Item 16 of this volume, for a summary of the policies and objectives of the Administration with respect to the monetary system.)

90 ❡ The President Advocates Legislation to Prevent Violation of Petroleum Code Regulating Production. May 23, 1934

My dear Mr. Chairman:

I HAVE received a disturbing letter from the Administrator for the Petroleum Industry, Hon. Harold L. Ickes, informing me of the continued daily production of oil in excess of the maximum amount determined on by the Administrator pursuant to authority under the Petroleum Code.

The Administrator states that the records of the Bureau of Mines during the first three months of this year show a daily average production of "illegal" oil of 149,000 barrels. Technically speaking, this may not all have been "hot" oil, but in a real sense it is, since it is oil produced in excess of the allowable. While the final figures of the Bureau of Mines are not available for the months of April and May, it is unquestionably true that there is a growing disregard for production orders issued under the Petroleum Code and that the trend of hot oil produced is upward. For example, it is stated on reliable authority that the daily excess production in the East Texas field alone is running at 60,000 to 75,000 barrels per day. Other estimators say that this figure should be much higher. The *Oil and Gas Journal* recently estimated that there was illegal production in the country as a whole of 198,475 barrels per day during the week ending May 12th.

If the principle of prorating production under a code is to be maintained, it seems necessary that the existing law should be strengthened by the passage of the Bill which has been introduced in the Senate by Senator Thomas and in the House by Congressman Disney and supported by the Oil Administrator.

It is a simple fact that as a result of the work of the Oil Administrator definite progress has been made both in eliminating unfair practices and in raising the price of crude petroleum to a reasonable level, which has brought added employment and more fair wages to those engaged in oil production.

I am frankly fearful that if the law is not strengthened, illegal production will continue and grow in volume and result in a collapse of the whole structure. This will mean a return to the wretched conditions which existed in the spring of 1933.

I hope therefore that the proposed legislation can be enacted. I do not want to see this important American industry reduced to the condition under which it was operating before the Oil Administration started its work.

Very sincerely yours,

Hon. M. M. Logan,
Chairman, Senate Committee on Mines and Mining,
and Hon. Sam Rayburn,
Chairman, House Committee on Interstate and
Foreign Commerce, Washington, D. C.

NOTE: As I pointed out in the foregoing letter addressed to the Chairman of the Interstate and Foreign Commerce Committee of the House and to the Chairman of the Senate Committee on Mines and Mining, the production limitations in the oil code were being violated to an increasingly dangerous extent. The pressure of this overproduction on the market was again threatening a collapse of the price structure of petroleum, which had been stabilized by the petroleum code adopted under N.I.R.A.

There was legislation pending at this time which would have provided for the establishment of a Petroleum Administrative Board in the Department of Interior and would have given the Department broad powers to enforce the production limits placed upon petroleum after investigation and determination of the national demand for petroleum. The legislation did not pass; but as a result of it a resolution providing for an investigation of the petroleum industry and of the regulation of commerce in petroleum and petroleum products was adopted by the House of Representatives (House Resolution 441, 73d Congress).

The Committee conducted extended hearings in Washington and in the oil States of Oklahoma, Texas and California; and made its report on January 2, 1935. A proposed bill was introduced, which gave the consent of the Congress to an interstate compact to conserve oil and gas, entered into on February 16, 1935. The proposed bill authorized a Petroleum Administrative Board as an independent agency of the Federal Government to make investigations, to determine the reasonable market demand for petroleum, and to make public its findings.

This legislation also did not pass. Instead a joint resolution was approved August 27, 1935 (Public Resolution No. 64, 74th Congress), consenting to an interstate oil compact to conserve oil and gas. On August 9, 1935, I had sent a message to the Congress recommending approval of this compact. This message is printed in Vol. IV, Item 103.

This compact was to have expired by its terms on September 1, 1937; but it has been renewed for an additional two-year period with the consent of the Congress, given by Public Resolution No. 57, 75th Congress, approved August 10, 1937.

In the meantime, the Secretary of the Interior proceeded to try to bring about some order in the industry. In October, 1934, he created the Federal Tender Board, pursuant to the authority given in N.I.R.A.; and required a certificate of clearance issued by the Federal Tender Board as a condition precedent to the movement of petroleum and petroleum products in interstate commerce.

Through a staff of examiners and by making physical checks, the Federal Tender Board functioned very effectively until January 7, 1935. On that date, however, the Supreme Court, in *Panama Refining Company vs. Ryan*, 293 U. S. 388, declared unconstitutional Section 9-C of the National Industrial Recovery Act under which the Secretary of the Interior had created the Federal Tender Board and had adopted rules and regulations for the conduct of the industry. The decision was predicated on the ground that the power attempted to be conferred on the President by the statute constituted an unconstitutional delegation to him of legislative authority.

Thereafter the Board ceased functioning and movements of "hot oil" increased immediately. Additional State legislation was passed, but it continued to fail to meet the situation. Commerce in hot oil steadily increased.

Finally, on February 22, 1935, the Connally Act (Public No. 14, 74th Congress; 49 Stat. 30) was passed by the Congress to deal with the situation. (See Vol. IV, Item 21.)

91 ⟨ The President Hails Plan to Draft Minimum Employment Standards by Interstate Compact. May 25, 1934

My dear Governor Winant:

THE Secretary of Labor has told me that on Tuesday, May 29th, representatives of the States of Connecticut, Maine, New Hampshire, New York, Rhode Island, Massachusetts and Pennsylvania are to convene at Concord, New Hampshire, under your chairmanship, to consider and to act upon a draft of an interstate compact establishing uniform minimum standards for conditions of employment.

You may recall that in January, 1931, when I was Governor of the State of New York, I called the first conference of officials of the Northeastern States to consider the possibility of proceeding by joint State action to maintain and improve industrial and labor standards. Because this meeting on the 29th of May is, at least in part, an outgrowth of our earlier discussions in Albany, I naturally have a deep personal satisfaction in it. But my interest goes much further, for the State action now proposed is complementary to the national action already taken in Washington to give American citizens a more ample and more secure life.

I hope you will extend to the representatives and guests who attend the conference my good wishes and my heartiest congratulations upon their substantial accomplishment.

Very sincerely yours,

Honorable John G. Winant,
Concord, New Hampshire,

NOTE: The first movement toward establishing a common standard for labor legislation among neighboring States was a conference of Governors called by me at Albany, New York, on January 23 and 24, 1931, for the purpose of considering unemployment. (See Item 99, Vol. I.)

At this meeting seven States participated — Massachusetts, Rhode Island, Connecticut, New York, New Jersey, Pennsylvania and Ohio. It was agreed that a comparative study of labor laws should be made and that a meeting of the representatives of the labor departments of the East-Central section of the United States should be called to discuss differences in the labor laws of the several States and to study the feasibility of making them more or less uniform.

Similar meetings to continue the discussion were held at Harrisburg, Pennsylvania, at which representatives of Delaware, Maryland and West Virginia were also present in addition to representatives of the seven States previously represented at Albany. Recommendations for more uniform laws relative to workmen's compensation, employment agencies, and women and minors in industry were presented to the conference.

On January 27 and 28, 1933, Governor Ely, of Massachusetts, called a similar conference at Boston and recommendations similar to those made at Harrisburg were again urged. Thereafter, representatives of the seven Northeastern States—Maine, New Hampshire, Massachusetts, Connecticut, Rhode Island, New York and Pennsylvania—met several times during 1933 and 1934, in an effort to draw up an interstate compact affecting labor legislation. On May 29, 1934, Governor Winant, of New Hampshire, called a conference at Concord, New Hampshire, to ratify an interstate compact which had been drawn up affecting labor legislation and providing particularly for a mandatory uniform minimum-wage law for minors and for women. The compact was signed on that date, subject of course to approval by the Legislatures of the respective States.

As soon as the compact was ratified by the Legislatures of Massachusetts, New Hampshire and Rhode Island, the compact was approved by Public Resolution No. 58, of the 75th Congress, and declared to be effective in those ratifying States and in such States as might thereafter ratify the same.

92 ❬ The One Hundred and Twenty-fifth Press Conference (Excerpts). May 25, 1934

(Strikes.)

Q. Mr. President, anything you care to say about the strike situation?

THE PRESIDENT: I don't think so. I think I had better not. It is awfully difficult to say anything without going into details and differentiations. I think it is better I should not. We are all working on it, as you know.

Q. You still need legislation of the type of the Wagner bill dealing with this?

THE PRESIDENT: It would be very helpful. There is no question about that. It would be very helpful, because it would clarify administrative procedure and at the same time would create methods that were perfectly clear under the law. In the individual strike cases people would know exactly the procedure on both sides — whom they come under, and to whom they go, and what authority there is in any given case.

Q. Is it fair to assume, then, that you want this legislation this Session?

THE PRESIDENT: I would like to have it very much. I think it would be helpful. I think you had better put this off the record.

Q. What you are saying now?

THE PRESIDENT: Yes, what I am saying now. It would be perfectly all right to say I am in favor of this legislation and hope it will go through; but, off the record, you all know that in any period of this kind, with a return of prosperity and reemployment and with an increase in values, you are bound to have more strikes. I look for a great many strikes in the course of this summer, a good many more. It is a normal and logical thing. I think I have said this before at a strike conference. They are brought about by a great many causes.

For instance, keeping this again entirely off the record, in this Toledo case the strike originated with only 400 employees in one factory, but there are a lot of other factors involved. They had pretty serious political trouble where a lot of graft and misgovernment, etc., was shown in the city. The result was that the population as a whole "got sore." It wasn't just these 400 men.

Yesterday, when this crowd of between 5,000 and 10,000 people started, they were, as a body, "sore" at certain definite people. As they went along, they would throw stones at one particular factory or shop, and then they would go along past several other factories or shops they were not "sore at," and then they would pick out the next fellow at whom they were "sore."

Charlie Taft telephoned to Miss Perkins about two hours ago and made the point that it is not an indiscriminatory strike; it is a strike against people they are "sore at," and it is not just the 400 strikers; it is a very large element of the population.

So each case really has to be taken up on the merits of that particular, individual case. There is no general statement that can be made relating to it. Miss Perkins used a parallel which, of course, has got to be entirely off the record. She said in conference today that it is not a general revolutionary feeling but a feeling against certain old-line politicians and a feeling against certain industrialists. It is a pretty discriminating opposition. It is based on reason of some kind.

In the Toledo situation, of course, the one thing that all of us ought to appreciate and write about is that there are methods of settlement, and that the attitude of employers in many cases has been so autocratic. Take, for instance, the man who said, in one of the papers this morning, that he would consider that he was demeaning himself if he sat in the same room with William Green. Now that kind of autocratic attitude on the part of a steel company official does not make for working things out. On the other hand, there are people on the other end of the camp, the labor end, who are just as autocratic. . . .

(See also Press Conference of September 5, 1934, on similar subject, Item 155, this volume.)

93 ❧ White House Statement on Executive Order No. 6723 Applying to Obligations of Service Industries under N.R.A. May 27, 1934

Most industries have a national community of economic interest even though the operation of some of their units is local. There are others which, notwithstanding their having national trade associations, do not actually integrate themselves nationally. Whether an industry can govern and police itself under the fair trade provisions of a national code depends on its degree of actual economic integration on a national scale and on the organization and solidarity within the whole industry. A trial period of some months has shown that while most industries, after organization for this work and a little experience with it, can secure uniform national results, there are others to which a greater degree of autonomous local self-government is desirable. Among these are some, but not all, of the so-called service industries — that is, industries engaged in the sale of services rather than of goods.

No industry would give up the gains we have made in the elimination of child labor and in the establishment of minimum wages and maximum hours of labor, and, of course, under the law, we cannot give up collective bargaining and the right of the President to cancel or modify codes, orders and agreements.

I am signing an order today which carries these principles into effect as to some of the so-called service industries. To put it simply: No matter where he is located, no member of any such service industry, as shall have previously been designated by the Administrator, may fly the Blue Eagle, unless he is living up to the present Code provisions governing child labor, maximum hours, minimum wages and collective bargaining. But trade practices shall be required as a condition of flying the Blue Eagle in these designated service industries only in particular localities in which at least 85 percent of the members there have proposed, as a local code of fair trade practice, a schedule of such practices. If the Administrator approves of any such proposed local code then no member in that locality may fly the Blue Eagle unless, in addition to complying with the Code provisions governing child labor, maximum hours, minimum wages, and collective bargaining, he also is complying with this local compact on trade practices.

The display of the Blue Eagle by any employer is notice to the people of the United States that he is dealing fairly with his workers in accordance with the letter and spirit of the Recovery Program, that he is not taking advantage of child labor and that he is living up to the prescribed high responsibility to the public and to his competitors. The absence of a Blue Eagle indicates that the employer has omitted or refused to adopt some of these standards and to cooperate with the Government and his economic and actual neighbors in trying to bring about a better day.

NOTE: N.I.R.A., in seeking to improve business conditions and wages and hours as a whole, had made no distinction, as to codification, between interstate and intrastate commerce. The law did provide that, when codes were violated, penalties should be attached only to transactween interstate and intrastate commerce. Confusion was inevitable because all businesses of all types were subject to voluntary codification, and particularly because the President's Reemployment Agreement could be voluntarily signed by businesses which were purely local — the local cleaner and dyer, the barber, the laundryman, the restaurant proprietor, the garageman, etc.

Although these so-called service trades are ordinarily thought of as insignificant in comparison with such industries as steel, oil or automobiles, the number of persons employed therein is actually as large as, and in many cases larger than, the number employed in some of what are usually thought of as major industries. Moreover, some of the worst labor conditions existed in these trades, which were likewise beset in many instances by various kinds of racketeering. In consequence, labor groups brought great pressure to bear to put codes for these trades into effect as soon as possible. Moreover, under the pinch of depression and in the face of the racketeering violence which arose in many cases out of acute price competition, the trades themselves clamored for codes of fair competition.

The code which became, in a sense, the typical case was the code for the cleaning and dyeing trade. This code was approved on November 8, 1933. The report of the Administrator to me on this code contains the following illuminating paragraph:

"The trade has been harassed for the past three years by cut-throat competition, which in many cases led to racketeering, brought about by slashing prices below cost, lowering wages, accompanied often by sweating labor, offering inferior quality and poor service. These conditions have almost completely demoralized the business of plant owners and have caused untold hardships to some 175,000 or more tailor shops serving as retail outlets for the wholesale dry-cleaning plants. There are but few concerns in the trade who have any credit, and in many cases there are substantial amounts owed to labor for past-due wages. Testimony at the hearing, for example, brought out the fact that over $600,000 in wages are long past due to workers in the city of New York."

To cope with these conditions, the code for the cleaning and dyeing trade contained provisions for minimum wages, maximum hours, collective bargaining, and the fixing of minimum prices.

When the problem of enforcement came, however, the statute required that the line must be drawn between interstate and intrastate transactions. This was a difficult matter to explain and a difficult policy to maintain. Some of the worst labor conditions persisted in local service industries, in local manufacturing and retail operations. In these local industries the code requirements could not, of course, be enforced by N.R.A. Trade associations usually did not exist in this type of industry, and attempts at self-discipline by the industry were wholly ineffectual.

Very soon considerable public clamor arose against the fixing of minimum prices in the code. The proponents of the code defended it hotly, and organized labor exhibited considerable apprehension lest the removal of price protection should result in further pressure upon wages. After an extended inquiry, which included reexamination of other service trades, the foregoing Executive Order No. 6723 was issued as the best working compromise which could be found. It was one of many efforts made to extricate N.R.A. from this impossible situation.

The significant features of Executive Order No. 6723 were: (a) retention of the provisions governing child labor, maximum hours, minimum wages, and collective bargaining; (b) the suspension of any attempt to regulate prices and trade practices on a nationwide basis. In place of this, it was provided that such price and trade practice provisions could be reinstated within any locality in which 85 percent of the members of the trade agreed to do so; (c) the only program of enforcement contemplated for price and trade practice provisions in localities in which they were reinstated by a vote of 85 percent of the members of the trade was the use of the Blue Eagle.

In addition, the various States were urged to adopt State industrial recovery acts to cover local trades and industries. One unhappy result of this was to cause much duplication and overlapping between State and Federal codes and between State and Federal authority.

For example, in the spring of 1934, Jacob Maged, a tailor of Jersey City, New Jersey, was convicted and sentenced for violating a code which had been adopted under a statute of New Jersey, a counterpart of the N.I.R.A. This code fixed a minimum price for the service of pressing, and Mr. Maged's offense consisted of doing pressing work at five cents under the code minimum price. He was sentenced to serve a thirty-day jail sentence, but after serving three days he was released on his promise to abide by the State code. Whether out of ignorance or design, a very large section of the press at the time reported the incident as one occur-

ring under the Federal N.I.R.A. itself, rather than under the local statute, and trumpeted it as an illustration of the extremes to which the N.R.A. had gone, and of the way Federal authority was creeping into local business.

Much as I regret the necessity of saying it, the continued insistence upon this misstatement by a certain type of newspaper owner and columnist, long after the truth had been fully explained that this New Jersey case concerned a violation of the local and not of the Federal statute, constitutes a glaring example of perversion of news.

It had become evident before the termination of N.R.A. that it would be necessary for it to withdraw as rapidly as possible from the field of local business and leave all regulatory efforts in this field to State and municipal action. The proposed revision of N.R.A. (see Vol. IV, note to Item 17) included such withdrawal.

94 ⟨ Request for Congressional Reconsideration of Processing Tax on Coconut Oil from the Philippine Islands. May 28, 1934

To the Congress:

Early in the present session of the Congress the Philippine Independence Act was passed. This Act provided that after the inauguration of the new interim or Commonwealth form of government of the Philippine Islands trade relations between the

United States and the Philippine Islands shall be as now provided by law. Certain exceptions, however, were made. One of these exceptions required levying on all coconut oil coming into the United States from the Philippine Islands in any calendar year in excess of 448,000,000 pounds, the same rates of duty now collected by the United States on coconut oil imported from foreign countries.

It is, of course, wholly clear that the intent of the Congress by this provision was to exempt from import duty 448,000,000 pounds of coconut oil from the Philippines.

Later in the present session, the Congress in the Revenue Act imposed a three cent per pound processing tax on coconut oil from the Philippines. This action was of course directly contrary to the intent of the provision in the Independence Act cited above.

During this same period, the people of the Philippine Islands through their Legislature accepted the provisions of the Independence Act on May 1, 1934.

There are three reasons why I request reconsideration by the Congress of the provision for a three cent per pound processing tax.

First, it is a withdrawal of an offer made by the Congress of the United States to the people of the Philippine Islands.

Second, enforcement of this provision at this time will produce a serious condition among many thousands of families in the Philippine Islands.

Third, no effort has been made to work out some form of compromise which would be less unjust to the Philippine people and at the same time attain, even if more slowly, the object of helping the butter and animal fat industry in the United States.

I, therefore, request reconsideration of that provision of the Revenue Act which relates to coconut oil in order that the subject may be studied further between now and next January, and in order that the spirit and intent of the Independence Act be more closely followed.

NOTE: I was opposed to the enactment of this tax from the moment that it was first suggested, on the grounds that it conflicted with the provisions of the Philippines Independence Act. Unfortunately, however, no action was taken by the Congress pursuant to the foregoing message.

95 ❴ The President Forbids the Shipment of Arms and Munitions to the Combatants in the Chaco. Proclamation No. 2087. May 28, 1934

WHEREAS Section 1 of a joint resolution of Congress, entitled "Joint resolution to prohibit the sale of arms or munitions of war in the United States under certain conditions," approved May 28, 1934, provides as follows:

"That if the President finds that the prohibition of the sale of arms and munitions of war in the United States to those countries now engaged in armed conflict in the Chaco may contribute to the reestablishment of peace between those countries, and if after consultation with the Governments of other American Republics and with their cooperation, as well as that of such other Governments as he may deem necessary, he makes proclamation to that effect, it shall be unlawful to sell, except under such limitations and exceptions as the President prescribes, any arms or munitions of war in any place in the United States to the countries now engaged in that armed conflict, or to any person, company, or association acting in the interest of either country, until otherwise ordered by the President or by Congress."

AND WHEREAS it is provided by Section 2 of the said joint resolution that—

"Whoever sells any arms or munitions of war in violation of Section 1 shall, on conviction, be punished by a fine not exceeding $10,000 or by imprisonment not exceeding two years, or both."

Now, THEREFORE, I, Franklin D. Roosevelt, President of the United States of America, acting under and by virtue of the authority conferred in me by the said joint resolution of Congress, do hereby declare and proclaim that I have found that the prohibition of the sale of arms and munitions of war in the United States to those countries now engaged in armed conflict in the Chaco may contribute to the reestablishment of peace between those countries, and that I have consulted with the Governments of other American Republics and have been assured of the cooperation of such Governments as I have deemed necessary as contemplated by the said joint resolution; and I do hereby admonish all citizens of the United States and every person to abstain from every violation of the provisions of the joint resolution above set forth, hereby made applicable to Bolivia and Paraguay, and I do hereby warn them that all violations of such provisions will be rigorously prosecuted.

And I do hereby enjoin upon all officers of the United States charged with the execution of the laws thereof, the utmost diligence in preventing violations of the said joint resolution and this my proclamation issued thereunder, and in bringing to trial and punishment any offenders against the same.

And I do hereby delegate to the Secretary of State the power of prescribing exceptions and limitations to the application of the said joint resolution of May 28, 1934, as made effective by this my proclamation issued thereunder.

NOTE: The foregoing Proclamation was issued by me pursuant to the Joint Resolution of the Congress quoted in the Proclamation. It prohibited the sale of arms and munitions of war in the United States to Bolivia and Paraguay, who were engaged in armed conflict over the Chaco. (See also Item 180 of Vol. II.)

After the Proclamation, the Administration continued its efforts to assist in the achievement of a settlement of the Chaco dispute. On July 12, 1934, the United States, Argen-tina and Brazil proposed a peace plan to the belligerents which was not adopted. The efforts of the League of Nations to bring about a peaceful settlement were also unsuccessful, and in fact resulted in the withdrawal of Paraguay from the League on February 23, 1935.

Finally, a mediatory group, composed of representatives of Argentina, Chile, Brazil, Peru, Uruguay and the United States, met in Buenos Aires in May, 1935, with the Ministers for Foreign Affairs of Bolivia and Paraguay. Again the United

States cooperated effectively in this peace effort and played a very important role in assuring the success of the negotiations. A peace Protocol was finally signed on June 12, 1935, and actual hostilities in the Chaco ceased on June 14, 1935. The Protocol provided for a peace conference to seek a settlement of all questions at issue between Bolivia and Paraguay. In the meantime hostilities have ceased, the armies have been demobilized, prisoners of war have been repatriated, and an agreement has been entered into between Bolivia and Paraguay to renew diplomatic relations. The conference is still at work on a final agreement upon the territorial issue.

The prohibition in the foregoing Proclamation remained in force until it was revoked by my Proclamation No. 2147, dated November 14, 1935 (see Vol. IV, Item 163). This latter Proclamation was issued after the conference in Buenos Aires had formally adopted, on October 28, 1935, a resolution declaring that the war between Bolivia and Paraguay had come to an end.

96 (Request for Approval of a New Treaty with Cuba. May 29, 1934

To the Senate:

To THE end that I may receive the advice and consent of the Senate to its ratification, I transmit herewith a Treaty of Relations between the United States of America and the Republic of Cuba, signed at Washington on May 29, 1934.

This treaty would supersede the Treaty of Relations between the United States and Cuba, signed at Habana on May 22, 1903.

I have publicly declared "that the definite policy of the United States from now on is one opposed to armed intervention." In this new treaty with Cuba, the contractual right to intervene in Cuba which had been granted to the United States in the earlier treaty of 1903 is abolished, and those further rights, likewise granted to the United States in the same instrument, involving participation in the determination of such domestic policies of the Republic of Cuba as those relating to finance and to sanitation, are omitted therefrom. By the consummation of this treaty, this Government will make it clear that it not only opposes the policy of armed intervention, but that it renounces those rights of intervention and interference in Cuba which have been bestowed upon it by treaty.

Our relations with Cuba have been and must always be especially close. They are based not only upon geographical proximity, but likewise upon the fact that American blood was shed as well as Cuban blood to gain the liberty of the Cuban people and to establish the Republic of Cuba as an independent power in the family of Nations. I believe that this treaty will further maintain those good relations upon the enduring foundation of sovereign equality and friendship between our two peoples, and I consequently recommend to the Senate its ratification.

NOTE: This treaty abrogated the old treaty of 1903, which contained the so-called Platt Amendment. Under the latter, Cuba had agreed to consent to United States intervention in certain specified circumstances, and had likewise agreed not to make treaties with foreign powers which tended to impair its independence, and not to contract any public debt beyond its ability to service from ordinary revenues.

The treaty of 1903, in the light of the situation existing a generation later, was an anachronism, and I early determined upon its replacement by a modern instrument responsive to changed conditions. The treaty of 1934, which constitutes the present basis for our relations with Cuba, abrogated all of the above mentioned provisions of the Treaty of Relations of 1903.

This action on our part in relinquishing the special rights and the potential control which we had in the internal and external affairs of Cuba, not only strengthened the friendship between Cuba and the United States, but very materially increased the good-will and confidence with which we are regarded by all the other American Republics. Here was additional definite proof that the United States was opposed to any further armed intervention in the American countries.

The treaty was ratified on June 9, 1934, on which date cablegrams of congratulations between Cuba and the United States were exchanged.

97 ⁋ "The Selfishness of Sectionalism Has No Place in Our National Life" — Address at Gettysburg. May 30, 1934

Governor Pinchot, Mr. Chairman, my friends:

WHAT a glorious day this is! I rejoice in it and I rejoice in this splendid celebration of it.

On these hills of Gettysburg two brave armies of Americans once met in contest. Not far from here, in a valley likewise consecrated to American valor, a ragged Continental Army survived a bitter winter to keep alive the expiring hope of a new Nation; and near to this battlefield and that valley stands that invincible city where the Declaration of Independence was born and the Constitution of the United States was written by the fathers. Surely, all this is holy ground.

It was in Philadelphia, too, that Washington spoke his solemn, tender, wise words of farewell — a farewell not alone to his generation, but to the generation of those who laid down their lives here and to our generation and to the America of tomorrow. Perhaps if our fathers and grandfathers had truly heeded those words we should have had no family quarrel, no battle of Gettysburg, no Appomattox.

As a Virginian, President Washington had a natural pride in Virginia; but as an American, in his stately phrase, "the name of American, which belongs to you, in your national capacity, must always exalt the just pride of patriotism, more than any appellation derived from local discrimination."

Recognizing the strength of local and State and sectional prejudices and how strong they might grow to be, and how they might take from the national Government some of the loyalty the citizens owed to it, he made three historic tours during his Presidency. One was through New England in 1789, another through the Northern States in 1790, and still another through the Southern States in 1791. He did this, as he said — and the words sound

272

good nearly a century and a half later — "In order to become better acquainted with their principal characters and internal circumstances, as well as to be more accessible to numbers of well-informed persons who might give him useful advices on political subjects."

But Washington did more to stimulate patriotism than merely to travel and mingle with the people. He knew that Nations grow as their commerce and manufactures and agriculture grow, and that all of these grow as the means of transportation are extended. He sought to knit the sections together by their common interest in these great enterprises; and he projected highways and canals as aids not to sectional, but to national, development.

But the Nation expanded geographically after the death of Washington far more rapidly than the Nation's means of intercommunication. The small national area of 1789 grew to the great expanse of the Nation of 1860. Even in terms of the crude transportation of that day, the first thirteen States were still within "driving distance" of each other.

With the settling and the peopling of the Continent to the shores of the Pacific, there developed the problem of self-contained territories because the Nation's expansion exceeded its development of means of transportation, as we learn from our history books. The early building of railroads did not proceed on national lines.

Contrary to belief of some of us Northerners, the South and the West were not laggard in developing this new form of transportation; but, as in the East, most of the railroads were local and sectional. It was a chartless procedure; people were not thinking in terms of national transportation or national communication. In the days before the Brothers' War not a single line of railroad was projected from the South to the North; not even one from the South reached to the national capital itself.

In those days, it was an inspired prophet of the South who said: "My brethren, if we know one another, we will love one another." The tragedy of the Nation was that the people did not know one another because they had not the necessary means of visiting one another.

Since those days, two subsequent wars, both with foreign Nations, have measurably allayed and softened the ancient passions. It has been left to us of this generation to see the healing made permanent.

We are all brothers now, brothers in a new understanding. The grain farmers of the West and in the fertile fields of Pennsylvania do not set themselves up for preference if we seek at the same time to help the cotton farmers of the South; nor do the tobacco growers complain of discrimination if, at the same time, we help the cattle men of the plains and mountains.

In our planning to lift industry to normal prosperity, the farmer upholds our efforts. And as we seek to give the farmers of the United States a long-sought equality, the city worker understands and helps. All of us, among all the States, share in whatever of good comes to the average man. We know that we all have a stake — a partnership in this Government of this, our country.

Today, we have many means of knowing each other — means that at last have sounded the doom of sectionalism. It is, I think, as I survey the picture from every angle, a simple fact that the chief hindrance to progress comes from three elements which, thank God, grow less in importance with the growth of a clearer understanding of our purposes on the part of the overwhelming majority. These groups are those who seek to stir up political animosity or to build political advantage by the distortion of facts; those who, by declining to follow the rules of the game, seek to gain an unfair advantage over those who are willing to live up to the rules of the game; and those few who, because they have never been willing to take an interest in their fellow Americans, dwell inside of their own narrow spheres and still represent the selfishness of sectionalism which has no place in our national life.

Washington and Jefferson and Jackson and Lincoln and Theodore Roosevelt and Woodrow Wilson sought and worked for a consolidated Nation. You and I have it in our power to attain that great ideal within our lifetime. We can do this by following the peaceful methods prescribed under the broad and resilient provisions of the Constitution of the United States.

Here, here at Gettysburg, here in the presence of the spirits of those who fell on this ground, we give renewed assurance that the passions of war are moldering in the tombs of Time and the purposes of peace are flowing today in the hearts of a united people.

98 ⟨ Message to the Congress on the Payment of War Debts to the United States. June 1, 1934

To the Congress:

IN MY address to the Congress, January 3, I stated that I expected to report later in regard to debts owed the Government and people of this country by the Governments and people of other countries. There has been no formal communication on the subject from the Executive since President Hoover's message of December 19, 1931.

The developments are well known, having been announced to the press as they occurred. Correspondence with debtor Governments has been made public promptly and is available in the Annual Report of the Secretary of the Treasury. It is, however, timely to review the situation.

Payments on the indebtedness of foreign Governments to the United States which fell due in the fiscal year ended June 30, 1932, were postponed on the proposal of President Hoover announced June 20, 1931, and authorized by the Joint Resolution of Congress approved December 23, 1931. Yugoslavia alone suspended payment while rejecting President Hoover's offer of postponement.

In the six months of July to December, 1932, which followed the end of the Hoover moratorium year, payments of $125,-000,000 from twelve Governments fell due. Requests to postpone the payments due December 15, 1932, were received from Great Britain, France, Belgium, Czechoslovakia, Estonia, Latvia, Lithuania and Poland. The replies made on behalf of President Hoover through the Department of State declined these requests, generally stating that it was not in the power of the Executive to grant them, and expressing a willingness to cooperate with the debtor Government in surveying the entire situation. After such correspondence, Czechoslovakia, Finland, Great Britain, Italy, Latvia and Lithuania met their contractual obligations, while Belgium, Estonia, France and Poland made no payment.

In a note of December 11, 1932, after the United States had declined to sanction postponement of the payment due December 15, the British Government, in announcing its decision to make payment of the amount due on December 15, made the following important statement:

"For reasons which have already been placed on record His Majesty's Government are convinced that the system of intergovernmental payments in respect of the War Debts as it existed prior to Mr. Hoover's initiative on June 20th, 1931, cannot be revived without disaster. Since it is agreed that the whole subject should be re-examined between the United States and the United Kingdom this fundamental point need not be further stressed here.

"In the view of His Majesty's Government therefore the payment to be made on December 15th is not to be regarded as a resumption of the annual payments contemplated by the existing agreement. It is made because there has not been time for discussion with regard to that agreement to take place and because the United States Government have stated that in their opinion such a payment would greatly increase the prospects of a satisfactory approach to the whole question.

"His Majesty's Government propose accordingly to treat the payment on December 15th as a capital payment of which account should be taken in any final settlement and they are making arrangements to effect this payment in gold as being in the circumstances the least prejudicial of the methods open to them.

"This procedure must obviously be exceptional and abnormal and His Majesty's Government desire to urge upon the United States Government the importance of an early exchange of views with the object of concluding the proposed discussion before June 15th next, in order to obviate a general breakdown of the existing intergovernmental agreements."

The Secretary of State, Mr. Stimson, replied to this note on the same day that acceptance by the Secretary of the Treasury of funds tendered in payment of the December 15 installment cannot constitute approval of or agreement to any condition or declaration of policy inconsistent with the terms of the agreement inasmuch as the Executive has no power to amend or to alter those terms either directly or by implied commitment.

No payment was made by France December 15, 1932, as the French Chamber of Deputies by a vote on the morning of December 14 refused authorization to make the payment. The resolution voted by the French Chamber at that time invited the French Government to convoke as soon as possible, in agreement with Great Britain and other debtors, a general conference for the purpose of adjusting all international obligations and putting an end to all international transfers for which there is no compensating transaction. The resolution stated that the Chamber, despite legal and economic considerations, would have authorized settlement had the United States been willing to agree in advance to the convening of the conference for these purposes.

This resolution of the French Chamber is to be read in relation with the public statements of policy made by President Hoover and by myself on November 23, 1932. President Hoover said, "The United States Government from the beginning has taken the position that it would deal with each of the debtor Governments separately, as separate and distinct circumstances surrounded each case. Both in the making of the loans and in the subsequent settlements with the different debtors, this policy has been rigidly made clear to every foreign Government concerned." I said:

"I find myself in complete accord with the four principles discussed in the conference between the President and myself yesterday and set forth in a statement which the President has issued today.

"These debts were actual loans made under distinct understanding and with the intention that they would be repaid.

"In dealing with the debts each Government has been and is to be considered individually, and all dealings with each Government are independent of dealings with any other debtor Government. In no case should we deal with the debtor Governments collectively.

"Debt settlements made in each case take into consideration the capacity to pay of the individual debtor Nations.

"The indebtedness of the various European Nations to our Government has no relation whatsoever to reparations payments made or owed to them."

Of the $125,000,000 due and payable December 15, 1932, the Treasury received $98,750,000, of which $95,550,000 was the British payment made subsequent to the above correspondence, and the other $3,000,000 represented payments by five other debtor Nations. The amounts due from Belgium, Estonia, France, Hungary and Poland which were not received amounted to $25,-000,000, of which $19,260,000 was due and payable by France.

In my statement issued November 23, 1932, I had said:

"I firmly believe in the principle that an individual debtor should at all times have access to the creditor; that he should have opportunity to lay facts and representations before the creditor; and that the creditor always should give courteous, sympathetic and thoughtful consideration to such facts and representations.

"This is a rule essential to the preservation of the ordinary relationships of life. It is a basic obligation of civilization. It applies to Nations as well as to individuals.

"The principle calls for a free access by the debtor to the creditor. Each case should be considered in the light of the conditions and necessities peculiar to the case of each Nation concerned."

On January 20, 1933, President Hoover and I agreed upon the following statement:

"The British Government has asked for a discussion of the debts. The incoming Administration will be glad to receive their representative early in March for this purpose. It is, of course, necessary to discuss at the same time the world economic problems in which the United States and Great Britain are mutually interested and therefore that representatives should also be sent to discuss ways and means for improving the world situation."

On March 4, 1933, the situation with regard to the indebtedness of other Governments to the United States was, in brief, as follows:

France — The French Parliament had refused to permit payment of $19,261,432.50 interest due on the $3,863,650,000 bonds of France owned by the United States;

Great Britain — With respect to the British bonded debt held by the Treasury in the principal amount of $4,368,000,000, Great Britain in meeting a due payment of $30,000,000 principal and $65,550,000 interest had stated that the payment was not to be regarded as a resumption of the annual payments contemplated under the funding agreement of June 19, 1923, but was to be treated, so far as the British Government was concerned, as a capital payment of which account should be taken in any final settlement;

Italy — With respect to the $2,004,900,000 principal amount of bonds of the Italian Government held by the United States Treasury, the Italian Government had paid the sum of $1,245,437 interest due December 15, 1932; but in doing so it referred to a resolution of the Grand Council of Fascism, adopted December 5, 1932, in which "a radical solution of the 'sponging of the slate' type was declared to be necessary for the world's economic recovery";

Czechoslovakia in making a payment of $1,500,000 principal due December 15, 1932, on its debt of $165,000,000 had stated that "this payment constitutes in the utmost self-denial of the Czechoslovak people their final effort to meet the obligation under such extremely unfavorable circumstances";

Belgium had declined to pay $2,125,000 interest due December 15, 1932, on its bonds of $400,680,000 held by the Treasury of the United States and in doing so had recited circumstances which it stated "prevent it from resuming, on December 15th, the payments which were suspended by virtue of the agreements made in July, 1931," adding, "Belgium is still disposed to collaborate fully in seeking a general settlement of intergovernmental debts and of the other problems arising from the depression";

Poland had not paid the $232,000 principal and $3,070,980 interest due December 15, 1932, on its bond in the principal amount of $206,057,000 held by the Treasury of the United States.

Of the nine other Governments whose bonds are held by the Treasury of the United States, *Estonia* and *Hungary* had not met payments due December 15, 1932;

Austria is availing itself of a contractual right to postpone payments;

Greece was making only partial payments on its foreign bonded indebtedness, including that held by the United States;

Yugoslavia had declined to sign any Hoover moratorium agreement and had stopped paying;

No payment by *Rumania* had fallen due since the close of the Hoover moratorium;

Finland, Latvia and *Lithuania* were current in their payments.

Although I had informal discussions concerning the British debt with the British Ambassador even before March 4, 1933, and in April there was further discussion of the subject with the Prime Minister of Great Britain and between experts of the two Governments, it was not possible to reach definitive conclusions. On June 13, the British Government gave notice that in the then existing circumstances it was not prepared to make the payment due June 15, 1933, but would make an immediate payment of $10,000,000 as an acknowledgment of the debt pending a final settlement. To this notice reply was made by the Acting Secretary of State, pointing out that it is not within the discretion of the President to reduce or cancel the existing debt owed to the United States or to alter the schedule of debt payments contained in the existing settlement. At the same time I took occasion to announce that in view of the representations of the British Government, the accompanying acknowledgment of the debt itself, and the payment made, I had no personal hesitation in saying that I would not characterize the resultant situation as a default. In view of the suggestion of the expressed desire of the British Government to make representations concerning the debt, I suggested that such representations be made in Washington as soon as convenient.

The Agricultural Adjustment Act, approved May 12, 1933, had authorized the President for a period of six months from that date to accept silver in payment of installments due from any foreign Government, such silver to be accepted at not to exceed a price of fifty cents an ounce. In the payments due June 15, 1933, the Governments of Great Britain, Czechoslovakia, Finland, Italy, Lithuania and Rumania took advantage of this offer.

On June 15, 1933, payments of about $144,000,000 were due from foreign Governments, the larger amounts being about $76,000,000 from Great Britain, almost $41,000,000 from France and $13,500,000 from Italy. The amounts actually paid into the Treasury were $11,374,000 of which $10,000,000 was paid by Great Britain and $1,000,000 by Italy. Communications were received from most of the debtor Governments asking a discussion of the debt question with the United States Government.

In October, 1933, representatives of the British Government arrived in Washington and conferred for some weeks with representatives of this Government. These discussions made clear the existing difficulties and the discussions were adjourned.

The British Government then stated that it continued to acknowledge the debt without prejudicing its right again to present the matter of readjustment and that it would express this acknowledgment tangibly by a payment of $7,500,000 on December 15. In announcing this I stated that in view of the representations, of the payment, and of the impossibility of accepting at that time any of the proposals for a readjustment of the debt, I had no personal hesitation in saying that I should not regard the British Government as in default.

On December 15, 1933, there was due and payable by foreign Governments on their debt funding agreements and Hoover moratorium agreements a total of about $153,000,000. The payments actually received were slightly less than $9,000,000, including $7,500,000 paid by Great Britain, $1,000,000 by Italy, and about $230,000 by Finland.

At the present time Finland remains the only foreign Government which has met all payments on its indebtedness to the United States punctually and in full.

It is a simple fact that this matter of the repayment of debts contracted to the United States during and after the World War has gravely complicated our trade and financial relationships with the borrowing Nations for many years.

These obligations furnished vital means for the successful conclusion of a war which involved the national existence of the borrowers, and later for a quicker restoration of their normal life after the war ended.

The money loaned by the United States Government was in turn borrowed by the United States Government from the people of the United States, and our Government in the absence of payment from foreign Governments is compelled to raise the shortage by general taxation of its own people in order to pay off the original Liberty Bonds and the later refunding bonds.

It is for these reasons that the American people have felt that their debtors were called upon to make a determined effort to discharge these obligations. The American people would not be disposed to place an impossible burden upon their debtors, but are nevertheless in a just position to ask that substantial sacrifices be made to meet these debts.

We shall continue to expect the debtors on their part to show full understanding of the American attitude on this debt question. The people of the debtor Nations will also bear in mind the fact that the American people are certain to be swayed by the use which debtor countries make of their available resources — whether such resources would be applied for the purposes of recovery as well as for reasonable payment on the debt owed to the citizens of the United States, or for purposes of unproductive nationalistic expenditure or like purposes.

In presenting this report to you, I suggest that, in view of all existing circumstances no legislation at this session of the Congress is either necessary or advisable.

I can only repeat that I have made it clear to the debtor Nations again and again that "the indebtedness to our Government has no relation whatsoever to reparations payments made or owed to them" and that each individual Nation has full and free opportunity individually to discuss its problem with the United States.

We are using every means to persuade each debtor Nation as to the sacredness of the obligation and also to assure it of our willingness, if it should so request, to discuss frankly and fully the special circumstances relating to means and method of payment.

Recognizing that the final power lies with the Congress, I shall keep the Congress informed from time to time and make such new recommendations as may later seem advisable.

99 ❬ The President Submits to the Congress Reports on a Comprehensive Plan for Control and Development of Water Resources. June 4, 1934

To the Congress:

ON FEBRUARY 2, 1934, by resolution, the Congress requested me to report on "a comprehensive plan for the improvement and development of the rivers of the United States, with a view of giving the Congress information for the guidance of legislation which will provide for the maximum amount of flood control, navigation, irrigation, and development of hydro-electric power."

Pursuant thereto I requested the Secretaries of the Departments of the Interior, War, Agriculture and Labor to advise on the development of a water policy and on the choice of projects. I am sending herewith copies of their report, together with separate letters from the Secretary of War and the Secretary of Labor, and also:

(1) List of Technical Advisory Committees of the President's Committee.
(2) Review of reports of Technical Sub-Committees on water flow.

(3) Review of report of Technical Sub-Committees covering additions in the Arid Section, prepared by the Bureau of Reclamation.

(4) Seven reports of Technical Sub-Committees covering various regions.

I ask that the Congress bear in mind certain obvious facts relating to these reports:

(1) That the time for the preparation of these reports was extremely limited.

(2) That the subject is one of enormous magnitude covering the whole of the United States.

(3) That the Resolution of the Congress, covering the subjects of flood control, navigation, irrigation, and development of hydro-electric power, automatically opened the door to all interrelated subjects which come under the general head of land and water use. This broader definition brings to our attention very clearly such kindred problems as soil erosion, stream pollution, fire prevention, reforestation, afforestation, marginal lands, stranded communities, distribution of industries, education, highway building, home building, and a dozen others.

(4) All of the reports were based primarily on information already at hand and further study is strongly recommended.

(5) For the purpose of making a preliminary test, I requested a wholly tentative trial selection of ten specific projects. As I had expected, the report strongly doubts the advisability of recommending these projects, on the ground that any selection at this point must necessarily omit many meritorious projects which further analysis may show to be preferable.

(6) The reports of the Technical Sub-Committees, covering various areas, are of definite value. But before any work is done, it is obvious that a competent coordinating body must go over all of these reports, as well as reports on other projects, and produce a comprehensive plan.

In view of the above, I, therefore, suggest that the Congress regard this message and the accompanying documents as merely a preliminary study and allow me, between now and the assembling of the next Congress, to complete these studies and to outline to the next Congress a comprehensive plan to be pursued over a long period of years. Further legislative action on this subject at this session of the Congress seems to me, therefore, unnecessary.

I expect before the final adjournment of this Congress to forward to it a broader outline of national policy in which the subject matter of this message will be presented in conjunction with two other subjects also relating to human welfare and security.

We should proceed toward a rounded policy of national scope.

NOTE: This report was prepared by the President's Committee on Water Flow, appointed by me during the previous winter, consisting of the Secretaries of the Interior, War, Agriculture and Labor. The report dealt primarily with navigation, flood control, irrigation and hydro-electric power. It was, however, calculated to lead to consideration of all the other multiple-use aspects of water planning and served to emphasize the regional water problems of the country. (See Vol. IV, Items 8 and 73.)

100 ❲ Request for Authority to Present to Haiti Buildings and Equipment Formerly Used by the U. S. Marines in Haiti. June 5, 1934

To the Congress:

NEXT October our Marine and Naval forces will be withdrawn from the Republic of Haiti. During a period of almost twenty years in which they have been stationed in Haiti they have rendered valuable assistance to the Haitian Government and people in training the Haitian Constabulary. This Constabulary known as the Garde, has been using certain equipment and material loaned to them by our Marine and Naval forces, and the Haitian Government would welcome the opportunity of retain-

ing this equipment and material. Also, there are various buildings, barracks, garages and workshops which our Marine and
Naval forces have constructed and which would be of practical
use to the Haitian Government. It would seem to me a fitting
climax to the close of the period of special relationship which has
existed between Haiti and the United States if our Government
were to make a gift of these buildings and of a portion of this material and equipment to the Haitian Government. In the joint
statement which the President of Haiti and I issued on April 17th,
following our conversations during President Vincent's visit to
Washington, I expressed my intention of seeking the necessary
authorization from the Congress of the United States in order to
make such a gift.

With the foregoing in mind, therefore, I recommend the enactment of legislation authorizing me in my discretion to convey
to the Government of Haiti, without cost to that Government,
such buildings, material, and equipment now in Haiti owned by
our Government as may appear to me to be appropriate.

NOTE: The foregoing recommen- gress, approved June 19, 1934, 48
dation was adopted by the enact- Stat. 1117. (See also Item 59, this
ment of Public No. 422, 73d Con- volume.)

101 ❡ Greetings to the American Newspaper Guild. June 5, 1934

So MANY of my friends are attending with you the second national convention of the American Newspaper Guild that it affords me real and personal pleasure to send a word of greeting
and best wishes. Newspapermen have been and are rendering real
and valued service to the Nation. It is gratifying that they accept
the great responsibilities that go at all times with their work. I
wish for you a most successful convention.

FRANKLIN D. ROOSEVELT

Heywood Broun,
President, American Newspaper Guild Convention,
St. Paul, Minnesota

102 ❡ Message to the Congress Reviewing the Broad Objectives and Accomplishments of the Administration. June 8, 1934

To the Congress:

You are completing a work begun in March, 1933, which will be regarded for a long time as a splendid justification of the vitality of representative government. I greet you and express once more my appreciation of the cooperation which has proved so effective. Only a small number of the items of our program remain to be enacted and I am confident that you will pass on them before adjournment. Many other pending measures are sound in conception, but must, for lack of time or of adequate information, be deferred to the session of the next Congress. In the meantime, we can well seek to adjust many of these measures into certain larger plans of governmental policy for the future of the Nation.

You and I, as the responsible directors of these policies and actions, may, with good reason, look to the future with confidence, just as we may look to the past fifteen months with reasonable satisfaction.

On the side of relief we have extended material aid to millions of our fellow citizens.

On the side of recovery we have helped to lift agriculture and industry from a condition of utter prostration.

But, in addition to these immediate tasks of relief and recovery we have properly, necessarily and with overwhelming approval determined to safeguard these tasks by rebuilding many of the structures of our economic life and of reorganizing it in order to prevent a recurrence of collapse.

It is childish to speak of recovery first and reconstruction afterward. In the very nature of the processes of recovery we must avoid the destructive influences of the past. We have shown the

287

world that democracy has within it the elements necessary to its own salvation.

Less hopeful countries where the ways of democracy are very new may revert to the autocracy of yesterday. The American people can be trusted to decide wisely upon the measures taken by the Government to eliminate the abuses of the past and to proceed in the direction of the greater good for the greater number.

Our task of reconstruction does not require the creation of new and strange values. It is rather the finding of the way once more to known, but to some degree forgotten, ideals and values. If the means and details are in some instances new, the objectives are as permanent as human nature.

Among our objectives I place the security of the men, women and children of the Nation first.

This security for the individual and for the family concerns itself primarily with three factors. People want decent homes to live in; they want to locate them where they can engage in productive work; and they want some safeguard against misfortunes which cannot be wholly eliminated in this man-made world of ours.

In a simple and primitive civilization homes were to be had for the building. The bounties of nature in a new land provided crude but adequate food and shelter. When land failed, our ancestors moved on to better land. It was always possible to push back the frontier, but the frontier has now disappeared. Our task involves the making of a better living out of the lands that we have.

So, also, security was attained in the earlier days through the interdependence of members of families upon each other and of the families within a small community upon each other. The complexities of great communities and of organized industry make less real these simple means of security. Therefore, we are compelled to employ the active interest of the Nation as a whole through government in order to encourage a greater security for each individual who composes it.

With the full cooperation of the Congress we have already

made a serious attack upon the problem of housing in our great cities. Millions of dollars have been appropriated for housing projects by Federal and local authorities, often with the generous assistance of private owners. The task thus begun must be pursued for many years to come. There is ample private money for sound housing projects; and the Congress, in a measure now before you, can stimulate the lending of money for the modernization of existing homes and the building of new homes. In pursuing this policy we are working toward the ultimate objective of making it possible for American families to live as Americans should.

In regard to the second factor, economic circumstances and the forces of nature themselves dictate the need of constant thought as to the means by which a wise Government may help the necessary readjustment of the population. We cannot fail to act when hundreds of thousands of families live where there is no reasonable prospect of a living in the years to come. This is especially a national problem. Unlike most of the leading Nations of the world, we have so far failed to create a national policy for the development of our land and water resources and for their better use by those people who cannot make a living in their present positions. Only thus can we permanently eliminate many millions of people from the relief rolls on which their names are now found.

The extent of the usefulness of our great natural inheritance of land and water depends on our mastery of it. We are now so organized that science and invention have given us the means of more extensive and effective attacks upon the problems of nature than ever before. We have learned to utilize water power, to reclaim deserts, to recreate forests and to redirect the flow of population. Until recently we have proceeded almost at random, making many mistakes.

There are many illustrations of the necessity for such planning. Some sections of the Northwest and Southwest which formerly existed as grazing land, were spread over with a fair crop of grass. On this land the water table lay a dozen or twenty feet below the surface, and newly arrived settlers put this land under the plow. Wheat was grown by dry farming methods. But in many of these places today the water table under the land has dropped to fifty or sixty feet below the surface and the top soil in dry seasons is blown away like driven snow. Falling rain, in the absence of grass roots, filters through the soil, runs off the surface, or is quickly reabsorbed into the atmosphere. Many million acres of such land must be restored to grass or trees if we are to prevent a new and man-made Sahara.

At the other extreme, there are regions originally arid, which have been generously irrigated by human engineering. But in some of these places the hungry soil has not only absorbed the water necessary to produce magnificent crops, but so much more water that the water table has now risen to the point of saturation, thereby threatening the future crops upon which many families depend.

Human knowledge is great enough today to give us assurance of success in carrying through the abandonment of many millions of acres for agricultural use and the replacing of these acres with others on which at least a living can be earned.

The rate of speed that we can usefully employ in this attack on impossible social and economic conditions must be determined by business-like procedure. It would be absurd to undertake too many projects at once or to do a patch of work here and another there without finishing the whole of an individual project. Obviously, the Government cannot undertake national projects in every one of the 435 Congressional districts, or even in every one of the 48 States. The magnificent conception of national realism and national needs that this Congress has built up has not only set an example of large vision for all time, but has almost consigned to oblivion our ancient habit of pork-barrel legislation; to that we cannot and must not revert. When the next Congress convenes I hope to be able to present to it a carefully considered national plan, covering the development and the human use of our natural resources of land and water over a long period of years.

In considering the cost of such a program it must be clear to all of us that for many years to come we shall be engaged in the task of rehabilitating many hundreds of thousands of our American families. In so doing we shall be decreasing future costs for the direct relief of destitution. I hope that it will be possible for the Government to adopt as a clear policy to be carried out over a long period, the appropriation of a large, definite, annual sum so that work may proceed year after year not under the urge of temporary expediency, but in pursuance of the well-considered rounded objective.

The third factor relates to security against the hazards and vicissitudes of life. Fear and worry based on unknown danger contribute to social unrest and economic demoralization. If, as our Constitution tells us, our Federal Government was established among other things "to promote the general welfare," it is our plain duty to provide for that security upon which welfare depends.

Next winter we may well undertake the great task of furthering the security of the citizen and his family through social insurance.

This is not an untried experiment. Lessons of experience are available from States, from industries and from many Nations of the civilized world. The various types of social insurance are interrelated; and I think it is difficult to attempt to solve them piecemeal. Hence, I am looking for a sound means which I can recommend to provide at once security against several of the great disturbing factors in life — especially those which relate to unemployment and old age. I believe there should be a maximum of cooperation between States and the Federal Government. I believe that the funds necessary to provide this insurance should be raised by contribution rather than by an increase in general taxation. Above all, I am convinced that social insurance should be national in scope, although the several States should meet at least a large portion of the cost of management, leaving to the Federal Government the responsibility of investing, maintaining and safeguarding the funds constituting the necessary insurance reserves.

I have commenced to make, with the greatest of care, the necessary actuarial and other studies for the formulation of plans for the consideration of the 74th Congress.

These three great objectives — the security of the home, the security of livelihood, and the security of social insurance — are, it seems to me, a minimum of the promise that we can offer to the American people. They constitute a right which belongs to every individual and every family willing to work. They are the essential fulfillment of measures already taken toward relief, recovery and reconstruction.

This seeking for a greater measure of welfare and happiness does not indicate a change in values. It is rather a return to values lost in the course of our economic development and expansion.

Ample scope is left for the exercise of private initiative. In fact, in the process of recovery, I am greatly hoping that repeated promises of private investment and private initiative to relieve the Government in the immediate future of much of the burden it has assumed, will be fulfilled. We have not imposed undue restrictions upon business. We have not opposed the incentive of reasonable and legitimate private profit. We have sought rather to enable certain aspects of business to regain the confidence of the public. We have sought to put forward the rule of fair play in finance and industry.

It is true that there are a few among us who would still go back. These few offer no substitute for the gains already made, nor any hope for making future gains for human happiness. They loudly assert that individual liberty is being restricted by Government, but when they are asked what individual liberties they have lost, they are put to it to answer.

We must dedicate ourselves anew to a recovery of the old and sacred possessive rights for which mankind has constantly struggled — homes, livelihood, and individual security. The road to these values is the way of progress. Neither you nor I will rest content until we have done our utmost to move further on that road.

103 ❨ The President Asks the Congress for Additional Funds to Carry on Drought Relief. June 9, 1934

To the Congress:

UNFORESEEN drought has visited disaster upon a large part of our country. Prompt and vigorous action to meet the emergency has been taken by the Federal Government through its various agencies. But the situation has become more grave as rainfall shortage has continued. Future rainfall cannot restore more than a small part of the damage to crops and livestock. An especially serious problem has developed because, while there is no prospect of shortage of human food, a shortage of animal food threatens over a wide area. This is causing losses to farmers and regions dependent upon the livestock industries. Large-scale assistance by the Federal Government is necessary to protect people in the stricken regions from suffering, to move feed to livestock, and livestock to feed, and to acquire and process surplus cattle to provide meat for relief distribution.

Organizations already exist in the Department of Agriculture, the Federal Emergency Relief Administration and the Farm Credit Administration to carry on the emergency program.

To finance operations of the magnitude planned, further funds are needed. After a conference with Members of Congress from the affected regions, a program along seven lines has been devised to meet the situation. These proposals and the funds required as estimated at this time are:

1. $125,000,000 for special work program and human relief.
2. $75,000,000 for livestock purchase in addition to the funds already available under the Jones-Connally Act.

3. $100,000,000 for shipping, processing and relief distribution of purchased cattle.

4. $100,000,000 for loans to farmers to finance emergency feed purchases and shipments.

5. $50,000,000 for emergency acquisition of submarginal farms and assistance in re-locating destitute farm families.

6. $50,000,000 for work camps to afford employment in the drought area for young men principally from cities and towns.

7. $25,000,000 for purchase of seed for 1935 plantings, and for loans to get seeds into farmers' hands.

These wholly tentative estimates have been made upon the basis of present and probable conditions. I believe the present emergency can be effectively met by the appropriation of $525,-000,000. Only such portion, of course, will be used as becomes absolutely necessary. We are dealing with a rapidly changing problem, and it is important that the authorization should be flexible so that funds can be allotted to the several Federal agencies as required.

NOTE: The foregoing message was sent by me while the various emergency relief agencies of the Government were already at work to meet the crisis in the drought areas (see Item 81, this volume). As a result of this message, the Congress, in full cooperation, voted $525,000,000 to be allocated among the various agencies engaged in drought relief measures. I appointed a President's Drought Relief Committee, consisting of the Secretary of Agriculture, the Administrator of the Agricultural Adjustment Administration, the Federal Emergency Relief Administrator and the Governor of the Farm Credit Administration. The various governmental agencies, cooperating in this joint drought relief drive, divided their functions among them as follows:

I. The Agricultural Adjustment Administration.
  (1) Purchase of surplus livestock.
  (2) Modification of "rented" acreage to encourage the production of forage crops.
  (3) Complete survey to determine feed and seed needs.
  (4) Coordination of feed acquisition through commercial channels and distribution of feed supplies to deficit areas.
  (5) Purchase of adapted seed grain.
  (6) Maintenance of farm income

through rental and benefit payments.

II. The Farm Credit Administration.

Granting emergency loans to farmers for buying and moving feed and seed with emphasis on the maintenance of foundation herds, for cattle movement and for other purposes.

III. The Federal Emergency Relief Administration.

(1) Processing of cattle purchased by the Agricultural Adjustment Administration into edible meats for relief distribution.

(2) Increasing employment and purchase of lands in stricken areas.

(3) Where necessary, supplying necessities of life to farm families made destitute by crop failure.

IV. The Civilian Conservation Corps.

(1) Increased enrollment of youths in drought area.

(2) Forestation and other measures to conserve moisture, prevent wind erosion, and minimize the effects of future drought.

The benefit payments under the existing crop-adjustment programs, being based on past average production, were not decreased by the widespread failure of crops in the drought area. Farmers participating in the adjustment programs were therefore assured of a certain amount of cash income. In this way the adjustment programs had the effect of crop insurance. In connection with 1934 crop production, the A.A.A. disbursed in benefit payments, in the States officially designated as within the drought area, a total of more than $470,000,000. These payments assisted in maintaining continued production on farms where the drought would have made it impossible otherwise to continue. They permitted the purchase of feed to carry livestock and to plant late feed and forage crops. Together with commodity loans they provided food, clothing and fuel for thousands of families whose income the drought had wiped out.

Under the Jones-Connally Act, approved April 7, 1934 (Pub. No. 142, 73d Congress, 48 Stat. 528), a program had already been developed for eliminating diseased cattle and for removing surplus cattle in cooperation with producers. This program enabled the A.A.A. to act without delay in purchasing cattle in drought areas where feed was so low that the animals could no longer be carried on the farms. Restrictions on raising feed which had been imposed by the crop reduction programs were modified in order to encourage replacement in part of the seed crops which had been destroyed by the drought.

To help in the administration of

relief a director of drought relief was appointed for each State within the area. The State directors were given general supervision of all the emergency drought activities in their respective States, under the Department of Agriculture, and in cooperation with regional and State representatives of the Federal Emergency Relief Administration, the Farm Credit Administration and other governmental agencies. County agricultural agents assisted by special county committees did much of the actual field work. In this way the program of administration throughout the drought areas was thoroughly decentralized, as had been the program of voluntary crop reduction under A.A.A.

In order to help the cattle and sheep industry, two principal measures of relief were adopted: shipment of feed into the drought areas and purchase and removal of cattle and sheep from the drought area. Because of the appropriations already available under the Jones-Connally Act, these measures could be initiated at once without waiting for the emergency appropriation which I requested in the foregoing message. As a matter of fact, even before the emergency appropriation was enacted on June 19, 1934, 213,-124 head of cattle had already been purchased.

The three principal methods of disposing of purchased animals were: (1) processing them into food products to be distributed by the various State emergency relief administrations through their county units to the destitute unemployed; (2) shipment to processing plants to be distributed by the Federal Surplus Relief Corporation in accordance with its usual practices (see Vol. II, Items 125 and 130); (3) destruction of all animals unfit for food. By December 31, 1934, 7,815,000 head of cattle had been purchased from 675,499 farms in twenty-four drought States at a total cost of $102,744,000. Not all of the cattle delivered to the Federal Surplus Relief Corporation were slaughtered immediately. More than a million and a half head of them were shipped to States where droughts had not affected pastures, and were there placed in grazing for later disposition.

The cattle-buying program, in addition to furnishing income not otherwise available to the cattle men, removed a surplus of stock which would have glutted all the commercial markets and would have ruined prices for producers outside the drought areas as well as within. It also acted as a vast culling process, which will undoubtedly improve materially the quality of our future herds. Farmers who found it necessary to sell their cattle because of shortage of feed naturally selected the least desirable for sale, and held on to their better quality animals.

By the middle of August, 1934, the Government also started a program for the purchase of sheep and goats whose grazing areas had been ruined by the drought. By the end of the year about 3,600,000 sheep and 354,000 goats had been purchased for a total of $7,136,000.

The problem of inadequate feed supplies was further met by encouraging increased seed planting through modification of the provisions of the crop adjustment contracts which had been executed. Lands taken out of cultivation of other crops were planted with forage and pasture crops, with the incidental benefits of helping to prevent erosion and to improve the soil.

The Federal Livestock Feed Agency was established in Kansas City in September as an agency to cooperate with the livestock feed trade, to encourage conservation and the most efficient utilization of available feed, to locate and help distribute regional surplus of feed. To protect the seed-corn supply, large quantities of seed-quality corn were purchased, and loans were made upon other supplies of seed corn by the Commodity Credit Corporation.

To make it easier to bring feed into the drought areas or to ship cattle out of them, the Government, in cooperation with the Western railroads, brought about an emergency reduction in freight rates for drought shipments.

Much of the material and arrangement of this note has been taken from the 1934 A.A.A. Report.

104 ❦ The President Appraises the Current Accomplishments of N.R.A. June 15, 1934

My dear Governor:

I AM happy to know that you have proclaimed next Saturday as a State holiday in honor of the first anniversary of the National Industrial Recovery Act.

One year ago, Congress placed this great Act before me and the people of the United States. It was the response of Government to the plea of prostrate industry for immediate and substantial help. It was also an expression of mutual trust, providing the means by which the faith and courage of our people might be given expression. When I signed the law, I observed that it created a challenge to industry, to labor, to Government and to the people as a whole.

Industry had desired and was given the right to act in unison for the prevention of unfair practices. The law was based on faith that industry would not violate a great public trust.

Workers had long sought, and now were given, a new Charter of Rights. Collective bargaining and the right of workers to choose their representatives were established.

Government was directed to establish a nationwide organization to set employers and employees to work and to protect the public.

The people as a whole were called on for aggressive support. They gave it.

Fear of disaster has given way to faith in united action. Millions of discouraged and suffering unemployed found their names on payrolls again. The evils of child labor and of starvation wages have almost everywhere been abolished. The Blue Eagle found its way into more than two million places of business.

Now that a year has passed, the National Recovery Administration under the leadership of General Johnson and with the assistance of thousands of unselfish men and women can rightfully and properly celebrate its first anniversary.

The first year under N.I.R.A. reveals significant and extraordinary increases in industry and business generally. We have spread employment, we have raised pay, and we are not through yet. It is a notable record of recovery. It has led the way for other Nations and has produced widespread and, I believe, permanent results. Certainly we have a right to celebrate this anniversary.

People who cannot see the forest for the trees make much of controversy in various groups which meet in N.R.A.—employers, consumers, employees. N.R.A. was deliberately conceived in controversy. It was deliberately set up as a forum where views of conflicting interest can meet in the open and where, out of controversy, may come compromise. If N.R.A. did not invite robust and unrestricted argument, it could not do the work assigned to it. Extreme views formerly held by any group, either of capital or labor, have already been modified in a better understanding of the simple fact that the broad interests of 125 million

Americans are paramount to the narrower interests of any such group.

The first phase of N.R.A. is drawing to a close. Ninety-five percent of industry has been codified. Very soon we shall be free to concentrate on the continuing task of code organization, code revisions, and compliance.

Before the people of this country accept either preconceived conjectures of ill-informed commentators, or the fulminations of minorities which still seek special and selfish privileges, we shall consider the results already achieved and look forward to greater gains on behalf of orderly progress for honest labor and honest industry. As time goes on experience will remove inequities which appear from time to time — and experience will, at the same time, point out to the country the names of those who seek unfair advantage over their fellow men.

Very sincerely yours,

His Excellency, H. G. Kump,
Governor of West Virginia,
Charleston, W. Va.

105 ❲ A Letter to the Advertising Federation of America. June 15, 1934

My dear Mr. Kobak:

THREE years ago it was my pleasure to meet personally with the twenty-seventh annual convention of the Advertising Federation of America. Unfortunately, I cannot be with you in person this year, but I welcome this opportunity of extending a message of greeting to you.

May I call your attention to a statement I made to your organization three years ago: "There is one field of human effort which today is insufficiently touched by the benefits of advertising. In spreading the doctrine of the necessity of advertising, which your profession has so thoroughly sold the American public, you can help also to establish in the minds of people the importance of advertising the functions and the operations of the various branches of Government. If ever one thing needed advertising publicity, it is Government — national, State, county and city. Our citizens are often in abysmal ignorance as to how Government functions or how it is intended to function." If this was true three years ago, it also is true today.

The drastic economic and social emergency required an unprecedented degree of governmental action and participation in functions not normally vested in the Government.

There are few groups which can accept and fulfill the responsibility of properly educating the public as well as the advertising fraternity. You have rendered conspicuous service thus far in presenting sound interpretations of the purposes and objectives of the recovery program.

I wish for you in your consideration of these broad and specific problems of advertising a most successful convention.

Very sincerely yours,

Edgar Kobak, Esq.,
The Advertising Federation of America,
New York, N. Y.

106 ⟨ The One Hundred and Thirtieth Press Conference (Excerpts). June 15, 1934

(Collective bargaining principle in labor legislation.)

Q. Did you tell Senator Robinson, sir, that you wanted labor legislation this session before adjournment?

THE PRESIDENT: Yes, quite a while ago.

Q. Have you agreed on a substitute form?

THE PRESIDENT: That you will have to find out up there on the Hill. In other words, the real situation is this: We have been trying to get some form of legislation which would not greatly delay the termination of the session. There have been at least a dozen different drafts of legislation, and it is a matter of discussion between Senator Robinson and Senator McNary, and has been for the last two days, a little over two days. That is really what it comes down to. I haven't heard anything since this morning when various other suggestions were made.

Q. Mr. President, can you comment on those three or four principal objections to the terms, such as limiting it to one year and restricting power?

THE PRESIDENT: There is no objection to restricting it to one year. There was definite objection to eliminating the word "organization" from the principle of representation. In other words, 7-A. This might just as well be made absolutely clear once and for all: About 120,000,000 people out of 125,000,000 understand plain English; there seems to be a very, very small minority that does not understand plain English. . . . Section 7-A says that the workers can choose representatives. Now if they want to choose the Ahkoond of Swat they have a perfect right to do so. If they want to choose the Royal Geographic Society, they can do that. If they want to choose a union, of any kind, they can do that. They have free choice of representation and that means not merely an individual or a worker, but it means a corporation or a union or anybody. And that has to be made absolutely clear in this legislation.

Q. How do you feel on the point of minorities?

THE PRESIDENT: The question of minorities is not a tremendously serious one, because that has to be worked out in each individual case. If there is a substantial minority, it seems fair and equitable that that minority should have some form of representation, but that is a matter of detail depending on the individual case. In some industries it is possible that neither side may want to have it.

Q. Suppose they do choose the National Geographic Society, then do the employers have to trade with them?

THE PRESIDENT: Absolutely.

NOTE: Section 7-A, discussed in the foregoing Conference, is the section in the National Industrial Recovery Act (see Items 59, 78 and 81 of Vol. II) which provides for collective bargaining between employer and employees. (48 Stat. 195.)

107 ❲Statement on Signing the Hayden-Cartwright Act, Formulating a Program of Stabilized Highway Building. June 18, 1934

As LONG as the roads of the Nation are used by more than 24,-000,000 automobiles and trucks, construction and improvement of roads will be of major importance.

The Hayden-Cartwright Act (48 Stat. 993; Pub. No. 393, 73d Congress) seeks to stabilize highway building with Federal and State funds by insuring a work program of far-reaching proportions and benefits for the next three years.

Highway work under the National Recovery Act now is more than 90 percent under contract or advertised for contract, and the new program is necessary to sustain highway employment on an adequate and reasonable scale for the remaining period of recovery.

The Act also provides for a gradual tapering off of emergency highway expenditures and lays the foundation for a return to normal expenditures.

Of the $522,000,000 authorized to be expended by the Act, $450,000,000 is allotted for Federal participation with the States in highway building, of which sum $200,000,000 will be a Federal grant, and the remaining $250,000,000, the Federal portion of regular Federal aid for the fiscal years 1936 and 1937, to be matched by the States on a 50-50 basis. The balance, $72,000,000, is to be applied at the rate of $24,000,000 annually to highway activities in the national forests, national parks, Indian Reservations and the public lands. Including the contributions to be made by the States and the $230,000,000 which will be carried over from the $400,000,000 appropriated by Congress last year, the total sum to be paid out for highway construction during the three-year period will be more than a billion dollars.

The Act provides that States, to be eligible for full participation in Federal Aid, must continue to use for roads at least whatever portion of their revenues from gasoline and other taxes on motor vehicles is now authorized by law to be expended for high-way purposes. Notice is also given to the forty-four State Legis-latures which will convene early next year that unmatched emer-gency grants are to be abandoned and that there is to be a return to the established plan which requires that the States shall meet the Federal Government half way in paying the cost of new con-struction.

Other important provisions of the Act provide safer traffic fa-cilities and the elimination of hazards to pedestrian and vehicu-lar traffic; preparation of advance surveys and plans for future highway construction; meeting emergency repairs on the Federal Aid highway system in the event of damage by floods or hurri-canes; and continuing the cooperative surveys for the proposed Inter-American Highway.

It is important to note that the sums mentioned above repre-sent only an authorization by the Congress and *not* an appropri-ation. Funds for work to be done the first year the Act is in effect are contained in the Deficiency Appropriation Bill.

108 ⟨ Statement on Signing Bill to Give the Supreme Court Power to Regulate Procedure in the Federal Courts. June 19, 1934

THE enactment by the Congress of this measure, which gives to the Supreme Court of the United States the power to prescribe uniform rules of practice and procedure for the Federal Courts in actions at law, represents one of the most important steps ever taken in the improvement of our judicial system. Its significance at once will be recognized in informed legal circles.

The procedure which has heretofore been followed is based upon a complicated patchwork of disconnected statutes and ju-dicial decisions, superimposed upon the varying practice in the several States. The confusion resulting from such an unscientific system has, of necessity, been productive of uncertainty, expense and delay.

For the complicated procedure of the past, we now propose to substitute a simplified, flexible, scientific, correlated system of procedural rules prescribed by the Supreme Court. The members of that great tribunal are preeminently qualified to discharge the duty which has been entrusted to them.

All of us who are seriously concerned with the problem of legal reform and the speeding up of the administration of justice regard the passage of this bill as a distinct achievement.

NOTE: The foregoing legislation was the result of the efforts of many leaders of the bench and bar for the past quarter of a century to simplify Federal legal procedure by means of court rules.

As early as 1792 the Supreme Court was empowered by statute to promulgate uniform rules of practice for the trial courts in equity and admiralty cases. In 1898 similar power was granted in respect to bankruptcy cases. On the other hand, the so-called Conformity Act barred progress along this line in respect of actions at law, as it required the Federal courts to conform as near as may be to State practice. The result has been that as to actions at law, there were forty-nine different procedures in the Federal courts — one for each State and for the District of Columbia. In many instances the practice was archaic and ponderous, and still enforced the technical intricacies and refinements that prevailed in England in the seventeenth and eighteenth centuries.

The Act about which the foregoing statement was issued empowered the Supreme Court to prescribe uniform rules of practice for the district courts in actions at law, and to provide for a single form of action for suits in equity and actions at law.

The flexibility of this type of regulation and its ready adaptation to the demands of justice will have a tendency to make technical procedure less important than it has been in the past.

109 ❧ The President Seeks to Adjust a Labor Dispute in the Steel Industry. June 19, 1934

I HAVE discussed with the Secretary of Labor every detail of the proposal that has been made by a committee of the Amalgamated Steel, Iron and Tin Workers on behalf of employees in the steel industry. The Secretary has described to me also the proposal that the employers in the Steel Industry made last week to the Administrator for N.R.A.

It is my hope that some method will be found to adjust all the points that are in controversy and to preserve orderly relations without sacrificing any principle that is involved.

I have referred the proposal to the Secretary of Labor for careful study and to undertake any negotiations that seem advisable. The Secretary is fully empowered to represent me in taking whatever action seems advisable under the circumstances and will, of course, consult and cooperate with all other agencies of Government concerned.

NOTE: The foregoing statement was issued by me at a time when the Amalgamated Steel, Iron and Tin Workers' Union was engaged in a dispute with employers. It was followed by Executive Order No. 6751 of June 28, 1934, setting up a National Steel Labor Relations Board, to handle labor problems relating to the iron and steel industry. (See Item 113, this volume.)

110 ❧ White House Statement on Presidential Practice in Explaining All Vetoes of Bills. June 26, 1934

THE Constitution of the United States, with reference to bills presented to the President by the Congress, provides:

"If any Bill shall not be returned by the President within ten Days (Sundays excepted) after it shall have been presented to him, the Same shall be a Law, in like Manner as if he had signed it, unless the Congress by their Adjournment prevent its Return, in which Case it shall not be a Law."

In the past, it has been customary in most cases involving vetoes for the President to withhold his signature, thereby, in effect, allowing the bill to die without becoming a law.

The President has desired, however, to take a more affirmative position than this, feeling that in the case of most legislation reasons for definite disapproval should be given. Therefore, he has written on the copy of each bill the words "Disapproved and Signature Withheld" and has appended in every case a brief statement giving the reason or reasons for disapproval.

The bills identified below have been vetoed by the President and the reasons which lead to their disapproval are contained in the following statements:

NOTE: In effect this policy means that the so-called pocket veto through silence and withholding signature is no longer in existence.

Fourteen vetoed bills accompanied ·this White House Statement.

111 ❪ The Procedure for Notice and Hearing on Any Proposed Reciprocal Trade Agreement. Executive Order No. 6750. June 27, 1934

Whereas Section 4 of the Act of Congress approved June 12, 1934, entitled "An Act to amend the Tariff Act of 1930" provides:

"Section 4. Before any foreign trade agreement is concluded with any foreign government or instrumentality thereof under the provisions of this Act, reasonable public notice of the intention to negotiate an agreement with such government or instrumentality shall be given in order that any interested person may have an opportunity to present his views to the President, or to such agency as the President may designate, under such rules and regulations as the President may prescribe; and before concluding such agreement the President shall seek information and advice with respect thereto from the United States Tariff Commission, the Departments of State, Agriculture, and Commerce and from such other sources as he may deem appropriate."

Now, THEREFORE, I, Franklin D. Roosevelt, President of the United States of America, acting under and by virtue of the authority vested in me by the aforesaid section, prescribe the following procedure with respect to the giving of public notice of the intention to negotiate trade agreements and with respect to the granting of opportunity on the part of interested persons to present their views:

1. At least 30 days before any foreign-trade agreement is concluded under the provisions of the Act notice of the intention to negotiate such agreement shall be given by the Secretary of State. Such notice shall be issued to the press and published in *Press Releases* of the Department of State, the weekly *Treasury Decisions*, and *Commerce Reports*.

2. Persons desiring to present their views with respect to any such proposed agreement shall present them to a committee to be known as the Committee for Reciprocity Information. Said Committee, hereinafter referred to as the Committee, shall consist of members designated from the personnel of their respective departments or offices by the Secretary of State, the Secretary of Agriculture, the Secretary of Commerce, the National Recovery Administrator, the Chairman of the Tariff Commission, the special adviser to the President on foreign trade, and the heads of such other Federal departments or offices as may be named from time to time by the Executive Committee on Commercial Policy. The Committee shall function under the direction and supervision of, and its chairman shall be designated from among the members of the Committee by, the Executive Committee on Commercial Policy.

3. The form and manner in which views may be presented, the place at which they shall be presented, and the time limitations for such presentation shall from time to time be prescribed by the Committee which may designate such subcommittees as it may deem necessary.

NOTE: A Committee on Trade Agreements was created on June 28, 1934, under the supervision of the Secretary of State, to assist in carrying out the provisions of the Trade Agreements Act, Pub. No. 316, 73d Congress; 48 Stat. 943, approved June 12, 1934 (see Item 33, this volume). It is made up of representatives of the Departments of State, Agriculture and Commerce, the Treasury Department and the Tariff Commission.

The Committee is the nucleus of the interdepartmental trade-agreements organization. It considers all matters of policy, directs the work on the trade agreements done in the various departments, examines in detail the recommendations of its sub-committee as to concessions to be given and obtained in the agreements, and directs the program generally. The Committee is assisted by approximately fifty interdepartmental sub-committees dealing with individual countries, individual commodities and special subjects. The personnel of these sub-committees usually consists of officers of the several governmental agencies in the interdepartmental trade-agreements organization.

The Committee, together with its sub-committees, has provided a very effective mechanism for the conduct of the trade-agreements program. Sixteen completed trade agreements already stand to the Committee's credit, and as many more are in various stages of preparation at this writing in July, 1937.

112 ⟨ Statement on Signing Bill for Federal Regulation of Grazing on Public Lands. June 28, 1934

THE passage of this Act marks the culmination of years of effort to obtain from Congress express authority for Federal regulation of grazing on the public domain in the interests of national conservation and of the livestock industry.

It authorizes the Secretary of the Interior to provide for the protection, orderly use, and regulation of the public ranges, and to create grazing districts with an aggregate area of not more than 80 million acres. It confers broad powers on the Secretary of the Interior to do all things necessary for the preservation of these ranges, including, amongst other powers, the right to specify from time to time the number of livestock which may graze within such districts and the seasons when they shall be permitted to do so. The authority to exercise these powers is carefully safeguarded against impairment by State or local action. Creation of a grazing district by the Secretary of the Interior and promulgation of rules and regulations respecting it will supersede State regulation of grazing on that part of the public domain included within such district.

Water development, soil erosion work, and the general improvement of such lands are provided for in the act.

Local residents, settlers, and owners of land and water who have been using the public range in the past are given a preference by the terms of the Act to the use of lands within such districts when placed under Federal regulation so long as they comply with the rules and regulations of the Secretary of the Interior. The Act permits private persons owning lands within a district to make exchanges for Federally owned land outside a grazing district if and when the Secretary of the Interior finds it to be in the best public interests.

The Federal Government, by enacting this law, has taken a great forward step in the interests of conservation, which will prove of benefit not only to those engaged in the livestock industry, but also to the Nation as a whole.

NOTE: The provisions of the foregoing statute, approved June 28, 1934 (Pub. No. 482, 73d Congress; 48 Stat. 1269), are described in the foregoing statement. The statute was amended later by an act approved June 26, 1936 (Pub. No. 827, 74th Congress; 49 Stat. 1976), which raised the number of acres from 80,000,000 to 142,000,000.

As soon as the bill had been approved on June 28, 1934, the Secretary of the Interior immediately sent representatives of the Department to the West to hold public meetings and hearings of the stockmen in each of the ten principal public domain States. They were held at various convenient points, and at these meetings the provisions and objectives of the Act were explained. Discussion from the floor was encouraged. Hearings were later held in each State at points convenient for the attendance of State officials and stockowners. Counsel was taken from the stockmen themselves with reference to selecting boundaries of grazing districts within the respective States.

In this way the policy of the Department was worked out in consultation with, and upon advice from, the men engaged in the industry themselves. After these hearings and discussions were held, the first Ex-

ecutive Order under the statute was   6910, printed as Item 187, this vol-
issued on November 26, 1934, No.   ume.

113 ❧ The National Steel Labor Relations Board Is Established. Presidential Statement. June 28, 1934

IN ACCORDANCE with the authority just conferred upon me by a Joint Resolution of Congress, I have today established a "National Steel Labor Relations Board." This Board consists of three impartial members, who will be thoroughly independent in their judgments and who are fully empowered to act under the law. They will make reports to me, through the Secretary of Labor, of their activities, from time to time.

The functions of the Board will be limited to labor relations in the iron and steel industry. In that field the Board is authorized to hear and determine cases of alleged violations of Section 7 (A) of the National Industrial Recovery Act, to mediate in labor questions, to serve as a board of voluntary arbitration and by secret ballot to conduct labor elections to determine who are representatives of workers for collective bargaining.

The general outline of this order was suggested by independent proposals which came from workers and from employers in the industry and which have been modified after conference with Government officials. It is from these proposals that the specific details of this order have been drawn. Though the order is in form by the President, it represents, in substance, suggestions of employers and recommendations of employees expressed to me. I am glad that such progress has been made, and I anticipate that the special board so created will serve to maintain industrial peace with justice and to further the establishment of sound standards of labor relations in this important industry. I appreciate the constructive and reasonable spirit which has prevailed in both groups. I confidently expect full cooperation of both sides with this Board.

NOTE: This Board was one of several which I created to handle industrial labor relations in the various industries. There was thus made possible a tribunal composed of three impartial persons before whom claims of discrimination on account of union activities could be heard and adjusted, and through whom negotiations looking to various adjustments of working conditions and disputes might take place.

The appointment of this Board for the iron and steel industry, the concurrence of both the employers and workers in accepting its good offices, and the general terms of its powers, had the effect of preventing a general strike in this field.

While the National Labor Board (see Items 109 and 182 of Vol. II) and the First National Labor Relations Board (see Items 118 and 118A of this volume) were in existence, several other boards having jurisdiction over labor relations in separate particular industries were created either by codes for the respective industries or pursuant to Public Resolution No. 44, 73d Congress, approved June 19, 1934. (See Item 118A, this volume.)

The National Bituminous Coal Labor Board (together with six divisional boards) and the Newspaper Industrial Board were established by codes. Various administrative orders, issued under the authority of codes for the respective industries, set up boards to handle labor disputes in the textile industries, and in the shipbuilding and ship-repairing industry. The Secretary of the Interior, as Administrator of the Petroleum Code, issued an administrative order establishing the Petroleum Labor Policy Board.

Pursuant to the authority of Public Resolution No. 44, the National Longshoremen's Labor Board (with jurisdiction limited to the Pacific coast), the National Steel Labor Relations Board, and the Textile Labor Relations Board were set up by me (Executive Orders No. 6748, 6751, 6858 respectively). The latter Board, composed of three representatives of the public, replaced the Cotton Textile Board, which had been composed of one representative each of labor, capital and the public.

The National Labor Relations Board made a study of these various boards, and concluded that separate boards for the various industries were not desirable. They reported that it was preferable to have one impartial national board to determine, in the last instance and subject only to court review, all labor questions; and that sub-agencies should handle the cases in the first instance in the various regions and localities. The results of this study helped to frame the legislation which was then being prepared to supersede, and which did supersede, Public Resolution No. 44 (see Items 118 and 118A of this volume).

114 ❨ The First "Fireside Chat" of 1934 — "Are You Better Off Than You Were Last Year?" June 28, 1934

I
T HAS been several months since I have talked with you concerning the problems of Government. Since January, those of us in whom you have vested responsibility have been engaged in the fulfillment of plans and policies which had been widely discussed in previous months. It seemed to us our duty not only to make the right path clear, but also to tread that path.

As we review the achievements of this session of the Seventy-third Congress, it is made increasingly clear that its task was essentially that of completing and fortifying the work it had begun in March, 1933. That was no easy task, but the Congress was equal to it. It has been well said that while there were a few exceptions, this Congress displayed a greater freedom from mere partisanship than any other peace-time Congress since the Administration of President Washington himself. The session was distinguished by the extent and variety of legislation enacted and by the intelligence and good-will of debate upon these measures.

I mention only a few of the major enactments. It provided for the readjustment of the debt burden through the corporate and municipal bankruptcy acts and the Farm Relief Act. It lent a hand to industry by encouraging loans to solvent industries unable to secure adequate help from banking institutions. It strengthened the integrity of finance through the regulation of securities exchanges. It provided a rational method of increasing our volume of foreign trade through reciprocal trading agreements. It strengthened our naval forces to conform with the intentions and permission of existing treaty rights. It made further advances toward peace in industry through the Labor Adjustment Act. It supplemented our agricultural policy through measures widely demanded by farmers themselves and intended to avert price-destroying surpluses. It strengthened the hand of the Federal Government in its attempts to suppress gangster crime. It took definite steps toward a national housing program through an act which I signed today designed to encourage private capital in the rebuilding of the homes of the Nation. It created a permanent Federal body for the just regulation of all forms of communication, including the telephone, the telegraph and the radio. Finally, and I believe most important, it reorganized, simplified and made more fair and just our monetary system, setting up standards and policies adequate to meet the necessities of modern economic life, doing justice to both gold and silver as the metal bases behind the currency of the United States.

In the consistent development of our previous efforts toward the saving and safeguarding of our national life, I have continued to recognize three related steps. The first was relief, because the primary concern of any Government dominated by the humane ideals of democracy is the simple principle that in a land of vast resources no one should be permitted to starve. Relief was and continues to be our first consideration. It calls for large expenditures and will continue in modified form to do so for a long time to come. We may as well recognize that fact. It comes from the paralysis that arose as the after-effect of that unfortunate decade characterized by a mad chase for unearned riches, and an unwillingness of leaders in almost every walk of life to look beyond their own schemes and speculations. In our administration of relief we follow two principles: first, that direct giving shall, wherever possible, be supplemented by provision for useful and remunerative work and, second, that where families in their existing surroundings will in all human probability never find an opportunity for full self-maintenance, happiness and enjoyment, we shall try to give them a new chance in new surroundings.

The second step was recovery, and it is sufficient for me to ask each and every one of you to compare the situation in agriculture and in industry today with what it was fifteen months ago.

At the same time we have recognized the necessity of reform and reconstruction—reform because much of our trouble today and in the past few years has been due to a lack of understanding of the elementary principles of justice and fairness by those in

313

whom leadership in business and finance was placed—reconstruction because new conditions in our economic life as well as old but neglected conditions had to be corrected.

Substantial gains well known to all of you have justified our course. I could cite statistics to you as unanswerable measures of our national progress—statistics to show the gain in the average weekly pay envelope of workers in the great majority of industries—statistics to show hundreds of thousands reemployed in private industries, and other hundreds of thousands given new employment through the expansion of direct and indirect Government assistance of many kinds, although, of course, there are those exceptions in professional pursuits whose economic improvement, of necessity, will be delayed. I also could cite statistics to show the great rise in the value of farm products—statistics to prove the demand for consumers' goods, ranging all the way from food and clothing to automobiles, and of late to prove the rise in the demand for durable goods—statistics to cover the great increase in bank deposits, and to show the scores of thousands of homes and of farms which have been saved from foreclosure.

But the simplest way for each of you to judge recovery lies in the plain facts of your own individual situation. Are you better off than you were last year? Are your debts less burdensome? Is your bank account more secure? Are your working conditions better? Is your faith in your own individual future more firmly grounded?

Also, let me put to you another simple question: Have you as an individual paid too high a price for these gains? Plausible self-seekers and theoretical die-hards will tell you of the loss of individual liberty. Answer this question also out of the facts of your own life. Have you lost any of your rights or liberty or constitutional freedom of action and choice? Turn to the Bill of Rights of the Constitution, which I have solemnly sworn to maintain and under which your freedom rests secure. Read each provision of that Bill of Rights and ask yourself whether you personally have suffered the impairment of a single jot of these great assurances. I have no question in my mind as to what your answer will be. The record is written in the experiences of your own personal lives.

In other words, it is not the overwhelming majority of the farmers or manufacturers or workers who deny the substantial gains of the past year. The most vociferous of the Doubting Thomases may be divided roughly into two groups: First, those who seek special political privilege and, second, those who seek special financial privilege. About a year ago I used as an illustration the 90 percent of the cotton manufacturers of the United States who wanted to do the right thing by their employees and by the public but were prevented from doing so by the 10 percent who undercut them by unfair practices and un-American standards. It is well for us to remember that humanity is a long way from being perfect and that a selfish minority in every walk of life—farming, business, finance and even Government service itself—will always continue to think of themselves first and their fellow beings second.

In the working out of a great national program which seeks the primary good of the greater number, it is true that the toes of some people are being stepped on and are going to be stepped on. But these toes belong to the comparative few who seek to retain or to gain position or riches or both by some short cut which is harmful to the greater good.

In the execution of the powers conferred on it by Congress, the Administration needs and will tirelessly seek the best ability that the country affords. Public service offers better rewards in the opportunity for service than ever before in our history—not great salaries, but enough to live on. In the building of this service there are coming to us men and women with ability and courage from every part of the Union. The days of the seeking of mere party advantage through the misuse of public power are drawing to a close. We are increasingly demanding and getting devotion to the public service on the part of every member of the Administration, high and low.

The program of the past year is definitely in operation and

that operation month by month is being made to fit into the web of old and new conditions. This process of evolution is well illustrated by the constant changes in detailed organization and method going on in the National Recovery Administration. With every passing month we are making strides in the orderly handling of the relationship between employees and employers. Conditions differ, of course, in almost every part of the country and in almost every industry. Temporary methods of adjustment are being replaced by more permanent machinery and, I am glad to say, by a growing recognition on the part of employers and employees of the desirability of maintaining fair relationships all around.

So also, while almost everybody has recognized the tremendous strides in the elimination of child labor, in the payment of not less than fair minimum wages and in the shortening of hours, we are still feeling our way in solving problems which relate to self-government in industry, especially where such self-government tends to eliminate the fair operation of competition.

In this same process of evolution we are keeping before us the objectives of protecting, on the one hand, industry against chiselers within its own ranks, and, on the other hand, the consumer through the maintenance of reasonable competition for the prevention of the unfair sky-rocketing of retail prices.

But, in addition to this our immediate task, we must still look to the larger future. I have pointed out to the Congress that we are seeking to find the way once more to well-known, long-established but to some degree forgotten ideals and values. We seek the security of the men, women and children of the Nation.

That security involves added means of providing better homes for the people of the Nation. That is the first principle of our future program.

The second is to plan the use of land and water resources of this country to the end that the means of livelihood of our citizens may be more adequate to meet their daily needs.

And, finally, the third principle is to use the agencies of government to assist in the establishment of means to provide sound and adequate protection against the vicissitudes of modern life — in other words, social insurance.

Later in the year I hope to talk with you more fully about these plans.

A few timid people, who fear progress, will try to give you new and strange names for what we are doing. Sometimes they will call it "Fascism," sometimes "Communism," sometimes "Regimentation," sometimes "Socialism." But, in so doing, they are trying to make very complex and theoretical something that is really very simple and very practical.

I believe in practical explanations and in practical policies. I believe that what we are doing today is a necessary fulfillment of what Americans have always been doing — a fulfillment of old and tested American ideals.

Let me give you a simple illustration:

While I am away from Washington this summer, a long-needed renovation of and addition to our White House office building is to be started. The architects have planned a few new rooms built into the present all too small one-story structure. We are going to include in this addition and in this renovation modern electric wiring and modern plumbing and modern means of keeping the offices cool in the hot Washington summers. But the structural lines of the old Executive office building will remain. The artistic lines of the White House buildings were the creation of master builders when our Republic was young. The simplicity and the strength of the structure remain in the face of every modern test. But within this magnificent pattern, the necessities of modern government business require constant reorganization and rebuilding.

If I were to listen to the arguments of some prophets of calamity who are talking these days, I should hesitate to make these alterations. I should fear that while I am away for a few weeks the architects might build some strange new Gothic tower or a factory building or perhaps a replica of the Kremlin or of the Potsdam Palace. But I have no such fears. The architects and builders are men of common sense and of artistic American tastes.

They know that the principles of harmony and of necessity itself require that the building of the new structure shall blend with the essential lines of the old. It is this combination of the old and the new that marks orderly peaceful progress, not only in building buildings but in building government itself.

Our new structure is a part of and a fulfillment of the old.

All that we do seeks to fulfill the historic traditions of the American people. Other Nations may sacrifice democracy for the transitory stimulation of old and discredited autocracies. We are restoring confidence and well-being under the rule of the people themselves. We remain, as John Marshall said a century ago, "emphatically and truly, a government of the people." Our Government "in form and in substance . . . emanates from them. Its powers are granted by them, and are to be exercised directly on them, and for their benefits."

Before I close, I want to tell you of the interest and pleasure with which I look forward to the trip on which I hope to start in a few days. It is a good thing for everyone who can possibly do so to get away at least once a year for a change of scene. I do not want to get into the position of not being able to see the forest because of the thickness of the trees.

I hope to visit our fellow Americans in Puerto Rico, in the Virgin Islands, in the Canal Zone and in Hawaii. And, incidentally, it will give me an opportunity to exchange a friendly word of greeting with the Presidents of our sister Republics, Haiti and Colombia and Panama.

After four weeks on board ship, I plan to land at a port in our Pacific Northwest, and then will come the best part of the whole trip, for I am hoping to inspect a number of our new great national projects on the Columbia, Missouri and Mississippi Rivers, to see some of our national parks and, incidentally, to learn much of actual conditions during the trip across the continent back to Washington.

While I was in France during the War our boys used to call the United States "God's country." Let us make it and keep it "God's country."

115 ❲ The President Places a Ban on the Exportation of Arms and Munitions to Cuba. Proclamation No. 2089. June 29, 1934

WHEREAS Section 1 of a joint resolution of Congress, entitled "Joint resolution to prohibit the exportation of arms or munitions of war from the United States to certain countries, and for other purposes," approved January 31, 1922, provides as follows:

"That whenever the President finds that in any American country, or in any country in which the United States exercises extraterritorial jurisdiction, conditions of domestic violence exist, which are or may be promoted by the use of arms or munitions of war procured from the United States, and makes proclamation thereof, it shall be unlawful to export, except under such limitations and exceptions as the President prescribes, any arms or munitions of war from any place in the United States to such country until otherwise ordered by the President or by Congress."

Now, THEREFORE, I, Franklin D. Roosevelt, President of the United States of America, acting under and by virtue of the authority conferred in me by the said joint resolution of Congress, do hereby declare and proclaim that I have found that there exist in Cuba such conditions of domestic violence which are or may be promoted by the use of arms or munitions of war procured from the United States as contemplated by the said joint resolution; and I do hereby admonish all citizens of the United States and every person to abstain from every violation of the provisions of the joint resolution above set forth, hereby made applicable to Cuba, and I do hereby warn them that all violations of such provisions will be rigorously prosecuted.

And I do hereby enjoin upon all officers of the United States, charged with the execution of the laws thereof, the utmost diligence in preventing violations of the said joint resolution and this my proclamation issued thereunder, and in bringing to trial and punishment any offenders against the same.

And I do hereby delegate to the Secretary of State the power of prescribing exceptions and limitations to the application of the said joint resolution of January 31, 1922, as made effective by this my proclamation issued thereunder.

NOTE: By a joint resolution of the Congress entitled "Joint resolution to prohibit the exportation of arms or munitions of war from the United States to certain countries, and for other purposes," approved January 31, 1922, the President was authorized to prohibit, under such limitations and exceptions as he may prescribe, the export of arms or munitions to any American country wherein conditions of domestic violence are found to exist.

Because of conditions in Cuba, I found it necessary to issue the foregoing Proclamation.

The Proclamation is still effective, and under it the exportation of arms and munitions to Cuba is permitted by license, only when the Department of State has been informed by the Cuban Embassy in Washington that it is the desire of the recognized Government of the country that the exportation be authorized.

116 ❨ A Typical Act of Protection and Conservation of Wild Life by Providing Suitable Refuges. Executive Order No. 6766. June 29, 1934

WHEREAS lands have been and are being acquired by the United States in order to provide suitable refuges for and to protect and conserve migratory birds and other wild life constituting depleted natural resources of the United States; and

WHEREAS the work and improvements necessary to be performed and made upon such lands to make them suitable and proper refuges for migratory birds and other wild life will provide protection for such lands from forest fires, floods and soil erosion, and plant pest and disease, and aid in the restoration of the country's depleted natural resources; and

WHEREAS the restoration, improvement, and development of such refuges will provide employment for citizens of the United States who are unemployed:

NOW, THEREFORE, by virtue of and pursuant to the authority vested in me, the sum of $2,500,000 is hereby allocated from the appropriations made by the said Deficiency Act of June 16, 1933, and the said Emergency Appropriation Act, fiscal year 1935, for carrying out the purposes of the said Act of March 31, 1933, to the Secretary of Agriculture, for the restoration, improvement, and development of such lands as wild-life refuges.

(See Item 23, Vol. II; Item 182, Vol. IV; Item 19, Vol. V.)

117 ❡ The Initiation of Studies to Achieve a Program of National Social and Economic Security. Executive Order No. 6757. June 29, 1934

BY VIRTUE of and pursuant to the authority vested in me by the National Industrial Recovery Act (ch. 90, 48 Stat. 195), I hereby establish (1) the Committee on Economic Security (hereinafter referred to as the Committee) consisting of the Secretary of Labor, Chairman, the Secretary of the Treasury, the Attorney General, the Secretary of Agriculture, and the Federal Emergency Relief Administrator, and (2) the Advisory Council on Economic Security (hereinafter referred to as the Advisory Council), the original members of which shall be appointed by the President and additional members of which may be appointed from time to time by the Committee.

The Committee shall study problems relating to the economic security of individuals and shall report to the President not later than December 1, 1934, its recommendations concerning proposals which in its judgment will promote greater economic security.

The Advisory Council shall assist the Committee in the consideration of all matters coming within the scope of its investigations.

The Committee shall appoint (1) a Technical Board on Economic Security consisting of qualified representatives selected from various departments and agencies of the Federal Government, and (2) an executive director who shall have immediate charge of studies and investigations to be carried out under the general direction of the Technical Board, and who shall, with the approval of the Technical Board, appoint such additional staff as may be necessary to carry out the provisions of this order.

NOTE: The foregoing Executive Order was a first step toward the adoption of the Social Security Act of 1935. It was the report of this committee which contained the recommendations which were on the whole incorporated in that Act (see Vol. IV, Item 107).

118 ❨ Creation of the First National Labor Relations Board. Executive Order No. 6763. June 29, 1934

By virtue of and pursuant to the authority vested in me under Title I of the National Industrial Recovery Act (ch. 90, 48 Stat. 195, Tit. 15, U.S.C., sec. 701) and under Joint Resolution approved June 19, 1934 (Public Res. 44, 73d Congress), and in order to effectuate the policy of said Title and the purposes of the said Joint Resolution, it is hereby ordered as follows:

CREATION OF THE NATIONAL LABOR RELATIONS BOARD

SECTION 1(a) There is hereby created in connection with the Department of Labor a board to be known as the National Labor Relations Board (hereinafter referred to as the Board), which shall be composed of Lloyd Garrison of Wisconsin, Chairman, Henry Alvin Millis of Illinois, and Edwin S. Smith of Massachusetts. . . .

ORIGINAL JURISDICTION OF THE BOARD

SECTION 2. The Board is hereby authorized

(a) To investigate issues, facts, practices, and activities of employers or employees in any controversies arising under Section 7(a) of the National Industrial Recovery Act or which are burdening or obstructing, or threatening to burden or obstruct, the free flow of interstate commerce; and

(b) To order and conduct elections and on its own initiative to take steps to enforce its orders in the manner provided in Section 2 of Public Resolution 44, 73d Congress; and

(c) Whenever it is in the public interest, to hold hearings and make findings of fact regarding complaints of discrimination against or discharge of employees or other alleged violations of Section 7(a) of the National Industrial Recovery Act and such parts of any code or agreement as incorporate said Section; and

(d) To prescribe, with the approval of the President, such rules and regulations as are authorized by Section 3 of Public Resolution 44, 73d Congress, and to recommend to the President such other rules and regulations relating to collective bargaining, labor representation, and labor elections as the President is authorized to prescribe by Section 10(a) of the National Industrial Recovery Act.

(e) Upon the request of the parties to a labor dispute, to act as a Board of Voluntary Arbitration or to select a person or agency for voluntary arbitration.

RELATIONSHIP TO OTHER LABOR BOARDS

SECTION 3(a) The Board is hereby authorized and directed —

(1) To study the activities of such boards as have been or may hereafter be created to deal with industrial or labor relations, in order to report through the Secretary of Labor to the President whether such boards should be designated as special boards and given the powers that the President is authorized to confer by Public Resolution 44, 73d Congress; and

(2) To recommend, through the Secretary of Labor, to the President the establishment, whenever necessary, of "Regional Labor Relations Boards" and special labor boards for particular industries vested with the powers that the President is authorized to confer by Public Resolution 44, 73d Congress; and

(3) To receive from such regional, industrial, and special boards as may be designated or established under the two preceding sub-sections reports of their activities and to review or hear appeals from such boards in cases in which (1) the board recommends review or (2) there is a division of opinion in the board or

(3) the National Labor Relations Board deems review will serve the public interest.

(b) The National Labor Board created by Executive Order of August 5, 1933, and continued by Executive Order No. 6511 of December 16, 1933, shall cease to exist on July 9, 1934; and each local or regional labor board, established under the authority of section 2(b) of the said Executive Order of December 16, 1933, if it is not designated in accordance with subsection 3(a)(1) of this order, shall cease to exist at such time as the National Labor Relations Board shall determine. The National Labor Relations Board shall have authority to conduct all investigations and proceedings being conducted by boards that are abolished by this subsection; and all records, papers, and property of such boards shall become records, papers, and property of the National Labor Relations Board. . . .

RELATIONSHIP TO OTHER EXECUTIVE AGENCIES

(c) The National Labor Relations Board may decline to take cognizance of any labor dispute where there is another means of settlement provided for by agreement, industrial code, or law which has not been utilized.

(d) Whenever the National Labor Relations Board or any board designated or established in accordance with subsections 3(a)(1) or 3(a)(2) of this order has taken, or has announced its intention to take, jurisdiction of any case or controversy involving either section 7(a) of the National Industrial Recovery Act or Public Resolution 44, 73d Congress, no other person or agency in the executive branch of the Government, except upon the request of the National Labor Relations Board, or except as otherwise provided in subsection 3(a)(3) of this order, shall take, or continue to entertain, jurisdiction of such case or controversy.

(e) Whenever the National Labor Relations Board or any board designated or established in accordance with subsections 3(a)(1) or 3(a)(2) of this order has made a finding of facts, or issued any order in any case or controversy involving section 7(a) of the National Industrial Recovery Act or Public Resolution 44,

73d Congress, such finding of facts and such order shall (except as otherwise provided in subsection 3(a)(3) of this order or except as otherwise recommended by the National Labor Relations Board) be final and not subject to review by any person or agency in the executive branch of the Government.

(f) Nothing in this order shall prevent, impede or diminish in any way the right of employees to strike or engage in other concerted activities.

(See following Item and note.)

118A ⟨ Statement by the President Accompanying the Foregoing Executive Order. June 30, 1934

THE Executive Order that I have just issued carries out the mandate of Congress, as expressed in Public Resolution No. 44, 73d Congress, approved June 19, 1934. It establishes upon a firm statutory basis the additional machinery by which the United States Government will deal with labor relations, and particularly with difficulties arising in connection with collective bargaining, labor elections and labor representation.

For many weeks, but particularly during the last ten days, officials of the Department of Labor, the National Recovery Administration and the National Labor Board have been in conference with me and with each other on this subject. It has been our common objective to find an agency or agencies suitable for the disposition of these difficult problems, and after making such selection to make clear to the public how this machinery works and how it can be utilized in the interest of maintaining orderly industrial relations and justice as between employers, employees and the general public, and enforcing the statutes and other provisions of law that relate to collective bargaining and similar labor relations.

The Executive Order creates in connection with the Department of Labor, but not subject to the judicial supervision of the Secretary of Labor, a National Labor Relations Board composed of three impartial persons, each of whom will receive a salary of $10,000 a year. This Board is given the power to make investigations, to hold labor elections, to hear cases of discharge of employees and to act as voluntary arbitrator. In addition, the Board is authorized to recommend to the President that in such cases as they deem it desirable, existing labor boards such as the industrial boards already created in the cotton textile industry or the petroleum industry, and such as the various Regional Labor Boards, should be reestablished under the authority of the Joint Resolution just passed by Congress and approved by me on June 19, 1934; and also to recommend that additional boards of a similar character should be newly created. Whenever any regional, industrial or special board is established or created under the authority of the Joint Resolution it will report for administrative purposes to the National Labor Relations Board, but the decisions of the regional, industrial or special boards will be subject to review by the National Board only where it is clear that such review will serve the public interest. Furthermore, the Board can utilize and refer cases to suitable State or local tribunals.

The existing National Labor Board is by this Executive Order abolished, effective July 9, 1934, but the new National Labor Relations Board will have the benefit of the expert personnel of the old Board and of such of the subordinate regional labor boards as it may deem necessary. The new Board will have the advantages of the experience of the old Board. . . .

One of the most important features of the new arrangement is that the National Labor Relations Board and all subordinate boards will make regular reports through the Secretary of Labor to the President. . . . Reports furnished regularly in this manner will be invaluable in the event that any permanent legislation is later contemplated and in developing a systematic knowledge of the general character of the labor relations problems in the United States of America, which must be justly and expeditiously handled.

The very presence of this Board and any boards it may authorize will have undoubtedly a salutary effect in making it possible for individual conciliators to arrive at settlements of local grievances promptly. Indeed it is my hope that so far as possible adjustment in labor relations and the correction of labor abuses can be effectively made at the source of the dispute without bringing the parties before national authorities located in Washington. . . .

This Executive Order, I believe, marks a great step forward in administrative efficiency and, more important, in governmental policy in labor matters. It meets the universal demand not only of employers and employees, but of the public, that the machinery for adjusting labor relations should be clarified so that every person may know where to turn for the adjustment of grievances.

NOTE: The foregoing Executive Order (Item 118) was issued by me pursuant to a Joint Resolution of the Congress approved by me June 19, 1934 (Public Res. 44; 73d Congress), which authorized the President to establish one or more boards to investigate the facts in labor controversies, arising under Section 7-A of N.I.R.A., or controversies which burdened or threatened to become a burden upon the free flow of interstate commerce.

The boards were given the right by the Resolution to hold elections among employees of industrial units in order to determine their representatives for collective bargaining; and provided for review by the United States Circuit Courts of Appeals of the complaints of orders made by the boards in election cases.

This first National Labor Relations Board, which I appointed, commenced its operations on July 9, 1934. Under its procedure, complaints of violations of Section 7-A of N.I.R.A. were filed with the various regional boards which were continued from the days of the old National Labor Board (see Items 109 and 182 of Vol. II). Attempt was then made to adjust the matter by mediation; if that failed, a hearing was held. Findings of fact were made, and if there was refusal by the employer to comply, the case was forwarded to the National Board in Washington, which after further oral argument, or submission of briefs, or in some cases, further hearing, issued its decisions. If no compliance resulted the cases would be sent to the Attorney General for prosecution and to the Compliance Division of the N.R.A. with a recommendation that the employer's Blue Eagle be revoked.

The life of the National Labor Relations Board was extended by successive Executive Orders 7074, 7090 and 7121 from June 16, 1935, the date of its expiration, to August 27, 1935, although, of course, the active work of the Board ceased immediately upon the decision of the

Supreme Court of the United States on May 27, 1935, declaring Title I of the N.I.R.A. unconstitutional. (See Items 65, 66, 67, 68 and Introduction of Vol. IV.)

The record of the accomplishments of this Board again clearly proved the beneficial effect of Federal intervention in the field of labor relations, and the necessity of a Government Board for this purpose.

During the period from July 9, 1934, to May 30, 1935, the Board settled 703 strikes involving 229,640 employees, and it succeeded in averting threatened strikes in 605 cases involving 536,398 employees. In addition, it settled about 14 disputes in cases where there were no strikes or threats of strikes. Elections under its supervision were conducted in 579 establishments covering 56,814 employees.

119 ❲ The One Hundred and Thirty-fourth Press Conference (Excerpts). June 29, 1934

(Identical bids for Government work under code provisions.)

THE PRESIDENT: I think the only news at the present moment is an order which I signed this morning to see if we could correct a very difficult situation in regard to the purchases of various articles by the Government. You know, we have been getting a series of identical bids on the plea from the bidders that they are precluded from putting in competitive bids by their filed prices with their respective Code Authorities. We are going to try something new to see if we can break that down.

The Executive Order provides—you can get a copy of it after the press conference so that you can see what it says— that any bidder for a Government contract of the United States or a State or municipality or other public authority, in other words, any kind of Government contract for goods on which the bidder has filed prices with his Code Authority, these bids from now on will be held to have complied with the Code requirements on two conditions: First, if the bidder quotes a price to the Government agencies not more than 15 percent below his filed price and, second, if he does quote a lower price than the filed price, he shall file that lower price with the Code Authority.

In other words, he gives the public the advantage of the same reduction that he offers to the Government.

The second part of it is that if any other member of the Code believes that this lower bid is made possible only by unfair practices, he has the right to complain to the Administrator of Industrial Recovery who shall thereupon make a finding as to whether the complaint is justified or not.

We hope by this means to restore competition on Government bids and, incidentally as a result of that, in a very large line of actual prices to private consumers, and at the same time we hope to prevent unfair trade practices.

Q. In other words, Mr. President, if they bid on a Government contract now they do not have to file their prices with the Code Authority?

THE PRESIDENT: Actually at the present time they all bid the same price with the Government on the excuse that that is the price they have filed with the Code Authority. . . .

120 ⟪ Statement by the President Approving the Railroad Retirement Bill. June 30, 1934

S. 3231 — An Act to provide a retirement system for railroad employees, to provide unemployment relief, and for other purposes.

DECISION on this bill has been difficult.

The principal arguments against the measure include:

(a) The Federal Coordinator of Transportation at much public expense is now engaged in a thorough survey of the whole subject of employment security on railroads. He requested many months ago that legislation be deferred until the completion of these studies and the filing of his report.

(b) The bill, although much improved in its final form, is still crudely drawn and will require many changes and amendments at the next session of Congress.

(c) Although the bill does not create very large additional financial obligations on the part of the railroads during the next four years, the financial burden will increase progressively after that date, and the bill makes no sound provision for this increase.

The arguments in favor of the bill are as follows:

(a) The actual burden on the railroads caused by enforced contribution will be far less than their figures would indicate.

(b) Superannuated employees will retire under the new pension plan and, though a considerable number of these older men will not be replaced, many others will be replaced by other employees. The net result will be to improve the morale of the entire force.

(c) The bill is in line with sound social policy.

(d) The bill provides for the creation of a board which will have the duty of accumulating all necessary data and recommending changes which will put the system on an adequate and permanent basis.

After a careful weighing of the advantages and disadvantages to the country I have come to the deliberate conclusion that I should approve the bill.

NOTE: Many railroads at this time had voluntary pension systems. Some of them had none. Those systems which did exist were not uniform and of course were not legally enforceable.

The foregoing Act set up a Railroad Retirement Board with a compulsory uniform retirement and pension system which was maintained by compulsory contributions from employees, and from the railroads. The carriers' contributions were double the amount of the employees'. Provision was made for compulsory retirement by employees at a certain age with pensions to be paid out of a separate fund in the United States Treasury into which these contributions had been deposited.

This statute was declared unconstitutional by the Supreme Court by a five to four vote in *Alton Railroad Co. vs. Railroad Retirement Board* (295 U. S. 330), as violating the due process clause and as not being "in purpose or effect a regulation of interstate commerce within the meaning of the Constitution." (See Introduction and Item 69 of Volume IV, and Item 232 of Vol. V.)

The Act was superseded in 1935 by two other statutes (Pub. No. 339, 74th Congress; 49 Stat. 967; and Pub. No. 400, 74th Congress; 49

Stat. 974), both approved August 29, 1935.

These statutes in effect divided the prior Act into two parts. The former set up a retirement and pension system with a retirement board, eliminating some of the provisions of the prior statute. The second statute provided for the levying of an excise tax upon the railroads and their employees, which was to be paid into the general treasury but not into a segregated fund as provided in the invalidated statute. The retirement allowances and pensions were to be paid out of the general funds of treasury.

These statutes were contested, but before a decision could be reached by the Supreme Court, I persuaded representatives of the carriers and of the employees to join in an effort to work out agreed legislation providing for a system of pensions which would be acceptable to all parties and be administered by Federal Government.

Extended negotiations resulted in an agreement pursuant to which the Congress passed a new retirement act, June 24, 1937, amending the Retirement Act of 1935. A few days later — June 29, 1937 — a taxing act was approved providing for taxes on carriers and employees to bring into the Treasury the funds necessary to meet the obligations of the retirement act.

The pension system provided by these Acts is now in effect, and is being administered by the Railroad Retirement Board. Apparently the validity of this legislation is conceded by all those affected.

121 ⟨ Statement by the President Approving Amendments to Bankruptcy Law. June 30, 1934

S. 3580 — An Act to amend an Act entitled "An Act to establish a uniform system of bankruptcy throughout the United States," approved July 1, 1898, and Acts amendatory thereof and supplementary thereto.

THIS is another bill on which many arguments pro and con have been made. There has been a serious lack of understanding of its provisions and it has been alleged that insurance companies and other mortgagees will suffer severely through the use of this law by farmers to evade the payment of debts that are within their capacity to meet.

I do not subscribe to these fears.

I have sufficient faith in the honesty of the overwhelming

majority of farmers to believe that they will not evade the payment of just debts.

Furthermore, contrary to the belief of many uninformed persons this is not a general or wholesale moratorium privilege. The provisions for appointment of appraisers under the Bankruptcy Act and for the judicial review of their appraisals furnish adequate checks against the possibility of unfair appraisals. The actual repugnance with which farmers, like other right-minded people, regard bankruptcy will prevent them from availing themselves of the provisions of this measure except under the force of necessity. The bill is intended to protect not only the farmers, but their creditors also.

In the actual operation of the law, I do not believe that losses of capital will greatly exceed, if they exceed at all, the losses that would be sustained if this measure were not signed.

On the other side of the picture, it is worth remembering that this act will stop foreclosures and prevent occasional instances of injustice to worthy borrowers. The mere threat of a use of this machinery will speed voluntary conciliation of debts and the refinancing program of the Farm Credit Administration. It will prevent deficiency judgments — a form of liability which, in the judgment of many thinking business men, ought to be abolished entirely.

The bill is in some respects loosely worded and will require amendment at the next session of Congress. Nevertheless, the reasons for signing it far outweigh the arguments on the other side.

NOTE: The foregoing statute was known as the Frazier-Lemke Act, of June 28, 1934 (48 Stat. 1289). Its purpose was to provide further relief to a farmer in composing or extending his indebtedness.

The statute was declared unconstitutional in the case of *Louisville Joint Stock Land Bank vs. Radford* (295 U.S. 555). A new bill was immediately prepared to meet the constitutional difficulties and within three months after the decision, the Congress had passed, and I had approved, substitute legislation which is popularly referred to as the Frazier-Lemke Act of August 28, 1935 (49 Stat. 943). The Supreme Court, by its decision in *Wright vs. Binton Branch of the Mountain*

Trust Bank (300 U.S. 440, March 29, 1937), has removed many of the   doubts regarding the validity of the new Frazier-Lemke Act.

122 (A Commission on Aviation Policy Is Established. June 30, 1934

Announcement was made of the appointment of the Commission created by the Act approved June 12, 1934, entitled "An Act to Revise Airmail Laws and to Establish a Commission to Make a Report to the Congress Recommending an Aviation Policy." The following will constitute this Commission:

> Clark Howell, *of Atlanta, Georgia*
> Jerome Clarke Hunsaker, *of New York*
> Edward P. Warner, *of Washington, D. C.*
> Franklin K. Lane, Jr., *of California*
> Albert J. Berres, *of California*

NOTE: This commission was appointed pursuant to the provisions of the Air Mail Act of June 12, 1934, with directions to report to the Congress not later than February 1, 1935. The report was made to me and I transmitted it to the Congress with a message on January 31, 1935 (see Volume IV, Item 12).

123 (The Industrial Emergency Committee Is Created. Executive Order No. 6770. June 30, 1934

By virtue of the authority vested in me by the National Industrial Recovery Act, approved June 16, 1933, and to effectuate the purposes of said Act and further to effectuate the purposes of the Executive Order of July 11, 1933, appointing a temporary Executive Council and the Executive Order of November 17, 1933, creating a National Emergency Council:

1. I hereby appoint Donald R. Richberg to serve (without compensation except as hereinafter provided) as Executive Secretary of the Executive Council and as Executive Director of the National Emergency Council from and after July 1, 1934, until

further order and during the absence of Frank C. Walker, who is hereby, at his request, temporarily relieved from the duties of said offices.

2. I hereby create an Industrial Emergency Committee, which shall be composed of:

> The Secretary of the Interior,
> The Secretary of Labor,
> The Administrator of Federal Emergency Relief,
> The Administrator for Industrial Recovery,

and a Director to be appointed by the President. It shall be the duty of said Industrial Emergency Committee to make recommendations to the President, through its director, with respect to problems of relief, public works, labor disputes and industrial recovery and to study and coordinate the handling of joint problems affecting these activities.

3. I hereby appoint Donald R. Richberg Director of said Industrial Emergency Committee and direct that he be given leave of absence as General Counsel of the National Recovery Administration until September 1st, with pay, in order that he may fulfill the duties of the positions to which he is hereby appointed and such further functions and duties as shall be prescribed by the President.

NOTE: The purpose of the foregoing Committee was to coordinate the activities of the Administration affecting relief and unemployment and in general the activities under the various emergency recovery measures. One primary reason for the creation of the Industrial Emergency Committee was to bring the N.R.A. into line with a coordinated Government policy, to see to it that each of the major agencies or departments concerned with the recovery program was working in harmony with the objectives of the others and was following reasonably consistent general policies.

In the autumn of 1934 it became evident that it was unnecessary to maintain both the Executive Council (see Item 94, Vol. II) and the National Emergency Council (see Item 163, Vol. II).

Accordingly, Executive Order No. 6889-A was issued on October 29, 1934 (see Item 172, this volume), transferring to the National Emergency Council the functions and duties of the Executive Council. The same Executive Order consolidated

the Industrial Emergency Committee with the National Emergency
Council as a subcommittee, direct-

ing that it continue to exercise its
functions and duties (see Item 172,
this volume).

124 ❬ The National Resources Board Is Established. Executive Order No. 6777. June 30, 1934

BY VIRTUE of the authority vested in me by the National Industrial Recovery Act (Public No. 67, 73d Cong.), I hereby establish the National Resources Board, consisting of the Secretary of the Interior (chairman), the Secretary of War, the Secretary of Agriculture, the Secretary of Commerce, the Secretary of Labor, the Federal Emergency Relief Administrator, Frederic A. Delano, Charles E. Merriam, and Wesley C. Mitchell.

An advisory committee, consisting of Frederic A. Delano (chairman), Charles E. Merriam, and Wesley C. Mitchell, is hereby constituted, to which additional members may be added from time to time by order of the President.

There is also established a technical committee with no fixed membership or tenure of office to be selected by the Board.

The functions of the Board shall be to prepare and present to the President a program and plan of procedure dealing with the physical, social, governmental, and economic aspects of public policies for the development and use of land, water, and other national resources, and such related subjects as may from time to time be referred to it by the President.

The Board shall submit a report on land and water use on or before December 1, 1934. The program and plan shall include the coordination of projects of Federal, State, and local governments and the proper division of responsibility and the fair division of cost among the several governmental authorities.

The National Planning Board of the Federal Emergency Administration of Public Works is hereby abolished, and all of its powers, duties, records, personnel, equipment, and funds are hereby transferred to the National Resources Board.

The Committee on National Land Problems, created by Executive Order No. 6693, of April 28, 1934, is hereby abolished.

The Federal Emergency Administration of Public Works is hereby directed to allot to the National Resources Board the sum of one hundred thousand dollars ($100,000), and such additional sums as may be approved from time to time by the President, to carry out its functions.

(See following Item and note.)

124A ❡ White House Statement on the Establishment of the National Resources Board. July 3, 1934

IN ORDER to grapple on a national scale with the problem of the millions of farm families now attempting unsuccessfully to wrest a living from worn-out, eroded lands, the President today issued an Executive Order creating the National Resources Board. The Board will study and plan for the better utilization of the land, water, and other national resources of the country.

The personnel of the Board includes the Secretary of the Interior, chairman; the Secretary of War, the Secretary of Agriculture, the Secretary of Commerce, the Secretary of Labor, the Federal Emergency Relief Administrator, Mr. Frederic A. Delano, Mr. Charles E. Merriam, and Mr. Wesley C. Mitchell. The last three named also constitute an Advisory Committee, of which Mr. Delano is chairman. The order at the same time abolished the National Planning Board, transferring its personnel, duties and records to the new organization. The relationships with State planning agencies heretofore established by the National Planning Board will be continued and developed by the new National Resources Board. The order provided for a Technical Committee as well, with no fixed personnel or tenure.

The Board will prepare a program and plan of procedure to be submitted to the President dealing with all aspects of the problem of development and use of land, water and other national resources, in their physical, social, governmental and economic aspects.

A report on land and water is called for in the order, to be submitted before December 1, 1934. The program and plan will include coordination of projects of Federal, State and local governments, defining the division of responsibility and costs among the various governmental authorities.

The new Board which will coordinate the diverse efforts of several government agencies in attacking the problems, supersedes the Committee on National Land Problems, which is abolished by today's order.

As an example of the major problems facing the new Board, there is the imperative need of saving those lands of the country now being rapidly turned into virtual deserts through wind and water erosion, and the relocation of those who are trying to wrest a living from this rapidly deteriorating land. Such lands include the flat prairie lands of the West where drought and wind combine to carry away the remaining fertile top-soil, and hill land where, after land has been cleared, rain has washed the formerly fertile hillsides clean of productive soil, with consequent gullying and virtual ruin of the land for productive purposes. Such lands can be saved by returning them to forest, or utilizing them for grazing rather than attempting to raise clean-tilled crops, which induce rapid erosion.

Coupled with this problem, of course, is that of relocating those farmers and their families on better land, where their efforts will bring them a better living and more certain economic security.

The program will be prepared with more in mind than better land utilization. It will give consideration to the better balancing of agricultural production and the solution of human problems in land use. It will aim to point the way to correction of the misuse of land and water resources, thereby improving the standards of living of millions of impoverished families.

Many agencies of the Federal Government will cooperate in this broad program, including the following:

337

Interior Department: National Park Service, Office of Indian Affairs, the General Land Office, the Bureau of Reclamation, the Geological Survey, the Subsistence Homesteads Division and the Soil Erosion Service.

Department of Agriculture: Bureau of Agricultural Economics, the Forest Service, the Agricultural Adjustment Administration, the Farm Credit Administration, the Bureau of Chemistry and Soils, the Biological Survey, the Bureau of Agricultural Engineering and the Extension Service.

Relief: The Federal Emergency Relief Administration and the Federal Surplus Relief Corporation.

In matters affecting navigable waters, the War Department will cooperate with the National Resources Board. Likewise, the Bureau of Fisheries of the Department of Commerce will cooperate in matters affecting that national resource.

NOTE: On July 20, 1933, the Administrator of Public Works had designated with my approval a National Planning Board "to advise and assist the Administrator . . . through the preparation, development and maintenance of comprehensive plans . . . through surveys and research . . . and through the analysis of projects for coordination and correlation of effort among the agencies of the Federal, State and local governments."

The report of the National Planning Board was submitted to me on June 24, 1934. I issued the foregoing Executive Order, reorganizing it as the National Resources Board, with some additional personnel. The new Board included the three former members of the National Planning Board and also the Secretary of the Interior as Chairman, the Secretaries of War, Agriculture, Commerce, Labor, and the Federal Emergency Relief Administrator.

The National Resources Board prepared a series of reports as required by the Executive Order. The most comprehensive was the one dated December 1, 1934, which I transmitted to the Congress on January 24, 1935 (see Vol. IV, Item 8).

125 ❨ The President Hails the Celebration in Denmark of the Anniversary of American Independence. July 4, 1934

I HAVE learned with much interest and pleasure of the celebration of the anniversary of the Independence of the United States which is to be held in Denmark at Rebild National Park, with participation by American citizens of Danish birth or descent, some of whom may possibly have been instrumental in founding this remarkable international monument.

It seems singularly fitting, and of good augury for the future of international relationships, that the commemoration of this milestone in the progress of the American people toward a fuller expression of their national and individual life should find a sympathetic response in the land of origin of many of my fellow citizens.

It is my belief that the Americans assembled at Rebild Park may, by serving as interpreters between their lands of origin and of adoption, do much to encourage the growth of helpful international understanding, and advance the cause of good-will throughout the world.

126 ❨ The National Power Policy Committee Is Established. July 5, 1934

My dear Mr. Secretary:

I WISH to establish in the Public Works Administration a Committee to be called the "National Power Policy Committee." Its duty will be to develop a plan for the closer cooperation of the several factors in our electrical power supply — both public and private — whereby national policy in power matters may be unified and electricity may be made more broadly available at cheaper rates to industry, to domestic and, particularly, to agricultural consumers.

Several agencies of the Government, such as the Federal Power and Trade Commission, have in process surveys and reports useful in this connection. The Mississippi Valley Committee of Public Works is making studies of the feasibility of power in connection with water storage, flood control and navigation projects. The War Department and Bureau of Reclamation have under construction great hydro-electric plants. Representatives of these agencies have been asked to serve on the Committee. It is not to be merely a fact-finding body, but rather one for the development and unification of national power policy.

As time goes on there undoubtedly will be legislation on the subject of holding companies and for the regulation of electric current in interstate commerce. This Committee should consider what lines should be followed in shaping this legislation. Since a number of the States have commissions having jurisdiction over intrastate power matters, it is necessary that whatever plan is developed should have regard to the powers of these various State commissions as well as of the States in general.

It is not thought that it will be necessary to have frequent meetings of the full Committee. An adequate administrative staff will be provided, and personal expenses of the members of the Committee in connection with its meetings will be met.

The Committee is to be advisory to the President. I hope that you will accept membership on this Committee and act as its Chairman.

Sincerely yours,

Hon. Harold L. Ickes,
The Secretary of the Interior,
Interior Building,
Washington, D. C.

NOTE: The foregoing communication was prepared before my departure on my trip to the outlying parts of the United States (see Item 127, this volume); but was not signed until July 9, 1934.

The purpose of this Committee was to coordinate the Administration's policy with respect to the development of electric power for the benefit of domestic, rural, commercial and industrial consumers.

There were in existence at the time several agencies of the Government making surveys and preparing reports on topics closely associated with the development and use of electric power. I thought that it was necessary to have a general organization for the development and unification of a national policy to form the basis of legislation and administrative activity. See Chaps. IV and VII, Vol. I.

The first subject studied by the Committee after its organization was the problem of the public utility holding company. Its report, submitted to the President, was transmitted to the Congress on March 12, 1935, and played a large part in the enactment of the Public Utility Holding Company Act of 1935 (see Vol. IV, Item 27).

It also began to consider, soon after its organization, the problem of rural electrification, and its notes on the subject, submitted to the President, were among the factors which led ultimately to the establishment of the Rural Electrification Administration.

The administrative work in connection with the organization of the Third World Power Conference was also carried on by this National Power Policy Committee (see Vol. V, Item 123).

127 ⟨ Joint Statement on Conversations in Haiti Between the President and President Vincent. July 5, 1934

DURING the conversations today, July 5th, in Cape Haitien between President Roosevelt and President Vincent, the following conclusions were reached:

(1) In view of the rapid progress made by the Garde d'Haiti, and upon the request of the Haitian Government, it has been agreed that the Garde d'Haiti will be turned over to complete Haitian command on August 1, 1934. All American Marine forces now in Haiti will be withdrawn a fortnight later.

(2) President Roosevelt informed President Vincent of the action of the Congress of the United States which authorized him to present to the Haitian Government a portion of the equipment belonging to the American Government now in use by the Garde d'Haiti and the Marine forces in Haiti.

(3) Negotiations will begin shortly between the two Govern-

ments for the conclusion of a commercial treaty, the underlying principles of which have been under discussion for some time. It is hoped that such a treaty will result in a mutually profitable increase in the commerce between the two countries.

The conversations held between the two Presidents at Cape Haitien have served to reaffirm the feeling of friendship and cordiality existing between the United States and Haiti, a feeling which was signally marked in the course of their conversations held last April in the City of Washington, D. C.

Presidential Palace,
Cape Haitien.

NOTE: Because I found myself confronted with many problems relating to outlying parts of the United States, and desired to obtain first-hand knowledge, I sailed from Annapolis on July 1, 1934, on the *U.S.S. Houston* for a 10,000-mile cruise.

The first stop was at Cape Haitien, on July 5, 1934, where I went ashore and was warmly greeted by President Vincent and his Cabinet. I also renewed acquaintance with old friends of January, 1917, when I visited Haiti as Assistant Secretary of the Navy. Puerto Rico was next visited. I landed at Mayaguez on July 6, 1934, and drove across the Island, stopping for a few minutes at San German, Sabana Grande, Yauco, Penuelas, Ponce, Juana Diaz, Coamo Springs, Coamo, Aibonita, Cayey, Jajome Alto, Caguas, Rio Piedras, and finally arrived at San Juan, where I spent the night with my old friend Governor Winship.

The next port of call was St. Thomas, followed by a visit to St.

Croix, the two principal islands in the American Virgin Island group, where I inspected the subsistence homesteads and other improvements (see Item 28, this volume).

The course from here to Panama passed close to the coast of Colombia, and President Olaya Herrera was good enough to invite me to land at the historic city of Cartagena. I spent a most delightful day there as his guest, reaching Panama the following day, July 11, 1934. There I was welcomed by President Arias of Panama, and saw many of the interesting spots of the Republic and of the Canal Zone.

Leaving Panama, *U.S.S. Houston* stopped at Cocos Island and Clipperton Island, at both of which the party had excellent fishing. On July 24th we arrived at the Island of Hawaii, visiting the volcanoes and proceeding the next day to Honolulu. While there I was delightfully entertained by the Governor and the citizens of Oahu. I inspected the Army and Navy bases, and left on

July 28th, for Portland, Oregon, where we arrived August 3d.

The return trip across the continent by train enabled me to visit several of the important new dams on which work had just commenced —Bonneville, Grand Coulee and Fort Peck. I returned to Washington on August 10, 1934.

The following items, Nos. 128-133 incl., 135, and 137-144 incl., are some of the speeches made by me on this interesting and instruc-

tive trip. There were other extemporaneous talks, not printed for lack of space, at the following places:

Spokane, Washington	Aug. 4th
Bonners Ferry, Idaho	Aug. 4th
Fargo, North Dakota	Aug. 7th
Willmar, Minn.	Aug. 7th
Lake City, Minn.	Aug. 8th
Wabasha, Minn.	Aug. 8th
Sparta, Wis.	Aug. 8th
Milwaukee, Wis.	Aug. 9th

128 ❧ Extemporaneous Remarks at Cape Haitien, Haiti. July 6, 1934

I AM very happy to come back to Cape Haitien. I shall always remember as long as I live the week which I had the privilege of spending in the Republic of Haiti.

I am glad to come back especially at a time when the relationship between the Republic of Haiti and the Republic of the United States will be restored to a basis of complete independence.

I am glad that, as a result of the visit of President Vincent to Washington, as he has so well said, two out of three points which we considered have already been consummated or are about to be consummated.

Very soon, I think within a month or six weeks, the last Americans who have served here with the Garde d'Haiti and with the Marines will leave the Republic of Haiti. That is not all. I am very hopeful and very certain that when these Americans leave your shores you will think of them with the spirit of friendship and that you will be happy in the days to come remembering that they tried to help the people of Haiti, and so when they go, Mr. President, I am certain also that you will carry on the same spirit of friendship between our peoples which must always

343

exist in the future. We shall have the same confidence, closer
relationships of commerce and also something that you desire far
more than commerce, and that is a spirit of understanding and a
spirit of friendship between not only our two peoples but also
our two Governments.

And so, Mr. President, I am happy to come here once more.
I wish that I had the opportunity again to go from one end of
the Republic to the other. In this short visit, I want to thank you
for your hospitality; and I want to thank you for the great pains
to which you have gone to make my visit most comfortable, and
I want to drink to the health of the President of Haiti, to the
Government of Haiti, and to the people of Haiti. May our friendship ever continue!

129 ❪ Extemporaneous Remarks in San Juan, Puerto Rico. July 7, 1934

My friends and fellow citizens of Puerto Rico:

NEVER as long as I live shall I forget the warmth of your reception to me yesterday and today. The drive from Mayaguez to
Ponce and then across the island to San Juan gave me again a
wonderful picture of your wonderful island.

I was here thirty years ago and it seems to me that in these
years a great deal of progress has been made; but I believe, also,
that the progress that you have made in the past is very small
compared with the progress that you are going to make in the
future.

One thing that seemed to be very clear was that your problems
here on the island are very much the same kind of problems that
we have in many other parts of the United States. They are social
problems and economic problems, and the same methods that we
use to solve them in other parts of the country will be applied
here in Puerto Rico.

I believe in better homes. That means bringing about a better
family life, better living conditions, a better chance for educa-

tion, and a better chance for every person to earn his livelihood. Then we shall have better health conditions because unhealthy conditions are caused by a lack of opportunity to earn one's bread. With the help of our Government in Washington and with the splendid help of the Island Government and of the Governor, I am looking forward to the solving of these problems here in the island just as quickly as we shall solve them in the continental part of the United States.

We cannot accomplish everything in one year. In fact, we must look ahead for a great many years, and that is why we have all come to an agreement in principle for the rehabilitation of Puerto Rico. That plan, of course, will take a great many years to accomplish, but I hope and I am confident that all of you will do your part in making the plan a success.

I wish very much that I could stay here for many weeks and see many parts of the island that I have not had the opportunity of visiting. I hope to come back here not once, but many times, and see what you have done. I hope to see that a great deal of progress has been made.

I know that you will cooperate with us in what we are trying to do for the United States, not only here but in all parts of the Nation. And so, my friends, I am not going to say good-bye but au revoir.

It has been good to see you again in Puerto Rico. Many thanks for your splendid spirit. I shall never forget how good you have been to me on this visit.

130 ⟪ Extemporaneous Remarks in St. Thomas, Virgin Islands. July 7, 1934

I just wanted to say a word while we are here in the family that I am very proud of the work that has been done down in the Virgin Islands because it shows what can be done with a little help from Washington and a great deal of cooperation down here toward improving the conditions of a great many thousands of human beings. Of course, we never expect the Virgin Islands to be a tremendous factor in trade but we do hope that they may be self-sustaining.

The experiment that we are working out in the Virgin Islands is being watched by Washington with a great deal of interest. We have a unit in the Virgin Islands where we can actually see the results of their work. I am very proud of what you have done. I hope to come here again before I leave Washington and see some more of these fine results. I am glad to see you all.

131 ⟨ Extemporaneous Remarks in St. Croix, Virgin Islands. July 8, 1934

MY FRIENDS in St. Croix—I am very glad to come here and I am very grateful to you for this splendid reception and very hearty welcome, and I want you to remember that today, more than ever before, the people of the continental United States remember and realize that you, also, are a part of the American family.

132 ⟨ Extemporaneous Remarks in Cartagena, Colombia. July 10, 1934

FROM the days of my youth when I was a small boy, it has been my dream to visit "La Ciudad Heroica" — this noble Cartagena of the New World which signifies so much to all Americans in every part of our continent.

Today that dream has come true, and more than true, for I little thought that it would be my happy privilege, as the representative of the United States, to be the guest of the President and of the People of Colombia. I am indeed grateful to you for the warmth of your reception and for the close spirit of friendship which you have shown me, and I am especially happy to be received by President Herrera, who has left behind such a multitude of warm friends which he made during all those years when he represented Colombia in Washington.

We, the citizens of all the American Republics are, I think, at the threshold of a new era.

It is a new era because of the new spirit of understanding that is best expressed in the phrase, "Let us each and every one of us live and let live." In all of our American Nations, there is growing insistence on the peaceful solution of international problems. Colombia and Peru have rendered an inestimable service to humanity in the settlement of their Letitia problem. The United States joins with Colombia in every effort she has made to end the unfortunate war in the Chaco, a war that is the only discordant note that remains in all the length and breadth of North and Central and South America.

We are entering a new era in accepting the plan that no one of our Nations must hereafter exploit a neighbor Nation at the expense of that neighbor. We shall all of us find methods for the development of the commerce and resources of the Americas, but we shall do this in the spirit of fair play and of justice.

Finally, I hope, my friends, that this new era is bringing a communion of understanding of the life and culture and ideals of the separate Nations that make up the Americas. It is right that each country should have its own cultural development, but every one of us can learn greatly from each other.

That is true of literature and of the arts, and it is true also of government.

We in the United States know of the universities in the lands to the South of us. Many of these were great institutions of learning long before white men founded Virginia or landed at Plymouth Rock. We know of your poets and of your painters and of your writers.

But it must be equally understood that the process of development in sociological and humanitarian lines is proceeding at a splendid pace in every American Republic. All of us are seeking to improve the condition of the average citizen and we give to social legislation an interest and an incentive which augurs well for succeeding generations.

And so, Your Excellency, it is in this spirit of seeking mutual understanding and mutual helpfulness that a President of the United States sets foot for the first time on the sacred soil of the Republic of Colombia. May your Nation greatly prosper and may both our countries from this day forth come to know and honor each other as good neighbors and as preservers of human liberty.

133 ⟪Extemporaneous Remarks in Panama. July 11, 1934

I AM grateful to you, Mr. President, and to the people of Panama, for the cordial welcome you have given me. It is a great pleasure to me to return to Panama after an absence of twenty-two years and to see the great progress which has been made and is being made in the well-being of the Republic.

But my interest in Panama may be said to be of a historic character as well, because it was my own great-uncle, Mr. William H. Aspinwall, who was instrumental in starting the Panama Railroad in 1848 and who in the face of many natural difficulties carried it to a successful conclusion in 1855.

It was this railway which began to restore to the Isthmus its former proud position of the crossroads of the Americas. When the work started there was no city where Colon now stands and Panama City had but 10,000 inhabitants. Through the succeeding years, you have become a Nation and an important nerve center of the commerce of the world.

The Canal serves all Nations in the needs of peaceful commerce. The United States is therefore a trustee for all the world in its peaceful maintenance. In that trusteeship, we have always had, and I am sure always will have, the complete cooperation of the Republic of Panama. The questions of administration and of methods of cooperation, which arise and will continue to arise in many new forms in the future as conditions change and new problems confront us, will, I am certain, be solved in the same spirit of justice which we are now displaying.

It was to me most delightful — and most helpful — to have President Arias visit Washington last winter. I appreciate the problems of the Republic of Panama, but I am happy to think that Panama and the United States have both definitely entered into the period of recovery from difficult days.

Both Nations are seeking a greater progress and a greater social justice. For you, Mr. President, and for Panama, I wish every happiness and every good.

134 ⟪ Message of Condolence on the Assassination of Chancellor Dollfuss of Austria. Sent from U.S.S. Houston. July 26, 1934

IT IS with horror and deep regret that I learn of the assassination of Engelbert Dollfuss, Minister of Foreign Affairs and Chancellor of Austria. I extend through you to the Austrian people sincere sympathy in my own name and on behalf of my fellow countrymen.

Mrs. Roosevelt joins with me in expressing to Madame Dollfuss our deepest sympathy in this great sorrow which has come to her.

His Excellency, Wilhelm Miklas,
President of the Confederation of Austria,
Vienna, Austria

135 ❨ Extemporaneous Remarks in Hawaii.
July 28, 1934

Governor Poindexter, my friends and fellow Americans of the Territory of Hawaii:

I LEAVE you today with reluctance, for the friendly spirit and the generous reception given me everywhere by the people of the Islands of the Territory make me greatly wish that my visit could be prolonged.

I leave also with pride in Hawaii — pride in your patriotism and in your accomplishments. The problems you are solving are the problems of the whole Nation, and your Administration in Washington will not forget that you are in very truth an integral part of the Nation.

In a fine old prayer for our country are found these words: "Fashion into one happy people those brought hither out of many kindreds and tongues." That prayer is being answered in the Territory of Hawaii. You have a fine historic tradition in the ancient people of the Islands and I am glad that this is so well maintained. You have built on it — built on it wisely — and today men and women and children from many lands are united in loyalty to and understanding of the high purposes of America.

You are doing much to improve the standards of living of the average of your citizenry. This is as it should be, and I hope that you will put forth every effort to make still further progress.

There are indeed many parts of the mainland where economic and educational levels do not come up to those which I find here.

May I compliment you also on the excellent appearance of neatness and cleanliness in the homes which I have seen in all parts of the Islands? They deserve emulation in every part of the Nation.

And on leaving, I want to say a word of congratulation on the efficiency and fine spirit of the Army and Navy forces of which I am Commander-in-Chief. They constitute an integral part of our national defense, and I stress the word, "defense." They must ever be considered an instrument of continuing peace, for our Nation's policy seeks peace and does not look to imperialistic aims.

And so, my friends, I leave you my gratitude for all the kindnesses you have shown me. I carry with me the hope that I shall have the opportunity to return.

My friends, I shall ever remember these days — days that are all too short — your flowers, your scenery, your hospitality, but, above all, the knowledge that America can well be proud of the Territory of Hawaii. And so I say to you: "Aloha from the bottom of my heart."

136 ❧ A Letter Urging the Fullest Opportunity for Exercise of the Right to Vote. From U.S.S. Houston. August 1, 1934

My dear Alben:

IN VIEW of the interest which we all feel in the processes by which public servants are selected throughout the country, as well as the results that flow therefrom, I am taking the liberty of expressing the hope that in your State, without regard to political parties, the greatest freedom and the widest opportunity may be accorded to all the people for participation in the selection of candidates, as well as in their final election.

One of the purposes of the present national Administration in most of its activities is to improve the lot of the men and women whose voices have not always been heard and whose welfare has not always been regarded by those in charge of our Government. The right to equality of treatment under that Government and in the choosing of that Government is inherent in democracy and its denial cannot anywhere be justified.

May I indulge the hope and belief that in your State and in all the States those who are charged with party responsibility will preserve and guarantee these indisputable rights to the people of every class?

Very sincerely yours,

Hon. Alben Barkley,
Washington, D. C.

137 ⟨ Extemporaneous Remarks at the Site of the Bonneville Dam, Oregon. August 3, 1934

Governor Meier, my friends of Oregon and Washington:

THERE is an old saying that "seeing is believing" and that is why I came here today.

Until today I have never been familiar with more than the lower course of the Columbia River, but as far back as 1920 I had the privilege of coming out through these States — through all of the great Northwest — and I conceived at that time the very firm belief that this wonderful valley of the Columbia was one of the greatest assets, not alone of the Northwest, but of the United States of America. Back there, fourteen years ago, I determined that if I ever had the rank or the opportunity to do something for the development of this great River Basin and for the territory that surrounds it, I would do my best to put this great project through.

Yes, "seeing is believing." Over a year ago, when we first established the principle of commencing great public works projects in every part of the Union, I became firmly convinced that the Federal Government ought immediately to undertake the construction of the Bonneville Dam and the Grand Coulee Dam, and so we got started. General Martin reminded me, as we were driving out here, that it was only on the 26th day of September last year — ten months ago only — that the definite allocation of money for the Bonneville project was made by me at the White House, and I think we have gone a long way in less than a year.

It has been my conception, my dream, that while most of us are alive we would see great sea-going vessels come up the Colum-

352

bia River as far as the Dalles, and it was only this morning that
the Secretary of War told me of a new survey that is being made
by the Army Engineers. From that survey I hope it will be found
to be, in the part of wisdom, to enlarge these locks so that ocean-
going ships can pass up as far as the Dalles. And, when we get
that done and moving, I hope that we can also make navigation
possible from the Dalles up, so we may have barge transportation
into the wheat country.

I am reminded a good deal of another river, with a problem
somewhat similar—a river on which I was born and brought up
—the Hudson. It was only a comparatively few years ago—within
the past ten years—that through the action of the Federal Government the channel of the Hudson River was so deepened that
Albany, 140 miles from the sea, was made a seaport. You have a
very similar case on the Columbia. In the same way, in the State
of New York, above Albany, you meet the rapids and the falls
of the Mohawk. It was over a hundred years ago that Dewitt
Clinton, a Governor of New York, built what was called "Clinton's Ditch," the Erie Canal, and carried through the possibility
of navigation by barge from the sea to the Great Lakes. And so
I believe that the day will come on the Columbia when we shall
not only extend sea-going navigation far back into the continent
but, at the end of sea navigation, we shall be able to extend barge
transportation still further back far north into the State of Washington and far into the State of Idaho. That is a dream, my
friends, but not an idle dream, and today we have evidence of
what man can do to improve the conditions of mankind.

There is another reason for the expenditure of money in very
large amounts on the Columbia. In fact there are a good many
reasons. While we are improving navigation we are creating
power, more power, and I always believe in the old saying of
"more power to you." I do not believe that you can have enough
power for a long time to come, and the power we shall develop
here is going to be power which for all time is going to be controlled by Government.

Two years ago, when I was in Portland, I laid down the principle of the need of Government yardsticks so that the people of this country will know whether they are paying the proper price for electricity of all kinds. The Government can create yardsticks. At that time one had already been started on the Colorado River. Since then two other yardsticks have been undertaken, one in the Tennessee Valley, one here on the Columbia River, and the fourth, the St. Lawrence, is going to be started.

In this Northwestern section of our land, we still have the opening of opportunity for a vastly increased population. There are many sections of the country, as you know, where conditions are crowded. There are many sections of the country where land has run out or has been put to the wrong kind of use. America is growing. There are many people who want to go to a section of the country where they will have a better chance for themselves and their children, and there are a great many people who have children and need room for growing families. As a Roosevelt I am thinking about growing families.

Out here you have not just space, you have space that can be used by human beings. You have a wonderful land — a land of opportunity — a land already peopled by Americans who know whither America is bound. You have people who are thinking about advantages for mankind, good education, and, above all, the chance for security, the chance to lead their own lives without wondering what is going to happen to them tomorrow. They are thinking about security for old age, security against the ills and the accidents that come to people and, above all, security to earn their own living.

Today I have seen a picture I knew before only in blueprint form. So far as topography goes, it conforms to the blueprints, and the chief engineer of this project tells me that nothing stands in the way of its being completed on time, on schedule and according to plan.

Within three years, I hope the Bonneville Dam will be an actual fact and, as a fact, it will from then on militate very greatly to the benefit of the lives, not only of the people of Oregon and Washington but of the whole United States.

I know you good people are heart and soul behind this project and I think most of you are heart and soul behind what your Government is trying to do to help the people of the United States. I wish I might stay here and survey everything in detail but, as you know, I have been on a long voyage and the sailor man does not stay put very long in one place.

I have been so much interested during this wonderful drive here that I have delayed things all along the road. That is why I am an hour late. Now I have to go to the train.

I want to tell you from the bottom of my heart what a privilege it is to come here and see this great work at first hand. May it go on with God's blessing and with your blessings.

138 ❨ Extemporaneous Remarks at the Site of the Grand Coulee Dam, Washington. August 4, 1934

Senator Dill, Governor Martin, my friends:

I GO back a long, long way in my interest in the Grand Coulee. Some people in this country think that this is a new project but I remember very well that in the campaign of 1920, when I was out through the Northwest, it was a very live subject.

My old friend, Senator Dill, being of a historical turn of mind, went back into the dark ages of fourteen years ago and dug up a speech I made in Spokane. He brought it to me on the train and I am going to read it to you—not the speech but about two sentences of it for the historical record—to show that people have been thinking about the Columbia River for a great many years.

In 1920, I said this: "Coming through today on the train" (I was coming through from Montana and Idaho) "has made me think pretty deeply. When you cross the Mountain States and that portion of the Coast States that lie well back from the ocean, you are impressed by those great stretches of physical territory, just land, territory now practically unused but destined some day to contain the homes of thousands and hundreds of thousands of citizens like us, a territory to be developed by the Nation and for the Nation. As we were coming down the river today" (this was fourteen years ago) "I could not help thinking, as everyone does, of all that water running down unchecked to the sea."

Well, there is the text of what we are trying to do in this country today. I went on and said:

"It is not a problem of the State of Washington; it is not a problem of the State of Idaho; it is a problem that touches all the other States in the Union." It is a problem, as I said then, that interests us way back in old New York State. We have made beginnings — scratching the soil — and I like to think that they are only beginnings; that even in our lifetime we are going to see with our own eyes these problems taken up on a vastly greater scale.

It took fourteen years for that prophecy to come true, but it is on its way. Most of us who are here today are going to be alive when this dam is finished and when the Bonneville and a lot of other dams are finished. As I said to the Secretary of the Interior when we were on the other side of the river a few minutes ago, we are in the process of making the American people "dam minded."

People are going to understand some of the implications of building dams in the higher stretches of rivers all over the country. The Chief Engineer here was telling me a few minutes ago that the eventual completion of this dam is going to mean the doubling of potential power of every site on the Columbia River between here and the mouth of the Snake, and that is a lot of power.

It is going to mean from the Snake down to sea level, adding 50 percent to potential power they have today. That means a lot. It is going to affect not only the Columbia River Basin, but the whole of the Mountain States and Pacific Coast territory. We are going to see, I believe, with our own eyes, electricity and power made so cheap that they will become a standard article of use, not merely for agriculture and manufacturing but for every home within the reach of an electric transmission line.

The experience in those sections of the world that have cheap power prove very conclusively that the cheaper the power, the more it is used in the homes and on the farms and in small businesses. And that makes me believe that this low dam which we are undertaking at the present time is going to justify its existence before it is completed by our being able to contract for the sale of practically all of the power that it will develop. If we are justified in that belief, and hope, then we come down to Chapter II, which is the building of the high dam.

I want to take this opportunity, my friends, of telling you something about the amount of money the Federal Government is spending in the three States of the Coast. I should have liked personally to have been able to say to the Secretary of the Interior to proceed from the very beginning by setting aside, allocating, the money for the complete project here. But the fact is that out of the total sum made available to the Administration by the Congress, we have allocated in these States of the Coast a much larger proportion of that fund than the population of the three States justifies. I am talking to you frankly. It has meant that by allocating a larger portion of the three-billion-dollar fund to the Coast than a mere figure of population would justify, we have had to take some money from other States and give them less than they would have got normally on a population basis. Many other States have got less than what might be called their normal quota. Why did we do it? We did it, in my judgment, with perfect propriety and with the knowledge that those States that did not get quite as much as the Coast got would understand and approve it. We did it because out here in the Mountain States and in the Coast States you have unlimited natural resources; you have vast acreage, capable of supporting a much larger population than you now have. We believe that by proceeding with these great projects it will not only develop the well-being of the Far West and the Coast, but it will also give an opportunity to many individuals and many families back in the older settled parts of the Nation to come out here and distribute the burdens which fall on them more heavily than they fall now on the West.

You have great opportunities and you are doing nobly in grasping them. A great many years ago, seventy-five or eighty, a great editor in the City of New York said, "Go west, young man." Horace Greeley is supposed to be out-of-date today, but there is a great opportunity for people in the East, in the South and some of the overcrowded parts of the Middle West. You here show them the opportunity of still going west.

I am going to try to come back here when the dam is finished and I know that this country is going to be filled with homes not only of a great many people of this State, but by a great many families from other States of the Union — men and women and children who will be making an honest livelihood and doing their best successfully to live up to the American standard of living and the American standard of citizenship.

So I leave here today with the feeling that this work is well undertaken; that we are going ahead with a useful project; and that we are going to see it through for the benefit of our country.

139 ❨ Radio Address Delivered at Two Medicine Chalet, Glacier National Park. August 5, 1934

I HAVE been back on the soil of the continental United States for three days after most interesting visits to our fellow Americans in Puerto Rico, the Virgin Islands, the Canal Zone and the Territory of Hawaii. I return with the conviction that their problems are essentially similar to those of us who live on the mainland and, furthermore, that they are enthusiastically doing their part to improve their conditions of life and thereby the conditions of life of all Americans.

On Friday and Saturday I had the opportunity of seeing the actual construction work under way in the first two national projects for the development of the Columbia River Basin. At Bonneville, Oregon, a great dam, 140 miles inland, at the last place where the river leaps down over rapids to sea level, will provide not only a large development of cheap power but also will enable vessels to proceed another 70 or 80 miles into the interior of the country.

At Grand Coulee, in North Central Washington, an even greater dam will regulate the flow of the Columbia River, developing power and, in the future, will open up a large tract of parched land for the benefit of this and future generations. Many families in the days to come, I am confident, will thank us of this generation for providing small farms on which they will at least be able to make an honest and honorable livelihood.

Today, for the first time in my life, I have seen Glacier Park. Perhaps I can best express to you my thrill and delight by saying that I wish every American, old and young, could have been with me today. The great mountains, the glaciers, the lakes and the trees make me long to stay here for all the rest of the summer.

Comparisons are generally objectionable and yet it is not unkind to say, from the standpoint of scenery alone, that if many, and indeed most, of our American national parks were to be set down anywhere on the continent of Europe thousands of Americans would journey all the way across the ocean in order to see their beauties.

There is nothing so American as our national parks. The scenery and wild life are native. The fundamental idea behind the parks is native. It is, in brief, that the country belongs to the people, that it is in the process of making for the enrichment of the lives of all of us. The parks stand as the outward symbol of this great human principle.

It was on a famous night, sixty-four years ago, that a group of men who had been exploring the Yellowstone country gathered about a campfire to discuss what could be done with that wonderland of beauty. It is said that one of the party, a lawyer from the State of Montana, Cornelius Hedges, advanced the idea that the region might be preserved for all time as a national park for the benefit of all the people of the Nation. As a result of that suggestion, Yellowstone National Park was established in 1872 by Act of Congress as a "pleasuring ground" for the people. I like that phrase because, in the years that have followed, our great series of parks in every part of the Union have become indeed a "pleasuring ground" for millions of Americans.

My old friend, Franklin K. Lane, Secretary of the Interior in the Wilson Administration, well described the policies governing the National Park Administration when he said:

"The policy to which the Service will adhere is based on three broad principles: First, that the national parks must be maintained in absolutely unimpaired form for the use of future generations as well as those of our own time; second, that they are set apart for the use, observation, health and pleasure of the people; and, third, that the national interest must dictate all decisions affecting public or private enterprise in the parks."

The present National Park Service stands as an example of efficient and far-seeing governmental administration and to its former duties I added last year by transferring from other departments many other parks, battlefield sites, memorials and national monuments. This concentration of responsibility has thus made it possible to embark on a permanent park policy as a great recreational and educational project — one which no other country in the world has ever undertaken in such a broad way for protection of its natural and historic treasures and for the enjoyment of them by vast numbers of people.

Today I have seen some of the work of the Civilian Conservation Corps boys in this Northwestern country. Of the three hundred thousand young men in these Camps, 75,000 are at work in our national parks. Here, under trained leadership, we are helping these men to help themselves and their families and at the same time we are making the parks more available and more useful for the average citizen. Hundreds of miles of firebreaks have been built, fire hazards have been reduced on great tracts of timberland, thousands of miles of roadside have been cleared, 2,500 miles of trails have been constructed and 10,000 acres have been reforested. Other tens of thousands of acres have been treated for tree disease and soil erosion. This is but another example of our efforts to build not for today alone, but for tomorrow as well.

We should remember that the development of our national

park system over a period of many years has not been a simple bed of roses. As is the case in the long fight for the preservation of national forests and water power and mineral deposits and other national possessions, it has been a long and fierce fight against many private interests which were entrenched in political and economic power. So, too, it has been a constant struggle to continue to protect the public interest, once it was saved from private exploitation at the hands of the selfish few.

It took a bitter struggle to teach the country at large that our national resources are not inexhaustible and that, when public domain is stolen, a twofold injury is done, for it is a theft of the treasure of the present and at the same time bars the road of opportunity to the future.

We have won the greater part of the fight to obtain and to retain these great public park properties for the benefit of the public. We are at the threshold of an even more important battle to save our resources of agriculture and industry from the selfishness of individuals.

The Secretary of the Interior in 1933 announced that this year of 1934 was to be emphasized as "National Parks Year." I am glad to say that there has been a magnificent response and that the number visiting our national parks has shown a splendid increase. But I decided today that every year ought to be "National Parks Year." That is why, with all the earnestness at my command, I express to you the hope that each and every one of you who can possibly find the means and opportunity for so doing will visit our national parks and use them as they are intended to be used. They are not for the rich alone. Camping is free, the sanitation is excellent. You will find them in every part of the Union. You will find glorious scenery of every character; you will find every climate; you will perform the double function of enjoying much and learning much.

We are definitely in an era of building, the best kind of building — the building of great public projects for the benefit of the public and with the definite objective of building human happiness.

I believe, too, that we are building a better comprehension of our national needs. People understand, as never before, the splendid public purpose that underlies the development of great power sites, the improving of navigation, the prevention of floods and of the erosion of our agricultural fields, the prevention of forest fires, the diversification of farming and the distribution of industry. We know, more and more, that the East has a stake in the West and the West has a stake in the East, that the Nation must and shall be considered as a whole and not as an aggregation of disjointed groups.

May we come better to know every part of our great heritage in the days to come.

140 ❲ Extemporaneous Rear Platform Remarks at Havre, Montana. August 6, 1934

I WISH I had a loud speaker on the train, but there is none. This is not a political campaign.

I have never been through this section of Northern Montana and the reason I chose this particular route was because I wanted to learn something at first hand both by talking to the people, and seeing conditions with my own eyes. As you know, we are trying to do a good many new things, but I believe the country understands what we are trying to do and is supporting our effort to make a better living for the average citizen.

I notice that here we are on the outskirts, the edge, of what we call the secondary drought area. I am glad it has not been any worse here than it actually has.

We have to provide in the days to come for the elimination of the causes not only of drought but of the conditions that come from drought. It is going to take a long time to do it, but, as I have said before, I think we are on our way and that you good people understand it and are supporting it.

I wish I had time to stop off here and spend a little longer time, but I have been away from Washington now for a little over five weeks — it was actually five weeks yesterday — having covered the Virgin Islands, Puerto Rico, the Canal Zone and Hawaii. I have to get back to the Nation's capital.

I hope when I come back through here next that things are going to be better than they are today. Many thanks.

141 ❡ Extemporaneous Remarks at Fort Peck Dam, Montana. August 6, 1934

My friends:

I CANNOT very well just say my friends of Montana, because in this group there are men and women of a great many States of the Union. That is one of the characteristics of this particular job. It is national in scope and it was undertaken with the idea that it would benefit the whole Nation. And it is going to do it.

It is a very delightful thing to form a mind picture of something from prints, drawings and figures, and then, a year later, come out and find that the project is just about twice as big and twice as fine as you thought it was.

I am tremendously impressed by the magnitude of this job. About three weeks ago the Secretary of War, who is with me today, met me down in the Canal Zone, Panama. We saw together one of the wonders of the world, the Gatun Dam. I had seen it many years ago when it was under construction. I did not believe then that anybody would build a dam bigger than the Gatun. I assure you it is a pigmy compared with Fort Peck.

Not only is this going to be, I am told, the largest earthwork dam in the world, but I believe also that in its construction we are going to do a very great amount of good for the elimination of unemployment. That means unemployment today and unemployment in the future. In so far as unemployment today goes, this type of dam probably uses more manpower, more hours of work in its completion, than concrete dams or other types.

It is also true, of course, that a very large proportion of the materials going into this dam come from other parts of the Union, some of them from Pittsburgh and New York and Birmingham, Alabama, and as far west as the Pacific Coast. There is the other feature — affording employment in the days to come.

I refer to the fact that, when this dam is completed, it is going to be an important factor in the navigation of the Missouri River. It is going to help to maintain a nine-foot channel. This channel will connect with the Mississippi. It will enable the wheat growers and farmers of the Northwest to get cheaper transportation rates from the middle of the country to the south and the east and to foreign countries.

Then, of course, there are other features: the power that will be generated; the effect on flood control and soil erosion. One of the things that makes me happiest is that downstream from this point they are going to be able to place under irrigation some 84,000 acres of land — land which today is not particularly fit for human habitation and which, when we get water on it, will be the means of support and honest livelihood for thousands of American families.

I understand that some people, seeking to misrepresent facts, have suggested that we are going out through the Northwest and saying to the families on marginal lands — families having a good deal of trouble making both ends meet — "You have to leave your homes tomorrow morning and get out."

Of course no person who thinks twice will believe silly tales of that kind.

It is a fact, however, and you and I know it, that there are many families in many States who are trying to make both ends meet without much success. It has been shown over a period of years that the land these families are using for agriculture ought not, for the best economic purposes, be used for agriculture.

Now, if those families want to go on farming that land and go deeper in the red every year, I take it it is their affair.

On the other hand, your Government believes in giving them a chance to go to better places — a voluntary chance. That is why this very broad national planning is seeking to provide farms where they will not have crop failures, where they will not be faced with starvation and where they may be able, I hope, to make not only both ends meet from the point of view of living, but also that they may come to own their farms free and clear of any debt.

Now people talk about the Fort Peck Dam as the fulfillment of a dream. It is only a small percentage of the whole dream covering all of the important watersheds of the Nation. One of those watersheds is what we call the watershed of the Missouri River, not only the main stem of the Missouri, but countless tributaries that run into it and countless other tributaries that run into those tributaries. Before American men and women get through with this job, we are going to make every ounce and every gallon of water that falls from the Heaven and the hills count before it makes its way down to the Gulf of Mexico.

It is because we have undertaken this gigantic task that will take us more than a generation to complete, because we have undertaken it now, and the people of the United States understand the objective of the idea, that I feel very certain we are going to carry it through to a successful completion.

That is one reason, my friends, the chief reason, that I am glad to be out in these parts today to see the work in its inception; to see the fine spirit of all the people who are engaged in the work. That is why, also, that I am very confident it is going to be carried through to the success and glory of the Nation.

142 ⟨ Extemporaneous Remarks at Devils Lake, North Dakota. August 7, 1934

Senator Nye, my friends of North Dakota:

I CANNOT honestly say that my heart is happy today, because I have seen with my own eyes some of the things that I have been reading and hearing about for a year and more. The reason I came here was that I wanted to see something at first hand of a problem that has perplexed me and perplexed many other people ever since I have been in office. It is a problem. I would not try to fool you by saying we know the solution of it. We do not.

I believe in being frank, and what I can tell you from the bottom of my heart, truthfully, is this: If it is possible for us to solve the problem, we are going to do it.

I saw some signs along the road that said: "You gave us beer, now give us water."

Well, the beer part was easy.

That was something that could be controlled very definitely by human agency. It was a question of what the people of this country wanted and when they made it clear they wanted beer back again, they got it. But, when you come to this water problem through here, you are up against two things. In the first place you are up against the forces of nature and, secondly, you are up against the fact that man, in his present stage of development, cannot definitely control those forces.

I think it was more than a year ago that the delegation of this State, in the Senate and the House, first talked to me about the problem of this watershed in Northern North Dakota. I have been studying it ever since.

It is all very well to say, "Let's have a dam across the Missouri River." I would love to do it, but when a great many engineers tell me they have not found a safe place for that dam, there is not a man or woman in the Devils Lake area who would ask me to build a dam that might go out and drown many thousand people.

In other words, I have a responsibility. I cannot build a dam unless I have the best engineering assurance that it is not only the right thing to do, but the safe thing to do.

And, the result is, my friends, that today there is more of what you might call Government talent, experts from different departments in the Government service, fine people with good knowledge and training. They are getting the views of civilians and State employees and are trying to find a solution of this problem.

Soon after I get back to Washington many of the studies being made this summer by engineering and agricultural officials will be completed. I expect to confer within the next few weeks with all of the experts. I shall give an opportunity to people who do not agree with their conclusions to come and be heard. As you know, I believe in action.

On the 4th of March, 1933, we had a parallel. It was not just one section of one State or a few sections in a few States. It was the whole of the United States. The United States was up against it. I asked the people of the United States at that time to have courage and faith. They did.

Today, out here, I do not ask you to have courage and faith. You have it. You have demonstrated that through a good many years. I am asking, however, that you keep up that courage and, especially, keep up the faith.

If it is possible for Government to improve conditions in this State, Government will do it.

I assure you the interests of these communities are very close to my heart. I am not going to forget the day I have spent with you.

We hope that Nature is going to open the Heavens. When I came out on the platform this morning and saw a rather dark cloud, I said to myself, "Maybe it is going to rain." Well, it did not. All I can say is, I hope to goodness it is going to rain, good and plenty.

My friends, I want to tell you that I am glad I came here. I want to tell you that I am not going to let up until I can give my best service to solving the problems of North Dakota.

143 ⟨ A Tribute to the Mayo Brothers. An Address Delivered at Rochester, Minnesota. August 8, 1934

I HOPE that the people of Rochester will not feel limited in their pride of possession when the Nation which I have the honor to represent claims the right to call Dr. Will and Dr. Charles by the good word "neighbor." You are beloved at home and abroad and a world deeply in your debt gives you inadequate return in external honors and distinctions. But your true distinction is in the simple fact that you have put men's sense of brotherhood and interdependence into a new setting and have given it a new meaning.

For fifty years you have given tireless, skillful and unselfish service here in this State and city. These fifty years, the span of your medical practice, have covered probably the most remarkable period in the history of science. You have seen practically all of modern medicine and surgery come into being. The rise of research, dating back to the days when you began your practice, has revolutionized the diagnosis, prevention and treatment of disease. The development of the branches of this science has revolutionized not only the science of medicine, but the entire field of effort that we sometimes call public welfare. You have seen surgical technique become one of the finest of all the arts of man. You have seen the development of the science of public health, which has brought the gospel of health to the school and clinic. You have seen the growth of hospitals, the creation of foundations for medical research, and a revolution in the teaching of medicine. You have seen isolated clinics come to be part of great universities, an association resulting in the enrichment of both.

But despite the progress that you have seen and that you have helped to accomplish, the restless spirit of science prompts you to see new visions of achievement. As you have pointed out so often in your predictions of what humanity may expect from medical science in the future, progress is only at its beginning. In the further development of the curative art, in the discovery of new means for the prevention of disease, in the creation of methods by which all of the people may be made aware of the knowledge of hygiene and public health developed in the laboratory clinic, your vision offers promise of a greater Nation and a happier people.

You have helped to give to the medical profession a unique place in the community and the Nation. By reason of his special opportunities, the physician has the occasion to perform a service in his community far beyond the bounds of his own professional duty. His infinitely complex relationships with the people of the community enable him to lead them in standards of ethical right which may profoundly affect human conduct in general. For this reason, the science of medicine comes to concern itself with many things besides the healing of the sick. It has been broadly interpreted as a major factor in the science of human welfare. The problems of disease and the circumstances related to it are to the science of modern medicine only the sequel of a long train of social cause and effect. Medicine has taught us how important it is to look beyond the result to the cause, not only of human sickness, but of those social disorders out of which individual difficulties necessarily arise.

Those of us who are concerned with the problems of government and of economics are under special obligation to modern medicine in two very important respects. In the first place, it has taught us that with patience and application and skill and courage it is possible for human beings to control and improve conditions under which they live. It has taught us how science may be made the servant of a richer, more complete common life. And it has taught us more than that, because from it we have learned lessons in the ethics of human relationships—how devotion to the public good, unselfish service, never-ending consideration of human needs are in themselves conquering forces.

Democracy looks to the day when these virtues will be required and expected of those who serve the public officially and unofficially. Modern medicine has set an exalted example. It has shown the way for us all.

You whom we honor today have rendered the highest form of patriotic service during the battles of the World War, but, even more than that, you deserve the Nation's thanks for the national service that you have rendered throughout your lives.

144 ❲ "A Wider Opportunity for the Average
Man" — Address Delivered at Green Bay,
Wisconsin. August 9, 1934

Governor Schmedeman, Mr. Mayor, my friends:

THIS is an inspiration to be here today. This is a wonderful setting on the shores of the Bay and I am glad to take part in this commemoration of the landing in Green Bay of the man who can truly be called the first white pioneer of this part of the United States. Over all the years, as your distinguished Representative in Congress has suggested, the purposes of the men and women who established civilization in Wisconsin and in the Northwest were the same as those that stimulated the earlier settlers of the Atlantic Seaboard. Men everywhere throughout Europe — your ancestors and mine — had suffered from the imperfect and often unjust Governments of their home land, and they were driven by deep desire to find not alone security, but also enlarged opportunity for themselves and their children. It is true that the new population flowing into our new lands was a mixed population, differing often in language, in external customs and in habits of thought. But in one thing they were alike. They shared a deep purpose to rid themselves forever of the jealousies, the prejudices, the intrigues and the violence, whether internal or external, that disturbed their lives on the other side of the ocean.

Yes, they sought a life that was less fettered by the exploitations of selfish men, set up under Governments that were not free. They sought a wider opportunity for the average man.

Having achieved that initial adventure of migrating to new homes, they moved forward to the further adventure of establishing forms of government and methods of operating these forms of government that might assure them the things they sought. They believed that men, out of their intelligence and their self-discipline, could create and use forms of government that would not enslave the human spirit, but free it and nourish it throughout the generations. They did not fear government, because they knew that government in the new world was their own.

I do not need to tell you that here in Wisconsin they built a State destined for extraordinary achievements. They set up institutions to enforce law and order, to care for the unfortunate, to promote the arts of industry and agriculture. They built a university and school system as enlightened as any that the world affords. They set up against all selfish private interests the organized authority of the people themselves through the State. They transformed utilities into public servants instead of private means of exploitation.

People know also that the average man in Wisconsin waged a long and bitter fight for his rights. Here, and in the Nation as a whole, in the Nation at large, this battle has been two-fold.

It has been a fight against Nature. From the time that the settlers started to clear the land until now, they have been compelled to assert the power of their brains and courage over the blind powers of the wind and the sun and the soil. They have paid no heed to the reactionaries who would tell them that mankind must stand impotent before the forces of nature. Year after year, as science progressed and mastery of the mysteries of the physical universe increased, man has been turning nature, once his hard master, into useful servitude.

That is why, on this trip across the northern part of this Continent, I have been so moved by the distressing effects of a widespread drought, and at the same time so strengthened in my belief that science and cooperation can do much from now on to undo the mistakes that men have made in the past and to aid the good forces of nature and the good impulses of men instead of fighting against them.

Yes, we are but carrying forward the fundamentals behind the pioneering spirit of the fathers when we apply the pioneering methods to the better use of vast land and water resources — what God has given us to use as trustees not only for ourselves but for future generations.

But man has been fighting also against those forces which disregard human cooperation and human rights in seeking that kind of individual profit which is gained at the expense of his fellows.

It is just as hard to achieve harmonious and cooperative action among human beings as it is to conquer the forces of Nature. Only through the submerging of individual desires into unselfish and practical cooperation can civilization grow.

In the great national movement that culminated over a year ago, people joined with enthusiasm. They lent hand and voice to the common cause, irrespective of many older political traditions. They saw the dawn of a new day. They were on the march; they were coming back into the possession of their own home land.

As the humble instruments of their vision and their power, those of us who were chosen to serve them in 1932 turned to the great task.

In one year and five months, the people of the United States have received at least a partial answer to their demands for action; and neither the demand nor the action has reached the end of the road.

But, my friends, action may be delayed by two types of individuals. Let me cite examples: First, there is the man whose objectives are wholly right and wholly progressive but who declines to cooperate or even to discuss methods of arriving at the objectives because he insists on his own methods and nobody's else.

The other type to which I refer is the kind of individual who demands some message to the people of the United States that will restore what he calls "confidence." When I hear this I cannot help but remember the pleas that were made by government and certain types of so-called "big business" all through the years 1930, 1931 and 1932, that the only thing lacking in the United States was confidence.

Before I left on my trip on the first of July, I received two letters from important men, both of them pleading that I say something to restore confidence. To both of them I wrote identical answers: "What would you like to have me say?" From one of them I have received no reply at all in six weeks. I take it that he is still wondering how to answer. The other man wrote me frankly that in his judgment the way to restore confidence was for me to tell the people of the United States that all supervision by all forms of Government, Federal and State, over all forms of human activity called business should be forthwith abolished.

Now, my friends, in other words, that man was frank enough to imply that he would repeal all laws, State or national, which regulate business — that a utility could henceforth charge any rate, unreasonable or otherwise; that the railroads could go back to rebates and other secret agreements; that the processors of food stuffs could disregard all rules of health and of good faith; that the unregulated wild-cat banking of a century ago could be restored; that fraudulent securities and watered stock could be palmed off on the public; that stock manipulation which caused panics and enriched insiders could go unchecked. In fact, my friends, if we were to listen to him and his type, the old law of the tooth and the claw would reign in our Nation once more.

The people of the United States will not restore that ancient order. There is no lack of confidence on the part of those business men, farmers and workers who clearly read the signs of the times. Sound economic improvement comes from the improved conditions of the whole population and not a small fraction thereof.

Those who would measure confidence in this country in the future must look first to the average citizen.

Confidence is returning to our agricultural population who, in spite of unpredictable and uncontrollable drought in a large area of the Nation, is giving understanding cooperation to practical planning and the ending of the useless bickering and sectional thinking of the past. Confidence is returning to the manufacturers who, in overwhelming numbers, are comparing the black ink of today with the red ink of many years gone by; to the workers who have achieved under the National Recovery Administration rights for which they fought unsuccessfully for a generation; to the men and women whose willing hands found no work and who have been saved from starvation by Government work and Government relief; to the youngsters whose childhood has been saved to them by the abolition of child labor; to the fair and sincere bankers and financiers and business men, big and little, who now, for the first time, find Government cooperating with them in new attempts to put the golden rule into the temples of finance; to the home owners who have been saved from the stark threat of foreclosure and to the small investors and savers of the Nation who, for the first time, rightly believe that their savings are secure.

These are the elements that make for confidence in the future. This Government intends no injury to honest business. The processes we follow in seeking social justice do not, in adding to general prosperity, take from one and give to another. In this modern world, the spreading out of opportunity ought not to consist of robbing Peter to pay Paul. In other words, we are concerned with more than mere subtraction and addition. We are concerned with multiplication also — multiplication of wealth through cooperative action, wealth in which all can share.

These high purposes must be accompanied by cooperation among those charged by the people with the duties of government. I am glad to be in a State from which I have greatly drawn in setting up the permanent and temporary agencies of the national Administration.

Your two Senators, Bob LaFollette and Ryan Duffy, both old friends of mine, and many others, worked with me in maintaining excellent cooperation, the kind I have been talking about, between the executive and legislative branches of the Government. I take this opportunity of expressing my gratitude to them.

Not only in Washington but also in the States it has been necessary, of course, for us to have cooperation by public officials in the achievement of the great purposes we seek. I thank Governor Schmedeman, another old friend of mine, for his patriotic cooperation with the national Administration.

We who support this New Deal do so because it is a square deal and because it is essential to the preservation of security and happiness in a free society such as ours. I like its definition by a member of the Congress. He said:

"The new deal is an old deal — as old as the earliest aspirations of humanity for liberty and justice and the good life. It is as old as Christian ethics, for basically its ethics are the same. It is new as the Declaration of Independence was new, and the Constitution of the United States; its motives are the same. It voices the deathless cry of good men and good women for the opportunity to live and work in freedom, the right to be secure in their homes and in the fruits of their labor, the power to protect themselves against the ruthless and the cunning. It recognizes that man is indeed his brother's keeper, insists that the laborer is worthy of his hire, demands that justice shall rule the mighty as well as the weak.

"It seeks to cement our society, rich and poor, manual worker and brain worker, into a voluntary brotherhood of freemen, standing together, striving together, for the common good of all."

Keep that vision before your eyes and in your hearts; it can, it will be attained.

NOTE: The quotation in the above speech on this page was from a widely published address by Congressman Edward Burke of Omaha, Nebraska, later a member of the United States Senate from Nebraska, and at that time a candidate for the United States Senate.

145 ⟮ Presidential Proclamation No. 2092 on the Coinage of Silver. August 9, 1934

WHEREAS, by paragraph (2) of Section 43, Title III, of the Act of Congress, approved May 12, 1933 (Public No. 10), as amended by the Gold Reserve Act of 1934, the President is authorized "by proclamation to fix the weight of the gold dollar in grains nine-tenths fine and also to fix the weight of the silver dollar in grains nine-tenths fine at a definite fixed ratio in relation to the gold dollar at such amounts as he finds necessary from his investigation to stabilize domestic prices or to protect the foreign commerce against the adverse effect of depreciated foreign currencies, and to provide for the unlimited coinage of such gold and silver at the ratio so fixed . . ." and "The President, in addition to the authority to provide for the unlimited coinage of silver at the ratio so fixed, under such terms and conditions as he may prescribe, is further authorized to cause to be issued and delivered to the tenderer of silver for coinage, silver certificates in lieu of the standard silver dollars to which the tenderer would be entitled and in an amount in dollars equal to the number of coined standard silver dollars that the tenderer of such silver for coinage would receive in standard silver dollars"; and "The President is further authorized to issue silver certificates in such denominations as he may prescribe against any silver bullion, silver, or standard silver dollars in the Treasury not then held for redemption of any outstanding silver certificates, and to coin standard silver dollars or subsidiary currency for the redemption of such silver certificates"; and

WHEREAS the Silver Purchase Act of 1934, approved June 19, 1934, provides in part, as follows:

"Whenever in the judgment of the President such action is necessary to effectuate the policy of this act, he may by Executive order require the delivery to the United States mints of any or all silver by whomever owned or possessed. The silver so delivered shall be coined into standard silver dollars or otherwise added to the monetary stocks of the United States as the President many determine; and there shall be returned therefor in standard silver dollars, or any other coin or currency of the United States, the monetary value of the silver so delivered less such deductions for seigniorage, brassage, coinage, and other mint charges as the Secretary of the Treasury with the approval of the President shall have determined: *Provided,* That in no case shall the value of the amount returned therefor be less than the fair value at the time of such order of the silver required to be delivered as such value is determined by the market price over a reasonable period terminating at the time of such order."

NOW, THEREFORE, finding it necessary, in my judgment, to effectuate the policy of the Silver Purchase Act of 1934, to assist in increasing and stabilizing domestic prices, to protect our foreign commerce against the adverse effect of depreciated foreign currencies, and to promote the objectives of the proclamation of the 21st day of December, 1933, relating to the coinage of silver; by virtue of the power in me vested by the acts of Congress above cited, and other legislation designated for national recovery, and by virtue of all other authority in me vested;

I, Franklin D. Roosevelt, President of the United States of America, do proclaim and direct that each United States mint shall receive for coinage or for addition to the monetary stocks of the United States, as hereinafter determined, any silver which such mint, subject to regulations prescribed hereunder by the Secretary of the Treasury, is satisfied was situated on the effective date hereof in the continental United States, including the Territory of Alaska.

The silver so delivered shall be added to the monetary stocks of the United States and shall be coined from time to time into standard silver dollars in such amounts as are required to carry out the provisions of this proclamation and to provide for the redemption of silver certificates; and there shall be returned therefor in standard silver dollars, silver certificates, or any other coin or currency of the United States, the monetary value of the silver so delivered (that is, $1.2929+ a fine troy ounce), less a deduction of 61%₂₅ percent thereof for seigniorage, brassage, coinage, and other mint charges, such deduction having been determined by the Secretary of the Treasury with my approval.

The provisions hereof are supplemental to the provisions of the proclamation of the 21st day of December 1933, and the United States coinage mints shall continue to receive for coinage in accordance with the provisions of such proclamation silver which such mint, subject to regulations prescribed thereunder by the Secretary of the Treasury, is satisfied has been mined subsequently to the date of such proclamation, from natural deposits in the United States or any place subject to the jurisdiction thereof: *Provided, however,* That the Director of the Mint shall, at the option of the tenderer of such silver, deliver silver certificates in lieu of the standard silver dollars to which the tenderer of such silver for coinage would be entitled and in an amount in dollars equal to the coined standard silver dollars that the tenderer of such silver for coinage would receive in standard silver dollars.

The Secretary of the Treasury is authorized to prescribe regulations to carry out the purposes of this proclamation.

Notice is hereby given that I reserve the right by virtue of the authority vested in me to revoke or modify this proclamation as the interest of the United States may seem to require.

(See next Item and note.)

146 ⟨ The Government Requires the Delivery of All Silver to the United States for Coinage. Executive Order No. 6814. August 9, 1934

BY VIRTUE of the authority vested in me by the Silver Purchase Act of 1934 and of all other authority vested in me, I, Franklin D. Roosevelt, President of the United States of America, do hereby require the delivery of all silver situated in the continental United States on the effective date hereof, by any and all persons owning, possessing, or controlling any such silver, and do hereby require any and all persons owning, possessing, or controlling any such silver to deliver the same in the manner, upon the conditions and subject to the exceptions herein contained, such action being in my judgment necessary to effectuate the policy of the Silver Purchase Act of 1934. . . .

SECTION 2. *Silver required to be delivered.* — There shall be delivered in accordance with the terms of this order all silver situated in the continental United States on the effective date hereof, except silver falling within any of the following categories so long as it continues to fall thereunder:

(a) Silver coins, whether foreign or domestic;

(b) Silver of a fineness of .8 or less, which has not entered into industrial, commercial, professional, artistic, or monetary use;

(c) Silver mined, after December 21, 1933, from natural deposits in the United States or any place subject to the jurisdiction thereof: *Provided, however,* That so much of such silver so mined in the continental United States on or before the effective date of this order which shall not have been deposited with a

United States mint under the proclamation of December 21, 1933, shall, if processed to a fineness greater than .8 within 75 days from the effective date of this order, be delivered in accordance with this order, not later than 90 days from the effective date hereof, or if processed to a fineness greater than .8 after 75 days from the effective date of this order, be delivered within 15 days thereafter in accordance with this order;

(d) Silver held for industrial, professional, or artistic use and unmelted scrap silver and silver sweepings in an amount not exceeding in the aggregate 500 fine troy ounces belonging to any one person;

(e) Silver owned on the effective date hereof by a recognized foreign government, foreign central bank, or the Bank for International Settlements;

(f) Silver contained in articles fabricated and held in good faith for a specific and customary use and not for their value as silver bullion; or

(g) Silver held under a license issued in accordance with Section 6 hereof.

SECTION 3. *Time and place of delivery.* — The silver required to be delivered hereunder shall be delivered not later than 90 days from the effective date hereof to the United States mint nearest to the place where the silver is situated immediately prior to delivery: *Provided,* That such silver temporarily falling within the exempt categories enumerated in Section 2, shall be delivered at the end of 90 days from the effective date hereof, or 15 days after the time when it ceases to fall within such categories, whichever date is later. Any person acquiring ownership, possession, or control of silver required to be delivered under this order after 75 days from the effective date hereof, shall deliver such silver within 15 days of such acquisition.

SECTION 4. *Amount returnable for silver.* — The silver herein required to be delivered shall be coined into standard silver dollars, or otherwise added to the monetary stocks of the United States in accordance with the proclamation, bearing the same date as this order, relating to the coinage of silver, and there shall be returned therefor in standard silver dollars, silver certificates, or any other coin or currency of the United States, the monetary value of the silver so delivered (that is, $1.2929+ a fine troy ounce), less a deduction of 61 ⅗ percent thereof for seigniorage, brassage, coinage, and other mint charges, as provided in such proclamation; that is, the amount returnable for the silver delivered in accordance herewith shall be an amount equal to 50+ ¢ a fine troy ounce, which amount is not less than the fair value, at the time of this order, of the silver required to be delivered hereunder as determined by the market price over a reasonable period terminating at the time of this order.

SECTION 5. *Reimbursement of costs.* — The Secretary of the Treasury shall pay all necessary costs, actually incurred, of the transportation of such silver and standard silver dollars, silver certificates, and other coin or currency of the United States, including the cost of insurance, protection, and such other incidental costs as may be reasonably necessary. Persons desiring reimbursement of such costs shall submit their accounts on voucher forms which may be obtained by writing to the Treasurer of the United States, Washington, D. C.

SECTION 6. *Licenses.* — The Secretary of the Treasury, subject to such regulations as he may prescribe, acting directly or through such agency or agencies as he may designate, shall issue licenses authorizing the withholding of silver which the Secretary of the Treasury, or such agency as he may designate, is satisfied

(a) is required for legitimate and customary use in industry, profession, or art by a person regularly engaged in such industry, profession, or art or in the business of processing silver or furnishing silver therefor;

(b) has been imported for reexport; or

(c) is required to fulfill an obligation to deliver silver in such amount to a third person, incurred or assumed by the applicant on or before the effective date of this order; *Provided,* That at the date of the application, the applicant owns such silver or holds the obligation of another to deliver to him such silver.

The Secretary of the Treasury may, with the approval of the President, issue licenses authorizing the withholding of silver for purposes deemed to be in the public interest and not inconsistent with the purposes of the Silver Purchase Act of 1934 and of this order.

SECTION 7. *Deliveries in fulfillment of obligations or to licensees.* — No person required to deliver silver owned by him or in his possession or control shall be deemed to have failed to comply with the provisions of this order, if such silver is delivered in fulfillment of an obligation incurred or assumed by such person on or before the effective date of this order or is delivered to a person licensed to acquire and withhold silver in such an amount under Section 6. . . .

NOTE: The foregoing Proclamation and Executive Order, both issued on the same day, required the delivery of certain silver to the United States Mints, and fixed the amount returnable for the silver at about 50 cents per fine ounce.

The purpose of this "nationalization" of silver was to secure for the Treasury part of the increment resulting from the rise in the price of silver.

Regulations were issued on August 17, 1934, relating to the delivery and receipt of silver under this Executive Order and Proclamation; and they have been amended since that date from time to time.

On April 10, 1935, by Proclamation No. 2124, the Proclamation of December 21, 1933 (see Vol. II, Items 187 and 187A) was amended to increase the amount returnable by the United States Mints to producers of domestic silver mined on or after April 10, 1935, from the equivalent of 64 cents per ounce to the equivalent of 71 cents per ounce. This action was taken in view of the rise in the world price of silver.

On April 24, 1935, by Proclamation No. 2125, the amount was increased on domestic silver mined on or after April 24, 1935, from the equivalent of about 71 cents per ounce to the equivalent of about 77 cents per ounce.

See Item 16, this volume, for a summary of the gold and silver policy of the Administration.

147 ⟨ Presidential Proclamation No. 2093 Allowing Importation of Duty-Exempt Feed for Livestock in Drought Areas. August 10, 1934

WHEREAS an unusual lack of rain in the States of North Dakota, South Dakota, Nebraska, Texas, Missouri, Utah, and Nevada, and to a lesser extent in other States, has caused an acute shortage of feed for livestock, particularly in the affected area and elsewhere in the United States. . . .

Now, THEREFORE, I, Franklin D. Roosevelt, President of the United States of America, by virtue of the authority vested in me by the said Section [318] of the Tariff Act of 1930, and by virtue of all other authority vested in me, do hereby proclaim an emergency to exist and do hereby authorize the Secretary of the Treasury to permit, until June 30, 1935 (unless before that date it has been determined by the President and declared by his Proclamation that the emergency has terminated), within such limits and subject to such conditions as he may deem necessary to meet the emergency, the importation of such feed for livestock as the Secretary of the Treasury may designate and under such regulations as he may impose, free of duty when imported by or directly for the account of any owner of livestock in any drought affected area, or by or for the account of any relief organization, not operated for profit, for distribution among distressed owners of livestock.

NOTE: The foregoing Proclamation, declaring a drought emergency and permitting the importation of food for livestock free of duty for the drought areas, was one of the many steps taken to meet the conditions created by the drought in many of the Western and mid-Western States during 1934 (see Items 81 and 103 of this volume).

148 ⟨ New Year's Greeting to the Jews of America. August 13, 1934

I am happy, at this festival season of Rosh Hashanah, to renew my good wishes to my fellow citizens of Jewish faith throughout the land.

It is a suitable opportunity to pause and, by dedicating ourselves anew to the responsibilities of the present day, to continue the work which, in common with all Americans, we have undertaken toward realizing the promise of the years which lie before us.

149 ⟨ Greeting to the Grand Army of the Republic. August 14, 1934

To the Commander-in-Chief, the Grand Army of the Republic:

Had circumstances permitted I would have been with you today in person. This being impossible, I have asked the Secretary of War to add to his own message to you a personal word from me.

You have lived to see the Nation face the profound problems of an unprecedented world-wide depression which has overthrown the Governments of many another Nation. How deep must have been your pride to see with what solidarity our united people met the demands of these difficult years. You are fortunate indeed to have lived to see the end of sectionalism and the final healing of the scars of conflict, and the achievement of a true unity of national purpose.

150 ⟨ Statement on the Death of Speaker Henry T. Rainey. August 19, 1934

IT MUST always be an occasion of national regret when a public servant who has given the greater part of his life to unselfish service passes away. This is especially true in the loss of Speaker Rainey at a time when the experience of many years had culminated in his useful leadership of the Nation's House of Representatives.

I had the privilege of knowing him first more than a score of years ago. I shall always think of him as a humanitarian whose fine patriotism thought first of what he conceived to be the well-being and the interests of the common man. Through all the years he kept the spirit of youth and he will be missed profoundly by old and young alike.

151 ⟨ An Episode of a Type Fortunately Rare— An Exchange of Letters and Telegrams between the President and Senator Thomas D. Schall. August 24, 1934

IN A statement read for you last night over the radio it was said: "A National press service . . . to take the place of the Associated Press, the Hearst News Services, and the United Press" and which would "have exclusive use of all Government news and be in a position to give its service only to those newspapers loyal to the Roosevelt dictatorship" is under consideration. The further statement was made that "The Roosevelt Administration is so determined on press censorship it may be interesting to the public to know how this un-American idea gets so much consideration." But for the fact that this statement was made for you, I would let it pass unnoticed. Since I should assume that these statements were not made without basis in fact, I request that you give me the benefit of such facts as you have in support of the charges you caused to be made. Once these facts are in my hands, they will receive immediate attention in order to make impossible the things you say will be done, because I am just as much opposed to them as you are. You will be rendering a real service if you will promptly let me have the facts on which you based the charges made.

FRANKLIN D. ROOSEVELT

Hon. Thomas D. Schall,
Senate Office Building,
Washington, D. C.

My dear Mr. Roosevelt:

Your telegram to me bears out the suggestion of the constant effort to mislead and fool the public. Your desire to make yourself appear before the people of the United States as a champion of a free press may be as insincere as your promises to the people when you accepted the Democratic nomination at Chicago with the statement that you were for their platform a hundred percent. To date you have not kept one of the covenants you pledged the people at that time. Let me recall your testy anger at your disappointment in keeping out of the press code the expression of a free press.

For me to chronicle all the attempts of your Administration to throttle the press and free speech — all known to you and approved by you in advance — would be but to recite incidents with which you are entirely familiar. If it were not for the fact that I see in your request for "information" an attempt on your part to appear as a victim of your own bureaucracy instead of its chief organizer, I would be inclined to ignore your telegram.

But since you assume a cloak of innocence and since your telegram to me is in the hands of the press, it becomes my duty as a sentinel of the people to do what little I can to mitigate their deception by citing specific evidence of your intention to force a censorship of the press so that your acts and the acts of your communistic bureaucrats might be hidden from public gaze.

I refer as you are quite aware to the statement of your chairman of the Judiciary Committee, Mr. Summers of Texas, in connection with the passage of the press censorship bill by the House in the special session of Congress called by you. Under your whip it passed the House and if the Senate had not taken out the poison a publisher who had not gained your approval or the approval of some of your appointees could be sentenced to ten years' imprisonment. The evidence convicting you of a desire to censor the press twenty-five days after you swore to uphold and defend the Constitution is in print in the archives of the House of Representatives. Mr. Summers in his statement says the bill was introduced at the request of the "Executive" and is necessary to the success of the recovery legislation. Mr. President, in my opinion, secrecy and press censorship are never necessary when motives are pure.

Every Government department under you is now cloaked in censorship. Almost every bill that has been forced through Congress by you has been in itself a little censorship, a little dictatorship either giving blanket powers to you or to some of your left or right hand bowers. According to Garrett Garet you usurped in the extra session of Congress 77 powers belonging, under the Constitution, to the Judiciary and Congress and when the next Congress met you asked that these powers be made permanent. How many powers you have taken from Congress and the Judiciary in this last session I have not been able to gather specifically as yet, but they are many. You have created some forty-seven bureaucracies. These bureaucracies are clothed with power to make their regulations law. These regulations cover something like 2,000 pages of dictatorship laws made by your appointees of whom not more than one percent has had the sanction of Congress.

Your Secretary of the Treasury has two billions of the people's money which he is expending under the protection of a press censorship which you demanded and approved.

You demanded and sanctioned passage of a bill permitting you to secretly fix tariff rates and clothe your acts with a press censorship second to nothing ever before even suggested in the legislative annals of the United States, and this, too, contrary to your Democratic Party platform and contrary to your former specific, vigorous and forceful denunciation of such.

The Communications bill originally introduced by you contained a press censorship clause which was stricken out before the bill was passed but it still gives you the power to inaugurate a Government telegraphic news service, under which as one example you immediately put out of business the three radio stations of Mr. Ford.

You ask me for "information" concerning what you yourself have done. Are you attempting to secure the facts so that you may be in a position to refute yourself?

Yours truly,

THOS. D. SCHALL

August 24th, 1934

Yesterday I sent you a telegram in good faith because you had made a statement that persons in the Administration were planning some form of press or radio Government-controlled news agency designed to supersede private news agencies. As any such plan would be contrary to the Administration's policy, I requested you with the utmost politeness to give me the facts behind your charges. Today I received from you a vituperative two-page letter which gives no facts and does not answer my simple request. The incident is closed.

FRANKLIN D. ROOSEVELT

Hon. Thomas D. Schall,
Senate Office Building,
Washington, D. C.

My dear Mr. President:

Your second open telegram to me in no wise explains the various attempts of your Administration to secure legislation censoring the press of the United States.

You requested evidence from me concerning your own acts. I cited you three instances of your efforts to keep the public from securing, through the press, facts concerning the attempts of your bureaucracy to communize the United States.

You say you are acting in "good faith." Then why not as a starter remove the censorship bars against the press that you have placed in all your departments?

Your conclusion to me that the "incident is closed" will in no way, Mr. President, satisfy the people of their fear of where you are un-

387

constitutionally steering their Republic. As a Representative of the people I dare not under my oath to support and defend the Constitution let it rest there. The people of the United States want to know from you why their Republic is being gradually cast aside for a dictatorship.

If you desire specific information as to the basis of my reasonable inference, that the Government is about to coordinate its various and sundry publicity functions into a national press service, you have only to assemble the following "makings" thereof:

The White House daily statements, political and economic, which in piecemeal form, not only determine the policies of the world's greatest bureaucracy, but likewise, the major part of political press publication. The free expression of an independent minority giving the public daily exposures of White House blunders and dangerous experiments is naturally disquieting and therefore must be controlled.

The press code which aims to dominate the publishers in the conduct of their business and your opposition to include therein the freedom of press demanded by the publishers' association of which there should have been no dispute, since it is a part of the Constitution and is guaranteed in the Bill of Rights.

The Rayburn Communications Act, controlling radio, telegraph, cable and telephone communication, which the American Newspaper Guild pronounces a menace and the foundation of the worst form of "dictatorship."

Your control of the business offices of the press by Government investment of $1,000,000,000 in the preferred shares of over 6,000 banks — without the credit support of which the publication of a great daily newspaper, or even a magazine and book publishing enterprise having national circulation, would be a business impossibility.

Your domination of all departments of the bureaucracy, in particular, all bureaus publishing current economic data, by which the great bulk of the data is politically "slanted" and damaging data suppressed, with the evident design to foist upon the public the sundry "bold experiments" of the "New Deal." In short it seems to me your Administration's intent is evident and it has become in lock, stock and barrel simply a group of publicity machinery not yet assembled for efficient and smooth operation but if the people return to you another spineless Congress the defects no doubt will be remedied and "what we fear will have come upon us."

Your Administration has set up its magazine, called *Today*, edited by Brain Truster Raymond Moley and financed by Admiral Vincent Astor of the Flagship *Nourmahal*. What is now needed is a day and night national news service that will cover the daily press field.

All dictatorships and most kings and emperors have their official organs. In Germany, President Hitler has created his ministry of publicity with Goebbels at the head. The Russian Soviet has the Taas Agency. Nothing goes out in Italy without Mussolini's sanction. The news service of the Washington Administration might appropriately be called the WHP — or White House Press — which would function as the official news service of the "New Deal."

In all fairness, Mr. President, you must admit that you have the "makings" all ready at hand. Is it too much for me to call the attention of the Nation to the danger threatened and as Patrick Henry well put it, when he was advocating that the Colonies throw off the yoke of George the Third, "I know of no way of judging the future but by the past"?

Sincerely yours,

THOS. D. SCHALL

NOTE: The above letters from Senator Schall are printed here only as an illustration of a type of utterance which is, fortunately, rare on the part of members of the legislative branch of the Government. Most public servants and most of the public realize that this form of vituperation and falsification results only in reaction against the author.

152 ⟨ A Letter to the National Conference on Street and Highway Safety. August 24, 1934

My dear Mr. Secretary:

As CHAIRMAN of the National Conference on Street and Highway Safety you are, no doubt, fully familiar with the very decided upward trend in highway fatalities, injuries and property damage in recent months.

I know you had this condition in mind when you called the fourth session of the National Conference during the latter part of last May. I was greatly impressed and pleased with the constructive steps taken, particularly as regards the perfection of the Uniform Motor Vehicle Code. I am more than ever convinced that the adoption of uniform, tested laws and their strict and impartial enforcement must be one of our primary objectives.

I have before me at the moment communications from a large variety of organizations and groups calling attention to the increasing gravity of the situation — attributable perhaps in part to heavier motor vehicle traffic as a result of improved economic conditions. The interest of these groups is in itself a splendid sign and indicates at least that serious thought is being given to the problem. But what we need most is organized and continuing action.

I note that the Governors of many States are issuing proclamations designating September as Safety Month. This should prove helpful if only to the extent that it serves as a focal point for more mobilization. It is also timely, since we are just entering on the period of the year which experience has shown takes the heaviest toll. However, we must steadfastly keep before us that we need more than a Safety Month. We must make every year a Safety Year, every month a Safety Month, and every day a Safety Day. We must attack the problem continuously and energetically in much the same way as we have conducted our attack on the depression.

I am expressing these thoughts so that you may be assured of my full sympathy and cooperation in whatever steps may seem feasible to you to give a greater degree of direction and force to a coordinated national effort looking to the prevention of largely needless fatalities, injuries and property damage, which we can ill afford at any time, and least of all now.

Very sincerely yours,

Hon. Daniel C. Roper,
The Secretary of Commerce,
Washington, D. C.

153 ⟨ Extemporaneous Remarks at Welcome-Home Party, Hyde Park, New York.

August 30, 1934

THIS is a very nice welcome-home party. I am certainly very glad to get back again.

As a matter of fact, as you know, I have only been here for about forty-eight hours since last fall, and in the meantime I made a good many voyages into a good many places. When I got back on Sunday, one of my neighbors gave me a very great shock. He came up, and shook hands, and looked at me and said, "My, how fleshy you have got." And then to cap the climax one of these people — special writers — I think they call them Columnists or something like that — made the assertion, and of course anything that you see in the paper in categorical form must be true, that I put on twelve pounds. Well, I resent it. But of course you cannot quarrel with the press. You all know that. He just added a little figure one in front of the true gain. I did gain two pounds, and I came up here with the perfectly serious intention of taking off five. But there is a certain quality to Dutchess County milk and my mother's cooking, and the air that you breathe; I do not believe I am going to make good my objective.

I have had, since Congress went home, an exceedingly interesting trip. I did the queer and strange thing of going almost to the Equator in July. As a matter of fact, just between ourselves, I went to Puerto Rico, the Virgin Islands, Cartagena, and Colombia, and the Canal Zone and Cocos Island, which is only a few degrees from the Equator, and Hawaii, and I never felt the heat until I got back in Northern Montana, up next to the Canadian border. It was a very wonderful trip. It took me to a lot of places I had not seen before. It took me to a number of territories and dependencies of the United States which I had wanted to see because of the fact that you and I as Americans are responsible for them. The people in Puerto Rico and the Virgin Islands, and the Canal Zone and Hawaii, no matter what their racial origin may have been, are still our fellow citizens, and as such we have a very distinct responsibility for them as long as the American flag floats over them. So I wanted to see at first hand what some of their problems were; to see whether this great Nation of ours was doing the right thing by these fellow Americans of ours.

And then, on the way back, coming across the continent, I had the opportunity of seeing a number of very large public works which had been undertaken, partly to relieve the unemployment of the present time, but equally to develop great regions of our country in the future for the benefit of future Americans.

Of course you have heard me before — you have heard me very often — talk about things growing up like Topsy. Things have grown up like Topsy in a great many places in the country and we are paying the penalty today. The simplest illustration, quite aside from the problem of this year's drought, is the fact, as you and I know, that a great deal of land that ought never to have been cultivated was taken up by people from the East and from the Middle West and put into cultivation. And we are engaged as a Nation in undoing mistakes of the past, rectifying them so that in the future we shall not be paying so much of a penalty for those mistakes as we are paying today.

In crossing the continent I always think about the people who went there — went out West — and I often wonder whether we people back home realize our responsibility. I think it was Dr. Poucher here today who first dug out the facts — Dr. Poucher or Miss Helen Reynolds. When I was a small boy I used to go hunting up in the town of Clinton, which is not far from here as you know, and when I was a boy people used to talk about a certain section north of the town of Clinton around Brown's Pond they called "Kansas." Nobody ever knew why it was called Kansas, but it was called Kansas locally. We dug into the facts, tried to look up the origin of the name and finally the best solution of the problem seemed to be this: That somewhere around 1850, when the State of Kansas — I guess it was not even a State then, just a territory that had been opened for the white man — was being developed by railroads that were being pushed across the prairie, the railroads sent agents back here through the older, settled parts of the country to get people to go out there. I take it that right here in our county there are a good many acres of what we might call "marginal land" that were settled by the Dutch and English and Scotch and Irish that ought never to have been settled, and in those days there were not only marginal lands in the county but marginal families.

This agent went to Poughkeepsie — and it all came out in the papers in Poughkeepsie in the period — and with a horse and buggy he went out through the town and county. He got up into the town of Clinton. He had what you and I would call prospectuses today about this far land of Kansas, and he persuaded about six or eight families north of Brown's Pond to accept his offer, and to get on an emigrant train which was to leave a week later from Poughkeepsie. They only had a week to move but these neighbors of ours of nearly a hundred years ago just closed up house and closed up the barn and went. They were behind in their taxes, probably. They were poor. They did not see any future living up here in the town of Clinton, so they decided they would move out to the new prairie land. So they went down to Poughkeepsie and got on the emigrant train and disappeared out of our county. Possibly they have kin who still live here.

And it is an interesting fact that when I go through the United States, west of the Mississippi, there is hardly a State that I go into on any trip, that somebody does not come up to me and say, "Governor," or "Mr. President, do you know a family back in Dutchess County named so-and-so?" And I say, "Why, yes, I have heard the name." And then they say, "Why, she was my grandmother" or "He was my grandfather." And they ask, "Do you know what part of Dutchess County they lived in?" Of course I do not know where grandpa had lived in Dutchess County seventy-five years ago.

But there are people from this county all over the United States, especially out through the Middle West and Far West and they have a certain amount of pride of ancestry and they are asking today, trying to find out something about grandmother

393

and grandfather and great-grandmother, wanting to know something about the place they came from.

I think I have spoken to you of this before, but it is always worth repeating — the comparison that Lord Bryce, the historian who was Ambassador in Washington twenty or thirty years ago, used to make between the United States and Europe. He pointed out that we here have come from all kinds of stock, all kinds of Nations in Europe, that most of us here have half a dozen different racial strains in us — and yet here we are, all Americans living in a land over three thousand miles one way and two thousand the other, talking the same language and thinking essentially along the same lines. It is a very thrilling thing.

Lord Bryce would express the thought: "You are singularly blessed in America, because when there are new things to be done you have — not a melting pot — but a trying-out system through the different States. You do not have to do new things all over the country at the same time except in crises and emergencies, and when you people have crises and emergencies you seem to get together and keep together very well until the crisis or emergency is past. You can try out experiments to solve some one economic problem or another, to see if they work, or compare them with other similar experiments in other parts of the same country and gradually work out the solution of problems that are cropping up every day."

And so while on the surface of things this country around here, Dutchess County, looks fine, looks the way we want it to look — no drought, pretty good crops — while on the surface things are in better shape than they have been in a good long time, I hope very much, and I know you will not mind my saying this, that the Home Club will have more and more meetings, and have people come to address those meetings who will tell the truth about conditions and about the methods that are being used to try to solve those conditions. The more we do that, the more we shall realize that if a farm family is on the verge of starvation in North Dakota, we people in the town of Hyde Park are helping to pay to keep that family from actual starvation; if we have made mistakes in the settling of the country in the past, we in the town of Hyde Park have to pay to correct those mistakes. In other words, we should realize that we have a definite stake in the whole country, not merely the spiritual side of it, or the social side of it, or the patriotic side, but the actual financial side of it. We people in the town of Hyde Park, no matter whether we like it or not, are paying, and will have to pay, for the correction of mistakes that were made in other parts of the country in the past, and will have to pay to get things better.

Most of us, the great majority, see the country as a whole, see that unless we help to raise other people up, they are going to drag us down. Most of us are very willing to bear our share and to work for the attainment of the national objective.

By the way, I did not know I was going to make an address until Moses told me so about five minutes ago, but I have been going on delivering not an address but a sermon.

I do wish that everybody in this country had a chance to know every part of the country. I am very proud of the country and very proud of the way we are realizing our national responsibilities. I am very certain that the good people of our town will be willing to go along and cooperate in a big program that has nothing to do with party and nothing to do with section, which is merely trying to be square to all Republicans and Democrats and Socialists, and everybody else, no matter what they call themselves, no matter to which party or church they belong.

I am glad to see you all, glad to be back, and sorry that Congress will probably be in session again in the spring, but I do hope that I shall be able to stay here for another month, and if possible, violate all precedents by taking off a few pounds.

154 ❨ Congratulations Cabled to the New Commander-in-Chief of the Salvation Army. September 4, 1934

Please accept my sincere congratulations on your election as General of the Salvation Army throughout the world. In these troubled times it is particularly important that the leadership of all good forces shall work for the amelioration of human suffering and for the preservation of the highest spiritual ideals. Through your efforts as Commander-in-Chief of the Salvation Army in the United States, you have earned the gratitude and admiration of millions of your countrymen. I am confident that, under your guidance, the Salvation Army will go steadily forward in service to the unfortunate of every land.

FRANKLIN D. ROOSEVELT

General Evangeline Booth,
Salvation Army,
London, England

155 ❨ The One Hundred and Forty-first Press Conference (Excerpts). September 5, 1934

(Labor troubles and strikes — Education of organized labor — English labor experiences.)

Q. Is there anything to say about Mayor LaGuardia's visit here?
THE PRESIDENT: No, I don't know what he is going to talk about. I suppose in general it will be about the city's financial problems and relief problems.

There is one thing you boys could ask about and get an awfully good story. About three months ago there appeared an editorial in the London *Times* which, of course, people over here still regard as the bailiwick of Toryism, and as I remember it — I have filed it away — the editorial ran something like this: That we in England are somewhat surprised, somewhat amazed at the resistance and the objections being offered by certain elements in American industry to Article 7-A (see Note to Item 106, this volume) which reads as follows — and then it quotes Article 7-A which, as you know, is very short. Then it goes on to say, "Our surprise is based on the fact, which every Englishman knows, that its principle has been accepted in England since" — when was the general strike?

Q. 1926.

THE PRESIDENT: "— since 1926, and the acceptance of the principles of 7-A since that time has prevented any serious labor difficulties in the British Isles, and therefore, perhaps, it is interesting to note that conservative old England has been for so many years several steps ahead of so-called radical young America in its dealing with social problems and labor problems."

(Addressing Lord Illiffe) I wish you could talk to these good people and tell them something about how you have worked out some of your labor problems, except that you are just about three jumps ahead of us.

LORD ILLIFFE (Joint owner of the London *Telegraph* and other papers): Of course, labor has had its experiences in England for a very much longer time than it has in the United States, has it not?

THE PRESIDENT: Taking it by far and large, yes.

LORD ILLIFFE: We have a responsible union system now; but, as you know, we have had very considerable troubles. But I think the same thing is going to apply to the United States. You have unions here that have only just begun to feel their power, and when a man gets power at first he does not know how to use it. But he does after a bit. I am perfectly certain it is going to turn out all right in the end.

THE PRESIDENT: Some of our unions are going to work out really well.

LORD ILLIFFE: The result of the general strike in England in 1926,

I think, is that it gave unions a greater feeling of responsibility than they felt before. They really thought that it was possible for them to do anything, and they did not consider the interest of the Nation as a whole. Before 1926 they played their own hand; after 1926 they realized that they had to consider the general good of the public. In the United States, as soon as they realize that, you will find that the union system will work all right.

In these days, when you have organized capital you have to have organized labor; and each side has to realize its responsibility for the public good as a whole.

Q. Does England recognize the principle of collective bargaining?

LORD ILLIFFE: Oh, yes; it does.

THE PRESIDENT: Did the bill pass the present House of Commons that was pending away back in June before I went off on my trip? It was a bill which would give the Government enforcement authority in the case of agreements which had been made in any particular industry between labor and capital. As I recall it, there was some bill pending of that kind and it was a Government measure.

LORD ILLIFFE: I don't remember it. Was it just recently?

THE PRESIDENT: It was in June before I went on my trip.

LORD ILLIFFE: I don't remember that. You mean to enforce agreements that have been arrived at voluntarily between capital and labor, that they should be enforced by Government?

THE PRESIDENT: Yes.

LORD ILLIFFE: I don't remember that.

THE PRESIDENT: There was something of that kind. I saw it in a newspaper story. It might not have been entirely accurate.

One thing—and this is off the record completely, just conversation between us—thinking people are beginning to realize certain elements in the situation. This brings in California again, but I have to keep it off the record.

In the San Francisco strike a lot of people completely lost their heads and telegraphed me, "For God's sake, come back;

turn the ship around." Stephenson and Roddan and Fred (three of the White House correspondents) would not let me turn the ship around. They insisted on Hawaii. Everybody demanded that I sail into San Francisco Bay, all flags flying and guns double shotted, and end the strike. They went completely off the handle.

Well, I kept in pretty close touch, which I would not admit to those Three Musketeers. It appeared very clear to me just as soon as there was talk about a general strike, that there were probably two elements bringing about that general strike. One was the hot-headed young leaders who had had no experience in organized labor whatsoever and said that the only thing to do was to have a general strike. On the other side was a combination of people out there on the Coast who were praying for a general strike. In other words, there was the old conservative crowd just hoping that there would be a general strike, being clever enough to know that a general strike always fails. Hence there was a great deal of encouragement for a general strike. . . . I could not prove this as a legal point, but it was there just the same.

The general strike started; and immediately the strikers, being young, did silly things like saying to the inhabitants, "You cannot eat in that restaurant, but you can eat in this restaurant." Naturally, the public resented it.

Of course they learn by things of that kind. They have got to learn by going through the actual processes, actual examples, and not by interference from the Federal Government or the President or the United States troops. People will learn from a certain number of examples. We have to conduct the country and essentially to educate labor to their responsibility.

LORD ILLIFFE: We realized in England, before 1926, that there would be a general strike, but, until the thing occurred, we were frightened by it. But I am inclined to agree that no general strike can succeed, and that the strike did a lot toward making the labor element realize its responsibility in Great Britain. . . .

Q. Mr. President, would it be possible for us to use this interview with Lord Illiffe, and bring in the fact that you questioned him a little bit about English labor conditions?

THE PRESIDENT: Submitting it to him first, submitting it to the editor.

I don't know that there is anything pending. I am nearly cleaned up. I was terribly far behind. . . .

156 ❬ The One Hundred and Forty-second Press Conference (Excerpts). September 7, 1934

(Proposed reorganization plans for N.R.A.)

Q. Have you given any thought, outside of the impending visit of Mr. Johnson, to your temporary reorganization plans for N.R.A.?

THE PRESIDENT: Not any more than I have been doing every day for the last three months. I give a certain amount of thought to it every day. Nothing out of the ordinary.

Q. Have you received any reports or any data from Washington?

THE PRESIDENT: Nothing for about a week. Of course I get reports all the time in the way of suggestions and recommendations. There isn't anything. I couldn't write a story if I tried. None of those reports and recommendations is news.

Q. Has the program for reorganization taken any fairly definite shape yet that you can talk about?

THE PRESIDENT: I haven't got to that point yet but things are "sort of shaping up." Certain aspects are becoming more and more clear in my mind. Now, as I think I told you before, the ultimate shaping-up is a matter of legislation for the next Congress. So it is not exactly a spot news story, and it is very difficult to write it as a dope story, because no program has been determined on and we are looking at all kinds of permanent administration. The trouble is that if I were to give you an

example it would give that particular thing undue promi-
nence in a very big program. That is why it is so difficult to
do. There are a lot of things, like child labor, for example.
You cannot alleviate that unless you talk about minimum
wages and hours of work, also the old-age pension and the interpretation of 7-A. You have to have the individual authorities getting together and exchanging views. Then, how far can
you go on the exchange of views before running afoul of the
anti-trust law—price fixing and things of that kind? You
might say they all have an equal value in the entire picture,
and we are considering them all.

Q. Mr. President, do you expect that you will get an N.R.A. reorganization, a temporary one, well under way during this
month or October, or are you going to wait until shortly
before Congress?

THE PRESIDENT: I think you can probably make a fairly good
guess on that. If I were writing the story I would say that
there will undoubtedly be a recommendation to the Congress
for permanent legislation. It does not matter whether it goes
up in January or does not go up until March, but something
will have to be done before the Congress adjourns that would
be permanent legislation in the sense that it would at least
tide over for one year. In other words, we are feeling our way
on all of these steps. You cannot at this time say that the
permanent form of N.R.A. is going to be A, B, C or D. Child
labor and collective bargaining, the collective principle of
bargaining, are examples of those things which should have a
permanent position in American life. Now, those things will
have to be taken up by the Congress, otherwise the whole
thing will have to be renewed for another year.

Then you come to the borderline; it is partly administrative and partly a question of whether the thing has worked or
not. If a part has not worked, should it be modified or abandoned, such as price fixing? That is one of the items on which
there is a question mark. We all know that. It runs afoul of
the Sherman Anti-Trust Law and other things.

Then, on the administrative end, it is probable that there will be certain temporary changes in the purely administrative set-up which is more a matter of detail than anything else, before the legislation of the next Session goes into effect. Again we are feeling our way, feeling our way toward the ultimate goal. What we do may not be permanent, it may be changed a half dozen times. There have been changes in the past, quite a number of them. There probably will be more as we work toward a simplification of the whole procedure.

Q. You are not including price-fixing policy and price posting, things of that sort, in the category of things that might be changed? After all, you don't need new legislation to change that.

THE PRESIDENT: They might be modified in the meantime. We are trying it out. After all, they were put in there to try out. But those things, as I said, are pretty vague and I would not go so far as to say that they are going to be done, because I don't know. They are among the things that are open for discussion and have been right along; very much so.

Q. On administrative set-ups, will there be a change in that in the near future, say, by the first of October?

THE PRESIDENT: Now you are getting too definite. I don't know. That is the trouble, you haven't a spot news story. You have an interpretative long-range story. I cannot tell you what will be done, because I don't know. But we are working gradually toward a simplification of N.R.A., throwing overboard or modifying the things that are not working — putting in eventually, through perhaps a process of several changes, a machinery that would seem to work better with a more permanent and more simplified organization. It is hard to say anything categorically about it. . . .

(See also Items 159 and 163, this volume, and Item 17, Vol. IV.)

157 ❰ The President Receives Report on Cotton Textile Strike. September 20, 1934

THE excellent report of the board of inquiry for the Cotton Textile Industry presents findings and recommendations which cover the basic sources of difficulties, and does this in a way which shows the wholly fair and reasonable approach with which the board undertook its task.

It is, I think, a good example of the practical way in which industrial problems can be calmly discussed and solved under a republican form of government.

It is, of course, greatly to be hoped that a fair solution can be had because of the good-will and intelligence which undoubtedly exist in the industry as a whole including both workers and plant owners.

157A ❰ The President Approves the Report and Urges Strikers to Return to Work. September 20, 1934

IN FORMALLY approving the report submitted to me by the Board of Inquiry for the Cotton Textile Industry, I want to express the very sincere hope that all employees now out on strike will return to work, and that all textile manufacturers will take back employees without discrimination. At the same time I am confident that manufacturers will aid the Government in carrying out the steps outlined.

NOTE: The threat of a general strike in the textile field had been growing since May, 1934. It was finally voted about the middle of August, 1934. The Cotton Textile National Industrial Relations Board offered, without success, to act as mediator. The National Labor Relations Board also tried without success. After these efforts to avert the strike had failed, I appointed on September 5, 1934, a Board of Inquiry for the Cotton Textile Industry to investigate the complaints of the workers and the conditions in the industry. The report of this

Board was filed with me on September 17, 1934; and the union terminated the strike.

In accordance with the recommendations of the Board and pursuant to the authority of Public Resolution No. 44, 73d Congress, approved June 19, 1934, I appointed a Textile Labor Relations Board on September 26, 1934, by Executive Order No. 6858, with an adequate staff and facilities, and with powers and duties similar to those of the Steel Labor Relations Board (see Item 113, this volume). It was authorized to administer the labor provisions of the cotton, silk and wool codes, in addition to the provisions of Section 7-A, of N.I.R.A.

The same Executive Order directed the Bureau of Labor Statistics of the Labor Department to prepare a comprehensive report of actual hours of employment, earnings and working conditions in the industry, and directed the Federal Trade Commission to study the financial condition of the industry and to report upon its wage-paying ability. The reports submitted showed that, broadly speaking, wage conditions of textile workers had been generally improved by the code, but that they still remained diverse and at a relatively low level.

On October 16, 1934, I signed four Executive Orders, Nos. 6875-6878, putting into effect some of the recommendations of the Board of Inquiry for the Cotton Textile Industry which I had appointed on September 5, 1934. These Executive Orders set up cotton, silk and wool textile work assignment boards and prescribed rules and regulations for their guidance.

158 ❨ Letter to the Veterans of Foreign Wars. September 24, 1934

My dear Commander Van Zandt:

It is with profound regret that I find myself unable to meet with you at your thirty-fifth encampment in Louisville this year. Only the pressure of public business prevents my foregathering with you men who have served your country on foreign fields and on the high seas during hostilities. My inability to be present in no wise affects the measure of my real interest in your proceedings, for I, too, am a member of your distinguished organization.

Not since the gunfire was stilled along the battle lines in 1918, have you overseas veterans been confronted with emergency conditions such as today demand the undivided attention and unselfish application of all of us. And just as we did in those days when we subordinated everything to the attainment of our great objective, so now we must carry on through until we are definitely clear of the mine fields of economic distress.

I do not hesitate to include you in that gallant company of men who hold the welfare of the entire country paramount, for your very membership in the Veterans of Foreign Wars of the United States shows that when the call came you were prepared to give your lives if need be for this Republic. Many and diverse may be your interests but greatest of all is that which we all share in common. It is the welfare of our Nation. That comes first. Let us look to that and the lesser things will follow in their due time.

I wish your convention every success. May the memories of your active service in other climes endure down the years, for these recollections are sacred. They are the cherished possessions of the favored few, the few who risked their all for a principle and survived to answer the roll call.

Very sincerely yours,

Mr. James E. Van Zandt,
Commander-in-Chief, Veterans of Foreign Wars,
Washington, D. C.

159 ❨ N.R.A. Is Reorganized—The National Industrial Recovery Board Is Established. Executive Order No. 6859. September 27, 1934

By VIRTUE of the authority vested in me by the National Industrial Recovery Act, approved June 16, 1933, and to effectuate the purposes of said act:

1. I hereby appoint Clay Williams, A. D. Whiteside, Sidney Hillman, Leon C. Marshall, and Walton Hamilton to serve as members of the National Industrial Recovery Board, which is hereby created to administer under my direction the provisions of Title I of the National Industrial Recovery Act.

2. I hereby appoint Blackwell Smith, legal adviser, and Leon Henderson, economic adviser, to said National Industrial Recovery Board. The legal adviser and economic adviser shall serve ex officio as members of said Board.

3. The said Board is hereby authorized, subject to the general approval of the Industrial Emergency Committee (created, constituted, and empowered by the Executive Order of June 30, 1934, No. 6770, and subsequent Executive Orders amending said Order), to promulgate administrative policies, to appoint, employ, discharge, fix the compensation, define the duties, and direct the conduct of the personnel necessary for its administration and to exercise all those powers heretofore conferred by Executive Orders upon the Administrator for Industrial Recovery.

4. The Board shall elect from its members a chairman and an executive secretary, both to serve at the pleasure of the Board and to perform such duties as may be prescribed by the Board, or by the President.

5. Any previous orders concerning the subject matter hereof are hereby modified and amended so far as necessary to make this order fully effective.

NOTE: After the resignation of General Hugh S. Johnson on September 24, 1934, I changed the nature of the control of the N.R.A. by the foregoing Executive Order, creating the National Industrial Recovery Board. Thereafter, this Board exercised all of the powers that the Administrator had exercised, subject to the joint approval of the Industrial Emergency Committee appointed June 30, 1934 (see Item 123, this volume), the membership of which was increased by adding the Chairman of the National Industrial Recovery Board and the Administrator of A.A.A. as a result of Executive Orders No. 6836 of August 31, 1934, and No. 6860 of September 27, 1934.

The Advisory Council which had been created on May 21, 1934, made up of three members each of the Labor, Consumers, and Industrial Advisory Boards, was continued with a slightly different membership, to act as a medium for deliberation and for consultation on various viewpoints. It took over the functions of the old Policy Group which had operated with the Administrator.

A few days after this Executive Order was issued, in a radio address on September 30, 1934 (see Item 163, this volume), I emphasized the fact that the formative period of code-making was at an end and that the reorganization was intended to meet the needs of preparing for legislation to determine a more permanent form of N.R.A. I pointed out that if any defects had crept into the administration of the Act, such as overcomplicated codes, price-fixing, and limitation of production, it was largely because the representatives of trade and industry had been permitted, within certain limits, to write their ideas into the codes. I stated at that time that it was time to review the entire situation in the light of past experience.

The National Industrial Recovery Board undertook a general survey of its task, and classified the more significant problems immediately ahead, which were, as the Board saw them, as follows:

1. Compliance and enforcement.

2. The decentralization of administration, but with centralized control of policy formulation.

3. The simplification of the code structure and improvement of code administration.

4. The determination of the appropriate functions of self-government in industry, which involved the functions of code authorities and to which were related the problems of the organization of code authorities and multiple code assessments on one enterprise.

5. Price control and production control in terms of encouragement of a sane competitive system that, by the very process of reasonable control, would stimulate the development of individual initiative.

6. The giving of needed elasticity to management under the labor provisions of the codes along with effective safeguards for labor.

7. The appropriate business areas for codification, particularly as to the service trades and small enterprises.

8. Determination of policies as to the imposition of codes and of changes in the codes.

9. The further reduction of unemployment — a problem which in the opinion of the Board required the cooperative action of other governmental agencies.

10. The policy of the stimulation of the volume of production.

11. The securing of more cooperative and more effective alignment with other agencies of the Government.

The Board did not undertake to change or revise the existing codes. It was chiefly engaged, in addition to its administrative work, in securing adequate information and developing policy for the framework of a new and more permanent N.R.A., should the N.I.R.A. be extended beyond its original expiration day.

See also Item 163, this volume, and Item 17, Vol. IV.

160 ❨ Greeting to the International Association of the Chiefs of Police. September 27, 1934

Mr. Chairman and Members of the International Association of Chiefs of Police:

IT AFFORDS me a great deal of pleasure to address this brief personal message of greeting and best wishes to my friends of the International Association of Chiefs of Police.

I wish to commend your organization for the cooperation which it is furnishing in the great movement which the agencies of government—national, State and local—are now organizing against the forces of crime. No undertaking is more vital to the welfare of society at this time than that of the prevention and detection of crime. The social order cannot exist except upon the basis of a respect for and observance of the law, and it is only when the people of a country are secure in their homes and in the normal activities of their lives from the depredations of the criminal classes that national progress can be maintained.

This respect for law and this security are possible only when the administration of justice is entrusted to wise, upright, patriotic and courageous officials.

It is of great importance that the International Association of Chiefs of Police shall press forward its vigorous efforts directed toward the elevation of the standards of police institutions and officials. Permit me, therefore, to wish you success in your great work.

161 ❨ A Message to the Conference on Current Problems. September 27, 1934

I WISH that I could have attended in person all of the sessions of the Conference on Current Problems because of the wide field of human endeavor which it has covered and because of the distinguished group of speakers to whom you have listened. The world as a whole is making progress in meeting current problems, because the world as a whole realizes that the problems are new and, as such, must be met with new answers.

If you were to ask me, I would tell you frankly that the greatest achievement of the past two years in the United States has been the fact that the American people have taken, and are taking, a greater interest in, and have acquired a better understanding of, current problems affecting their welfare and the world's welfare than at any time at least during the present generation. That is a very heartening thought to all of us who believe in the republican form of government as carried into effect by majority rule.

In every walk of life in every part of the country, it has become a normal and an interesting thing when two or more persons are gathered together for them to talk over methods of improving the economic and social lot of our citizenry.

More and more people are doing their own thinking. The number of poll-parrots in our midst is steadily declining—for which we must be very thankful. More and more men and women are looking up their own facts and forming their own opinions.

We are learning to discriminate between news and rumor. As a people we put our tongues in our cheeks when a fact or a series of facts are distorted, no matter what motive is the cause of that distortion.

We as a people are less inclined to believe those who would create fear or encourage panic. We as a people pay small attention to those gossip-mongers who invent tales, generally with a selfish objective behind the tales.

You and I as sensible Americans know of daily instances which mar rather than help our efforts for calm discussion of current problems. Just for example, I cite one which occurred this very day. A rumor which started in Wall Street spread to Chicago, and came back to Washington for verification. The rumor was the immediate retirement of three members of my Cabinet—the Secretary of Agriculture and his Undersecretary, the Secretary of Labor and the Secretary of the Treasury. It even went to the extent of announcing the name of a new Secretary of the Treasury.

The origin of the report comes from what is politely called "an anonymous source." I urge that every one of you consider and analyze the source and motive back of every report you read.

Fortunately the overwhelming mass of the American people pay no more attention to this kind of rumor than I do. Today's story happens to be wholly untrue.

It is with a very definite sense of gratification and thanks that I tell you of my conviction that our people have both feet on the ground; that they are increasingly interested in the truth and increasingly interested in arriving at sound conclusions regarding our national progress in meeting current problems.

For that reason I am glad to have this opportunity of sending my greetings to a gathering of intelligent men and women, who know how to discriminate in making up their minds about the current problems of American life.

162 ❬ Address to the Conference on the Mobilization for Human Needs. September 28, 1934

I AM happy that for the second time the Conference on the Mobilization for Human Needs comes here to the White House. In doing this you are emphasizing with me the national character of our common task. I like to feel that I share the responsibility with all of you who are here representing every part of the country.

Your work in the past has been of such outstanding success that I am confident that this year you will achieve an all-time record.

Last year, when I had the privilege of speaking to you, I emphasized the simple fact that the responsibility of the individual and of the family for the well-being of their neighbors must never cease. If we go back in our own history to those earliest days of the white man in America, with those first winters of suffering in Jamestown and at Plymouth, we know it has been the American habit from that time on continuously to render aid to those who need it. Through the centuries, as the first struggling villages developed into communities and cities and counties and States, destitution and want of every description have been cared for, in the first instance by community help, and in the last instance as well.

With the enormous growth of population we have had, with the complexities of the past generation, community efforts have now been supplemented by the formation of great national organizations. These organizations are designed to coordinate and stimulate local groups which are striving not only to take care of those in need but also to stimulate better conditions of health, of child welfare, of mental hygiene, of recreation, and to attain all those many other splendid objectives which are part and parcel of our national life today.

The mere reading of the names of the organizations that are working solidly behind this great task is enough to make this country realize the unity of purpose, the solidarity, behind what we are doing. It is right, I think, for us to emphasize that the American family must be the unit which engages our greatest interest and concern. With this we must stress once more the task of each community to assist in maintaining and building up that family unit.

No thinking or experienced person insists today that the responsibility of the community shall be eliminated by passing this great and humane task on to any central body at the seat of Federal Government. You and I know that it has been with reluctance and only because we have realized the imperative need for additional help that the Federal Government has been compelled to undertake the task of supplementing the more normal methods which have been in use during all the preceding generations.

I repeat what I told you last year because it is something that is a fundamental of our present-day civilization: that the primary responsibility for community needs rests upon the community itself. That if every effort has been used by any given community and has proven insufficient, then it is the duty of the State to supplement, with the resources of the State, the additional needs up to the limit of the power of the State. And that, finally, and only finally, it is only when both of these efforts, taken together, have proven insufficient that the Federal Government has any duty to add its resources to the common cause.

It is inevitable, of course, that in carrying on relief—whether in the form of work relief or home relief—in an area that includes every State, every county and every city in the Union, local inefficiency is bound to exist in some instances. It is very definitely your task, and mine, to see to it that during the coming winter there shall be increased vigilance in every locality, vigilance against the giving of relief or of aid of any kind except to those who definitely and clearly need it and are entitled to it.

In this great emergency system we are establishing, with each passing month, a greater degree of efficiency, and we are eliminating many of the evils which of necessity attended our first efforts of over a year ago. The trained workers who belong to the many organizations represented in this conference have an opportunity and a duty to see to it, first of all, that destitution is relieved and, secondly, that no family and no individual shall receive public assistance if that individual or that family does not deserve it.

Your work and the work of local, State and Federal agencies are so closely associated that your success is very vital to the success of Government itself. I am confident that the people of this country, in each and every community, will understand the true importance of cooperating in this great mobilization for human needs.

I always like to emphasize the word "privilege" rather than the word "duty"; for it is clearly the privilege of the individual American to bear his personal share in a work which must be kept personal in so far as it is possible to make it so. It is that personal appeal, that personal service, which has carried us through all these trying years. A unity of effort for a little while longer will, I am confident, bring national success to our nationally unified efforts to bring Old Man Depression to the point where we can finally master and destroy him.

The church groups and the social groups organized on private lines, whether they act separately or jointly through Community Chests, or in any other way, are an essential part of the structure of our life. The American people believe in you, believe in the work you are doing. The American people support your fine objectives. That support will attend again this year the excellent enterprise you are launching today.

NOTE: In addition to the foregoing speech, I made a radio address on behalf of the 1934 Mobilization for Human Needs on October 22, 1934, which is, however, not printed in these volumes for lack of space. The other volumes in this series also contain addresses to the annual Conferences on the Mobilization for Human Needs for the respective other years of my Administration. See Item 123, Vol. II; Item 150, Vol. IV; Item 127, Vol. V.

163 ⟨ Second "Fireside Chat" of 1934 — "We Are Moving Forward to Greater Freedom, to Greater Security for the Average Man." September 30, 1934

THREE months have passed since I talked with you shortly after the adjournment of the Congress. To-night I continue that report, though, because of the shortness of time, I must defer a number of subjects to a later date.

Recently the most notable public questions that have concerned us all have had to do with industry and labor and with respect to these, certain developments have taken place which I consider of importance. I am happy to report that after years of uncertainty, culminating in the collapse of the spring of 1933, we are bringing order out of the old chaos with a greater certainty of the employment of labor at a reasonable wage and of more business at a fair profit. These governmental and industrial developments hold promise of new achievements for the Nation.

Men may differ as to the particular form of governmental activity with respect to industry and business, but nearly all are agreed that private enterprise in times such as these cannot be left without assistance and without reasonable safeguards lest it destroy not only itself but also our processes of civilization. The underlying necessity for such activity is indeed as strong now as it was years ago when Elihu Root said the following very significant words:

"Instead of the give and take of free individual contract, the tremendous power of organization has combined great aggregations of capital in enormous industrial establishments working through vast agencies of commerce and employing great masses of men in movements of production and transportation and trade, so great in the mass that each individual concerned in them is quite helpless by himself. The relations between the employer and the employed, between the owners of aggregated capital and the units of organized labor, between the small producer, the small trader, the consumer, and the great transporting and manufacturing and distributing agencies, all present new questions for the solution of which the old reliance upon the free action of individual wills appears quite inadequate. And in many directions, the intervention of that organized control which we call government seems necessary to produce the same result of justice and right conduct which obtained through the attrition of individuals before the new conditions arose."

It was in this spirit thus described by Secretary Root that we approached our task of reviving private enterprise in March, 1933. Our first problem was, of course, the banking situation because, as you know, the banks had collapsed. Some banks could not be saved but the great majority of them, either through their own resources or with Government aid, have been restored to complete public confidence. This has given safety to millions of depositors in these banks. Closely following this great constructive effort we have, through various Federal agencies, saved debtors and creditors alike in many other fields of enterprise, such as loans on farm mortgages and home mortgages; loans to the railroads and insurance companies and, finally, help for home owners and industry itself.

In all of these efforts the Government has come to the assistance of business and with the full expectation that the money used to assist these enterprises will eventually be repaid. I believe it will be.

The second step we have taken in the restoration of normal business enterprise has been to clean up thoroughly unwholesome conditions in the field of investment. In this we have had assistance from many bankers and business men, most of whom recognize the past evils in the banking system, in the sale of securities, in the deliberate encouragement of stock gambling, in the sale of unsound mortgages and in many other ways in which the public lost billions of dollars. They saw that without changes in the policies and methods of investment there could be no recovery of public confidence in the security of savings. The country now enjoys the safety of bank savings under the new banking laws, the careful checking of new securities under the Securities Act and the curtailment of rank stock speculation through the Securities Exchange Act. I sincerely hope that as a result people will be discouraged in unhappy efforts to get rich quick by speculating in securities. The average person almost always loses. Only a very small minority of the people of this country believe in gambling as a substitute for the old philosophy of Benjamin Franklin that the way to wealth is through work.

In meeting the problems of industrial recovery the chief agency of the Government has been the National Recovery Administration. Under its guidance, trades and industries covering over 90 percent of all industrial employees have adopted codes of fair competition, which have been approved by the President. Under these codes, in the industries covered, child labor has been eliminated. The work day and the work week have been shortened. Minimum wages have been established and other wages adjusted toward a rising standard of living. The emergency purpose of the N.R.A. was to put men to work and since its creation more than four million persons have been reemployed, in great part through the cooperation of American business brought about under the codes.

Benefits of the Industrial Recovery Program have come, not only to labor in the form of new jobs, in relief from overwork and in relief from underpay, but also to the owners and managers of industry because, together with a great increase in the payrolls, there has come a substantial rise in the total of industrial profits — a rise from a deficit figure in the first quarter of 1933 to a level of sustained profits within one year from the inauguration of N.R.A.

Now it should not be expected that even employed labor and capital would be completely satisfied with present conditions. Employed workers have not by any means all enjoyed a return to the earnings of prosperous times, although millions of hitherto underprivileged workers are today far better paid than ever before. Also, billions of dollars of invested capital have today a greater security of present and future earning power than before. This is because of the establishment of fair, competitive standards and because of relief from unfair competition in wage cutting which depresses markets and destroys purchasing power. But it is an undeniable fact that the restoration of other billions of sound investments to a reasonable earning power could not be brought about in one year. There is no magic formula, no economic panacea, which could simply revive overnight the heavy industries and the trades dependent upon them.

Nevertheless the gains of trade and industry, as a whole, have been substantial. In these gains and in the policies of the Administration there are assurances that hearten all forward-looking men and women with the confidence that we are definitely rebuilding our political and economic system on the lines laid down by the New Deal — lines which as I have so often made clear, are in complete accord with the underlying principles of orderly popular government which Americans have demanded since the white man first came to these shores. We count, in the future as in the past, on the driving power of individual initiative and the incentive of fair private profit, strengthened with the acceptance of those obligations to the public interest which rest upon us all. We have the right to expect that this driving power will be given patriotically and whole-heartedly to our Nation.

We have passed through the formative period of code making in the National Recovery Administration and have effected a reorganization of the N.R.A. suited to the needs of the next phase, which is, in turn, a period of preparation for legislation which will determine its permanent form.

In this recent reorganization we have recognized three distinct functions: first, the legislative or policy-making function; second, the administrative function of code making and revision; and, third, the judicial function, which includes enforcement, consumer complaints and the settlement of disputes between employers and employees and between one employer and another.

We are now prepared to move into this second phase, on the basis of our experience in the first phase under the able and energetic leadership of General Johnson.

We shall watch carefully the working of this new machinery for the second phase of N.R.A., modifying it where it needs modification and finally making recommendations to the Congress, in order that the functions of N.R.A. which have proved their worth may be made a part of the permanent machinery of government.

Let me call your attention to the fact that the National Industrial Recovery Act gave business men the opportunity they had sought for years to improve business conditions through what has been called self-government in industry. If the codes which have been written have been too complicated, if they have gone too far in such matters as price fixing and limitation of production, let it be remembered that so far as possible, consistent with the immediate public interest of this past year and the vital necessity of improving labor conditions, the representatives of trade and industry were permitted to write their ideas into the codes. It is now time to review these actions as a whole to determine through deliberative means in the light of experience, from the standpoint of the good of the industries themselves, as well as the general public interest, whether the methods and policies adopted in the emergency have been best calculated to promote industrial recovery and a permanent improvement of business and labor conditions. There may be a serious question as to the wisdom of many of those devices to control production, or to prevent destructive price cutting which many business organizations have insisted were necessary, or whether their effect may have been to prevent that volume of production which would make possible lower prices and increased employment. Another question arises as to whether in fixing minimum wages on the basis of an hourly or weekly wage we have reached into the heart of the problem which is to provide such annual earnings for the lowest paid worker as will meet his minimum needs. We also question the wisdom of extending code requirements suited to the great industrial centers and to large employers, to the great number of small employers in the smaller communities.

During the last twelve months our industrial recovery has been to some extent retarded by strikes, including a few of major importance. I would not minimize the inevitable losses to employers and employees and to the general public through such conflicts. But I would point out that the extent and severity of labor disputes during this period have been far less than in any previous comparable period.

When the business men of the country were demanding the right to organize themselves adequately to promote their legitimate interests; when the farmers were demanding legislation which would give them opportunities and incentives to organize themselves for a common advance, it was natural that the workers should seek and obtain a statutory declaration of their constitutional right to organize themselves for collective bargaining as embodied in Section 7-A of the National Industrial Recovery Act.

Machinery set up by the Federal Government has provided some new methods of adjustment. Both employers and employees must share the blame of not using them as fully as they should.

The employer who turns away from impartial agencies of peace, who denies freedom of organization to his employees, or fails to make every reasonable effort at a peaceful solution of their differences, is not fully supporting the recovery effort of his Government. The workers who turn away from these same impartial agencies and decline to use their good offices to gain their ends are likewise not fully cooperating with their Government.

It is time that we made a clean-cut effort to bring about that united action of management and labor, which is one of the high purposes of the Recovery Act. We have passed through more than a year of education. Step by step we have created all the Government agencies necessary to insure, as a general rule, industrial peace, with justice for all those willing to use these agencies whenever their voluntary bargaining fails to produce a necessary agreement.

There should be at least a full and fair trial given to these means of ending industrial warfare; and in such an effort we should be able to secure for employers and employees and consumers the benefits that all derive from the continuous, peaceful operation of our essential enterprises.

Accordingly, I propose to confer within the coming month with small groups of those truly representative of large employers of labor and of large groups of organized labor, in order to seek their cooperation in establishing what I may describe as a specific trial period of industrial peace.

From those willing to join in establishing this hoped-for period of peace, I shall seek assurances of the making and maintenance of agreements, which can be mutually relied upon, under which wages, hours and working conditions may be determined and any later adjustments shall be made either by agreement or, in case of disagreement, through the mediation or arbitration of State or Federal agencies. I shall not ask either employers or employees permanently to lay aside the weapons common to industrial war. But I shall ask both groups to give a fair trial to peaceful methods of adjusting their conflicts of opinion and interest, and to experiment for a reasonable time with measures suitable to civilize our industrial civilization.

Closely allied to the N.R.A. is the program of public works provided for in the same Act and designed to put more men back to work, both directly on the public works themselves, and indirectly in the industries supplying the materials for these public works. To those who say that our expenditures for public works and other means for recovery are a waste that we cannot afford, I answer that no country, however rich, can afford the waste of its human resources. Demoralization caused by vast unemployment is our greatest extravagance. Morally, it is the greatest menace to our social order. Some people try to tell me that we must make up our minds that for the future we shall permanently have millions of unemployed just as other countries have had them for over a decade. What may be necessary for those countries is not my responsibility to determine. But as for this country, I stand or fall by my refusal to accept as a necessary condition of our future a permanent army of unemployed. On the contrary, we must make it a national principle that we will not tolerate a large army of unemployed and that we will arrange our national economy to end our present unemployment as soon as we can and then to take wise measures against its return. I do not want to think that it is the destiny of any American to remain permanently on relief rolls.

Those, fortunately few in number, who are frightened by boldness and cowed by the necessity for making decisions, complain that all we have done is unnecessary and subject to great risks. Now that these people are coming out of their storm cellars, they forget that there ever was a storm. They point to England. They would have you believe that England has made progress out of her depression by a do-nothing policy, by letting nature take her course. England has her peculiarities and we have ours, but I do not believe any intelligent observer can accuse England of undue orthodoxy in the present emergency.

Did England let nature take her course? No. Did England hold to the gold standard when her reserves were threatened? No. Has

England gone back to the gold standard today? No. Did England hesitate to call in ten billion dollars of her war bonds bearing 5 percent interest, to issue new bonds therefor bearing only 3½ percent interest, thereby saving the British Treasury one hundred and fifty million dollars a year in interest alone? No. And let it be recorded that the British bankers helped. Is it not a fact that ever since the year 1909, Great Britain in many ways has advanced further along lines of social security than the United States? Is it not a fact that relations between capital and labor on the basis of collective bargaining are much further advanced in Great Britain than in the United States? It is perhaps not strange that the conservative British press has told us with pardonable irony that much of our New Deal program is only an attempt to catch up with English reforms that go back ten years or more.

Nearly all Americans are sensible and calm people. We do not get greatly excited nor is our peace of mind disturbed, whether we be business men or workers or farmers, by awesome pronouncements concerning the unconstitutionality of some of our measures of recovery and relief and reform. We are not frightened by reactionary lawyers or political editors. All of these cries have been heard before. More than twenty-one years ago, when Theodore Roosevelt and Woodrow Wilson were attempting to correct abuses in our national life, the great Chief Justice White said:

"There is great danger it seems to me to arise from the constant habit which prevails where anything is opposed or objected to, of referring without rhyme or reason to the Constitution as a means of preventing its accomplishment, thus creating the general impression that the Constitution is but a barrier to progress instead of being the broad highway through which alone true progress may be enjoyed."

In our efforts for recovery we have avoided, on the one hand, the theory that business should and must be taken over into an all-embracing Government. We have avoided, on the other hand, the equally untenable theory that it is an interference with liberty to offer reasonable help when private enterprise is in need of help. The course we have followed fits the American practice of Government, a practice of taking action step by step, of regulating only to meet concrete needs, a practice of courageous recognition of change. I believe with Abraham Lincoln, that "The legitimate object of Government is to do for a community of people whatever they need to have done but cannot do at all or cannot do so well for themselves in their separate and individual capacities."

I am not for a return to that definition of liberty under which for many years a free people were being gradually regimented into the service of the privileged few. I prefer and I am sure you prefer that broader definition of liberty under which we are moving forward to greater freedom, to greater security for the average man than he has ever known before in the history of America.

164 ⟨ An Excerpt from the One Hundred and Forty-seventh Press Conference. October 3, 1934

(Annual wage income.)

Q. Any plans for taking up the annual wage question referred to in your speech Sunday night?

THE PRESIDENT: The annual wage thing?

Q. Yes, sir.

THE PRESIDENT: You mean the annual wage to Government employees?

Q. Insuring workmen an annual income.

THE PRESIDENT: I don't think I mentioned that, did I, in the speech?

Q. Yes, sir; you spoke of the inadequacy or possible inadequacy of wage minimums for a given short length of time such as a week or an hour or two, to establish living standards.

THE PRESIDENT: That I merely mentioned as one of the things people are beginning to think about.

Q. Would you call it an immediate problem?

THE PRESIDENT: Frankly, I don't know. I just mentioned it as something people are thinking about. As a matter of fact, when I first dictated that speech the other day I had an example which would have made more clear that phase of the wage problem.

Last winter, as you will recall, the automobile workers were down here. They were a pretty young crowd, most of those fellows were about thirty-five years or along there. I said to one of them, "What are you getting? What is your hourly wage?" He said, "A dollar and a quarter an hour." I said, "Eight hours?" He said, "Yes, sir." I said, "That is $10 a day?" He said, "Yes, sir; that is right." I said, "It seems to me that is a pretty good wage. What are you, a machinist?" "Yes, sir." I said, "I think that is a pretty good wage."

Then he said, "Mr. President, that is a pretty good wage, yes, but last year I only worked 65 days. My total gross income was $650."

I think that particular story emphasizes the thought better than anything else that you or I can use as to the reason for thinking in terms of how much a fellow gets by December 31st instead of how much he gets per hour. That is what I was driving at. . . .

(See also Item 180, Vol. V.)

165 ❪ The President Congratulates the C.C.C. — "This Kind of Work Must Go On."

October 6, 1934

Dear Mr. Fechner:

I have been greatly interested and encouraged by the fine report of your visits to C.C.C. camps in many parts of the country.

This kind of work must go on. I believe that the Nation feels that the work of these young men is so thoroughly justified and, in addition, the benefits to the men themselves are so clear that the actual annual cost will be met without much opposition or much complaint.

Very sincerely yours,

Hon. Robert Fechner,
Civilian Conservation Corps,
Washington, D. C.

NOTE: The C.C.C. program was by this time not only a success in the saving of hundreds of thousands of young men, but also in the accomplishment of inestimable good in the parks and forests. See Items 21, 31, 90, and 113 of Vol. II.

During its second year, which began on April 1, 1934, the authorized enrollment was 303,000 men. In July, 1934, by Executive Order No. 6747, funds were provided to enroll 50,000 men from the drought areas in the Central States, which increased the strength of the Corps to 353,000 men.

During this second year, steps were taken to return about 50,000 men who had been enrolled in the East but who had been sent to the Western national forests and parks because of the shortage of work projects in the East. With the establishment of more work projects in the East, the policy was followed to give as many men as possible employment in the State from which they were enrolled.

During the summer of 1934, the number of camps was increased to 1,625 through the establishment of additional camps in the drought areas.

The 1,625 camps in operation were widely distributed, and by late 1934 they had become a familiar sight in hundreds of communities. A typical camp of this period of the C.C.C.'s growth consisted usually of about twelve wooden buildings including four barracks, each capable of holding fifty men, a mess hall and necessary supplemental buildings, such as officers' quarters, garages, tool houses, bath houses, etc. A reserve officer called to active duty by the War Department was in charge of the camp. The camps, however, were civilian rather than military in character. Usually the men awoke to the stirring command of the bugle but there was no military drill, no manual of arms, no military discipline. Enrolled men had no military obligations. At each camp there were 200 enrolled men, two or three Army reserve officers, a medical officer, and from eight to ten members of a technical agency of the Department of Agriculture or the Department of the Interior. The officers had charge of the camps but their jurisdiction did not extend to the work projects. A project superintendent at each camp had supervision over all work done, and the men were turned over to him eight hours a day for five days a week. In the field they worked under the direction of the project superintendent, who was responsible for the amount and character of the work done.

The regular enrollees were single young men whose families were on relief or eligible for public aid, war veterans who were enrolled without regard to age or marital status, and a few experienced men, usually about sixteen per camp, from the vicinity of the camp.

At the end of the first two years, which was the expiration date of the original C.C.C. statute, there was almost unanimous opinion that the C.C.C. should be continued.

Accordingly, the Emergency Relief Appropriation Act of 1935, approved April 8, 1935 (Pub. Res. No. 11, 74th Congress; 49 Stat. 115), provided funds for its continuance and authorized the operation of the camps until March 31, 1937. By Executive Order No. 7029, April 30, 1935, funds were allocated for this work. The maximum age limit was extended to include men between the ages of 18 and 28, and the minimum age limit was later reduced to 17.

The enlarged program authorized the employment of as many as 600,000 enrollees. At the same time a new regulation was made requiring that enrollees could be selected only from families on the relief roll, except for war veterans and the local experienced men. On August 31, 1935, the enrolled strength had been increased to 505,782, and the number of camps to 2,652. That was the peak both in enrollees and the number of camps which the C.C.C. reached. Including all the persons connected with the organization as of that date, the total number of persons receiving employment from the C.C.C. was close to 600,000 men.

From that point the strength of the Corps was gradually reduced as conditions became better and as the size of the relief rolls diminished.

See Item 50, Vol. V, for a further discussion of C.C.C.

166 ⟨A Letter to the Annual Convention of the American Legion. October 8, 1934

My dear Commander Hayes:

I WAS delighted to receive your very cordial invitation to attend and address the Sixteenth Annual National Convention of the American Legion to be held at Miami, Florida, commencing October twenty-second. I well recall meeting with the American Legion last year in Chicago when you were elected to your present high office. My reception there always will be keenly appreciated.

It is with sincere regret, therefore, that this year I find it will be impossible to join with the American Legion at Miami. Other commitments and pressure of public business preclude the acceptance of your invitation.

My failure to be there, however, will in no sense lessen my distinct interest in your proceedings. The American Legion is a significant American organization, patriotic in its concepts and strong in its influence. Comprised of veterans of the World War and perpetuating the memory of those who have passed on, you can well stand as a beacon to guide your country's further national security.

While I realize your interests are in many directions, our national welfare is paramount. I urge you to carry such a spirit into your convention. Your country expects this of you and I am confident it will not be disappointed.

I wish your convention every success.

Very sincerely yours,

National Commander E. A. Hayes,
The American Legion,
Indianapolis, Indiana.

167 (Message of Condolence on the Assassination of King Alexander of Yugoslavia.

October 9, 1934

Mrs. Roosevelt and I are deeply shocked and grieved at the great calamity which has befallen you and your children. In your hour of distress we extend to you our heartfelt sympathy. In the death of His Majesty King Alexander the Yugoslav people have lost a courageous leader who worked untiringly for their well-being.

Her Majesty, Queen Marie,
Belgrade, Yugoslavia

168 ⟨ Address at the Dedication of Veterans' Hospital at Roanoke, Virginia. October 19, 1934

Governor Perry, Mr. Chairman, my friends:

I COULD not have failed to receive inspiration during this past hour from the generous welcome that so many of you good people have given me since I got off the train in Roanoke and during my motor trip out here, and now, at the end at this hospital site, from the view of these magnificent buildings and, almost more than anything else, I think, from the glorious hills of this lovely country of Virginia.

And I am honored, too, in the escort that you have given, the Virginia National Guard, these young men from two schools which are known throughout the length and breadth of the land, V. M. I. and V. P. I.

In coming here today, in coming to take part in the dedication of the latest addition to our chain of veterans' hospitals, I do not seek to enumerate or to catalogue the many steps which have been taken by your Federal Government to care for its veterans of many wars, — generous steps, fine steps, and of late years, adequate steps.

Most of you in this great audience are from this neighborhood and in the years to come you will see how your Government treats the men who have served it, treats the men who will occupy this hospital. They will be your friends and your neighbors. I commend them to your care, and I am very certain that you will give it to them.

You see before you today a monument which is a very definite representation of the national policy of your Government, that its disabled and sick veterans shall be accorded the best treatment which medical and surgical science can possibly supply.

In a larger sense these buildings are a symbol of the broader policy, the policy that the Government is seeking to give aid not only to the veterans of its wars, but also to hundreds of thousands of other citizens — men, women and children who are handicapped by environment or by circumstance and are lacking to-day in what reasonable people call the essentials of modern civilization.

For a great many years we have seen a constantly growing realization of the fact that any large or small group in any community which lacks the elementary necessities of proper food, of decent housing, of adequate medical attention, of essential education, drags down the level of the whole country, and of necessity retards the progress of the whole country. It is the same thought, to put it into naval terms, as to say that the speed of a fleet is the speed of the slowest vessel in the fleet. Or, to put it in military terms, the speed of an army is the speed of the slowest unit comprising that army.

In one sense these men and women and children that I am talking about are not forgotten people — I believe you have heard that phrase before — for the very good reason that we have known of their existence and have appreciated their plight for many years. But, in another sense they have been forgotten, for it has only been in recent years that Government, as such, has undertaken to help them on a national scale.

The further we go in our survey to find out who these people are and where they live, the more appalled I am by the magnitude of our task. Most of us know in general terms of the slum conditions which exist in many of the cities of America. Most of us know, from hearsay or from personal knowledge, of people who have lived for generations in back eddies remote from the active stream of life. But, I think, we have failed to realize the existence of those underprivileged people who are present and largely forgotten in practically every single one of the more than three thousand counties that make up the forty-eight States of the Union.

The improvement of their hard lot — for they exist in every community — is a definite obligation on all of our citizens and I am confident that the veterans of our American wars will be among the first to recognize this fact.

The improvement of their hard lot compels our immediate

exertions, not only because of the individual human beings who are suffering today, but also because future generations of American citizens will be the descendants of those who are now in need. In this thought also the veterans of our wars will go along.

Let it be well remembered that the hundreds of thousands of men and women and children to whom I have referred, scattered throughout our Nation, have no splendid hospitals for their care, have no medical attention, such as will be provided in this veterans' home, have no opportunities for adequate education, and can but suffer the ills of their lives according to their own individual circumstances.

You have heard it said that we must restore prosperity. You have heard some kind people say that the country is distinctly better off from a material point of view than it was last year. I am inclined to agree with them. But, other people, who fail to think things through, forget that one cause of the depression which we are beginning to leave behind, was the very existence of millions of men, women and children who have been and continue to be a definite drag against the return of prosperity.

It must remain our constant objective to eliminate the causes of depression and the drags on prosperity. It must be our constant objective to do what we can to raise these people up to a higher standard of living, to a better chance in life. It will cost money to do it. In the spending of this money, it goes without saying that we must have due regard for the good credit of the Government of the United States. That, my friends, means that we cannot spend at once or in any given year all that we could possibly spend.

I mentioned once upon a time that we must do first things first. The care of the disabled, the sick, the destitute and the starving in all ranks of our population — that, my friends, is the first thing. To this the Veterans of American Wars give their approval in agreement with the overwhelming majority of our other citizens.

I make this statement in regard to the Veterans of America because I believe in them, because I am confident of their patriotism, their understanding of our national needs; and I make it because of two other reasons. The first is that our Federal Government and our State Governments have given to them many privileges not accorded to other citizens; and the other reason is that it has been amply demonstrated that the Veterans of the World War, today in the prime of life, are better off on the average, from the point of view of employment and of annual income than the average of any other great group of our citizens. That is why I know they will go along with my thought of caring first for the great masses of people in this country who are crying for care and who need it now.

So, my friends, as I look out on these beautiful mountains, I cannot help feeling that we should let these facts about our country, together with this great monument — this veterans' hospital and all the other institutions of their kind throughout the country — serve as a symbolic and bold denial of any careless statement that the United States does not take care of those who have served it in war. But, more than that, I should like to have this monument and all the others throughout the length and breadth of the land serve as a symbolic affirmance of our American belief in the underlying patriotic willingness of everybody in the country — veterans, non-veterans, men, women and children — to put first things first.

That is the way of American progress. This symbol, which we dedicate today, will live all through the years to remind us that we are going to make progress in an American way.

169 ❪ Address upon Receiving Honorary Degree at the College of William and Mary, Williamsburg, Virginia. October 20, 1934

Mr. President, Governor Perry, my fellow students of William and Mary, my friends:

I VALUE far beyond the sentiment conveyed by my mere acknowledgment in words the honor that you, in behalf of this historic institution, have conferred upon me today.

I well know the great tradition that the College of William and Mary has carried through the centuries. You have taught, you have inspired and you have honored the great and devoted men who were responsible in such large part for the shaping of the cause of American liberty.

President Bryan, on this occasion of your inauguration as President of this institution, I congratulate you on the opportunity for service that lies before you. In my official capacity, I can bring to you the greetings of the Nation and I think I can take it upon myself, as a son of Harvard, to extend her greetings to the oldest of a long line of distinguished sisters.

The first time I came to Williamsburg was more than twenty years ago. I shall always remember my arrival. I landed at Jamestown from a boat and started to walk to Williamsburg. Fortunately I was picked up by an old Negro in a horse and buggy and driven here over what was at that time an almost impassable road. In those days there was no capitol building, there was no palace of the Royal Governors, there was no Raleigh Tavern. Instead modern buildings had crept into this historic place, almost to the extent of crowding out the fine old colonial structures which were still standing.

What a thrill it has been to me to return today and to have the honor of formally opening the Duke of Gloucester Street, which rightly can be called the most historic avenue in America; what a joy it has been to come back and see the transformation

431

which has taken place, to see the capitol, the Governor's palace, all the other buildings which have arisen even since I was here two and a half years ago, to see sixty-one colonial buildings restored, ninety-four colonial buildings rebuilt, the magnificent gardens of colonial days reconstructed—in short, to see how through the renaissance of these physical landmarks the atmosphere of a whole glorious chapter in our history has been recaptured. Something of this spiritual relationship between the past, the present and the future was well described by the first man who sought to colonize America, Sir Walter Raleigh. He said:

"It is not the least debt that we owe unto history that it hath made us acquainted with our dead ancestors; and out of the depth and darkness of the earth delivered us their memory and fame."

I am happy to say that the Federal Government, inspired by the fine vision and example of Mr. Rockefeller in recreating Williamsburg, has effectively taken up the preservation of other historic shrines near by. Six miles to the west of us, we have acquired Jamestown Island and we are now carrying on the necessary archaeological and research work to determine what should be done in the preservation of that hallowed spot. Fourteen miles to the east of us at Yorktown the National Park Service has acquired many thousand acres of land, and is actively carrying out the restoration of the symbol of the final victory of the war for American independence. When the work in these three places is completed, we shall have saved for future generations the Nation's birthplace at Jamestown, the cradle of liberty at Williamsburg, and the sealing of our independence at Yorktown.

Nearly two centuries ago it was to William and Mary College that Thomas Jefferson came in 1760. Here he studied for two years, remaining five years longer in Williamsburg to pursue the study of law. It was here in Williamsburg that he was admitted to the bar. It was to Williamsburg that he returned, first as a member of the House of Burgesses, then as Governor of Virginia, following Patrick Henry. He lived in the Governor's palace during his term and later served on the Board of Visitors of the college. It was largely the result of his recommendations, I am told, that the curriculum of the college was broadened to provide education in law, medicine, modern languages, mathematics and philosophy. No doubt inspired by his reflections on government, human liberty and the necessity of education, Jefferson throughout his life was interested in designing a system of education for his State and for the Nation. I like to think of him, not only as a statesman, but as the enlightened father of American education.

And, strange as it may seem, I believe it is entirely fitting that a statesman should have also been an educator. As education grows it becomes, of necessity, a partner of government.

When Jefferson wrote his "Notes on Virginia," he discussed the education then prevailing at William and Mary, pointing out the essentially liberal education that this college was giving to its students. He observed that in order to provide a more advanced type of education, the subjects of the six professorships had been changed after the Revolutionary War. It is a matter of very great importance to all of us that one of the six was the professorship of law and of what is now called political science. The teaching of law and of the science of government thus established as an academic discipline in this institution was made significant by the intellectual leadership of George Wythe, who was appraised by Jefferson as "one of the greatest men of his age." The study of this subject, because essentially it touches every human impulse, every human problem, becomes one of the greatest means for the broad education of men who enter every walk of life. It can become the touchstone of universal culture.

Law in itself is not enough. Man must build himself more broadly. The purpose of education, shown by these various subjects of instruction indicated by the builders of William and Mary, was not to train specialists, but to educate men broadly. They were attempting to train not merely doctors, lawyers and business men, but broad-gauged citizens of the Nation and of the world. They were, in short, training men for citizenship in our great Republic.

This was in the spirit of the Old America, and it is, I believe, in the spirit of America today. The necessities of our time demand that men avoid being set in grooves, that they avoid the occupational pre-destination of the older world, and that in the face of the change and development in America, they must have a sufficiently broad and comprehensive conception of the world in which they live to meet its changing problems with resourcefulness and practical vision.

There is in the spirit of a liberal education something of the self-confidence and the adaptability that is characteristic of our country. The pioneer does not call his life a failure if he comes to the end of one path. He knows that there are others, and with a sense of direction and a will to persevere, his life can go on with confidence into the uncertainties of the future.

All of us must honor and encourage those young men and young women whose ambitions lead them to seek specialization in science and in scholarship. Our great universities are properly providing adequate facilities for the development of specialists in science and in scholarship. The Nation is using their services in every form of human activity. Private business employs them. Private enterprise and government will continue to do so.

But at the same time there is a definite place in American life —an important place—for broad, liberal and non-specialized education. Every form of cooperative human endeavor cries out for men and women who, in their thinking processes, will know something of the broader aspects of any given problem. Government is using many men and women of this type — people who have the non-specialized point of view and who at the same time have a general and extraordinarily comprehensive knowledge not of the details, but of the progress and the purposes which underlie the work of the specialists themselves.

The noble list of those who have gone out into life from the halls of William and Mary is in greater part distinguished because these graduates came to know and to understand the needs

434

of their Nation as a whole. They thought and acted, not in terms of specialization, not in terms of a locality, but rather in the broad sense of national needs. In the olden days those needs were confined to a narrow seaboard strip. Later the needs gradually extended to the Blue Ridge and across through the mountains to the fair lands of Tennessee and Kentucky. Later still they spread throughout the great Middle West and across the plains and the Rockies to the Pacific Ocean.

It is in the realization of these needs in their national scope of today that the present and future generations of William and Mary can best carry forward the fine traditions of their centuries.

So I would extend my heartiest good wishes to the College of William and Mary, built early in the morning of American life, dedicated to the education of the makers of a great Republic, seeking to enrich and broaden the meaning of education, and seeking, above all things, to recognize that republican institutions are, in the last analysis, the application to human affairs of those broad human ideals that a liberal education preserves, enriches and expands in our beloved land.

170 ⟨Address at Constitution Hall, Washington, D. C., Bankers' Convention — "The Time Is Ripe for an Alliance of All Forces Intent Upon the Business of Recovery." October 24, 1934

I AM glad to be here tonight at your invitation to speak to you informally about some of our common problems. As many of you know by personal experience, it is not a new thing for me to talk with bankers. I have been seeing many of your number almost daily during the past year and a half, and let me make it quite clear that in these meetings I have not done all the talking. I have been a good listener and I have asked many questions. I am frank in saying to you that I have found that there is the same striking lack of unanimity of opinion among bankers that characterizes many other groups in the country. It has been my purpose to seek out underlying agreement in the opinions that bankers have expressed and to encourage agreement.

You will recognize, I think, that a true function of the head of the Government of the United States is to find among many discordant elements that unity of purpose that is best for the Nation as a whole. This is necessary because government is not merely one of many coordinate groups in the community or the Nation, but government is essentially the outward expression of the unity and the leadership of all groups. Consequently the old fallacious notion of the bankers on one side and the Government on the other side as being more or less equal and independent units, has passed away. Government by the necessity of things must be the leader, must be the judge of the conflicting interests of all groups in the community, including bankers. The Government is the outward expression of the common life of all citizens.

What is a bank and what are its relations with the people? Why do the people through their Governments supervise banks? The people put their money into banks. They do this in order to protect it and in some cases to have it earn a small income. It costs money to provide this service and, therefore, the banks are permitted to invest these deposits in order to pay their expenses and to provide a reasonable profit to their stockholders. The public has no means of knowing whether the bank is safe, whether it is making safe investments, so the public turns to its Government to supervise the bank. Government has accepted this responsibility.

In its relations with bankers, the purpose of government should be threefold: first, to promote the confidence of the people in banks and banking in view of the important service that banks and banking may perform for the people as a whole; second, to make this confidence a real and living thing by assisting banks to render themselves useful, to render themselves worthy of this confidence through wise supervision. A third purpose now offers itself, and I wish with all earnestness to press this point tonight.

436

Government should assert its leadership in encouraging not only the confidence of the people in banks, but the confidence of the banks in the people. In March, 1933, I asked the people of this country to renew their confidence in the banks of the country. They took me at my word. Tonight I ask the bankers of this country to renew their confidence in the people of this country. I hope you will take me at my word.

I need not recount the situation of the banks in the spring of 1933. I found that the restoration of banking activity itself was my first responsibility on assuming office. It was necessary that the Government throw itself squarely into the task of bringing back to the banks the deposits of millions of citizens. As a result of my appeal the people responded by restoring their confidence in the banks of the United States.

The primary purpose accomplished, it became necessary that the Congress and the Administration enact measures to build up the banking structure so that it could once more provide support for the economic life of the country. Moreover, it had to be built —and we built it—strong enough so that it could resist future stresses and strains. Government found it necessary to create and get under way new emergency credit agencies and to use to the fullest extent the already existing Reconstruction Finance Corporation. These credit agencies moved with heroic energy, and it was a source of the utmost satisfaction to find that when the Federal Deposit Insurance Corporation went into operation the banking structure had regained a very considerable amount of its strength and its vitality. I think it is only fair to say that never since the formation of our Government has such a task been achieved in so short a time. Happily, the present security of our banks bears witness to the wise course that we pursued.

I find almost universal agreement among bankers that these agencies must continue until such time as the banks and other private credit agencies are themselves able and ready to take over these lending functions; and when that time comes, I shall be only too glad to curtail the activities of these public agencies in proportion to the taking up of the slack by privately owned agencies. I venture to suggest to you that when the history of these years comes to be written, while the closing and the reopening of the banks will occupy a prominent place, even greater interest will be centered in the fact that within a few months not only was the banking structure strengthened but the great governmental lending agencies went into action and also saved from disastrous deflation, liquidation and loss a vast portion of the farms, homes, railroads and corporations of America. That action definitely rescued the security and happiness of millions of our people.

Just as it is to be expected that the banks will resume their responsibility and take up the burden that the Government has assumed through its credit agencies, so I assume and expect that private business generally will be financed by the great credit resources which the present liquidity of banks makes possible. Our traditional system has been built upon this principle, and the recovery of our economic life should be accomplished through the assumption of this responsibility. The present steady and unmistakable revival of public demand for goods and services should provide the assurance necessary to the financing of industrial life. The Government is bending every effort through the Treasury, the Federal Reserve system, the Reconstruction Finance Corporation, the Securities and Exchange Commission and the Federal Housing Administration to facilitate and encourage the revival of private investment. I commend the objectives of the Housing Administration to your immediate consideration, but at the same time I ask you to note that all of these new agencies are seeking consultation and cooperation with you bankers.

While there lies before us still the necessity for large expenditures for the relief of unemployment, I think we should all proceed in the expectation that the revival of business activity will steadily reduce this burden.

I am gratified to know of the expressions of belief, public and private, by your members that the speed that we shall make toward this objective is something that no one has the wisdom or the hardihood to estimate. This recognition reflects a growing appreciation of the problems resting upon a responsible Chief Executive.

With respect to international relationships, I have been glad to note the growing appreciation in other Nations of the desirability of arriving, as quickly as possible, at a point of steadiness of prices and values. This objective of a greater steadiness of prices and values we have constantly kept before us as our own national American policy.

The fact that American business men and bankers are devoting more and more individual study and attention to the wider problems of our Nation, to the wider problems of international affairs, is manifesting itself today in many ways. It seems to me that this is a very important development. Let me make it clear to you that the Government of the United States has daily and even hourly contact with sources of information which cover not only every State and section of our own country, but also every other portion of the habitable globe. This information, my friends, is more complete, more informative and, I believe, more accurate than that possessed by any private agency.

I need not tell you that true wealth is not a static thing. It is a living thing made out of the disposition of men to create and to distribute the good things of life with rising standards of living. Wealth grows when men cooperate; but it stagnates in an atmosphere of misunderstanding and misrepresentation. Here, in America, the material means are at hand for the growth of true wealth. It is in the spirit of American institutions that wealth should come as the reward of hard labor — hard labor, I repeat — of mind and hand. That is a pretty good definition of what we call the profit system. Its real fulfillment comes in the general recognition of the rights of each factor of the community. It is not in the spirit of partisans, but it is in the spirit of partners, that America has progressed. The time is ripe for an alliance of all forces intent upon the business of recovery. In such an alliance will be found business and banking, agriculture and industry, and labor and capital. What an all-America team that would be! The possibilities of such a team kindle the imagination. They encourage our determination. They make easier the tasks of those in your Government who are leading it.

My friends, the Nation does not merely trust or hope that we will always do our duty. No, it is more than that. The Nation is justified in expecting that all of us will do our duty.

171 ❲ Letter to the Navy on Navy Day. October 27, 1934

My dear Mr. Secretary:

IT IS gratifying to learn of the plans to observe Navy Day in accordance with the custom which has been followed annually since 1922 of setting apart the birthday of the late President Theodore Roosevelt for that occasion.

From the very beginning of our national life, the Navy has always been, and justly deserves to be, an object of special pride to the American people. Its record is indeed one to inspire such sentiments. I am very sure that the commemoration of this day each year tends to bring the Navy into closer contact with our people, from whom it draws its inspiration.

It is with real pleasure and a feeling of deep personal pride for our Navy that I send to the officers and men of the Navy the Nation's congratulations on this Navy Day, and I am certain that they will continue to justify the confidence of their countrymen and perpetuate the high endeavor, efficiency and tradition that has marked the service of the Navy to the Nation.

Very sincerely yours,

The Honorable,
The Secretary of the Navy,
Washington, D. C.

172 ❡ Consolidation of the National Emergency Council, the Executive Council and the Industrial Emergency Committee. Executive Order No. 6889-A. October 31, 1934

WHEREAS it is desirable in the public interest that all members of the Executive Council be included in the National Emergency Council and that their functions and duties be consolidated, and that the functions and duties of the Industrial Emergency Committee be coordinated with those of said Council:

Now, THEREFORE, by virtue of the authority vested in me as President of the United States, by legislation (enacted by the Congress of the United States to meet the national economic emergency and to provide relief necessary to protect the general welfare of the people) or otherwise, I hereby order that the Executive Order of July 11, 1933, No. 6202-A, creating the temporary Executive Council; the Executive Order of November 17, 1933, No. 6433-A, creating the National Emergency Council; the Executive Order of December 18, 1933, No. 6513, amending said order; the Executive Order of June 30, 1934, No. 6770, creating the Industrial Emergency Committee; the Executive Order of August 31, 1934, No. 6836, amending said order; and the Executive Order of September 27, 1934, No. 6860, amending said order, shall conform to the following orders:

(1) The National Emergency Council shall be composed of the following and such other members as the President may designate:

The President of the United States	The Secretary of the Navy
The Secretary of State	The Secretary of the Interior
The Secretary of the Treasury	The Secretary of Agriculture
The Secretary of War	The Secretary of Commerce
The Attorney General	The Secretary of Labor
The Postmaster General	The Director of the Budget
	The Secretary to the President

The Hon. L. W. Robert, Jr., Assistant Secretary of the Treasury

The Administrator of Agricultural Adjustment

The Administrator of Federal Emergency Relief

The Chairman of the Board of the Reconstruction Finance Corporation

The Chairman of the Board of the Tennessee Valley Authority

The Chairman of the Federal Home Loan Bank Board

The Chairman of the Federal Trade Commission

The Director of Emergency Conservation Work

The Federal Coordinator of Transportation

The Governor of the Farm Credit Administration

The Adviser on Consumer Problems

The Chairman of the National Industrial Recovery Board

The Chairman of the Federal Alcohol Control Administration

The Federal Housing Administrator

The President of the Export-Import Banks of Washington, D. C.

The Chairman of the Federal Deposit Insurance Corporation

The Chairman of the Federal Power Commission

The Chairman of the Federal Communications Commission

The Chairman of the Securities and Exchange Commission

The Governor of the Federal Reserve Board

The Executive Director

(2) It shall be the purpose of the National Emergency Council (a) to provide for the orderly presentation of business to the President; (b) to coordinate inter-agency problems of organization and activity of Federal agencies; (c) to coordinate and make more efficient and productive the work of the field agencies of the Federal Government; (d) to cooperate with any Federal agency in performing such activities as the President may direct; and (e) to serve in an advisory capacity to the President and the Executive Director of the National Emergency Council.

(3) The Industrial Emergency Committee, as heretofore established, shall continue to exercise all the functions and duties heretofore imposed upon it and serve as a sub-committee of the National Emergency Council.

(4) The functions and duties of the Council shall be prescribed from time to time by the President, and such rules and regula-

442

tions as may be necessary to effectuate the purposes for which the Council is created shall be prescribed by the Executive Director and approved by the President.

(5) The Executive Director, Donald R. Richberg (whose leave of absence as General Counsel of the National Recovery Administration is hereby extended until further order, with pay, in order that he may fulfill the duties of Executive Director of the National Emergency Council and Director of the Industrial Emergency Committee), is authorized to execute the functions and to perform the duties vested in the Council by the President through such persons as the Executive Director shall designate, and he is further authorized to prescribe such rules and regulations as he may deem necessary to supplement, amplify, or carry out the purposes and intent of such rules and regulations as may be prescribed by him and approved by the President under the provisions of this order.

(6) The Executive Director may appoint, subject to the approval of the President, without regard to the Civil Service laws or the Classification Act of 1923, as amended, fix the compensation and prescribe the duties and authority of such officials and employees, and make such expenditures (including expenditures for personal services, and rent at the seat of the Government and elsewhere, for law books and books of reference, and for paper, binding, and printing) as may be necessary to carry into effect the provisions of this order. The Executive Director may also, with the consent of any board, commission, independent establishment, or executive department of the Government, including any field service thereof, avail himself of the services of the officials, employees, and the facilities thereof and, with the consent of the State or municipality concerned, may utilize such State and local officials and employees as he may deem necessary.

(7) All the members of the Executive Council having been now included in the National Emergency Council, the functions and duties of the Executive Council are hereby transferred to and vested in the National Emergency Council, and the separate existence of the Executive Council is hereby terminated. All rec-

ords, papers, and property of the Executive Council shall become records, papers, and property of the National Emergency Council; and all of the unexpended funds and appropriations for the use and maintenance of the Executive Council shall be available for expenditure by the National Emergency Council as above provided; and all employees of the Executive Council shall be transferred to and become employees of the National Emergency Council at their present grades and salaries, but such transfer shall not be construed to give such employees any civil service or other permanent status.

(8) The powers and duties herein conferred upon the National Emergency Council are in addition to, and not in derogation of, any powers and duties conferred upon such Council by any other order made by me.

NOTE: The foregoing Executive Order consolidated the Executive Council which was established July 11, 1933, by Executive Order No. 6202-A (see Item 94, Vol. II) with the National Emergency Council, which was established by Executive Order No. 6433-A, November 17, 1933 (see Item 163, Vol. II).

In addition there were some members added to represent the agencies created subsequent to the formation of the two councils.

173 ❈ Letter to the American Veterans' Association. October 31, 1934

My dear Commander Kinsolving:

WILL you please extend my greetings to the chapter leaders of the American Veterans' Association now gathered in national conference in New York City?

I have observed the aims of your organization and the Federal policy with regard to veterans' relief which it proposes. Briefly, you urge "Justice to the War Wounded, Justice to the War Dead, Justice to the American People." No one may dispute the fact that these interests are paramount.

It is, however, in the application of this policy that we find wide differences of opinion which keep this national problem so continuously before the American people and before the legislative and executive branches of their Government. These differences are augmented by the consideration required for those who served their country honorably under arms and who now find themselves too old or too ill to carry on.

Frank discussion among organized veterans' groups of the several phases of this problem I am convinced would be most helpful in its ultimate solution. That the tenor of these discussions becomes public information is also helpful, for, in the final analysis, the character of our Federal policy regarding veterans' relief rests with our citizens. We may, I am sure, depend upon our American people continuously to honor our veterans of whatever war and to fully meet the Nation's obligation to those who suffered in her service.

Very sincerely yours,

Commander Charles M. Kinsolving,
The American Veterans' Association, Inc.,
New York, New York.

174 ⟨ An Appeal for Support of the American Red Cross. November 1, 1934

OUR people continue to look to the American Red Cross as the kindly and always helpful good neighbor to whom they turn for practical aid in emergency. They do so with the assurance that this national relief agency, with an organization in thirteen thousand American communities, has not and will not fail them.

In the difficult twelve months which have elapsed since last November Red Cross volunteers throughout the land have worked in close cooperation with the Federal, State and local governments in their humanitarian labors. Their service has not been limited to aid in furnishing the actual necessities of life, but has extended to the equally important field of safeguarding public health and of training their neighbors in the proper methods of caring for the sick or the injured.

At the same time the organization has continued to fulfill its obligation as our agency of relief for every community visited by disaster.

The Red Cross is looked upon as the representative of all of our people in times of distress. In order that it may continue its service to humanity it is highly important that we lend our support through individual membership.

I hope everyone who possibly can do so will respond generously to the Red Cross appeal.

NOTE: A similar appeal for the support of the American Red Cross has been issued by me each year during my Administration.

175 ❲ White House Statement on Cost of Distribution of Electricity by the New York Power Authority. November 12, 1934

A REPORT on Cost of Distribution of Electricity adopted as a basis for the marketing of 1,100,000 horse power of current from the St. Lawrence River was filed today by the Power Authority of the State of New York with the President, after a three-year survey initiated under his administration as Governor.

This represents the first field survey and analysis ever undertaken and successfully completed on costs specifically segregated to cover distribution of electricity from the sub-station to the customer's meter. Generating and transmission costs of electricity have long been known and may readily be estimated for new power developments.

The report filed today establishes a yardstick on rates for the Northeastern area of the United States which can be applied to every city, town and rural community in connection with the development of the St. Lawrence River as a public power project. By use of this yardstick a saving of $194,000,000 a year for customers in New York, Pennsylvania, New Jersey and New England is shown by detailed figures included in the report.

The report has been filed simultaneously with the President, Governor Lehman and the Federal Power Commission. Local cost-of-distribution figures and reports are being made available to the mayors of seventeen municipalities in New York, including New York City, and of twelve cities in five other States in the Middle Atlantic, South Atlantic, North Central and Pacific Coast areas to which the study extended. A total of twenty-nine cities in six States were included in the survey.

The findings in the report vitally affect 7,000,000 customers for electricity throughout the Northeast and link the public power development on the St. Lawrence River with the national yardstick policy already in effect on the Tennessee, Columbia and Colorado Rivers.

Its major conclusions are as follows:

1. The cost of distributing electricity to homes and farms in New York State warrants a rate schedule which would charge not more than 3½¢ a kilowatt hour for a use of 50 kilowatt hours a month instead of the average of 6¢ which these customers are now paying. In terms of the monthly bill this would mean a reduction from $3.00 to $1.65, representing a saving of $1.35 a month, or more than $16.00 a year for this service.

2. The monthly savings would be even greater for the increased use of electricity which will follow such rate reductions. As home consumption rises above 50 kilowatt hours per month the rate schedule which this survey justifies would provide current at a steadily diminishing average cost per kilowatt hour. For a monthly use of 100 kilowatt hours the bill should not exceed $2.70, for 200 kilowatt hours, $4.20, and for 400 kilowatt hours used in a single month the home should not pay more than $6.80.

3. This means that when rate schedules are reduced to the measure provided by the public yardsticks being set up under the national power program, a majority of homes should get more than 100 kilowatt hours for the monthly bills under which they

447

now get only 50 kilowatt hours. In some cities in New York State bills are being paid for 50 kilowatt hours which should buy 200.

4. The reduction in charges to small business customers in the commercial class, to correspond with the cost of distribution found to be justifiable by this survey, would similarly cut the monthly bill of $9.00 for an average use of 184 kilowatt hours to about $5.40. This would mean a saving of $3.60 a month, or about $43.20 a year to the average customer in this class of service. With larger commercial use the monthly and annual savings would be greater.

5. The costs upon which these conclusions rest are for private operation of electric systems, including a 6 percent return on all useful fixed capital, and an additional 5½ percent to cover depreciation, taxes and insurance. Municipalities owning their own electrical systems, the report shows, could provide service even more cheaply while carrying the full burden of fixed charges, including property, franchise and state and federal income taxes today borne by private companies.

6. When it is considered that the total electric bill of New York State is nearly $300,000,000 a year and that the consumers of electricity in the Northeastern States which will be affected by this yardstick pay over $681,000,000 annually for this service, it is apparent that the savings will be very large and will materially reduce the overhead cost which depresses the spending power of consumers throughout these states. The report estimates savings totaling $63,000,000 a year for New York State alone, or a reduction of 22 percent in the total electric bill. For the Northeastern area which will be affected by the yardstick the savings, including those on municipal street lighting, are estimated at $194,-000,000, representing a reduction of 27 percent in the total now paid for electricity.

(With respect to the foregoing report of the New York State Power Authority, see Chapter IV, Vol. I and note to Item 34, Vol. V.)

176 (A Letter to the United States Conference of Mayors on Mutual Problems.

November 13, 1934

My dear Sirs:

I AM glad to have this opportunity to extend my greetings to the United States Conference of Mayors, and through your organization to thank the mayors of the various cities of this country for the help and support the cities have given the National Administration in carrying out its program for national recovery.

During the past year I have conferred, from time to time, with the official committees of the Conference in an attempt to appraise and consider those problems which mutually confront our several levels of government. Through this contact with the representatives of our larger urban areas, it has been possible to secure a first-hand picture of conditions existing in and facing municipal governments. This fine cooperation has enabled the Federal Government to develop national policies and programs which have taken local needs into consideration.

Our efforts along the road of economic recovery have been productive of substantial results. It is undoubtedly true that the coming session of Congress will give further attention to proposals involving unemployment relief, public works, unemployment insurance, old-age pensions and housing, all of which vitally affect the city governments. I cannot say what final action Congress will take with reference to these subjects, but I assure you the Federal Government is anxious to work effectively and cooperatively on all of these common problems.

It is through teamwork of all governmental units that victory may be attained.

I wish you all success in your discussions and regret that I cannot personally meet with you.

Very sincerely yours,

United States Conference of Mayors,
Chicago, Illinois.

177 ❧ White House Statement on Creation of a Loan Committee to Coordinate Federal Lending Activities. November 14, 1934

To obtain improved cooperation among Federal agencies engaged in lending Government funds, either directly or indirectly, the President has created a Loan Committee comprising the heads of the following departments and agencies, with the Secretary of the Treasury designated as Chairman:

Henry Morgenthau, Jr.,	*Secretary of the Treasury*
Harold L. Ickes,	*Secretary of the Interior*
and as ——	*Administrator of the Emergency Administration of Public Works*
	Administrator of the Emergency Public Works Housing Corporation
W. I. Myers,	*Governor of the Farm Credit Administration*
John H. Fahey,	*Chairman of the Federal Home Loan Bank Board*
and as ——	*Chairman of the Home Owners Loan Corporation*
Chester C. Davis,	*Administrator of the Agricultural Adjustment Administration*
George N. Peek,	*President of the Export-Import Bank*
Lynn P. Talley,	*President of the Commodity Credit Corporation*
Leo T. Crowley,	*Chairman of the Federal Deposit Insurance Corporation*
Jesse H. Jones,	*Chairman of the Reconstruction Finance Corporation*
Marriner S. Eccles,	*Governor of the Federal Reserve Board*
James A. Moffett,	*Administrator of the Federal Housing Administration*

NOTE: The object of this committee was as stated, "the general coordination of all phases of the Government's activities with respect to the lending of money or the taking of evidence of indebtedness by governmental corporations or agencies in connection with their operations." It was understood that the committee would act also as a clearing house to consider and discuss banking and financial legislation proposed in the Congress.

The committee considered and discussed the financial needs of farm credit agencies, housing agencies, the various activities of the Reconstruction Finance Corporation and the other lending activities conducted in furtherance of the Government's recovery program. Efforts were made to coordinate and consolidate activities conducted in the same field by various agencies, particularly those interested in banking supervision and in housing.

The committee was especially active and helpful in the 1934-35 session of Congress in coordinating and clearing the legislative programs and proposals of the various lending agencies, such as the Banking Act of 1935, the Federal Deposit Insurance Act, the United States Savings Bond legislation, the extension of the lending powers of the Reconstruction Finance Corporation, the continuance of the Export-Import Banks and the Commodity Credit Corporation, the perfecting of facilities for the extension of agri-cultural credit, and an increase in the lending power of the Home Owners Loan Corporation.

The committee has also been a convenient medium for the consideration of special problems that arise from time to time in the field of Government finance. In 1936 it made a survey of possible reductions in authorized appropriations and savings that might be effected by the financial agencies of the Government.

The Interdepartmental Loan Committee has served to fit in with the general financing program of the Treasury, the borrowings of the Government agencies, such as the Federal Intermediate Credit Banks and the Home Owners Loan Corporation, which sell their securities directly to the investment market.

In this way the functions of this committee have been to coordinate the entire financial program of the Government in the matters of securing needed funds, extending credit to the various and numerous classes of borrowers to whom the Government lends, and recommending the necessary banking and financial legislation.

178 ⟨A Message to the National Grange. November 14, 1934

To the members of the Grange:

F OR many years, as you know, I have been a member of the Grange. I have felt at home in it because it embodies the fine flavor of rural living which I myself have known and loved. Beyond this it has been an instrument for expressing in useful activity the highest sentiments and deepest loyalties of Americans. Now, as perhaps never before, the Grange has an opportunity to extend its service to Agriculture and to the Nation in helping to adapt the democratic process to an age of fundamental economic change. Only from the thoughts and efforts of such groups as the members of the Grange can the new American democracy be built to stand the tests of time.

Mr. L. J. Taber,
Master, The National Grange,
Hartford, Connecticut

179 ❬Address to Advisory Council of the Committee on Economic Security on the Problems of Economic and Social Security. November 14, 1934

I AM glad to welcome you to the White House and to tell you that I am happy that there is so much interest in the problem of economic security. Last June I said that this winter we might well make a beginning in the great task of providing social insurance for the citizen and his family. I have not changed my opinion. I shall have recommendations on this subject to present to the incoming Congress.

Many details are still to be settled. The Committee on Economic Security was created to advise me on this matter. It will bring to me, not any preconceived views, but a mature judgment after careful study of the problem and after consultation with the Advisory Conference and the cooperating committees.

On some points it is possible to be definite. Unemployment insurance will be in the program. I am still of the opinion expressed in my message of June eighth that this part of social insurance should be a cooperative Federal-State undertaking. It is important that the Federal Government encourage States which are ready to take this progressive step. It is no less important that all unemployment insurance reserve funds be held and invested by the Federal Government, so that the use of these funds as a means of stabilization may be maintained in central management and employed on a national basis. Unemployment insurance must be set up with the purpose of decreasing rather than increasing unemployment. It is, of course, clear that because of their magnitude the investment and liquidation of reserve funds must be within control of the Government itself.

For the administration of insurance benefits, the States are the most logical units. At this stage, while unemployment insurance is still untried in this country and there is such a great diversity of opinion on many details, there is room for some degree of difference in methods, though not in principles. That would be impossible under an exclusively national system. And so I can say to you who have come from all parts of the country that not only will there have to be a Federal law on unemployment insurance, but State laws will also be needed. In January the great majority of the State Legislatures will convene, as well as Congress. You who are interested in seeing that unemployment insurance is established on a nationwide basis should make your plans accordingly.

We must not allow this type of insurance to become a dole through the mingling of insurance and relief. It is not charity. It must be financed by contributions, not taxes.

What I have said must not be understood as implying that we should do nothing further for the people now on relief. On the contrary, they must be our first concern. We must get them back into productive employment and as we do so we can bring them under the protection of the insurance system. Let us profit by the mistakes of foreign countries and keep out of unemployment insurance every element which is actuarially unsound.

There are other matters with which we must deal before we shall give adequate protection to the individual against the many economic hazards. Old age is at once the most certain, and for many people the most tragic of all hazards. There is no tragedy in growing old, but there is tragedy in growing old without means of support.

As Governor of New York, it was my pleasure to recommend passage of the Old-Age Pension Act which, I am told, is still generally regarded as the most liberal in the country. In approving the bill, I expressed my opinion that full solution of this problem is possible only on insurance principles. It takes so very much money to provide even a moderate pension for everybody, that when the funds are raised from taxation only a "means test" must necessarily be made a condition of the grant of pensions.

I do not know whether this is the time for any Federal legislation on old-age security. Organizations promoting fantastic schemes have aroused hopes which cannot possibly be fulfilled. Through their activities they have increased the difficulties of getting sound legislation; but I hope that in time we may be able to provide security for the aged—a sound and a uniform system which will provide true security.

There is also the problem of economic loss due to sickness—a very serious matter for many families with and without incomes, and therefore, an unfair burden upon the medical profession. Whether we come to this form of insurance soon or later on, I am confident that we can devise a system which will enhance and not hinder the remarkable progress which has been made and is being made in the practice of the professions of medicine and surgery in the United States.

In developing each component part of the broad program for economic security, we must not lose sight of the fact that there can be no security for the individual in the midst of general insecurity. Our first task is to get the economic system to function so that there will be a greater general security. Everything that we do with intent to increase the security of the individual will, I am confident, be a stimulus to recovery.

At this time, we are deciding on long-time objectives. We are developing a plan of administration into which can be fitted the various parts of the security program when it is timely to do so. We cannot work miracles or solve all our problems at once. What we can do is to lay a sound foundation on which we can build a structure to give a greater measure of safety and happiness to the individual than any we have ever known. In this task you can greatly help.

NOTE: The Committee on Economic Security had been appointed by me on June 29, 1934 (see Item 117, this volume). On November 10th, I announced the appointment of an Advisory Council to assist the Committee on Economic Security in formulating a program for social insurance. It was composed of representatives of industry, labor and social welfare. The Chairman of the Advisory Council was Frank P. Graham, President of the University of North Carolina. It met at the White House on November 14, 1934, and on that occasion I made the foregoing address.

The work of this Council and Committee led to the recommendations made by me to the Congress and to the adoption by the Congress of the Social Security Act of 1935 (see Vol. IV, Item 107).

180 ⟨ A Thanksgiving Day Proclamation.
November 15, 1934

I, FRANKLIN D. ROOSEVELT, President of the United States of America, hereby designate Thursday, the twenty-ninth day of November, 1934, as a Day of Thanksgiving for the people of the Nation.

Thus to set aside in the autumn of each year a day on which to give thanks to Almighty God for the blessings of life is a wise and reverent custom, long cherished by our people. It is fitting that we should again observe this custom.

During the past year we have been given courage and fortitude to meet the problems which have confronted us in our national life. Our sense of social justice has deepened. We have been given vision to make new provisions for human welfare and happiness, and in a spirit of mutual helpfulness we have cooperated to translate vision into reality.

More greatly have we turned our hearts and minds to things spiritual. We can truly say, "What profiteth it a Nation if it gain the whole world and lose its own soul."

With gratitude in our hearts for what has already been achieved, may we, with the help of God, dedicate ourselves anew to work for the betterment of mankind.

NOTE: For the other Thanksgiving Day Proclamations issued by me during my first term as President, see Item 165, Vol. II; Item 160, Vol. IV; Item 215, Vol. V.

181 ❨ Address at George Rogers Clark Celebration, Harrodsburg, Kentucky — "Survival Calls for a New Pioneering on Our Part." November 16, 1934

Senator Barkley, Governor Laffoon, and, after what your Senior Senator has said, I think I can say, "My Fellow Pioneers":

WE, PIONEERS of 1934, are come together today to honor the pioneers of a century and a half ago. On my journey hither I have been reading once more of those thrilling days which saw the first peopling of these fair lands beyond the mountains. It was the perfect moment which destiny offered to our forebears to create these United States.

It has seemed to me in reading history that Harrodsburg can lay claim to having been the scene of more historical first things than any spot I have ever known, and as you know, I am very much in favor of first things. It seems not enough that this delightful and historic place was the first permanent settlement well beyond the mountains; that there were here the earliest pioneer homes; that here came the first school teacher and the first doctor; that here was the first court of the West. That seems not enough; to this you must add many other firsts — the first corn raised in Kentucky, the first peach trees and apple trees planted, the first wheat fields, the first grist mill and, perhaps most important of all, the first spinning wheel.

That is why I am happy that, in addition to paying tribute to

456

the memory of George Rogers Clark who led his men from here to his great invasion and preservation of the inland empire for the United States, you are also honoring the men and women who made his expedition possible and who followed him with the permanency of home building.

It has come to be a generally accepted rule of civilized Nations that mere discovery of new lands conveys no sovereignty; and, indeed, that mere conquest conveys but little better title. It is, after all, only the peopling of the wilderness which gives permanency to the form of an ordered society.

There is a very definite analogy between those days and our days. Upon the pioneers of these great stretches of the Central West were forced new activities because of the circumstances of their surroundings. They were compelled to hew out a new path —a path that was dependent not on the ax and the rifle alone, but upon their ability to govern themselves in new ways as well.

To most of the pioneers the necessities of the new life called for efforts and experiments to which they had not been accustomed in their earlier years in the more ordered civilization of the Atlantic seaboard. For them, survival itself demanded immediate and new action.

I have called those of us who are here today "pioneers of 1934." And I mean everything that that word "pioneer" implies. We, too, in these latter years throughout the length and breadth of our land have come to a realization of the pregnant fact that the accustomed order of our formerly established lives does not suffice to meet the perils and the problems which today we are compelled to face. Again, mere survival calls for a new pioneering on our part.

Some portion of the blood of the Colonists and the pioneers who worked their way, through generations, across the mountains and across the plains and again across the mountains until they came to the Pacific, is present in very large part in the veins of millions of our people today and, in even greater part, in the veins of those whom I see before me today. More than that, the

457

example and the spirit of those earlier Americans are present in the mind and the heart of all our population.

The events we celebrate today were so vital in the extension of the new Nation, that it has been thought proper for Congress to commemorate them not only in the spirit of gratitude, but in the spirit of emulation, as an example to guide us in the conquest of new frontiers of the spirit, frontiers of the spirit that are neither physical nor geographical.

We are carrying on, we shall carry on the purposes of these men and women of Harrodsburg. They were hewing out a Commonwealth, and I like that word "Commonwealth."

All over this Nation we are hewing out a Commonwealth — a Commonwealth of the States which we hope will give to its people more truly than any that has gone before, the fulfillment of security, of freedom, of opportunity and of happiness which America asks and which America is entitled to receive.

NOTE: This was the beginning of a trip which I made to inspect the work of the Tennessee Valley Authority. After my trip through the Tennessee River Valley, I stopped at Warm Springs for a stay until my return to Washington on December 5, 1934. Items 182, 183, 184, 185, 189 are speeches made by me on this trip.

182 ⟨ Extemporaneous Remarks at Clinch River Below the Norris Dam. November 16, 1934

My friends:

I AM getting a great thrill out of this. I was thinking today that it was only a year ago last January, less than two years ago and before I became President, that I came down to Muscle Shoals with Senator Norris and a number of other gentlemen. At that time a very great idea was just beginning to take shape. It was only an idea then, and when I think of the very small period of time that has elapsed since then I am very proud to have had something to do with it. But I am much prouder of the way you good people are carrying that idea into actual fact. All of you who are working here at this great dam project and all of the good people throughout the Tennessee Valley who are working on the rest of this great program some day will be known as veterans. You will be known as veterans of a new kind of war, the kind of war that is going to improve conditions for millions and millions of our fellow American citizens.

All I can say to you is "God speed the work." You are going at it with a splendid spirit, and I am coming back here again some time when you get this work done.

183 (Extemporaneous Remarks at Corinth, Miss. November 17, 1934

My friends:

I AM glad to come into the district of my friend, John Rankin, to come back to Mississippi after an absence of six long years.

We have had a great day today. We started with a great friend of the people this morning — Andrew Jackson. We are ending up the day with another friend of the people — the Tennessee Valley Authority. As you all know, I have been tremendously interested in the work that you good people have been carrying on. You are carrying out the ideal of working out things for the benefit of the average man and average woman by meeting new problems with new methods.

I want to say a special word of commendation for the way you in Alcorn County have worked out an experiment that is going to succeed — the Alcorn County Electric Power Association. There are two points in regard to what you have done that ought to be known all over the United States — north and south and east and west. The first is that you are treating your county as a unit and, in treating it that way, you are giving an opportunity to the people who live on the farm equal with the people who live in the city. The other interesting fact, I am told, is that with cheaper rates of electricity than you have ever had before, you are going to pay off in five and a half years the money you have borrowed.

My friends, in this you are doing something not only for yourselves, but for the rest of the United States. You are proving something that some of us have believed to be true for a great many years. And, in proving it to the rest of the United States, you are going to make life easier for the average family in a great many other places. That is why I am very glad to stop here tonight. I wish I could come here by daylight and see more of you. I will do that some time later on.

I want to congratulate you and tell you how happy I am in hearing about the fine public spirit that Corinth and Alcorn County are showing to the United States of America.

184 ⟨ Extemporaneous Remarks at Tupelo, Miss. November 18, 1934

Senator Harrison, Governor Conner, Mr. Mayor, my friends:

I SHALL not make a speech to you today because we are assembled on this glorious Sunday morning more as neighbors than as anything else.

I have had a very wonderful three days; and everywhere that I have gone, the good people have come as neighbors to talk with me, and they have not come by the thousands — they have come literally by the acres.

This is the first time in my life that I have had the privilege of seeing this section of the State of Mississippi. Many, many years ago, when Pat Harrison and I were almost boys, I became acquainted with his stamping ground down on the Gulf. Today I am especially glad to come into the northern part of the State.

Two years ago, in 1932, during the campaign, and again in January, 1933, I came through Kentucky — through the Tennessee Valley — and what I saw on those trips, what I saw of human beings, made the tears come to my eyes. The great outstanding thing to me for these past three days has been the change in the looks on people's faces. It has not been only a physical thing. It has not been the contrast between what was actually a scarcity of raiment or a lack of food two years ago and better clothing and more food today. Rather it is a something in people's faces. I think you understand what I mean. There was not much hope in those days. People were wondering what was going to come to this country. And yet today I see not only hope, but I see determination and a knowledge that all is well with the country, and that we are coming back.

I suppose that you good people know a great deal more of the efforts that we have been making in regard to the work of the Tennessee Valley Authority than I do, because you have seen its application in your own counties and your towns and your own homes; and, therefore, it would be like carrying coals to Newcastle for me to tell you about what has been done.

But perhaps in referring to it I can use you as a text—a text that may be useful to many other parts of the Nation; because people's eyes are upon you and because what you are doing here is going to be copied in every State of the Union before we get through.

We recognize that there will be a certain amount of—what shall I say?—rugged opposition to this development, but I think we recognize also that the opposition is fading as the weeks and months go by—fading in the light of practical experience.

I cite certain figures for the benefit of the gentlemen of the press, who have come hither from many climes. I am told that from March of this year, when you started using T.V.A. power, the consumption of power for residential purposes has risen from 41,000 kilowatts to 89,000 kilowatts—an increase of 126 percent. I understand that from the financial point of view, in spite of various fairy tales that have been spread in other parts of the country, your power system is still paying taxes to the municipality. That is worth remembering. Furthermore, I understand that, as a whole, it is a remarkable business success.

461

I talk about those figures first, for it has been so often wrongly alleged that this yardstick which we are using could not be applied to private businesses, because a Government yardstick receives so many favors, because it is absolved from paying this and paying that and paying the other thing. Well, we are proving in this Tennessee Valley that by using good business methods we can instruct a good many business men in the country.

And there is another side of it. I have forgotten the exact figures and I cannot find them in this voluminous report at this moment, but the number of new refrigerators that have been put in, for example, means something besides just plain dollars and cents. It means a greater human happiness. The introduction of electric cookstoves and all the other dozens of things which, when I was in the Navy, we used to call "gadgets," is improving human life. They are things not especially new so far as invention is concerned, but more and more are they considered necessities in our American life in every part of the country.

And I have been interested this morning in seeing these new homesteads — not just the buildings, not just the land that they are on, not just the excellent landscaping of the trees among which those homes have been set, but rather the opportunities that those homes are giving to families to improve their standard of living.

And finally, my friends, there is one significant thing about all that you are doing here in Tupelo, that others are doing in Corinth, in Athens and Norris, and the various other places where accomplishment can be seen today — aye, the most important thing of all I think is that it is being done by the communities themselves. This is not coming from Washington. It is coming from you. You are not being Federalized. We still believe in the community; and things are going to advance in this country exactly in proportion to the community effort. This is not regimentation; it is community rugged individualism. It means no longer the kind of rugged individualism that allows an individual to do this, that or the other thing that will hurt his neighbors. He is forbidden to do that from now on. But he is going to be encouraged in every known way from the national capital and the State capital and the county seat to use his individualism in cooperation with his neighbors' individualism so that he and his neighbors together may improve their lot in life.

Yes, I have been thrilled by these three days, thrilled not only in the knowledge of practical accomplishment but thrilled also in the deep-seated belief that the people of this Nation understand what we are trying to do, are cooperating with us and have made up their minds that we are going to do it.

And so, in saying "Good-bye" to you for a short time — because I am coming back — I ask all of you, throughout the length and breadth of the Tennessee Valley and those areas which form an economic portion of that Valley, to remember that the responsibility for success lies very largely with you, and that the eyes of the Nation are upon you. I, for one, am confident that you are going to give to the Nation an example which will be a benefit not only to yourselves, but to the whole one hundred and thirty millions of Americans in every part of the land.

185 ⟨ Extemporaneous Remarks at Birmingham, Ala. November 18, 1934

My visit through the Tennessee Valley region would be incomplete without a stop here, brief as the visit must be on this trip. I remember with greatest pleasure the last time I was here, nearly two years ago, when as President-elect I acquired some first-hand information of the problems of Tennessee and of Northern Alabama.

I speak of Birmingham as being in the Tennessee region because, while I appreciate that you are located south of the Tennessee watershed, still there are a great many economic and social relationships between this city and the great territory which lies north of you.

I know something of the many difficulties under which you have been laboring in recent years. I well understand the problem, for example, of the heavy industries, such as iron, steel and coal on which you so largely depend. I can assure you that they are matters of the keenest concern to the whole Administration.

The great program of public works, which you know something about, which is in full swing, calls for vast quantities of the iron and steel and other capital goods this area produces. That program is going to help Birmingham and the surrounding territory.

Definite improvement has made its appearance, as you know, in the coal industry. The success of the N.R.A. Coal Code appears not only in the more orderly mining of coal but also in something that lies very close to my heart, steady employment and bigger pay envelopes for the thousands of miners who were in sore straits before the Government acted.

Of course, for you who live in the economic area of which this is the southern end, the Tennessee Valley Authority must continue to receive your growing interest, as it receives the growing interest and approval of so many other communities. The whole project can succeed fully only if it has the whole-hearted support and cooperation of the people here, and it is getting that support. I particularly request of the people of Birmingham an active cooperation with the Tennessee Valley Authority, and I know that you will give it.

You know, I am always frank, and I am aware, of course, that a few, just a few, of your citizenry are leaving no stone unturned to block, to harass and to delay this great national program. I am confident, however, that these obstructionists, few in number as I have said, few in comparison with the whole population, do not reflect the views of the overwhelming majority of the people of Birmingham or the neighboring cities. I know, too, that the overwhelming majority of your business men, big and little, are in hearty accord with the great undertaking of regional planning now being carried forward. They stand and you stand shoulder to shoulder with T.V.A. — eager to carry forward the development of this region in which Birmingham plays so important a part.

It is good to be with you again. I am glad to have this splendid reception; and I am looking forward to coming back here at a time when I hope I can spend the whole day.

186 ❰ The One Hundred and Sixtieth Press Conference (Excerpts). Warm Springs, Ga. November 23, 1934

(Power policy — The larger objectives of T.V.A. — Relationship of T.V.A. to local business and local power companies — Cheap power as a means of improving living standards — Financial pyramiding in holding companies.)

Q. Mr. President, is there anything you can tell us on the record concerning the visit of your various power officials here today?

THE PRESIDENT: They are members of a committee, I could not tell you the name of it, that has on it somebody from the Federal Trade Commission, somebody from T.V.A., somebody from Interior and one or two from the Power Commission. They have been working — I think the whole thing came out last spring — on a general survey of the power situation, and they are going to talk with me about that tonight.

Q. Is that your National Resources Committee?

THE PRESIDENT: No, it is separate from that. It relates only to power.

MR. TUGWELL: Manly can tell them about it. I have forgotten the name of the committee too.

THE PRESIDENT: It is one of the inter-departmental committees to report on the general situation.

Q. With recommendations for legislation?

THE PRESIDENT: Yes, and policy.

Q. Still on the record, does that visit here mean that you have in mind any new moves of a concrete nature in the immediate future in connection with what you were telling us the other day?

THE PRESIDENT: This has nothing to do with the trip or T.V.A. or anything like that, except in so far as it relates to general power policy. . . .

Q. I feel I am doing a lot of talking here, but the other day you spoke of power and there are a lot of interpretations on it. Purely . . .

THE PRESIDENT: Oh, the interpretations are all pure. (*Laughter*)

Q. Do you mind telling us what your ideas are regarding private power companies?

THE PRESIDENT: All right, I shall give you something on that, but this has to be off the record because I don't want to be in the position of interpreting what I said. (*Laughter*)

It is a perfectly simple thing. Two years ago, in this room, you were here, Fred . . .

MR. STORM: I was here.

THE PRESIDENT: We spent an hour and a half. I think it was in January, 1933, and we had been down with Norris to see the Wilson Dam. And I had said up there publicly that we were going ahead with the development of Muscle Shoals. That is all I said at that time publicly. We came down here and we had this talk in which I outlined what developed into T.V.A. . . .

I can put it this way: Power is really a secondary matter. What we are doing there is taking a watershed with about three and a half million people in it, almost all of them rural, and we are trying to make a different type of citizen out of them from what they would be under their present conditions. Now, that applies not only to the mountaineers — we all know about them — but it applies to the people around Muscle Shoals. Do you remember that drive over to Wheeler Dam the other day? You went through a county of Alabama where the standards of education are lower than almost any other county in the United States, and yet that is within twenty miles of the Muscle Shoals Dam. They have never had a chance. All you had to do was to look at the houses in which they lived. Heavens, this section around here is 1,000 percent compared

with that section we went through. The homes through here
are infinitely better.

So T.V.A. is primarily intended to change and to improve
the standards of living of the people of that valley. Power is,
as I said, a secondary consideration. Of course it is an important one because, if you can get cheap power to those people,
you hasten the process of raising the standard of living.

The T.V.A. has been going ahead with power, yes, but it
has been going ahead with probably a great many other things
besides power and dam building. For instance, take fertilizer.
You talk about a "yardstick of power."

Dr. H. A. Morgan is running the fertilizer end of it and at
Muscle Shoals he is turning out, not a nitrate — the plant was
originally built for a nitrate plant — but he is turning out a
phosphate. He is conducting a very fine experiment with phosphate of lime. They believe that for this whole area around
here, and that would include this kind of soil around here,
phosphate of lime is the best thing you can put on land in
addition to being the cheapest.

Now at once, the fertilizer companies, the National Fertilizer Association that gets out figures (*laughter*), say, "Are you
going into the fertilizer business?" The answer is a very simple one. The plant is primarily an experimental plant. That
is the primary purpose. Therefore, they are going to take this
year a thousand acres of Government land, worn-out land typical of the locality, and they are going to use this phosphate of
lime on these thousand acres and show what can be done with
the land. They are going to give a definite demonstration.
They will compare it with the other fertilizers, putting them
in parallel strips, and they will see which works out best and
at the lowest cost. Having the large plant, they will be able to
figure out what is a fair price for the best type of fertilizer.

Having done that and having figured out the fair price, it
becomes a process of education. If the farmers all through
that area can be taught that that type of fertilizer at x number of dollars a ton is the best thing for them to use, then it is

up to the National Fertilizer Association and its affiliated companies to meet that price. Now, that is the real answer, and we hope that they will meet that price, adding to the cost of manufacture a reasonable profit. We shall know what the cost of manufacture is, and it is very easy to say what a reasonable profit is. Now, if those gentlemen fail to avail themselves of this magnificent opportunity to conduct a sound business and make a profit, well, it is just too bad. Then somebody will get up in Congress and say, "These fellows are not meeting their opportunities and the farmers will have to have the fertilizer and of course we shall have to provide it." But I, for one, hope that that day will never come. Now, that is not holding a big stick over them at all. It is saying to them, "Here is your opportunity. We go down on our knees to you, asking you to take it."

Q. Just a little guiding light.

THE PRESIDENT: In other words, what we are trying to do is something constructive to enable business . . .

MRS. ROOSEVELT: An intimation. (*Laughter*)

THE PRESIDENT: No, it is not even an intimation. No, it is a generous offer.

Now, coming down to power. You take the example of Corinth we went through the other day. In Corinth, without Government assistance — they did it themselves — they had a county electric-power association and they used to buy their juice from the Mississippi Power Company. Because they were on a through line to Tupelo, the T.V.A. came along and stepped in as a middleman, and still bought the power from the Mississippi Power Company at a lower cost per kilowatt on the agreement with the Mississippi Power Company that it would take more juice. The result was that the Mississippi Power Company gets the same gross profit as it was getting before, but it is selling more power. Then the T.V.A., merely acting as middleman without any profit to itself, turns around and sells it to the county electric-power association. That part of it does not change the existing situation at all. The Mississippi Power Company merely gave a lower rate to the Alcorn County people, but it did it via the T.V.A., instead of direct. It was merely a bookkeeping matter. It does not cost the T.V.A. anything, and it does not receive anything.

Now the Alcorn County people, that is the Alcorn County Electric Power Association, did a very interesting thing. There they had Corinth, which is a good-sized town, and they found they could distribute in Corinth — these are not accurate figures — they found they could distribute household power at about two cents a kilowatt hour. But if they were to run an electric line out to a farm, they would have to charge three cents. In other words, the farmer would have had to pay more.

What did the Corinth people do? They said, "We can get cheaper power than the farmer, but we think he should have the same rates we are getting." Voluntarily they agreed to take and to pay for two-and-a-half-cent power which enabled the farmer to get two-and-a-half-cent power. That is an extraordinary thing. That is community planning. Now, there was no reason in God's world why the Mississippi Power Company could not have gone to Corinth and said the same thing — no reason in the world. It just never thought of it. It could have done that same thing. But it was the T.V.A. that went down and sold the idea to the people in that county and said, "Let us have a uniform power rate for the man next to the powerhouse and the same rate for the man who lives twenty-five miles up the Valley. We don't want to concentrate any more people in Corinth. We want to increase the rural population."

The result of that operation is that they are increasing — they have more nearly doubled the consumption of power. Furthermore, they have gone ahead and formed another association, tied up with this county one, by which people can buy refrigerators and electric cookstoves and all the other gadgets at a figure which is somewhere around 60 or 70 percent of what they were paying before.

Now, the process behind what they were paying before amounted to this: A subsidiary of the Mississippi Power Company in the business of selling refrigerators, generally owned — I am just saying this as a mean aside — generally owned by a son of a president of a power company — there is a lot of that nepotism — would go around and say, "We will sell you a refrigerator. The cost is two hundred dollars. You can pay for it over thirty months. The total cost to you at the end of thirty months will be three hundred dollars." In other words, it was a hundred dollars extra for instalment payments. It did not say that, but that is what it amounted to. In other words, it was selling them the thing at two hundred dollars, and it was making an average of 18 to 20 percent on that sale during this thirty months.

Now, who else profits? That selling corporation, of course, made not only its 15 or 20 percent, but also made quite a lot on what it had paid for the machine. It had probably paid a hundred and seventy-five dollars for the machine, so it made twenty-five dollars on the machine. Now, whom did it buy it from? It did not buy it from the General Electric or the Westinghouse. It bought it from the middleman, and he also made a twenty-five-dollar profit on it, and the General Electric Company got only a hundred and fifty dollars for the machine. Therefore, when the consumer paid three hundred dollars, it was just 100 percent more than the General Electric Company got for the machine.

We went to the General Electric Company and said, "Will you give us your wholesale rate on machines?" It said, "Sure." And we went to all the other refrigerator manufacturers so as to have a complete line, and then we said to the householder, "You can buy this for a hundred and fifty dollars plus a five-dollar handling charge, paying for it over thirty months at 5 percent interest instead of 18 percent." The net result is that instead of paying three hundred dollars, he pays a hundred and seventy-five or a hundred and eighty dollars. His instalment cost is at 5 percent instead of 18 percent. He gets it at the wholesale price, which the Mississippi Power Company could have done exactly as well as the T.V.A. In other words, we are teaching him something.

Q. Whom is Corinth getting its power from now?

THE PRESIDENT: Mississippi Power Company.

Q. I don't quite understand the power company getting its same profit. Mr. Ruble, who runs a department store down there, told us that the building had its bill cut from sixty dollars a month to forty dollars and he doubled his consumption.

THE PRESIDENT: That is the point; what does it do? Suppose it were selling—well, let us put it in algebra. Suppose it were selling x kilowatt hours times y cents per kilowatt hour. The total receipts of the company amounted to z. Now, we come in and tell these local people that if they will buy 2x kilowatts times $\frac{1}{2}$y—in other words, half the price—you will still have z. In other words, if they buy twice as much power at half the cost, the gross will be exactly the same at the end of the month. Now, that is what we have been trying to do.

I don't know the consumption back in Corinth, but in Tupelo we estimated it would take a year at a three-cent rate running down to one, instead of a rate starting at six cents and running down to three. We figured it would take a year for the consumption of power to double. Actually, it took only four months. The consumption of power in Tupelo has doubled in four months.

The result is that the local company has an even bigger gross in the way of receipts than it had before, and yet the consumers of that power, whether shopkeepers or farmers or householders or anything else, are getting their electricity for less than half the price—about 45 percent—of what they were paying before.

Q. Isn't there a considerable change in the cost of having to step up its power production to meet a demand like that?

THE PRESIDENT: Very little. The only overhead is when you get an extension of rural lines. There you have a larger inspection force to watch the lines. That is about all.

Then we are doing a third thing along the same lines. The power companies did a silly thing when it came to rural electrification. They put out all kinds of specifications for rural lines that were out of the question. There was a certain rural line we wanted here in Warm Springs, and the specifications of the power company, as I remember them, called for thirty-five-foot poles, white oak, that had to come from North Georgia. They had to be hauled here by railroad. Then I think it charged eighty dollars for the transmission line into the farmhouse. The net result is that a line for five or six farmers would cost somewhere on the average of four or five hundred dollars. That is a pretty big debt for a farmer to assume. Then it said to him, along the same line as the refrigerator, "You can pay that over a number of years with a small charge for interest." The interest ran from 18 to 20 percent.

What we are trying to do is to build a rural line which will be substantial. We will put in transformers, actually at cost from the electric supply company, the General Electric Company or the Westinghouse, and then let the farmer pay for his power line at 5 percent instead of 18 or 20 percent. It means that on the average he can put in his power line for about 60 percent of what it costs the other way.

Now, we come back to the old simile we used before. I hope that the proper power-company officials will accept this free education that the Government is giving them. It is a fine offer and a grand chance. If they come in and do it right with a reasonable profit on their actual cost, that is all we are asking. No threat. . . .

Q. Or else?

THE PRESIDENT: No "or else." . . .

Q. In Atlanta the Georgia Power Company runs its auxiliary plant in Atlanta with gas. It buys gas from Mississippi, makes electricity from the gas — converts the gas into electricity —

and sells it at a profit. It uses about twenty million cubic feet
a day.

THE PRESIDENT: Do you know, about gas — Ickes told me this on
the train the other day — there is going to waste every year in
the Texas oil fields $72,000,000 worth of gas. It is just escap-
ing into the air. Now, if that gas were turned into electricity,
think what it would mean to Texas. That is $6,000,000 worth
of gas a month.

Q. They pipe the gas into Atlanta from Mississippi.

Q. If that much is going to waste in Texas, what is the gas wasted
on Capitol Hill? (*Laughter*)

THE PRESIDENT: That would run the District, anyway. It might
cut the District tax rate.

Q. The trouble is that that is nonconvertible gas.

THE PRESIDENT: Now, coming back to the point, this statement
shows a balance available for construction and retirement of
35 percent of the gross. If you were to analyze the financing of
most of the private power companies, you will find that in
the majority of cases they have been following the pernicious
rule of the railroads. They get out a twenty- or thirty-year
bond issue and they don't start a sinking fund. When the
bonds mature they don't pay them off. For example, in the
paper yesterday morning, there is one company that is seeking to refund an issue of bonds which were issued twenty
years ago. That is what has hurt the railroads. The railroads
never paid off a single bond which had matured. They never
set up a sinking fund. . . .

Q. The logical question that that raises is, can the average private
utilities undergo the reorganization necessary to cut the rates
and take advantage of the opportunity given them?

THE PRESIDENT: Only if they reorganize. Of course, we all know
they do a lot of talking about widows and orphans. Now,
whose fault is it? I will give you an example: A certain friend
of mine, who makes or perhaps saves two or three thousand
dollars a year, started in about 1928 to put aside a savings
fund, realizing that some day he would get old and could not

work any more. Wanting a little more than 4 percent, he went to two banks in New York City, the most reputable, old-fashioned banks he could find. I was partly responsible and told him where to go. As a result, today he finds that the fifteen or twenty thousand dollars he put in is invested, about two-thirds, in bonds of utilities, not stocks but bonds. What kind of utilities? Holding companies, all of them holding companies, none of them operating companies. He was advised to buy the bonds of these holding companies as the best form of investment he could get. They were 6 percent and 7 percent bonds and he bought them at 102, 103 and 104. He bought them above par. Today the average of those bonds is about 40. The result is that he has lost over half of the savings that he put into those bonds.

Now, why are they selling at 40? For the simple reason that you have to find out what is behind them. That starts you back over a chain. Let us take Associated Gas & Electric, as an example, or Commonwealth & Southern, or any of the big holding companies. Those bonds have printed on them that behind them is so much stock. Let us call the first company the A Company, and its bonds state that it has so much stock of B Company, C Company, D Company, in the treasury of the A Company, as security for those bonds. Then you analyze and you ask, what is the common stock of B, C and D Companies? You will find that they are holding companies. And you will also find that they have outstanding certain bonds which are backed by the common stocks of E, F, G, H and I Companies. And then you will come down to those companies and perhaps they are operating companies or perhaps they are holding companies too. Sometimes you get the pyramid of the holding company principle up to the fourth dimension. . . .

The banker who does the merging gets a lot of common stock, and dumps it off on the market. Now what Charlie (Hurd) said was right. I don't like the expression "squeezing the water out," but if the utility companies in this country could recapitalize on the basis of the money put into them, every one of them would be making a profit today and every one of them could reduce the rates.

Q. But a lot of people have taken their money and gotten out.

THE PRESIDENT: And a lot of widows and orphans are holding the bag, having been persuaded by the best banks in New York City to buy that kind of bonds, which is not at all honest.

Q. The answer is that they hold the bag anyway, so that in reorganization it would not make any difference.

THE PRESIDENT: In a reorganization it is just too bad about people badly advised. It is not the Government's fault. In other words, somebody is bound to get hurt. There isn't any question about it.

It is a very simple proposition. Suppose, for the sake of argument, you can save the consumers of power one hundred million dollars at the rate of two hundred dollars a year. That would be five hundred thousand people who would benefit in a year. They would benefit from that kind of saving through cheaper power. You would hurt a lot of people. You might hurt twenty or thirty or forty thousand people in materially benefiting five hundred thousand. But, after all, that is one thing that Government cannot do, and that is to protect widows and orphans against bad advice they have had on investing. . . .

To give you a thought, what we are after primarily is to improve the standard of living for the country as a whole.

Q. And power is merely one of the things?

THE PRESIDENT: Merely one of the things. Better homes, slum clearance, better roads, they all tie in together. Better education is very, very important. . . .

Q. Do you think it is necessary to go ahead with the Tennessee Valley experiment on a national scale to bring about the plans you have outlined?

THE PRESIDENT: Not the same kind of governmental power development if the other fellows will do it. They have every chance in the world to do it.

You take a simple example: Eight miles over here to the eastward is a place called the Cove where they make the best corn liquor in Georgia.

Q. The best is none too good. (*Laughter*)

THE PRESIDENT: Throw him out. (*Laughter*) Now, in the Cove the Georgia Power Company owns one of the most favorable power sites in the State. It can turn out at that power site something between forty and fifty thousand kilowatts at a cost of less than half a cent. It has owned it for fifteen years and it bought the whole power site for a total of fifteen thousand dollars. In other words, it bought it as a farm lot. It has sought in other years to carry it on its books for a million dollars. It is an undeveloped power site and I think the old Public Service Commission of this State allowed it to do it for a while.

Farther up, where we are going to picnic, is a place where it can develop 30,000 kilowatts, and I think it paid fifteen or eighteen thousand dollars for all the land comprising that site. It has a grand chance to make cheap electricity for the whole region and we are just giving it the opportunity as well as showing it how.

Q. None of this, I take it, is on the record.

THE PRESIDENT: No, it is just so that when you talk about it in the future you will know all about it.

Q. Can't we write this as background?

THE PRESIDENT: I think not. You had better keep it. If you write anything at all it will look like trying to explain something. . . .

Q. Can't we use this, what you said this afternoon about Tennessee Valley and before—can't we use that?

THE PRESIDENT: Instead of using it right now, jot your notes down and let me give you a hint. The National Resources Board preliminary report is coming out, and it ties right in with it. Let me dig that up for you. Don't use it today—use it for a Sunday story or a Monday story.

Q. These notes are worth a thousand dollars at least, minimum.

THE PRESIDENT: Wait until you learn more about it. You don't know enough about it to write a story. . . .

Q. Mr. President, if you were going to write a story today for the morning papers, what would you write?

THE PRESIDENT: I would write that the power people were all down here and were discussing power policy and legislation, just a preliminary talk.

(With respect to holding companies, see Chapter VII, Vol. I.)

187 ❡ A Typical Executive Order (No. 6910) on Withdrawal of Public Lands to be Used for Conservation and Development of Natural Resources. November 26, 1934

WHEREAS, the Act of June 28, 1934 (ch. 865, 48 Stat. 1269), provides, among other things, for the prevention of injury to the public grazing lands by overgrazing and soil deterioration; provides for the orderly use, improvement and development of such lands; and provides for the stabilization of the livestock industry dependent upon the public range; and

WHEREAS, in furtherance of its purposes, said Act provides for the creation of grazing districts to include an aggregate area of not more than eighty million acres of vacant, unreserved and unappropriated lands from any part of the public domain of the United States; provides for the exchange of State owned and privately owned lands for unreserved, surveyed public lands of the United States; provides for the sale of isolated or disconnected tracts of the public domain; and provides for the leasing for grazing purposes of isolated or disconnected tracts of vacant, unreserved and unappropriated lands of the public domain; and

WHEREAS, said Act provides that the President of the United States may order that unappropriated public lands be placed under national-forest administration if, in his opinion, the land be best adapted thereto; and

WHEREAS, said Act provides for the use of public land for the conservation or propagation of wild life; and

WHEREAS, I find and declare that it is necessary to classify all of the vacant, unreserved and unappropriated lands of the public domain within certain States for the purpose of effective administration of the provisions of said Act;

Now, THEREFORE, by virtue of and pursuant to the authority vested in me by the Act of June 25, 1910 (ch. 421, 36 Stat. 847), as amended by the Act of August 24, 1912 (ch. 369, 37 Stat. 497), and subject to the conditions therein expressed, it is ordered that all of the vacant, unreserved and unappropriated public land in the States of Arizona, California, Colorado, Idaho, Montana, Nevada, New Mexico, North Dakota, Oregon, South Dakota, Utah and Wyoming be, and it hereby is, temporarily withdrawn from settlement, location, sale or entry, and reserved for classification, and pending determination of the most useful purpose to which such land may be put in consideration of the provisions of said Act of June 28, 1934, and for conservation and development of natural resources.

The withdrawal hereby effected is subject to existing rights.

This order shall continue in full force and effect unless and until revoked by the President or by act of Congress.

NOTE: The foregoing Executive Order was the first issued by me pursuant to the Taylor Grazing Act of June 28, 1934, 48 Stat. 1269 (see Item 112 this volume). It was amended by Executive Order No. 7048, dated May 20, 1935, Executive Order No. 7235, dated November 26, 1935, and Executive Order No. 7274, dated January 14, 1936.

The effect of these orders was to withdraw all of the vacant, unreserved and unappropriated public lands, with some exceptions, in the States of Arizona, California, Colorado, Idaho, Montana, Nevada, New Mexico, North Dakota, Oregon, South Dakota, Utah and Wyoming, from settlement, location, sale or entry.

Executive Order No. 6964, dated February 5, 1935, as amended by Executive Order No. 7363, dated May 6, 1936, withdrew all the vacant, unreserved and unappropriated public lands, with some exceptions, in the States of Alabama, Arkansas, Florida, Kansas, Louisiana, Michigan, Minnesota, Mississippi, Nebraska, Oklahoma, Washington and Wisconsin, from settlement, location, sale or entry.

The effect of these orders was to set aside millions of acres of land not suitable for the raising of agricultural products, and to use them for purposes of grazing, conservation and the development of natural resources.

A primary object was, of course, to carry out the purposes and provisions of the Act tending toward conservation, rehabilitation and regulated use of this public resource. There was full cooperation with State associations and agencies interested in wild life and recreation, with railroads, with local and State associations of stockmen and with the land-grant colleges. Advisory committees of stockmen were formed in all grazing districts with

original responsibility of recommending the issuance of grazing licenses and rules of fair range practices in each district. The users of the range themselves choose their own Board of Directors, who make recommendations to the Secretary of the Interior on all matters pertaining to the internal affairs of the grazing district they represent. This autonomous feature is responsible very largely for the excellent results which have been attained as a result of the establishment of grazing districts. Forty-nine grazing districts have been set up, involving 110,000 acres of vacant public lands.

At the time of these withdrawals there was a total of approximately 166,240,000 acres of unappropriated and unreserved lands in the States involved in the withdrawals.

188 ⟨ The One Hundred and Sixty-first Press Conference (Excerpts). Warm Springs, Ga. November 28, 1934

(Public housing — Slum clearance — Assistance to private housing.)

Q. Mr. President, would you care to tell us about the dispute between Moffett and Ickes over housing? That all came out of Washington. We didn't get anything here at all.

THE PRESIDENT: Do you want me to talk, off the record?

Q. That will be fine.

THE PRESIDENT: This has to be off the record. There is no use of injecting me into it, because somebody will say it was denial, and some it is affirming, and some it is settling a row. . . .

Now, the real answer is a perfectly simple one. We have

four and three-quarter million people on relief. Probably half of them are living under very terrible conditions. There are probably another four and three-quarter million people who are not on the relief rolls. Now, that just does not mean people, that means that the four and three-quarter million people on the relief rolls represent eighteen million people on relief.

Taking the two groups living under undesirable conditions, it means that there are nearly forty million people who are of such low earning capacity that they cannot get credit. They cannot get credit, and private capital won't give them credit — I am not saying "improperly." You take the ordinary person, if he hasn't a job or any special capacity, private capital isn't going in and lending him money to build a house. Obviously not. Now, what are we going to do? Are we going to leave him where he is just because he hasn't security to offer for a private loan?

If he falls into the higher class, he comes to Moffett. Now, the simplest illustration is this: that of all the loans made through the Housing Administration today, the average earning capacity of the people getting loans is $2,750 a year. Now, that figure of $2,750 a year is nearly three times the average family income in the United States. Therefore the Housing Administration is taking care of people with sufficient earning capacity to obtain a private loan, and it is doing a grand job. It is taking care of the very large number of people, millions of people, who fall into the category of having an income of somewhere, let us say, between $1,500 and $3,500 a year. Those people have found it difficult to go to the bank and get a loan at a low rate of interest because the bank was not certain of things. Therefore Moffett's organization (*Federal Housing Administration*) goes to the bank and says, "If you put this thing through, it is your responsibility, but you will get Government insurance up to a certain point."

Now, that is doing well for certain people, for that group, but it was never intended that the Housing Administration could persuade banks to lend people with incomes of $750 a year. There is not enough security there. Nor could they do it for people on relief who haven't any income except what they are getting from a Government job or through relief.

That raised the question, "Are we going to call ourselves licked?"

The very simple fact is that in the City of New York there are probably a million people — there are probably two hundred thousand families alone — that is probably a rough guess — whose earning capacity brings them under the thousand dollar a year class. They probably ought not to pay, out of that thousand dollars or less, more than a hundred and fifty dollars a year, let us say, for their rent. They cannot afford it because they have to eat and buy clothes.

Now, what does that mean if the cheapest rooms in the City of New York rent for $12 a room? That means that the whole family can afford to live only in one of those $12 rooms and no other room. They have to cook, to eat, and everything else in one room. If, on the other hand, you can get them rooms for $6 a month, the family can use two rooms.

What is the result? They are living today under most terrible conditions, in old tenement flats, on the East Side, on the West Side. We all know the conditions they live under. They are able to get, on the average, perhaps two rooms at $5 to $6 a room. There is no sanitation, no light — nothing. They are pretty terrible living conditions.

Now, some say, "We are licked. Private capital could not afford to build for $5 or $6 a room. That is not enough." That is their answer, "We are licked."

They say it is not the prerogative of the Government. It is unconstitutional. Like T.V.A., it is illegal. They say the thing, over a period of years, will work itself out some way. Then they also say, "If you go in and tear down these tenements, you are going to cut real-estate values very much." Well, that is true. The value of tenements in the City of New York, including the city-assessed valuations, is much too high. They are being held at those high prices with the hope of the

481

owners that some fairy godmother is going to come along and take them off their hands at this price.

And that is the great difficulty of the Government going in to remove slum conditions in the big cities — the fictitious cost we would have to pay for that land. Yet I suppose there are tens of thousands of parcels of land in the City of New York which are only bringing in 1½ or 2 percent on the assessed value, which is higher than what they can sell them for. But there is always the hope on the part of the owner that something is going to happen.

Q. If the Government built these homes, who would own them?

THE PRESIDENT: In the case of a tenant there are practically only two methods. One is tenant ownership, which has been used in a great many buildings in the City of New York, such as the Bronx buildings that the labor people put up. The tenant, by making extra payments over and above the rent, eventually, in twelve or fifteen years, owns his own apartment. That is tenant ownership.

The other method, especially in those places where you have a floating population that moves out and in a great deal, is a straight Government proposition which, after the Government has been paid back, could probably be sold to private people. In other words, it does not mean that the Government would stay in forever.

Some people also talk about the terrible socialism in what has been done in Germany and England and Vienna in cleaning up slums. They say it was just straight socialism and of course that we couldn't do anything like that. But if you had knowledge of what happened in Germany and England and Vienna, you would know that that so-called socialism has probably done more to prevent communism and rioting and revolution than anything else in the last four or five years. Vienna has practically cleaned out her slums and has done a grand job.

Then, of course, there are the other phases, such as rural housing. We talked about that the other day and you understand the whole objective of it. There, again, we have to put up homes that private capital cannot put up. We have to reach an entirely different group in the community. . . .

Now, who can buy, for example, a $3,800 house? None of the people on relief. It is too much. It will be taking too much of a chance for private capital to take a fellow off the relief rolls and put him into that house. Now, there are what I call the "marginal" people who are just out on the line, people who have a job, a little bit of a job, making $20 a week as a family. Private capital cannot afford to put them into a $3,800 house. They are too close to the line. It is not a good risk. So, what we are trying to do is to put up houses where these people can go in and where, because of the much lower monthly payments, there is a chance of getting the money back. Private capital cannot do it. It is a field into which Government alone can go, and Government only can do it.

Government cannot say, "We are licked." Other countries have done it and have put up good houses at $1,500 and $1,600. We can come close to doing it here. It does not interfere in any way with the outlet for private capital, not one bit, because they would not go into that field at all.

Q. How much money does it cost the Government?

THE PRESIDENT: It depends on the program. In other words, when it comes down to that, you can take your program and run it from $100 to a hundred billion. I mean, that becomes a matter of financing rather than a matter of policy.

Q. Is this on the record?

THE PRESIDENT: No, this is all off the record.

Q. On this housing program we were just talking about, has that been decided on at all?

THE PRESIDENT: In figures, no. In policy, yes.

Q. Could we use that fact?

THE PRESIDENT: Depends on what you use with it. In other words, if I were writing the story today I think it would be perfectly all right to say this, without putting it on me: It has been made increasingly clear by people coming to Warm Springs to see the President (*laughter*), meaning the press (*laughter*), that the Government recognizes as a matter of policy its obligation to those people in the United States whose standards of living are so low that something has to be done about it, but whose pocketbooks are so small that private capital cannot properly lend them money. And if somebody asks the question, "Is Government going to consider itself licked in its effort to take care of people who cannot otherwise be taken care of?" the answer is, obviously, "No!" And further, as a matter of policy, the Government is going to continue every reasonable effort — that answers Stevie's question, and I cannot give you any figures — continue every reasonable effort to give the lowest income group in the United States a chance to live under better conditions, for the very simple reason that if Government does not do it, nobody else will or can.

Now, of course, a Government program of that kind is not all one-sided. My "missus" suggests a very excellent addition to it: that it means a very definite lift to the heavy industries not only during the construction period, but also after that period is over. For there will be an additional consumers' demand because, once people get a better standard of living, they are going to insist on maintaining it.

In other words, the policy story is all right, as long as you don't try to get too factual about it, because I haven't any more idea than you have as to the dollars and cents, or whether it will be done, or anything of that kind. . . .

MR. MCINTYRE: In connection with what you said about housing policy, would you have any objection to the use of that part in which you pointed out that there is no conflict?

THE PRESIDENT: That is perfectly all right to use. There was absolutely no conflict. The private dollar won't go into the Government housing that we are going ahead on. If private dollars show any desire to come in, we will be willing to give them every opportunity so to do.

As to F.H.A., see Item 82, this volume; as to housing in P.W.A., see Item 117, Vol. II.

189 ⟨ Extemporaneous Remarks at Thanksgiving Day Party at Warm Springs, Georgia — an Informal History of the Institution.

November 29, 1934

It has been the custom, ever since our first Thanksgiving party of 1926, for me to call attention to the fact that the particular evening is a bigger party than ever before.

We started out with our first Thanksgiving party, as I remember it, with forty people, and it got up to sixty and to a hundred and then to a hundred and fifty, and two years ago, the last Thanksgiving dinner we had at good old Meriwether Inn, we had about two hundred and forty people in the dining room. That big dinner was what really compelled us to build Georgia Hall, because, while we do not know whether it was the turkey or the people, the old dining room settled six inches during that party.

It is the earliest settlers who have handed down the story to us that long before the white people came here, Warm Springs was a place where people came to get well, and in the tribal wars between the Crees and the Cherokees and the Coyatees and the other tribes around here, any wounded Indian seeking to come to Warm Springs had only to hold up his hand and give the sign that he was coming here, and from that time on he was not molested.

The story has it that when the Indians came here to get cured of their wounds, they lived here, different tribes all together, as in a place of sanctuary where war was forbidden. That tradition, I think, has been rather faithfully carried out right down to the present day.

Yes, this is a sanctuary for people, for wars of the body and wars of the mind are absolutely taboo. They do not have to be forbidden because of a thing that perhaps came down to us all the way from the Indians — what we call "the spirit of Warm

Springs." It has been here at least as long as I have been here, and I am quite sure it is still here and I am quite sure it will always rest upon these buildings.

Tonight marks the tenth anniversary of my coming to Warm Springs. Some of you have heard the story before but it occurred to me that a good many of you have not heard of the origin of the Foundation so, if you will permit me, I shall tell you some things that perhaps many of you know.

In the spring of 1924 I was taking treatments from Dr. Lovett in Boston who, at that time, was believed, I think, by everybody to have done more in the after-treatment of infantile paralysis than almost anybody. In June I went on up to Boston and spent a week getting my braces fixed up and learning some new exercises. I got talking with Dr. Lovett about his experimental work with Polio and he said, "You know, I found an interesting thing last summer. Most of my patients come from New England, and a great many of them come from seashores. I told all of them to swim as much as they possibly could and it is an interesting fact that the patients who went down to Buzzards Bay and Long Island Sound, where the waters were warm and where they could spend a great many minutes of the day in the water swimming around, seemed to improve in their muscles a great deal more than those of my patients who went to the North Shore or to the coast of Maine where the water is cold and you can only stay in for three or four or five minutes. Therefore," he said, "I have started a little shallow tank in the Children's Hospital of Boston to see if we cannot learn something from exercising muscles in the medium of water instead of just exercising them on tables."

I did not give very much time to it; I thought he was pursuing an interesting course in developing this theory. And then came a period that was known as the Democratic National Convention in Madison Square Garden, New York City—a party which lasted nearly three weeks. Then came a political campaign, in which I had some small part.

About September first, I think it was, I got a letter from Mr. Peabody and Mr. Peabody said, "Here is an interesting letter that I am enclosing from Mr. Tom Loyless, who is running Warm Springs for me."

Mr. Loyless told about a young man by the name of Josephs from Columbus who had come up here after an attack of infantile paralysis. He could not walk at all. There was just a public pool here then, but he had taught himself to use his legs in the water, to get his feet down to the bottom and to walk around on the bottom. Later on he found he could walk in shallower water all the time, and he kept on doing that until he found that he could walk on dry land.

Well, I put two and two together and I said to myself, "This confirms Dr. Lovett's theory." Meanwhile, Dr. Lovett had gone on a trip to Europe and unfortunately had died over there, so I was unable to consult him anyway.

But I spoke to Peabody and it was arranged for me to go to Hart's Cottage, now Mr. Pierson's cottage. We came down in the autumn. The only people who were here when we arrived were Mr. and Mrs. Loyless and old Mr. Watts, the postman, and it is perfectly true that he read everybody's postcards. In fact, he read so many postcards that it took him almost all day to make the delivery of the mail to the Loyless cottage and mine.

When we came down, there was no doctor around here; there was nobody in charge, or anything of a medical nature. I went down to what is now the public pool. It was rather simple in those days.

I stayed here for a month and I improved so much that I came back the following spring. But people had heard about it.

One day Mr. Loyless and some of the neighbors—the Harts, Miss Wilkins and Josephs and some of us—were sitting around when a messenger came up the hill to Mr. Loyless and said, "Two people have been carried off the train down at the station. What shall we do with them? Neither of them can walk."

Well, we held a consultation. It was long before anything was done here in the way of a hotel or cottages. We decided that we could take care of them in the village overnight, and then, in a couple of days we could fix up what is now "The Wreck," and put them in it. Well, before we could put that cottage in order, eight others had arrived. They came like Topsy and got here before we knew it.

We did not know what to do with them so I sent for Dr. Johnson. He came and looked them over and guaranteed that they did not have heart trouble or something from which they would suddenly die, and he recommended cream and fattening diets for some and he recommended very little food for some of the others.

And then I undertook to be doctor and physio-therapist, all rolled into one. I taught Fred Botts to swim. I taught them all at least to play around in the water. I remember there were two quite large ladies; and when I was trying to teach them an exercise which I had really invented, which was the elevating exercise in the medium of water, one of these ladies found great difficulty in getting both feet down to the bottom of the pool. Well, I would take one large knee and I would force this large knee and leg down until the foot rested firmly on the bottom. And then I would say, "Have you got it?" and she would say, "Yes," and I would say, "Hold it, hold it." Then I would reach up and get hold of the other knee very quickly and start to put it down and then number one knee would pop up. This used to go on for half an hour at a time; but before I left in the spring, I could get both those knees down at the same time.

I called that my medical practice, the first and last time that I have ever practiced medicine and physio-therapy. After I get through at the White House, I hope the medical fraternity will allow me to come back and practice here. I feel I would be rather good at giving exercises in the water. At least, I have had more exercise in the water, over a longer period of time, than anybody else in captivity in this country.

And then, we came down the following year, 1926, which, in a way, was the most interesting period we have ever had here because for the first time we had adequate medical supervision. We were a very small group of patients; I think there were twenty-five. Dr. Hubbard and Miss Mahoney were in charge, and every step we took was an experiment. In order to make both

488

ends meet, we tried to run the Inn as a hotel at the same time that we were taking care of these twenty-five patients.

Mr. Pope and I were the Foundation that year. Mr. Pope and I had long conferences. We started with a band of five pieces; but I think we spent an hour talking over the question of whether we could afford a band of five pieces or whether we should reduce it to three pieces. However, we managed to get by, and the following spring of 1927 the Foundation itself was truly launched.

Just see how that child has grown from 1927 to 1934 — in seven years. They are seven years that have shown a continuous growth, a growth not only in the number of patients we are treating, but also in the physical facilities that we have.

I hinted to you — and I am not going to do more than hint again — that as a result of our action today, I hope that the Warm Springs family next year is going to be even larger than it has been this year. That has been made possible by the very splendid fund that was collected all over this country under the leadership of Colonel Doherty on the thirtieth of January last. This year we are not asking any more funds for the Foundation.

The Birthday Party will give 70 percent of all funds raised to the care of infantile paralysis in the various localities throughout the country where they have Birthday Balls; the other 30 percent is going to be spent to do something we have always had in mind. It is going to further the cause of research. As I said this afternoon in the dedication of the two buildings, you must always remember that you who are here, those of us who are here under medical care, only represent a tiny fraction of the people throughout the land, grown-ups and children, who have infantile paralysis. Therefore, even if we were to double in size or quadruple in size, we could treat only a small fraction of the people of this country who need treatment.

We need to do everything we can to spread the knowledge we are gaining at Warm Springs, the treatments which we are so successfully carrying out, so that, throughout the country, the facilities for taking care of grown-ups and children who have Polio can be vastly improved. That is why Warm Springs may be called a pioneer; but it is also an example for a great many other people to follow all over the United States.

NOTE: On the day the above speech was delivered, I made several other extemporaneous talks at Warm Springs, which were reported in the newspapers, but which are not printed here for lack of space. See also note to Item 181, this volume.

190 ❦ A Letter in Behalf of the United Hospital Campaign. December 4, 1934

My dear Mr. Pyle:

While the Federal Government has necessarily stepped in to aid the States and localities in providing relief for the needy unemployed in their homes, it is impossible to make Government funds available to the hospitals for the care of the sick who lack funds to pay. Yet such patients are among the most needy of all the victims of unemployment. I have repeatedly stated my feeling that the care of the sick is a local responsibility. All over the land communities are rising manfully to fulfill this obligation.

I am interested to know of the campaign of the United Hospital Fund of New York on behalf of its fifty-six member hospitals, which depend wholly upon voluntary contributions and do not receive any tax aid.

I have been familiar with the work of this organization for many years. I commend its cause heartily to citizens of New York.

Very sincerely yours,

Mr. David H. McAlpin Pyle,
President, United Hospital Fund,
New York, N. Y.

191 ❡ Greetings to the American Foundation for the Blind. December 5, 1934

I am very happy to know of the ceremony at which you are officiating this afternoon. It is a milestone in the career of an organization, founded on sympathy and understanding, which has served not only to guide those who are without light, but to show the path to their fellow citizens, so that in our worldly progress we may come to recognize our obligation to them, and in the recognition and performance of that obligation benefit ourselves.

Hon. John Finley
New York, New York

192 ❡ A Greeting to the Farm Bureau. December 10, 1934

My friends of the Farm Bureau:

You and I know that the year now ending has been one of significant accomplishment for agriculture. Despite the worst drought of record, farm income is running about a billion dollars above last year.

All of us would like to see an even larger increase in 1935, but we know that this cannot come unless, in the first place, industrial production increases sufficiently to expand the market for farm products; unless, in the second place, more of our export trade is paid for by increased imports; and unless, in the third place, agriculture continues to adjust its total production to the market that actually exists.

To fulfill these three requirements, I ask a continuation of the splendid support you have so unselfishly given in the past.

I wish very much that it were possible for me to be with you today, and I give you my warm regards.

American Farm Bureau Federation
Nashville, Tenn.

193 ❲ Address to the Conference on Crime
Called by the Attorney General of the
United States. December 10, 1934

D URING the past two years there have been uppermost
in our minds the problems of feeding and clothing
the destitute, making secure the foundations of our
agricultural, industrial and financial structures, and
releasing and directing the vital forces that make for
a healthy national life. As a component part of the large objective
we include our constant struggle to safeguard ourselves against
the attacks of the lawless and the criminal elements of our
population.

Relentlessly and without compromise, the Department of Justice has moved forward in its major offensive against these forces.
With increasing effectiveness, State and local agencies are directing their efforts toward the achievement of law enforcement; and
with them, in more marked degree than ever before, the Federal
Government has worked toward the common objective.

It is a privilege to pay tribute to the men and women who, in
many capacities, official and otherwise, have contributed to our
growing success. To a much greater extent than is generally realized our law enforcement officers throughout the country have
rendered devoted, conscientious and effective service, often under
exasperating and hazardous circumstances.

Their effectiveness has, unfortunately, been impaired because
of inadequate organization, unscientific administration and lack
of public support and understanding. In many instances, we may
as well frankly admit, bandits have been better equipped and
better organized than have the officials who are supposed to keep
them in check. This is particularly true because of the lack of coordination between local agencies within the States. It is, also,
contributed to in serious measure by the lack of facilities for
training skilled men for the work of detection, apprehension and
prosecution of accused persons, and by similar lack of facilities

for the study and supervision of certain types of criminals capable of rehabilitation.

It is important, too, that we recognize clearly the increasing scope and complexity of the problem of criminal law administration. Undoubtedly there are unfortunate aspects of our national life which seriously threaten the American home, increase the danger of juvenile delinquency and multiply offenses against the good order of society. The regulation of the illicit traffic in drugs, the prevention of commerce in stolen goods and, generally, the interstate character of offenses attributable to the roving criminal have presented national problems against which primitive forms of law enforcement are relatively powerless.

It is equally necessary that we realize the importance of common action all along the line, starting with crime prevention itself and carrying this common action all the way through to prosecution and punishment.

Effective detection of criminals may be rendered useless by ineffective prosecution or by unintelligent judicial disposition. Beneficent and promising procedures, such as probation and parole, may actually become sources of danger, if ignorantly or indifferently administered. So, too, reliance on mere repression cannot take the place of intelligent training and guidance of youth.

We have come to a time when our need is to discover more fully and to direct more purposefully into useful channels that greatest of all natural resources, the genius of the younger generation. Crime is a symptom of social disorder. Widespread increase in capacity to substitute order for disorder is the remedy.

This can come only through expert service in marshalling the assets of home, school, church, community and other social agencies, to work in common purpose with our law enforcement agencies. We deceive ourselves when we fail to realize that it is an interrelated problem of immense difficulty. Scientific research, highly trained personnel, expert service are just as necessary here as in any field of human endeavor. To the extent that we provide, instead, unscientific methods, poorly trained personnel and hit-

493

or-miss procedures, we may expect bungling, heartbreaking re-sults.

I am delighted, therefore, that the Attorney General has called you together for this Conference. The country knows that under his leadership we are getting better results than ever before.

It is heartening and reassuring to the people of the United States that you have gathered here for this purpose. They are looking to you for guidance and intelligent leadership. They have a right to expect from you a constructive program of action in which they as individuals, and collectively as communities and organizations, may participate. It should be a challenge to you to respond to these expectations.

The task of this thoroughly representative conference is two-fold.

First, I ask you to plan and to construct with scientific care a constantly improving administrative structure—a structure which will tie together every crime-preventing, law-enforcing agency of every branch of Government—the Federal Govern-ment, the forty-eight State governments and all of the local gov-ernments, including counties, cities and towns.

Your second task is of equal importance. An administrative structure that is perfect will still be ineffective in its results un-less the people of the United States understand the larger pur-poses and cooperate with these purposes.

I ask you, therefore, to do all in your power to intepret the problem of crime to the people of this country. They must realize the many implications of that word "crime." It is not enough that they become interested in one phase only. At one moment popu-lar resentment and anger may be roused by an outbreak of some particular form of crime such, for example, as widespread ban-ditry; or at another moment, of appalling kidnappings; or at another, of widespread drug peddling; or at another, of horrify-ing lynchings.

It is your positive duty to keep before the country the facts in regard to crime as a whole—great crimes, lesser crimes and little crimes—to build up a body of public opinion which, I regret to

be compelled to say, is not in this day and age sufficiently active or alive to the situation in which we find ourselves.

I want the backing of every man, every woman and every adolescent child in every State of the United States and in every county of every State for what you and the officers of law and order are trying to accomplish.

The sustained interest and assistance of the organizations here represented can become a public service of high significance in the social life of the Nation—a service to which the American people, I am confident, will not fail to respond.

NOTE: For a discussion of the events leading up to this Crime Conference, called by the Attorney General of the United States, and of the efforts of the Department of Justice to stamp out crime since March 4, 1933, the reader is referred to Item 85 of this volume, and the note thereto.

The foregoing address was made at this conference. Experts on such subjects as the causes of crime, de-tection, apprehension and punishment, procedural reforms and rehabilitation of criminals also made addresses.

The conference lasted four days; and while the tangible results can never be measured, it did more than any other one thing to center national interest on the breadth of the crime problem and on constructive measures to deal with it.

194 ❰ The Federal Prison Industries, Inc. Is Established. Executive Order No. 6917.

December 11, 1934

By VIRTUE of the authority vested in me by the Act of June 23, 1934 (Public No. 461, 73d Congress), it is hereby ordered that a corporation of the District of Columbia be and is hereby created, said corporation to be named as

Federal Prison Industries, Inc.

1. The governing body of said corporation shall consist of a board of five directors to hold office at the pleasure of the Presi-

dent. The following persons shall constitute the first Board of Directors:

> Mr. Sanford Bates
> Mr. Thomas A. Rickert
> Hon. John B. Miller
> Dr. M. L. Brittain
> Mr. Sam A. Lewisohn

2. The principal office of said corporation shall be in the City of Washington, District of Columbia, but the corporation shall have power and authority to establish such other offices or agencies as it may deem necessary or appropriate.

3. The said corporation shall have power to determine in what manner and to what extent industrial operations shall be carried on in the several penal and correctional institutions of the United States and shall, so far as practicable, so diversify prison industrial operations that no single private industry shall be forced to bear an undue burden of competition with the products of the prison workshops. It shall also have power to do all things it is authorized to do by the said Act of June 23, 1934, and all things incident to or necessary or proper in the exercise of its functions. . . .

NOTE: One of the problems raised by the depression was the production by prison labor of articles which came into competition with private industries manufacturing the same articles. The use of labor in Federal prisons for the manufacture of articles required by the Federal departments and agencies did not create opposition so long as private plants were able to maintain their normal output. With a continuation of the depression, protests began to come in from private industry, beginning in 1931, against the continued operation of industrial plants in Federal institutions.

On the other hand, unless Federal prisoners were put to work in prison, the disciplinary and custodial problem would become almost impossible. It was difficult to meet complaints from private commercial firms and at the same time keep prisoners at work for proper administration and discipline in the prison. See Items 83, 86 of Vol. I for similar State difficulty.

On March 7, 1934, after consideration of the problem for some time, I called a conference at the White House between representatives of the Department of Justice and of the American Federation of Labor, to see what could be done. As a result of the conference, legislation was finally agreed upon, drafted and passed, and approved by me on June 23, 1934 (Public No. 461, 73d Congress; 48 Stat. 1211).

The bill authorized the establishment of a Federal corporation to manage and operate industrial activities in Federal prisons.

At the time I signed the bill I issued the following statement: "I am glad to approve this bill because it represents a distinct advance in the progress of prison industries. Without any important competition with private industry or labor, the Government can provide increasingly useful work for those who need to learn how to work, and to learn that work in itself is honorable and is a practical substitute for criminal methods of earning one's livelihood."

Pursuant to the authority given in this statute I issued the foregoing Executive Order creating the "Federal Prison Industries, Inc."; and appointed its first Board of Directors in accordance with the statute, which provided that one of them should be a representative of industry, one a representative of labor, one a representative of agriculture, one a representative of retailers and consumers, and one a representative of the Attorney General.

The problems which the Board of Directors had to solve were: to provide additional employment for inmates so as to reduce idleness in the institutions, to diversify the production of prison shops so that no individual industry would be substantially affected, to hear complaints by private industry and labor with respect to the prison-industry program, and at the same time to make sufficient money so that additional appropriations would not be required from the Congress.

The Corporation took over the operation of all industrial enterprises in Federal penal and correctional institutions on January 1, 1935, and since then has operated these industries on a basis which has been satisfactory to the particular industries involved. It has made sufficient earnings so as not to require any additional appropriation from the Congress, although the prices at which it has furnished materials and supplies to the various departments have never exceeded the lowest current market quotations. It has diversified its operations into some twenty industries including cotton textiles, shoes, clothing, foundry, furniture, rubber mats, laundries, print shops, dry cleaning and canvas goods.

With the operations of the Corporation has come a great improvement in morale and discipline. The vocational training given to prisoners has made it possible for many of them to secure subsequent employment in private industry.

The operations of the Corpora-

tion have pointed the way and served as an example to the various States in organizing their prison industrial activities.

195 ❡ Remarks on Receiving Medal of the Pan-American Society. December 12, 1934

IT IS with the greatest appreciation that I receive from your hands the medal of the Pan-American Society, particularly because it comes to me from an institution which was formed over twenty-two years ago and which has devoted its efforts ever since to the development of mutual knowledge and understanding and true friendship among the American Republics and their peoples. Through your hospitality to visitors from the other Republics to the United States and through your constant attention to the development of closer cultural and educational relations with our neighbors to the South you have been one of the links in the chain of attachment to our sister Republics which has fortunately helped so greatly in the promotion of good feeling between us.

I see among you certain members who, in addition to the helpful attention they have given to the aims of your Society, are also devoting themselves now to provide practical means of insuring the continuance of amicable relations between the American Republics through the means of the Inter-American Commercial Arbitration Commission. I have been very interested to learn of the substantial establishment of this Commission and I look to it with great hope and with full confidence that through its measures of friendly and reliant facilities it will afford an opportunity to harmonize the relations between the citizens of our American Republics in a phase of their relations which does not lie within the sphere of activities of our several Governments. The relations between Nations are after all dependent upon the relations between the individuals of those various Nations. In this Commission you are attacking a problem which is fundamental, and the solution of which will be most helpful, in promoting the welfare and advance of all the twenty-one Republics of America.

Permit me to thank you and, through you, the members of the Pan-American Society for this expression of support in a policy which has long been close to my heart and the fulfillment of which I consider one of the greatest privileges of this office.

196 ❧ Letter from the Federal Housing Administrator Explaining Need for State Legislation to Supplement the National Housing Act. December 18, 1934

My dear Mr. President:

In order that the Federal Housing Administration may attain a full measure of success throughout the country, it is essential that banks, insurance companies, building and loan associations, trust companies, fiduciaries, and other investors be able legally to make insured mortgage loans, and to invest in insured mortgages and in national mortgage association obligations, as provided by the National Housing Act. . . .

At the present time there are in the States various statutory limitations upon loans and investments by the aforementioned investing institutions, which restrict their ability to benefit fully from the National Housing program. A similar limitation upon the lending power of national banks has already been removed by the Congress.

The Legislatures of many States will convene during the next few months. Could you not, with propriety, suggest to the Governors of these States that their statutes should be amended as soon as possible so that banks, insurance companies, building and loan associations, trust companies, fiduciaries and all other investors under statutory restrictions might be permitted legally to make insured mortgage loans and to invest in insured mortgages and in national mortgage association obligations as provided by the National Housing Act?

Respectfully yours,

J. A. MOFFETT, Administrator.

(See next Item)

196A ❨ The President Requests Legislation by the States to Supplement the National Housing Act. December 11, 1934

My dear Governor:

I AM enclosing a copy of a letter to me from Mr. James A. Moffett, the Administrator of the Federal Housing Administration. This letter calls my attention to the need for certain legislation to make Titles II and III of the National Housing Act more effective.

Amendments to existing State laws seem to be called for in practically every State — forty-four of them — in which State Legislatures are meeting this winter.

Mr. Moffett tells me that the bill passed by the Legislature of the State of New York, in Special Session last August, seems to meet the general needs. I am enclosing a copy of this bill.

It would give me great satisfaction if you would give this matter your most careful consideration with the object, if you approve, of obtaining legislation in your State in 1935.

If you would care to have any further information in regard to the details or objects relating to this subject, I shall be glad to have you call on Mr. Moffett at any time.

Very sincerely yours,

(The foregoing letter was sent to the Governors of forty-four States.)

197 ❨ A Christmas Greeting to the Nation. December 24, 1934

THIS is the second year that I have joined with you on this happy occasion. Then, as now, with millions of others we celebrate the happy observance of Christmas.

The year toward which we looked then with anticipation and hope has passed. We have seen fulfilled many things that a year ago were only hopes. Our human life thus goes on from anticipation and hope to fulfillment. This year again we are entitled to new hopes and new anticipations.

For all those who can hear but not see this gathering, let me explain that here before us in the park in front of the White House is the monument of a man who will live forever as the embodiment of courage — Andrew Jackson. His was a long, long life in the public service, distinguished at all times by a chivalrous meeting of problems and difficulties that attended that service, a fast belief in people and a profound love for them. His patriotism was unstained and unafraid. Carved into that monument is his expression of the necessity for union. That message grows in importance with the years.

In these days it means to me a union not only of the States but a union of the hearts and minds of the people in all the States and their many interests and purposes, devoted with unity to the human welfare of our country.

Just across the street is the house he occupied one hundred years ago, the house the people of the country have built for their Presidents. From its windows I see this monument to this man of courage. It is an inspiration to me, as it should be to all Americans.

And so let us make the spirit of Christmas of 1934 that of courage and unity. It is the way to greater happiness and well-being. That is, I believe, an important part of what the Maker of Christmas would have it mean.

In this sense, the Scriptures admonish us to be strong and of good courage, to fear not, to dwell together in Unity.

I wish you one and all, here and everywhere, a very, very Merry Christmas.

197A ❡ A Christmas Greeting Sent to the Members of the Foreign Diplomatic Service. December 24, 1934

Toward the close of my second year in office, I send to you and to the members of the Foreign Service in the country of your residence, as well as to your family, personal and official, my cordial Christmas and New Year's greetings.

I want all of you to know that in spite of the distance which separates you from the National Capitol, you are often in my thoughts. We in the United States appreciate the service which all of you are giving to your country.

In a time of great difficulties in almost every part of the world, we are proud of the American Foreign Service. Once more I send you my warm greetings.

198 ❡ Greetings to the National Student Federation. December 27, 1934

I send greetings to the student leaders of America and wish for your meeting every success in clarifying your problems, and in deepening your determination to solve them in the spirit of devotion to that high idealism characteristic of youth.

This Administration has been engrossed perforce in the problems of economic recovery. I am fully aware, however, that economic recovery is ultimately to be appraised in terms of the enrichment it makes possible in human lives. Human resources are above physical resources. The purposes which inspire the college youth of today will determine largely the value of the human resources of tomorrow. Your opportunity and your responsibility are alike great.

Mr. John Lang,
President, National Student Federation,
Boston, Massachusetts.

199 ❡ The President Expresses His Views on the Soldiers' Bonus Issue. December 27, 1934

Dear Commander Farmer:

I APPRECIATE your letter of recent date, and it is particularly interesting in that it confirms an impression that I have had for some time; that is, that the bonus question is not well understood even among the veterans themselves.

I am also particularly impressed with one paragraph of your letter which confirms another conviction I have that the service men generally have the interests of their country and Government at heart. I have had prepared for me a memorandum which outlines in detail exactly what the Congress did in 1924 when they authorized the issuing of the Adjusted Service Certificates known generally as the "bonus." This memorandum I am inclosing herewith. I am sure that you will find in this memorandum sufficient information to enable you to decide for yourself the stand you should take on this issue as well as to be in a position, as I feel you should be, to advise legionnaires who come to you seeking information in regard to the immediate payment of the balance due on the Adjusted Service Certificates.

It is quite apparent from your letter in which you advise me of the reasons why the service men are demanding immediate payment of the bonus, that there is a general misunderstanding in regard to the Government's obligation in this matter. When, in 1924, the Congress decided to issue the Adjusted Service Certificates, they actually authorized a bonus of $1,400,000,000, but because of the stand taken at that time by those advocating the measure who felt that it would be in the interest of the service men themselves, this cash outlay was not made immediately, but was deferred for twenty years. Because of this deferment the initial bonus was increased 25 percent so that the $1,400,000,000 invested for the service men at 4 percent compounded annually, would mature in twenty years at $3,500,000,000. Or putting it another way, suppose that a veteran's original grant by the Congress in 1924 was $400 and that the veteran did not borrow on his certificate, permitting the interest to accumulate to maturity. The $400 would grow so that it would pay the veteran $1,000 when due in 1945. In other words, the amount which is printed upon the face of every Adjusted Service Certificate is not the amount of the basic or original bonus voted by the Congress, but is an amount plus 25 percent added for deferred payment which, with interest at 4 percent compounded annually over a twenty-year period, will produce the face or maturity value. This would seem to dispose of the question as to whether the obligation is immediately due.

There is another feature in connection with this matter that impresses me, and that is the fact that out of 3,500,000 certificates outstanding, 3,038,500 veterans have borrowed thereon approximately $1,690,000,000. In other words, some have borrowed more than the present worth of their bonus certificates. This is brought about by the action of the Congress permitting a veteran to borrow up to 50 percent of the face or maturity value of his certificate, even though that certificate may have been issued only a few days before the loan is made. Of course, all the certificates were not issued at the same time in 1925, but have been issued from that date up to the present time, so their present value or earned value, as we may put it, is not the same in all cases, but taking the aggregate of all the certificates issued they have a present value of $2,100,000,000, whereas their face value is $3,500,000,-000. Then, too, I believe it has been suggested that the interest paid or now accumulated be canceled or remitted. If this plan were carried out the total amount would increase to $3,720,-000,000; or putting it another way making the cost $1,620,000,000 over and above the present value and $2,320,000,000 above the amount which the Congress fixed as the original basic adjustment.

I feel sure that many of the veterans have not given the question sufficient study to realize the vast sums required to meet the demands suggested.

Your statement advising me that those who favor the immediate payment of the bonus feel that a good reason for doing so is because the Government has spent millions of dollars on the recovery program, and that much of these funds will not be repaid, while by the payment of the bonus the Government will be discharging an obligation, and by so discharging this obligation the money spent by the veterans will do much in a practical way of stimulating recovery, is interesting.

I know that you appreciate that all expenditures for relief have been made in the interest of recovery and for all our citizens, non-veterans as well as for veterans. All citizens in need have shared in the direct distribution for relief, and in employment, as you no doubt are aware, a very definite and distinct preference is given to veterans. I am advised that at the time the issue of paying the balance of the bonus was up and a compromise was made by increasing the loan value to 50 percent of the face value, there resulted a distribution of approximately a billion dollars, and at that time the same argument was advanced that the expenditure of such a large amount of money by the veterans would greatly stimulate business and aid recovery. A survey of the results showed otherwise. This large payment resulted in little stimulation of business, and in many of the larger cities no material change was indicated at all. It was found that indebtedness created by the veterans prior to the payment was liquidated, and the money advanced to veterans went to clear that indebtedness rather than to create new business. No doubt the same results would obtain if the balance were now paid. However, in this connection what to me is very important, having in mind that the bonus certificate is a paid-up endowment policy payable either to the veteran upon its maturity or to his beneficiary, generally the wife and children in the event of his death, is the fact that of the veterans who die, approximately 85 percent of them leave no other asset to their family but the Adjusted Service Certificate or the balance due on the certificate. I feel, therefore, that those who advocate the payment of these certificates at this time for the purpose of stimulating business certainly cannot have given the interests of the veterans much thought.

I appreciate your truly patriotic interest in desiring to obtain full information on an issue so vital to the service men and our country. I am giving you this information with the hope that it will be useful in enabling you to reach a conclusion in your own mind regarding the matter as well as helping others to determine the fair thing to do.

Very sincerely yours,

Commander Garland R. Farmer
American Legion Post
Henderson, Texas

199A ❪ Memorandum Enclosed by the President in the Foregoing Letter.

December 27, 1934

THE CONGRESS, by the passage of the Act of May 19, 1924, provided for the granting of additional compensation to each veteran, with certain specified exceptions, of $1 per day for services in the United States and $1.25 per day for services over seas, in excess of the first sixty days of services. The amount thus determined was increased by 25 percent because of deferment of payment. Using the aggregate as a net single premium according to the American Experience Table of Mortality with interest at 4 percent per annum, entitlement was granted to the veterans to payment, twenty years after 1925 or date of application, of a sum approximately two and one-half times that of the basic adjustment. The 150 percent increase represents the additional amount granted because of deferment of payment and the compounded interest. Thus an original grant of $400 in 1925 would enlarge itself to $1000 in 1945. If in 1925 the $1 and $1.25 per day adjustment had been paid in cash the veterans would have received a total of $1,400,000,000, but by deferring the payment twenty years the sum became $3,500,000,000.

Under the original law, veterans were permitted to borrow on their certificates according to the reserve value thereof, but in

February 1931 an amendment increased, without regard to actuarial value, the amount which could be borrowed to 50 percent of the maturity value. This amendment also fixed the maximum interest which could be charged on loans at 4½ percent, which rate was subsequently reduced to 3½ percent by the Act of July 21, 1932. The amount, including interest charges now outstanding because of loans made to veterans, is slightly less than $1,690,-000,000. Of this amount, $1,470,000,000 is represented by actual payments disbursed by the Veterans' Administration. The difference between the maturity value and the present liens on certificates is $1,810,000,000. However, the difference between the present value of the certificates, actuarially computed, and the amount outstanding as liens is only $410,000,000. As the major portion of this difference is represented by the value of the one-half million certificates which have not been borrowed upon, only $130,000,000 would be payable on the present value basis to the three million men who have borrowed on their certificates, representing an average equity of about $43 on the average certificate in contrast to the $500 which is now sought to be paid by the resolution of the American Legion.

In substance, this resolution seeks the remitting of interest in an amount in excess of $220,000,000 charged to the veterans' accounts, but would require the immediate payment by the Government of interest that will not have been earned until 1945, which together with the amount granted on account of deferred payments totals $2,100,000,000 more than the $1 and $1.25 a day adjustment provided by the original Act. The present value of the certificates in force is $2,100,000,000, whereas it is sought to have now paid $3,720,000,000 (the maturity or face value plus remittance of interest), or an additional amount of $1,620,000,000 over and above the present value and $2,320,000,000 more than the original basic adjustment.

See also Item 62, Vol. IV; and Item 12, Vol. V, for veto messages on bonus bills.

Index

Adjusted Compensation Payment Act, 1936 (Note) Item 55, p 180-181; See also Bonus Bill

Adjusted Service Certificates
Issuance of, Item 199, p 503; Borrowing on, Item 199, p 504; Deferred payment of, Item 199, p 504; Sole asset of majority of veterans who die, Item 199, p 505; Present value of, Item 199, p 507; Borrowing on, Item 199A, p 506-507; See also Bonus; Bonus Bill

Administration
The three great tasks of the first fifteen months of, Item 102, p 287-288; Three great objectives of, Item 102, p 288-292

Advertising
Value of — letter to Advertising Federation of America, Item 105, p 299-300

Advisory Council
Creation, members and functions of, (Note) Item 159, p 406

Advisory Council of Committee on Economic Security
Work of this council and committee led to Social Security Act of 1935, (Note) Item 179, p 455

Advisory Council on Economic Security
Established, Executive Order 6757, Item 117, p 321

Agricultural Adjustment Act
As an aid toward restoration of farm prices to parity, Item 1, p 11; Consumer interest recognized, (Note) Item 11, p 58; Suggested amendment to make sugar beets and sugar cane basic agricultural commodities, Item 21, p 87; Suggested amendment authorizing Secretary of Agriculture to direct marketing of sugar, Item 21, p 87; Marketing agreement of sugar disapproved by the Secretary of Agriculture, (Note) Item 21, p 89; Recommendations for amendment re sugar, (Note) Item 21, p 90; May 12, 1933, authorized President to accept silver in payment of instalments due from any foreign Government for a period of six months, Item 98, p 282

Agricultural Adjustment Administration
Increase in farm population, temptation for entering cotton-production business arising from increased prices led to belief efforts of — to be impeded, (Note) Item 27, p 100; Overwhelming desire on part of cotton producers for some form of compulsory control, (Note) Item 27, p 100; Voluntary reduction program complete success, (Note) Item 27, p 100; Bankhead Bill to safeguard voluntary — program by compulsory control over non-cooperators, (Note) Item 62, p 190; Invalidity of — decision of Supreme Court, (Note) Item 62, p 191; Invalidation of processing tax and production control features ended sugar program except for quota provisions, (Note) Item 76, p 221; Functions in the drought relief drive, (Note) Item 103, p 294-295; Drought-stricken area greatly assisted by the benefit payments of, (Note) Item 103, p 295

Agricultural Adjustment Administration, Administrator of
Member President's Drought Relief Committee, (Note) Item 103, p 294; Added to membership of Industrial Emergency Committee, Executive Order 6860, (Note) Item 159, p 406; Member National Emergency Council, Item 172, p 442

Agriculture
Relief for needy in rural areas must be identified with, Item 31, p 109; Request for authority to modify existing duties and import restrictions to benefit, Item 33, p 113; Will find expanded opportunities and productive capacity in foreign markets, Item 33, p 115; Increase in farm income dependent on continued adjustment of production to existing market, Item 192, p 491

Agriculture, Department of
Questionnaires show 95 percent favoring compulsory reductions in crop, Item 29, p 105; Relief program calls for complete cooperation with, Item 31, p 109; Representative of — on Interdepartmental Committee on Trade Agreements, (Note) Item 33, p 116; Re report on Inter-American Highway prepared by Bureau of Public Roads, Item 38A, p 133

Agriculture, Secretary of
Created office of Consumers' Counsel, (Note) Item 11, p 58; Questionnaires re Bankhead Act, (Note) Item 27, p 101;

Index

521

(Note) Item 29, p 106; Number of loans made, average loss, (Note) Item 29, p 107

Emergency Crop Production Loan Bill
Explanation of, Item 29, p 104; See also Emergency Crop and Feed Loan

Emergency Education Program
Effort made to adapt work relief to occupational skills, etc., of unemployed, (Note) Item 31, p 111

Emergency Expenditures
Control of, Item 3, p 23; Need of, Item 83, p 237-238

Emergency Farm Credit Act of 1933
Suggested amendment to provide responsibility for payment by Government of principal of, as well as interest on, bonds issued, Item 6, p 27

Emergency Farm Mortgage Act of 1933
Insufficiency of available funds for refinancing loans, (Note) Item 6, p 28; Transfer of funds and mortgages to Federal Farm Mortgage Corporation, (Note) Item 6, p 28

Emergency Relief Appropriation Act of 1935
Extension of Civilian Conservation Corps, (Note) Item 165, p 425

Emergency Work Relief Program
Number of Civil Works Administration projects and employees transferred to, (Note) Item 31, p 111

Employee Organization
Government favors no particular, Item 51, p 167

Employee Representation
Free choice of representative by employees; Government's right and duty to see law carried out, Item 37, p 129-130

Employees
Retention through working capital loans for small industries, Item 44, p 153

Employer-Employee Relations
Permanent machinery being created to maintain orderly, Item 114, p 316

Employers
Represented on boards of N.R.A., Item 37, p 125; Abuses against — not to be tolerated, Item 37, p 130

Employment
Increases in, Item 114, p 314; Created by Public Works Program, Item 163, p 420

Employment Standards
President hails plan to draft minimum employment standards by Interstate Compact, Item 91, p 259

England
Recognizes collective bargaining, Item 155, p 398; Departure from gold standard, Item 163, p 420-421; Refunding of war bonds at lower interest, Item 163, p 421

Erosion
Deterioration of land through wind and water erosion, Item 124A, p 337

Erie Canal
Built by De Witt Clinton, Item 137, p 353

Erie, Lake
And St. Lawrence Seaway, Item 43, p 146

Estonia
Indebtedness to U. S., March 4, 1933, Item 98, p 280

Europe
U. S. cannot take part in political situation of, Item 1, p 12

Evasions, Income Tax
How to determine, Item 43, p 151

Ever-Normal Granary
Item 80, p 229

Evolution
"When people talk to you about the word 'revolution' in this country, you tell them that they have one letter too many in that word," Item 64, p 195

Executive Committee on Commercial Policy
See Commercial Policy, Executive Committee on

Executive Council
Functions and duties transferred to National Emergency Council, (Note) Item 123, p 334; Consolidation of National Emergency Council, the Industrial Emergency Committee and, Executive Order 6889A, Item 172, p 441-444; Members, functions and duties transferred to National Emergency Council, separate existence terminated, Item 172, p 443-444

Index

Consolidated with National Emergency Council, subcommittee to, (Note) Item 123, p 334-335; Membership increased, (Note) Item 159, p 406; Consolidation of National Emergency Council, Executive Council and, Executive Order 6889A, Item 172, p 441-444; To continue to exercise function and duties imposed on it and serve as subcommittee of National Emergency Council, Item 172, p 442

Industrial Peace
Government agencies created to insure, Item 163, p 419

Industrial Problems
Solution of, Item 157, p 403

Industrial Recovery, Administrator for
May make exception to Executive Order 6646 to serve justice or public interest, Item 42, p 144; See also National Recovery Administration

Industry
Request for authority to modify existing duties and import restrictions to benefit, Item 33, p 113; Will find expanded opportunities and productive capacity in foreign markets, Item 33, p 115; Representative Government in — under N.R.A., Item 37, p 126; Immediate task of — to reemploy more people, Item 37, p 127; Obligations clearly set forth in settlement of threatened automobile strike, Item 51, p 169; 90 percent has been codified, Item 104, p 299; Self-government in, Item 114, p 316; Statement of Elihu Root, Item 163, p 414; Need of governmental assistance and safeguards, Item 163, p 414; Protests re continued operation of industrial plans in Federal institutions, (Note) Item 194, p 496

Infantile Paralysis
The problem of, Item 78, p 225; Dr. Lovett's work in connection with; Swimming as treatment for, Item 189, p 486

Insurance Companies
Government Loans to, Item 163, p 414-415; Federal Housing Administrator explains need of removing State restrictions on lending powers of, Item 196, p 499

Inter-American Commercial Arbitration Commission
To harmonize relations between citizens of American Republics in a phase of their relations not within sphere of governmental activities, Item 195, p 498-499

Inter-American Highway
A message transmitting to Congress a report on, Item 38, p 133; Letter from Secy. of State Hull submitting a report on — for transmission to Congress, Item 38A, p 133-136; Important socially and economically, (Note) Item 38A, p 134-135; Approval of Act of Congress authorizing continuation of reconnaissance survey, (Note) Item 38A, p 135; Surveyed route of, (Note) Item 38A, p 135-136; Appropriation made in Emergency Appropriation Act of 1935, (Note) Item 38A, p 135; In 1928 Congress passed resolution that U. S. take utmost interest in proposed, (Note) Item 38A, p 135; Bridges built in Panama, Guatemala, Nicaragua and Honduras with appropriation made by Emergency Appropriation Act of 1935, (Note) Item 38A, p 136; Total length of, (Note) Item 38A, p 136; Highway from U. S. to Panama City most practical part of proposed highway through North and South America, (Note) Item 38A, p 135

Inter-departmental Committee
Creation of Federal Communications Commission based on recommendations by, (Note) Item 30, p 108

Inter-departmental Committee on Trade Agreements
See Trade Agreements, Inter-departmental Committee on

Inter-departmental Loan Committee
Object of, (Note) Item 177, p 450; Activities of, (Note) Item 177, p 451

Interior, Department of
Remedial measures which will affect "stranded populations," Item 31, p 110; Petroleum Administrative Board, (Note) Item 90, p 257; Represented on committee conferring on power with President, Item 186, p 465

Interior, Secretary of
Member of Advisory Council to assist in formulation of comprehensive plan for social and economic advancement of people of Virgin Islands, Item 28, p 101; Act of March 7, 1902, permitted — to authorize Indian heirs to sell their lands; Act of March 1, 1907, permitted

544

Index

Index

Index

Index by Miss K. C. Blackburn